Child Sexual Abuse

This fully revised volume provides a rigorous assessment of the latest research relating to the disclosure of childhood sexual abuse, along with the practical and policy implications of the findings.

Leading researchers and practitioners from diverse and international backgrounds offer critical commentary on these findings gathered from both field and laboratory research. Building on the first edition, this book presents the research from the past twenty years on why delayed disclosure or denial is so common and what we can do about it. Chapters focus on field research interviewing reluctant children, including suspected victims of sexual abuse and other crimes, victims of trafficking, as well as young, suspected perpetrators of sexual abuse. Adding emphasis on research-based methods for overcoming reluctance, it also explores the different dynamics and circumstances which affect disclosure patterns and the ways in which interviewers can facilitate disclosures.

Child Sexual Abuse is for researchers and practitioners from child, forensic, and clinical psychology, social work, and all legal professionals who need to understand this crime. It will also be of interest to trainee social workers specializing in child welfare and intervention.

Michael E. Lamb PhD is Professor Emeritus of Psychology at the University of Cambridge and has written or edited approximately 50 books, including the first edition of this book.

Irit Hershkowitz is Professor Emerita of Social Work at the University of Haifa and has led research on interviewing reluctant children for over a decade.

Margaret-Ellen Pipe is Professor Emerita of Psychology at the City University of New York and was the principal editor of the first edition of this book.

"The editors are world renowned for their research and writings on child forensic interviews. They have assembled a group of international experts on disclosure... Readers will learn about the latest research advances as well as how to tackle relevant legal, policy, and professional dilemmas. Anyone who cares about child protection ... will find this volume invaluable...this book helps us learn how and when to listen to children."

Gail S. Goodman, *Distinguished Professor of Psychology, University of California-Davis* and **Tina Goodman Brown,** *in private practice*, from the Foreword to the 1st edition.

"Law and Psychology have not been able to fully coalesce and work together in the interests of the children rather than in the interests of the respective discourse. This book provides the empirical evidence to overcome any remaining inertia and shows that where there is a genuine will there are ways to successfully challenge such divisions."

Kim Stevenson, *Plymouth University, UK*

"This book should be at hand for all practitioners in the field of child welfare who need to understand this crime. It is an invaluable resource."

Peter Reeften, *Addiction Today*

"In summary, Child Sexual Abuse: Disclosure, Delay, and Denial offers one of the most comprehensive reviews of literature in this area and presents important new research findings [...] This book is a must read for anyone directly involved with victims of child sexual abuse and can be very effective in disseminating important information about child interviewing to mental health practitioners."

April R. Bradley & Holly M. Rusinko, *PsycCRITIQUES*

Child Sexual Abuse

Why Children Disclose or Deny Being Abused

Second Edition

Edited by
Michael E. Lamb, Irit Hershkowitz, and Margaret-Ellen Pipe

Routledge
Taylor & Francis Group
NEW YORK AND LONDON

Cover image: StockPlanets via Getty Images

Second edition published 2026
by Routledge
605 Third Avenue, New York, NY 10158

and by Routledge
4 Park Square, Milton Park, Abingdon, Oxon, OX14 4RN

Routledge is an imprint of the Taylor & Francis Group, an informa business

First edition published by Routledge 2007

ISBN: 9781032731919 (hbk)
ISBN: 9781032702223 (pbk)
ISBN: 9781003427155 (ebk)

DOI: 10.4324/9781003427155

Typeset in Galliard
by codeMantra

Contents

Contributors

Uri Blasbalg, Department of Psychology, University of Cambridge, Cambridge, UK

Ros Burnett, Department of Criminology, University of Oxford, Oxford, UK

Deborah A. Connolly, Department of Psychology, Simon Fraser University, Burnaby, Canada

Angela Crossman, Department of Psychology, John Jay College of Criminal Justice, City University of New York, New York City, USA

Irit Hershkowitz, School of Social Work, University of Haifa, Haifa, Israel

Carolyn Hoyle, Department of Criminology, University of Oxford, Oxford, UK

Malin Joleby, Department of Clinical Neuroscience, Karolinska Institute, Stockholm, Sweden

Yael Karni-Visel, School of Social Work, Bar-Ilan University, Ramat Gan, Israel

Sarah C. Kim, Department of Psychological Science, University of California-Irvine, Irvine, USA

Julia Korkman, Department of Psychology, Abo University, Turku, Finland

Michael E. Lamb, Department of Psychology, University of Cambridge, Cambridge, UK

Thomas D. Lyon, Gould School of Law, University of Southern California, Los Angeles, USA

Rosaleen McElvaney, Children's Health Ireland, Dublin, Ireland

Margaret-Ellen Pipe, Department of Psychology, College of Staten Island, City University of New York, New York City, USA

Heather L. Price, Department of Psychology, Thompson Rivers University, Kamloops, Canada

Jodi A. Quas, Department of Psychological Science, University of California-Irvine, Irvine, USA

Emma Simpson, Department of Psychological Science, University of California-Irvine, Irvine, USA

Zsofia A. Szojka, School of Law and Criminology, University of Greenwich, London, UK

Victoria Talwar, Department of Psychology, McGill University, Montreal, Canada

Tal Weissman Ben-Shahar, School of Social Work, University of Haifa, Haifa, Israel

Breanne E. Wylie, Department of Psychology, North Carolina State University, Raleigh, USA

Preface

Over the last four decades of research and controversy about child sexual abuse, a handful of key questions have waxed and waned in prominence. Intense debate about the extent to which children might come to make false allegations after being subjected to suggestive and/or coercive questioning, or, conversely, fail to report abuse because they didn't understand the questions directed to them, quickly followed recognition that even quite young children are often able to remember and talk about their experiences. There also arose concerns about the possibility that children might repress memories of serious abuse, only to retrieve memories of those experiences in adulthood, often following some kinds of therapeutic interventions. Whether or not forgetting took place, many adults reported histories of abuse they had not reported earlier, prompting debates about the frequency with which abuse remained undisclosed across extended delays or, indeed, indefinitely. Together, these controversial issues have continued to be the focus of research, debate, and speculation, with the associated concepts of disclosure, delay, recantation, and denial dominating the literature.

In 2007, Pipe et al. edited a book (*Child Sexual Abuse: Disclosure, Delay, and Denial*) exploring this vexed and confusing literature. That collection of essays illuminated debates about the frequency with which victims of abuse delay disclosure, and the conditions or circumstances in which delay or disclosure are fostered or, conversely, in which false allegation might be provoked. Complementing these discussions, other authors considered ways in which practitioners should act to facilitate timely and accurate disclosures of abuse while avoiding the elicitation of false allegations.

Nearly two decades later, it is clear that the 2007 book brought attention to these important questions and helped catalyse both basic research and the development of more effective tools and approaches, signalling a move from understanding the phenomena to overcoming the associated challenges. The present book brings together a series of chapters that illustrate how much we have learned in the interim while drawing attention to issues that remain controversial or in need of intensive research. Several of the contributors wrote important chapters for the previous book and so are well placed to summarise developments and newly grasped understanding from the last two decades while highlighting the topics that remain inadequately addressed. In addition, this volume includes chapters on topics and perspectives that received little attention in the earlier book and have since attracted significant interest from professionals in the field. The present book thus includes several discussions designed to help researchers and practitioners better understand the abilities and tendencies of children and adolescents to make false or misleading claims, and the factors that foster these, as well as those addressing the complex challenges facing those working with abused children in either forensic or therapeutic roles. Categories of offending that attracted little attention 20 years ago – including technology-facilitated sexual abuse or abuse perpetrated by other children – receive detailed attention in this volume.

All of the chapters in the present volume were written specifically for this volume and are thus entirely original. The contributors are researchers, practitioners, and applied academics working in the North American, European, and Asian countries where the relevant research and practice has received the most attention. The accounts they provide will be of value to scholars and practitioners worldwide who strive to understand and serve the many children whose lives are blighted by the scourge of child sexual abuse.

Michael E. Lamb, Irit Hershkowitz, and
Margaret-Ellen Pipe
July 2025

1

Child sexual abuse

Who, when, and what to tell?

Michael E. Lamb, Margaret-Ellen Pipe, and Irit Hershkowitz

Over the last few decades, criminal justice and child protection professionals, along with researchers, therapists, and the public at large, have come to recognize that child sexual abuse, once viewed as a rarity, is actually surprisingly common, with many millions of victims identified every year. That widely accepted consensus disguises a great deal of uncertainty, however. For example, many victims only identify themselves as such in adulthood, meaning that their status was not recognized when they were children. In some cases, abuse was suspected but denied; in others, victimization was reported, sometimes obliquely, but not believed. More alarmingly, many experts believe that some victims never report or acknowledge their experiences. Factors such as these make it impossible to specify exactly how widespread child sexual abuse is and underscore the importance of better understanding why children do and do not report their experiences of abuse, why some delay making such reports and others deny such experiences, and what professionals can do to foster timely and accurate reports when abuse occurs. Answers, or at least tentative answers, to these and related questions are the focus of this book.

Attention to the prevalence of victimization denials and of true and false disclosures, burgeoned more than four decades ago when a clinician named Roland Summit (1983) published an article about failures to disclose abuse, arguing that non-disclosure, denial, delayed reporting, and recantation commonly occurred because children sought to protect an abusive caregiver on whom they were dependent. He initially used the label "child sexual abuse accommodation syndrome" (CSAAS) to describe these related phenomena, although within a decade Summit (1993) backtracked, accepting that the syndrome label was inappropriate. Unfortunately, despite Summit's retraction, the label is still widely applied, especially in clinical circles, and is still accepted in some US courtrooms, where reference to the syndrome is used to rehabilitate young complainants who made delayed, partial, or inconsistent disclosures. As we discuss below, key questions remain: just how common are delayed or partial disclosures? Are initial (false) denials common?

DOI: 10.4324/9781003427155-1

To what extent should we view delay, denial or recantation as indices of reliability or markers of potential suggestibility? Especially in forensic contexts, these questions are as relevant today as when they were when provocatively articulated by London, Bruck, Ceci, and Schuman (2005) more than two decades ago in a trenchant critique of Summit's well-known hypotheses.

The answers to these questions have important implications in a variety of legal, personal, and academic domains. For example, if nondisclosures are taken to mean that the children were not abused as may have been suspected, then forensic and child welfare investigations should be suspended, even if that might deny some (abused) children the individual and systemic interventions they deserve. Such suspensions would leave both the victimized children and their peers potentially at risk of abuse in the future while the suspected abuser goes unpunished. If suspected victims later make allegations about incidents they previously denied, how should we judge the reliability and credibility of their delayed and contradictory reports? If false denials (and recantations) are not uncommon should children be formally interviewed more than once when there are suspicions of abuse whether or not the children deny having been abused? Surely information about the frequencies of delayed disclosures and false denials – and, conversely, false allegations of abuse – can and should be reported to courts and children's protective service agencies striving to make those judgments and decisions. Crucially, however, how good, reliable, and widely accepted are the available answers to those questions? Sadly, the answers have long been controversial even as research and scholarship have continued apace. In this volume, we review the literature and insights that have advanced our understanding over the past two decades.

It initially appeared straightforward to determine whether nondisclosure of abuse was common or infrequent but that confident hope quickly evaporated when reported rates of non-disclosure in individual studies ranged from 4% (Bradley & Wood, 1996) to 75% (Sorenson & Snow, 1991). To avoid biases associated with the characteristics of specific studies, it was suggested that researchers could, for example, take cases in which there is incontrovertible evidence of abuse (such as the presence of sexually transmitted diseases) and ask how frequently children with such infections reported being abused. As London et al. (2007) and Lyon (2007) showed in the first edition of this book, however, there were serious issues of sampling bias and questions regarding the generalizability of findings from highly selected samples of children in those unusual circumstances: in truth, almost all the relevant studies involved samples that were not representative but characterized by a variety of unique and special circumstances. This realization made it impossible to state with any certainty exactly how common delay, non-disclosure, or recantation really were, prompting a debate that animated many chapters in the first edition of this book, in the literature since, and even in the chapters that follow.

Further, unclear definitions of concepts such as nondisclosure have complicated efforts to reconcile disparate findings. Is nondisclosure the same as denial of abuse when interviewed or independent of whether the child was formally interviewed? Thus, when adults report that they were abused during childhood but had not disclosed to anyone, are those examples of nondisclosure whether or not the children had ever been asked about possible abuse? And do delayed disclosures, by definition, include a period during which the child was a "nondiscloser"?

Debates about patterns of disclosure differ in important ways from those that characterized the "memory wars" that divided researchers and practitioners in the late 1980s and 1990s. At that time, the focus was on adults' memories of childhood sexual abuse and on the possibility and frequency of repression and recovered memories, neither of which have been important concepts in debates about children's disclosure. Instead, the focus in the latter case has been on developmental limitations (e.g. lack of understanding, poor verbal skills) and characteristics as well as motivational issues that might hinder disclosure.

Some (probably many?) instances of abuse are not disclosed or even suspected because sexual abuse is typically a private, well-concealed crime without witnesses or visible consequences, leaving us reliant on verbal disclosure for estimates of its incidence. This makes it impossible to know the true incidence of childhood sexual abuse which in turn makes it impossible to estimate the rate of nondisclosure precisely. Other consequences are also frustratingly problematic. For example, when a suspected victim *does not* disclose abuse when interviewed, how do we know whether the child has not been abused (a true negative) or rather is unwilling to disclose abuse that has occurred (a false negative)? The corresponding question – when a child *does* disclose abuse, how do we distinguish between true and false positives? – was the focus of an enormous literature on suggestibility and the implantation of false memories, particularly in the late 1980s and 1990s. Research on the phenomenon of nondisclosure, by contrast, rose to prominence in the early 2000s, animating both the previous edition of this anthology as well as the present collection. Identifying both the barriers to disclosure and conditions under which both disclosure and nondisclosure are most likely to occur are crucial steps towards ensuring that abused children will disclose their abuse in a timely and accurate manner.

Overview of the first edition

In the prior volume, Pipe et al. (2007a) compiled a set of chapters comprising the first rigorous examination of the available evidence relating to the patterns of disclosure and nondisclosure of childhood sexual abuse, and the first systematic consideration of the practical and policy implications of the research findings. The contributors critically and comprehensively analysed how children disclose abuse and, in turn, how child protection workers, clinicians, forensic interviewers, and the courts should react to the emergent information. In the first two chapters, London et al. (2007) and Lyon (2007) reviewed the literature on disclosure, highlighting difficulties confronting researchers striving to determine how often children fail to disclose sexual abuse, delay disclosing it, provide incomplete accounts, and/or recant their disclosures, particularly when most of the research was either based on analyses of investigative interviews with suspected victims or on retrospective surveys of adults.

London et al. argued that because the highest rates of nondisclosure were associated with the weakest evidence that the abuse had, in fact, occurred, most nondisclosures were true negatives. Lyon, on the other hand, argued that children may deny being abused even when there is strong evidence that it happened (such as STDs), and that many studies reporting low rates of nondisclosure were tainted by "suspicion" and "substantiation" biases.

Despite their different emphases, however, the chapters by London et al. and Lyon converged on two conclusions. First, at least some children do not disclose abuse even when questioned about it, and second, delayed disclosures of sexual abuse is quite common. Research identifying the conditions under which nondisclosures are most likely to occur, the reasons why children delay disclosing abuse, and, importantly, what precipitates disclosure after a delay was addressed by the authors of four chapters. These focused on the individual and contextual factors determining whether, when, and how childhood sexual abuse tends to be disclosed, showing for the first time how the way children were interviewed affected disclosure patterns.

In all four studies, forensic interviewers followed the National Institute of Child Health and Human Development (NICHD) investigative interview protocol (Orbach et al., 2000), which emphasized the value of open-ended recall and nonintrusive interviewer support. Hershkowitz, Horowitz, and Lamb (2007) examined a data set comprising information about more than 25,000 suspected incidents of physical and sexual abuse in Israel investigated during a five-year time period. Unlike convenience samples or samples drawn from specific agency files, therefore, the sample was not subject to the usual selection biases. Contrary to concerns that heavy reliance on open-ended interview strategies may lead to elevated rates of nondisclosure, the disclosure rates reported by Hershkowitz et al. (just under two-thirds overall) were well within the range expected, and varied depending on the children's ages, relationship to the suspected abusers, and type of abuse concerned.

In a much smaller and more selective US sample, Pipe, Lamb, Orbach, Stewart, Sternberg, and Esplin (2007b) reported similarly high rates of disclosure when using the NICHD Protocol's open-ended approach to interviewing. Because they were able to examine a broad range of information about the children, suspects, and alleged offences, Pipe et al. were able to elucidate the associations between nondisclosure and these variables as well as the ways in which they were qualified by interactions, in particular with age. The authors reported, for example, that nondisclosure of abuse was likely to be multiply determined and that the correlates of nondisclosure were different at different ages. Discrepant rates of nondisclosure in the studies reviewed by London et al. (2005, 2007) may thus have depended, at least in part, on variations among the groups sampled.

Hershkowitz, Orbach, Lamb, Sternberg, Pipe, and Horowitz (2007) and Orbach, Shiloach, and Lamb (2007) both placed individual investigative interviews under the microscope, examining the dynamics of interviews conducted with children who did disclose, disclosed reluctantly, or did not disclose at all. Specifically, they examined in detail the types of prompts used by interviewers, and the children's responses to these, as well as the interviewers' supportive and non-supportive comments. Hershkowitz et al. (2007) found that, compared to children who disclosed abuse, children who did not disclose (despite good reason to believe that they had been abused) appeared reluctant early in the pre-substantive phase of the interview, before any focus on the suspected abuse. Importantly, Hershkowitz et al. pointed to the influence of such reluctance on the interviewers' behaviour: The latter appeared frustrated and unsupportive, asking many narrow, even leading, questions. Orbach et al. (2007) similarly found that children who were reluctant to disclose appeared reluctant even in the pre-substantive phases of the interview, and that when they did disclose they remained relatively uninformative. As noted below (see especially Hershkowitz et al., Chapter 9), these observations greatly influenced later efforts to counteract reluctance by interviewing more supportively, as exemplified by creation of the Revised NICHD Protocol (Lamb et al., 2018). Hershkowitz et al. noted how important it was to establish and maintain trustful rapport and suggested that it might sometimes be necessary to delay discussing possible abuse until the child is more forthcoming, even if it means interviewing reluctant witnesses on more than one occasion – an option suggested by Horowitz (2007) and discussed more fully below in Chapter 9.

Drawing on experimental rather than observational research, Bottoms, Quas, and Davis's (2007) chapter on the importance of interviewer approaches and characteristics correspondingly showed that interviewers who were warm and supportive elicited more and more accurate information than those who were cold and unempathetic. They suggested that interviewer demeanour would be even more important when children were reluctant, fearful, embarrassed or shy than in the analogue studies they reviewed, although little was known at the time about strategies for overcoming reluctance in these children (Saywitz, Esplin, & Romanoff, 2007).

Cederborg, Lamb, and Laurell (2007) closely examined a harrowing case to illustrate some of the strategies that perpetrators use to maintain children's silence. None of the 12 children abused by a Swedish paedophile who videotaped his abusive behaviour disclosed what had happened before the videotapes were discovered. Cederborg et al. suggested that the children may have failed to disclose abuse because they were unable to understand what they had experienced or had been manipulated into silence by the perpetrator. As they noted, developmental issues need to be taken into account when considering the reasons children delay disclosure or fail to disclose abuse. Barriers to disclosure may change during childhood, and approaches to dealing with them will need to be developmentally sensitive.

Pursuing a different angle to understand prolonged non-disclosure, Bottoms, Rudnicki, and Epstein (2007) reported studies of American college students who had been asked whether they had experienced different forms of abuse and whether they had disclosed that previously. Many of the students reported never disclosing their abuse as children, leading to what Bottoms et al. described as "huge under-reporting" of child maltreatment. Interestingly, furthermore, many of the adults who confirmed having been abused did not consider themselves to be victims of abuse. Unlike most other researchers, Bottoms et al. also failed to find that prior disclosure of either physical or sexual abuse was less likely when the perpetrator was a close family member.

Through comparisons between adults who had made criminal complaints of abuse that allegedly took place in the distant past (historical child sexual abuse) and those who had made "timely" disclosures, Connolly and Read (2007) found that delayed complaints were more likely when family members were suspected and when the abuse was more severe. These findings matched those reported in the studies reviewed by London et al. (2007) and Lyon (2007) although this was not true of the studies reviewed by Bottoms et al. Specifying what constitutes abuse continues to arouse controversy, and self-labelling may clearly lead to different estimates of disclosure than sampling specific behaviours. These observations were amplified by Lindblad (2007) who noted that apparently straightforward and unambiguous concepts are laden with implicit meanings so that labels (like disclosure or abuse) may be used quite differently in scientific, clinical, and legal contexts.

When children do not verbally disclose abuse, yet childcare professionals remain concerned about the children's well-being, what should happen next? As Saywitz et al. (2007) highlighted, forensic investigations are part of a larger process aimed at childcare, well-being, and protection and the investigative process can conflict with clinical considerations. Saywitz et al. (2007) and Gumpert (2007) thus challenged researchers and clinicians alike to pursue agendas much more sensitive to the overlapping challenges and goals than they had been.

Overview of this book

Nearly two decades have now passed since Pipe et al.'s (2007a) anthology was published. As the present collection of essays shows, the perspectives articulated in the earlier book profoundly affected practitioners and researchers who became aware of how difficult it is to identify true and false allegations and denials and thus how careful professionals need to be when planning investigations and interventions, whether they are individual (therapy), systemic, or legal.

While it is beyond the scope of the current volume to review the wealth of research that, over the past two decades, has informed our understanding of children's abilities to talk about their experiences, it is important to acknowledge the very fruitful ongoing dialogue between researchers and practitioners that has informed many of the chapters in the present volume. To take one example, Hershkowitz et al.'s (2007) emphasis on the counterproductive dynamics of the interactions between suspected victims and forensic interviewers directly and indirectly fostered considerable efforts to better understand reluctance, rapport, and interviewer support (Hershkowitz et al., 2005; Saywitz et al., 2015, 2019) and prompted development of the Revised NICHD Investigative Interview Protocol (e.g. Lamb et al., 2018; Hershkowitz et al., Chapter 9) which focuses on providing children with non-suggestive and developmentally appropriate emotional and cognitive support during forensic interviews.

Moreover, research examining children's abilities to remember and report specific instances of a repeated experience (e.g. Brubacher, Powell, & Roberts, 2014; Earhart et al., 2024; Price, Connolly & Gordon, 2016; Woiwod & Connolly, 2017; Woiwod et al., 2019); the effects of repeated and delayed interviewing (La Rooy et al., 2009; Quas et al., 2010); the use of specific prompts to cue reports of emotions associated with specific events (Lyon et al., 2012); strategies for providing support and building rapport (Saywitz et al., 2019), and research on children's changing tendencies to lie and to judge lying and truth telling (Talwar & Crossman, Chapter 4) has further enhanced our understanding of the factors affecting children's accounts of abusive experiences. Many of these and other fruits of scholarship during the last two decades are highlighted in the chapters comprising this book.

At the same time, new areas of concern have come to the forefront of efforts to protect and safeguard children. It is sobering to note that the same year that the previous anthology was published saw the introduction of the iPhone, contributing to the rapid expansion of social media usage by children. In turn this has led to increases in children's vulnerability, specifically to internet-assisted abuse. Internet-related abuse was undoubtedly already affecting the lives of many children prior to the proliferation of smartphones, but in the intervening years children have become more accessible to malevolent agents exploiting social media and the internet, while the means of investigating these crimes have changed drastically (see Korkman & Joleby, Chapter 7). Similarly, attention to and awareness of the sex trafficking of minors has increased significantly in response to media campaigns highlighting the prevalence of this previously hidden crime (see Quas et al., Chapter 3). Lastly, developmental psychopathologists and epidemiologists have drawn attention to the surprisingly large number of children who sexually abuse other children (Silovsky, Letourneau & Bonner, 2020; Letourneau et al., 2024), underscoring the need to develop techniques designed to interview these children about their behaviour (Hershkowitz et al., Chapter 8).

Summaries of the chapters that follow

The 2007 book began with chapters by London and her colleagues and Lyon and his colleagues providing competing and contrasting reviews of the literature on the prevalence of delayed, true and false disclosures and recantations. Their detailed analyses and criticisms of specific studies are not included here because these have been discussed at length by both of the opposing groups (e.g. London et al., 2005, 2007, 2008, 2020; Lyon 2007, 2009, 2023; Lyon et al., 2020; McGuire & London, 2020) and we wanted to highlight new scholarship and emerging areas of consensus, with all chapters written specifically for this volume.

Expanding on their earlier essays, Lyon et al. (Chapter 2) ask how professionals should interpret delayed disclosure, initial denial, and recantation, drawing attention to the competing concerns about suggestive influence and diverse motivations to avoid disclosure. Highlighting a parallel between the concerns about each, they argue that evidence for suggestibility reduces the evidentiary value of disclosures, and evidence for reluctance reduces the evidentiary value of delay and denial. They also show that the child's closeness to the suspect and the supportiveness of the child's family are important factors and stress the importance of prior disclosures, whether the child is being asked about abuse for the first time, and characteristics of the interview, including supportiveness and the questions asked. Concluding with an examination of the New Jersey Supreme Court decision in *New Jersey v. J.L.G.* (190 A.3d 442, 2018), which rejected expert testimony explaining to juries why abused children might deny abuse on the grounds that the evidence was inconclusive, Lyon et al. note that the court misinterpreted statistics regarding the proportions of abused children who delay and deny while overlooking selection biases when estimating the likelihood that abused children will deny abuse.

Of course, if denial and false recantations are as common as Lyon et al. believe, there are serious implications for investigators, who must walk a tightrope between techniques that promote the elicitation of true allegations while avoiding suggestive or coercive techniques that risk eliciting false allegations. Complicating the didactic tasks for expert witnesses are the barriers to conducting research involving representative samples in which there is certainty about the abuse status of the participants; these barriers and impediments make it impossible to specify precisely the probability that any allegation or denial is objectively true or false in the absence of additional corroboration.

Quas, Simpson, and Kim (Chapter 3) then discuss challenges surrounding the identification of young victims of sex trafficking whose unique characteristics and their deviation from common trafficking stereotypes often make it difficult both to identify victims and to question them effectively in ways that elicit clear and complete disclosures. Fortunately, Quas et al.'s recent research allows them to advise readers regarding practices designed to improve our knowledge, identification, and interviewing strategies.

To help us better understand why some child witnesses lie about victimization in the form of delays, denials, or recantations and when these behaviours are most likely to occur, Talwar and Crossman (Chapter 4) explore the development and evolution of lying and truth-telling in childhood and adolescence. As they note, children become more effective liars with age as their conceptual and moral understanding blossom. The chapter closes with the recommendation of techniques that support honest and accurate reporting in spite of potential countervailing motivations and challenges.

In Chapter 5, Connolly and Price observe that the delayed prosecutions of child sexual abuse has become "a thriving legal industry" which has persisted for more than 20 years in countries around the world. They discuss a number of sociolegal explanations why it remains necessary to prosecute cases so long after the alleged offences, especially given the frequency (discussed by many other contributors as well) with which victims delay disclosure of those offences. As Connolly and Price note, however, cases involving historical offences raise special concerns about the credibility of the available testimony and pose novel challenges for courts grappling with the frequent unavailability of some key witnesses and sources of evidence as well as the obvious frailties of fading memories.

In Chapter 6, Burnett and Hoyle then discuss the possibility that false allegations may arise as unintended consequences of child-safeguarding and victim-centred policies aimed at facilitating the apprehension, investigation, and conviction of child abusers. They examine the definitions and types of false allegations (including intentional or mistakenly false allegations, including those made by adults on behalf of children), their prevalence, reasons why they may arise, the changing cultural and sociolegal context of responses to allegations of child sexual abuse, and the impact of false allegations on those falsely accused – especially in "historical/non-recent" cases – when "believing the victim" in the absence of physical evidence has often been sufficient to presume guilt.

As explained by Korkman and Joleby (Chapter 7), modern digital technology has created new ways for perpetrators to sexually exploit children and has resulted in increasing numbers of online child sexual abuse crimes with more severe consequences for victims than we previously recognized. As with other forms of child sexual abuse, children may find it difficult to disclose their experiences of victimization. Researchers have demonstrated that factors such as guilt, shame, active participation by victims, the ability of perpetrators to conceal their identity, and victims' fears of being blamed, misunderstood, or having abuse images spread widely hinder disclosure. In some cases, children may even deny the abuse despite existing evidence. This chapter aims to improve understanding of online child sexual abuse, the barriers to disclosure, and of the ways in which victims of online crimes should be interviewed sensitively and effectively using an adaptation of the well-established Revised NICHD Protocol, specifically modified for the unique challenges of online child sexual abuse cases.

In Chapter 8, Hershkowitz, Weissman Ben-Shahar, and Lamb shift focus to the available research on young suspects, emphasizing their vulnerability and thus the need for forensic interviewers to embrace developmentally appropriate practices when questioning these children about their experiences and behaviour. As with the young alleged victims discussed by most of the contributors, many young suspects are scared and reluctant to talk about their experiences, so interviewers must provide the same kinds of socio-emotional support afforded to suspected victims while making sure they understand their rights and can make informed decisions about what information they should disclose. Drawing on the available literature, Hershkowitz et al. describe a newly developed model for forensic interviewing, the Revised Suspect Interview Protocol (RSP). This recently evaluated Protocol is developmentally oriented and includes research-informed practices for reducing distress and reluctance.

Hershkowitz et al. (Chapter 9) then focus on socio-emotionally based practices for addressing children's reluctance to disclose abuse in forensic interviews. They present research showing that skilful management of child reluctance is possible by enhancing rapport, encouraging emotional expression, and providing social and emotional support to reluctant children. Those practices, which are at the heart of the Revised NICHD Protocol, were shown in a series of studies to help reduce emotional barriers to disclosure and enhance the quality and quantity of information obtained from children.

The chapter summarizes evidence regarding the effectiveness of the protocol as well as the mechanisms by which the protocol works.

In the final chapter, McElvaney (Chapter 10) then explores the challenges inherent in working therapeutically with children and adolescents who are reluctant to disclose sexual abuse despite persistent concerns that they have been abused. In particular, she examines how therapists can maintain a delicate balance between the need to support a disclosure, protect the integrity of the child's narrative, and support the child's autonomy while keeping paramount the best interests of the child. Keeping an open mind about whether abuse has occurred ensures that therapists do not influence children's narratives about their experiences.

References

Bottoms, B. L., Rudnicki, A. G., & Epstein, M. A. (2007). A retrospective study of factors affecting the disclosure of childhood sexual and physical abuse. In M.-E. Pipe, M. E. Lamb, Y. Orbach, & A.-C. Cederborg (eds), *Child sexual abuse: Disclosure, delay, and denial* (pp. 175–194). Lawrence Erlbaum Associates.

Bottoms, B. L., Quas, J. A., & Davis, S. L. (2007). The influence of interviewer-provided social support on children's suggestibility, memory, and disclosures. In M.-E. Pipe, M. E. Lamb, Y. Orbach, & A.-C. Cederborg (eds), *Child sexual abuse: Disclosure, delay, and denial* (pp. 135–158). Lawrence Erlbaum Associates.

Bradley, A. R., & Wood, J. M. (1996). How do children tell? The disclosure process in child sexual abuse. *Child Abuse & Neglect*, *20*(9), 881–891. https://doi.org/10.1016/0145-2134(96)00077-4

Brubacher, S. P., Powell, M. B., & Roberts, K. P. (2014). Recommendations for interviewing children about repeated experiences. *Psychology, Public Policy, and Law*, *20*(3), 325–335. https://doi.org/10.1037/law0000011

Cederborg, A.-C., Lamb, M. E., & Laurell, O. (2007). Delay of disclosure, minimization, and denial when the evidence is unambiguous: A multi-victim case. In M. E. Pipe, M. E. Lamb, Y. Orbach, & A.-C. Cederborg (eds), *Child sexual abuse: Disclosure, delay, and denial* (pp. 159–173). Mahwah, NJ: Lawrence Erlbaum Associates.

Connolly, D. A., & Read, J. D. (2007). Canadian criminal court reports of historic child sexual abuse: Factors associated with delayed prosecution and reported repression. In M.-E. Pipe, M. E. Lamb, Y. Orbach, & A.-C. Cederborg (eds), *Child sexual abuse: Disclosure, delay, and denial* (pp. 195–217). Lawrence Erlbaum Associates.

Earhart, B., Deck, S. L., Brubacher, S. P., & Powell, M. B. (2024). Children's long-term memory for a staged repeated event: A preliminary investigation. *Applied Cognitive Psychology*, *38*(2), e4191. https://doi.org/10.1002/acp.4191

Gumpert, C. H. (2007). Clinical and organizational perspectives on denial and delayed disclosure. In M. E. Pipe, M. E. Lamb, Y. Orbach, & A.-C. Cederborg (eds), *Child sexual abuse: Disclosure, delay, and denial* (pp. 251–264). Mahwah, NJ: Lawrence Erlbaum Associates, 2007.

Hershkowitz, I., Horowitz, D., & Lamb, M. E. (2005). Trends in children's disclosure of abuse in Israel: A national study. *Child abuse & neglect*, *29*(11), 1203–1214. https://doi.org/10.1016/j.chiabu.2005.04.008

Hershkowitz, I., Horowitz, D., & Lamb, M. E. (2007). Individual and family variables associated with disclosure and non-disclosure of child abuse in Israel. In M. E. Pipe, M. E. Lamb, Y. Orbach, & A.-C. Cederborg (eds), *Child sexual abuse: Disclosure, delay, and denial* (pp. 65–75). Mahwah, NJ: Lawrence Erlbaum Associates, 2007.

Hershkowitz, I., Orbach, Y., Lamb, M. E., Sternberg, K. J., Pipe, M. E., & Horowitz, D. (2007). Suspected victims of abuse who do not make allegations: An analysis of their interactions with forensic interviewers. In M. E. Pipe, M. E. Lamb, Y. Orbach, & A.-C. Cederborg (eds), *Child sexual abuse: Disclosure, delay, and denial* (pp. 97–113). Mahwah, NJ: Lawrence Erlbaum Associates.

Horowitz, D. (2007). The silence of abused children in Israel: Policy implications. In M. E. Pipe, M. E. Lamb, Y. Orbach, & A.-C. Cederborg (eds), *Child sexual abuse: Disclosure, delay, and denial* (pp. 281–290). Mahwah, NJ: Lawrence Erlbaum Associates.

Lamb, M. E., Brown, D. A., Hershkowitz, I., Orbach, Y., & Esplin, P. W. (2018). *Tell me what happened: Questioning children about abuse* (second edition). Hoboken NJ: Wiley.

La Rooy, D., Lamb, M. E., and Pipe, M.-E. (2009). Repeated interviewing: A critical evaluation of the risks and potential benefits. In K. Kuehnle & M. Connell (eds), *The evaluation of child sexual abuse allegations: A comprehensive guide to assessment and testimony* (pp. 327–361). Hoboken, NJ: Wiley.

Letourneau, E. J., Schaeffer, C. M., Bradshaw, C. P., Ruzicka, A. E., Assini-Meytin, L. C., Nair, R., & Thorne, E. (2024). Responsible behavior with younger children: results from a pilot randomized evaluation of a school-based child sexual abuse perpetration prevention program. *Child maltreatment*, *29*(1), 129–141. https://doi.org/10.1016/j.chiabu.2008.09.012

Lindblad, F. (2007). Reflections on the concept of disclosure. In M. E. Pipe, M. E. Lamb, Y. Orbach, & A.-C. Cederborg (eds), *Child sexual abuse: Disclosure, delay, and denial* (pp. 291–301). Mahwah, NJ: Lawrence Erlbaum Associates.

London, K., Bruck, M., Ceci, S., & Shuman, D. (2005). Disclosure of child sexual abuse: What does the research tell us about the ways that children tell? *Psychology, Public Policy, and Law*, *11*, 194–226. https://doi.org/10.1037/1076-8971.11.1.194

London, K., Bruck, M., Ceci, S., & Shuman, D. (2007). Disclosure of child sexual abuse: A review of the contemporary empirical literature. In M. E. Pipe, M. E. Lamb, Y. Orbach, & A.-C. Cederborg (eds), *Child sexual abuse: Disclosure, delay, and denial* (pp. 11–40). Mahwah, NJ: Lawrence Erlbaum Associates.

London, K., Bruck, M., Miller, Q. C., & Ceci, S. J. (2020). Analyzing the scientific foundation of Child Sexual Abuse Accommodation Syndrome: A reply to Lyon et al. *Behavioral Sciences & the Law*, *38*(6), 648–653. https://doi.org/10.1002/bsl.2489

London, K., Bruck, M., Wright, D. B., & Ceci, S. J. (2008). Review of the contemporary literature on how children report sexual abuse to others: Findings, methodological issues, and implications for forensic interviewers. *Memory, 16*(1), 29–47. https://doi.org/10.1080/09658210701725732

Lyon, T. D. (2007). False denials: Overcoming methodological biases in abuse disclosure research. In M. E. Pipe, M. E. Lamb, Y. Orbach, & A.-C. Cederborg (eds), *Child sexual abuse: Disclosure, delay, and denial* (pp. 51–72). Mahwah, NJ: Lawrence Erlbaum Associates, 2007.

Lyon, T.D. (2009). Abuse disclosure: What adults can tell. In B. Bottoms, C. Najdowski, & G. Goodman (eds), *Children as victims, witnesses, and offenders: Psychological science and the law* (pp. 19–35). Guilford.

Lyon, T. D. (2023). Child maltreatment, the law, and two types of error. *Child Maltreatment, 28*(3), 403–406. https://doi.org/10.1177/10775595231176454

Lyon, T. D., Williams, S., Stolzenberg, S. N. (2020). Understanding expert testimony on child sexual abuse denial after New Jersey v. J.L.G.: Ground truth, disclosure suspicion bias, and disclosure substantiation bias. *Behavioral Sciences & the Law, 38*, 630–647. https://doi.org/10.1002/bsl.2490

Lyon, T. D., Scurich, N., Choi, K., Handmaker, S., & Blank, K. (2012). "How did you feel?" increasing child sexual abuse witness' production of evaluative information. *Law & Human Behavior, 36*, 448–457. doi:10.1037/h0093986

McGuire, K., & London, K. (2020). A retrospective approach to examining child abuse disclosure. *Child Abuse & Neglect, 99*, 104263. https://doi.org/10.1016/j.chiabu.2019.104263

Orbach, Y., Hershkowitz, I., Lamb, M. E., Sternberg, K. J., Esplin, P. W., & Horowitz, D. (2000). Assessing the value of structured protocols for forensic interviews of alleged child abuse victims. *Child Abuse and Neglect, 24*(6), 733–752. https://doi.org/10.1016/s0145-2134(00)00137

Orbach, Y., Shiloach, H., & Lamb, M. E. (2007). Reluctant disclosers of child sexual abuse. In M. E. Pipe, M. E. Lamb, Y. Orbach, & A.-C. Cederborg (eds), *Child sexual abuse: Disclosure, delay, and denial* (pp. 115–134). Mahwah, NJ: Lawrence Erlbaum Associates.

Pipe, M. E., Lamb, M. E., Orbach, Y., & Cederborg, A.-C. (eds) (2007a). *Child sexual abuse: Disclosure, delay, and denial.* Mahwah, NJ: Lawrence Erlbaum Associates.

Pipe, M. E., Lamb, M. E., Orbach, Y., Stewart, H. L., Sternberg, K. J., & Esplin, P. W. (2007b). Factors associated with nondisclosure of suspected abuse during forensic interviews. In M. E. Pipe, M. E. Lamb, Y. Orbach, & A.-C. Cederborg (eds), *Child sexual abuse: Disclosure, delay, and denial* (pp. 77–96). Mahwah, NJ: Lawrence Erlbaum Associates.

Price, H. L., Connolly, D. A., & Gordon, H. M. (2016). Children who experienced a repeated event only appear less accurate in a second interview than those who experienced a unique event. *Law and Human Behavior, 40*(4), 362–373. https://doi.org/10.1037/lhb0000194

Quas, J. A., Alexander, K. W., Goodman, G. S., Ghetti, S., Edelstein, R. S., & Redlich, A. (2010). Long-term autobiographical memory for legal involvement: Individual and sociocontextual predictors. *Cognitive Development, 25*(4), 394–409. https://doi.org/10.1016/j.cogdev.2010.08.005

Saywitz, K., Esplin, P. W., & Romanoff, S. (2007). A holistic approach to interviewing and treating children in the legal system. In M. E. Pipe, M. E. Lamb, Y. Orbach, & A.-C. Cederborg (eds), *Child sexual abuse: Disclosure, delay, and denial* (pp. 219–250). Mahwah, NJ: Lawrence Erlbaum Associates.

Saywitz, K. J., Larson, R. P., Hobbs, S. D., & Wells, C. R. (2015). Developing rapport with children in forensic interviews: Systematic review of experimental research. *Behavioral sciences & the law*, *33*(4), 372–389. https://doi.org/10.1002/bsl.2186

Saywitz, K. J., Wells, C. R., Larson, R. P., & Hobbs, S. D. (2019). Effects of interviewer support on children's memory and suggestibility: Systematic review and meta-analyses of experimental research. *Trauma, Violence, & Abuse*, *20*(1), 22–39. https://doi.org/10.1177/1524838016683457

Silovsky, J. F., Letourneau, E. J., & Bonner, B. L. (2020). Introduction to CAN special issue: Children with Problem Sexual Behavior. *Child Abuse & Neglect, 105.* https://doi.org/10.1016/j.chiabu.2020.104508.

Sorensen, T., & Snow, B. (1991). How children tell: The process of disclosure in child sexual abuse. *Child Welfare, 70*(*1*), 3–15.

Summit, R. (1983). The child sexual abuse accommodation syndrome. *Child Abuse & Neglect*, *7*(*2*), 177–193. https://doi.org/10.1016/0145-2134(83)90070-4

Summit, R. (1993). Abuse of the child sexual abuse accommodation syndrome. *Journal of Child Sexual Abuse*, *1*(*4*), 153–163. https://doi.org/10.1300/J070v01n04_13

Woiwod, D. M., & Connolly, D. A. (2017). Continuous child sexual abuse: Balancing defendants' rights and victims' capabilities to particularize individual acts of repeated abuse. *Criminal Justice Review*, *42*, 206–225. doi.org/10.1177/0734016817704700

Woiwod, D. M., Fitzgerald, R. J., Sheahan, C. L., Price, H. L., & Connolly, D. A. (2019). A meta-analysis of differences in children's reports of single and repeated events. *Law and Human Behavior*, *43*, 99–116. doi.org/10.1037/lhb0000312

2

Understanding child sexual abuse

Disclosures, delays, and denials

Thomas D. Lyon, Breanne E. Wylie, and Zsofia A. Szojka

A key question for child abuse investigators is how to interpret delayed disclosure, initial denial, and recantation of sexual abuse, which we refer to as delay and denial. When a child alleges abuse only after a delay and denies abuse when questioned at some point in the investigation, this might be due to false suggestion. That is, the delay and denial could mean that the child was never in fact abused, but over time succumbed to pressures leading to a false report. On the other hand, delay and denial might be due to reluctance. That is, the child was abused, but delayed disclosing, and sometimes denied abuse when questioned, because of motivational reasons deterring disclosure.

Concerns about suggestibility and reluctance arise at several points in the investigation and adjudication of sexual abuse claims. Interviewers need to be mindful of the risks of suggestibility and reluctance in deciding how to question a child who has never disclosed (or denied) before the interview, fails to disclose (or actively denies) during the interview, or subsequently recants. Awareness of the dangers of both suggestibility and reluctance has influenced the development of protocols for interviewing children, which seek to minimize suggestiveness while maximizing the provision of non-suggestive support in response to reluctance (Lamb et al., 2018).

Once an investigation is complete and the case is adjudicated, factfinders must also be mindful of suggestibility and reluctance in interpreting a child's disclosure history. In the United States and a number of other English-speaking countries, experts may testify about the ways in which suggestion can lead to false allegations (*Pennsylvania v. McGinnis*, 2023 [citing US cases]; Zajac et al., 2013 [New Zealand]) and the ways in which reluctance can lead to false denials (*California v. Munch*, 2020 [41 states allow expert testimony]; Horan & Goodman-Delahunty, 2020 [Australia, Canada, New Zealand, and the UK]). Experts on suggestibility and reluctance are usually prohibited from expressing opinions about whether a particular child was abused. Doing so violates judicial views about the proper role of the jury, which is asked to make the ultimate judgment about the child's credibility (Boals, 2023). Instead, experts are allowed to present "framework" evidence,

DOI: 10.4324/9781003427155-2

which describes how children as a group behave (Brown et al., 2023; Horan & Goodman-Delahunty, 2020). Furthermore, although appellate courts might consider percentages of delay and denial in determining whether experts will be allowed to testify in individual cases (*New Jersey v. J.L.G.*, 2018), experts in individual cases are routinely prohibited from citing percentages because of fears that juries will interpret them as reflecting the likelihood of guilt (e.g. *California v. Julian*, 2019). Instead, experts on suggestibility will testify to factors that increase the likelihood of false allegations, and experts on reluctance will testify to factors that increase the likelihood of false denials.

In this chapter we discuss suggestibility and reluctance as different perspectives on delay and denial. We introduce the likelihood ratio (from Bayes' theorem) as a means of understanding how to think about the issues. The likelihood ratio reminds us that to assess the evidentiary significance of disclosures, delays, and denials, we consider both abused children and non-abused children. We demonstrate a parallel between concerns about suggestibility and reluctance: Evidence for suggestibility reduces the evidentiary value of disclosures, and evidence for reluctance reduces the evidentiary value of delay and denial.

We then discuss factors that influence the likelihood of delayed disclosure and denial in abused children, examining population surveys, studies of children questioned about abuse, and studies questioning offenders about grooming behaviours. We show that the child's closeness to the suspect and the supportiveness of the child's family are important factors. With respect to interview characteristics that influence disclosure, we stress the importance of prior disclosures, whether the child is being asked about abuse for the first time, and characteristics of the interview, including supportiveness and the questions asked.

In the final section, we compare our analysis to that conducted by the New Jersey Supreme Court in *J.L.G.* (2018), in which the court severely restricted expert testimony explaining to juries why abused children might delay disclosure and at some point deny abuse. We discuss how the court focused on overall percentages of children who delay and deny, rather than the factors that influence abused children's reluctance, and how the court overlooked selection biases that lead to underestimation of the likelihood that abused children will deny abuse.

How to think about suggestibility and reluctance

Alternative interpretations of delay and denial

Delay and denial signals suggestion

Whether children are reluctant to disclose child sexual abuse is important for assessing child abuse allegations. On the one hand, initial silence and denial may be reasons to believe that an allegation of sexual abuse is false. If a child was never abused, but adults suspected that they were, and suggestively questioned the child about abuse, then one might observe non-disclosure, followed by initial denial (when the child was first questioned), followed by a disclosure (when the child acquiesced to suggestion). Similarly, recantations, which are denials that occur after an initial disclosure, may be evidence of false allegations. The disclosure may have occurred due to suggestive questioning, and the recantation may occur when the child is questioned in a less suggestive fashion (London et al., 2005).

In criminal trials involving allegations of child sexual abuse, defence attorneys frequently challenge children's credibility based on delayed disclosure and inconsistencies over time in children's reports (Stolzenberg & Lyon, 2014). They may present the testimony of an expert in children's suggestibility, who will describe the factors that may induce children to make false reports, including overt suggestions, suggestive questions, selective reinforcement, and guided imagery (for reviews of children's suggestibility, see London et al., 2021; Poole et al., 2015).

Delay and denial signals reluctance

On the other hand, concealment and denial may instead flow from a true allegation and reveal something about the dynamics of child sexual abuse. A child may have concealed and at some point denied abuse because the child was motivated to keep abuse a secret. The child may have avoided the negative consequences of disclosure, to themselves, to the suspect, and to others close to the suspect (often their mother and others in the child's family). They may feel embarrassment, shame, and blame themselves for the abuse, and they may anticipate disbelief and blame from adults to whom they might disclose. We review research on delay and denial in this chapter. Of course, there are other reasons for false allegations and false denials: children may make false accusations on their own without suggestion, and children may forget true abuse. In this chapter we focus on distinguishing between suggestibility and reluctance.

Weighing the significance of disclosure, delay, and denial

To consider whether a child was abused, one should weigh how both abused children and non-abused children behave. For evidence of a behaviour to increase the likelihood that a child was abused, the behaviour must be more common among abused than non-abused children. Conversely, evidence of a behaviour decreases the likelihood that the child was abused if the behaviour is more common among non-abused children. If the behaviour is equally common among abused and non-abused children, then evidence of that behaviour neither increases nor decreases the likelihood of abuse (Lyon, 2023). Disclosures of sexual abuse increase the likelihood that abuse occurred as long as abused children are more likely to disclose than non-abused children. Conversely, denials of sexual abuse decrease the likelihood that abuse occurred because non-abused children are more likely to deny than abused children.

The extent to which disclosures and denials increase or decrease the likelihood of abuse depends on the ratio of percentages, also known as the likelihood ratio. Assume that a behaviour is more common among abused children than non-abused children. The likelihood ratio is the ratio of the percentage of abused children who exhibit the behaviour to the percentage of non-abused children who exhibit the behaviour. The likelihood ratio will allow one to estimate the probability of abuse given the evidence, starting with the base rate (or prior odds) of abuse, and multiplying that number by the likelihood ratio to arrive at the posterior odds of abuse. The higher the ratio, the more the behaviour increases the likelihood that abuse occurred (Wood, 1996). In the law, the likelihood ratio is analogous to the "probative value" of the evidence (Lyon & Koehler, 1996; Ceci and Friedman, 2000). Understanding the strength or probative value of evidence in terms of the likelihood ratio has a long tradition in the law (Lempert, 1977).

Applying the logic of probabilities to false allegations and false denials

False allegations and suggestibility

Researchers who study suggestibility acknowledge that "children's reports are quite accurate when they are questioned by unbiased interviewers, even if they are occasionally asked leading questions, and even if they are questioned after long intervals following the event" (Bruck et al., 2002, p. 522). They warn, however, that many children will make false claims if suggestively questioned, including by concerned adults prior to formal interviews (Principe & London, 2022), and they argue that by extension, there is a substantial likelihood that a non-abused child would allege sexual abuse if suggestively questioned about abuse (Bruck & Ceci, 2013).

Suggestibility researchers do not claim that in the face of suggestion, non-abused children are *more* likely than abused children to alleged abuse. In such a case, allegations induced by suggestiveness would decrease the likelihood that abuse occurred. They do not attempt to estimate the likelihood that abused children allege abuse when suggestively questioned. Rather, they argue that suggestion *reduces the probative value* of abuse allegations. Regardless of the likelihood that abused children allege abuse when asked suggestive questions, the probative value of allegations will be limited if a substantial percentage of non-abused children are likely to allege abuse when questioned suggestively. A large denominator – a large percentage of allegations made by non-abused children – lowers the probative value of the allegation. In the law, statements with minimal probative value are often called "unreliable" (Mueller et al., 2018), and this is the language used by expert witnesses to describe abuse claims that they argue were tainted by suggestive questioning (London et al., 2020).

False denials and reluctance

Researchers who study reluctance do not argue that abused children are *more* likely than non-abused children to delay and deny. In such a case, delay and denial would increase the likelihood that abuse occurred. Their argument is that a substantial percentage of abused children delay and deny, which makes delay and denial weak evidence against abuse. Just as suggestibility research argues that the probative value of abuse disclosures in *proving* abuse *decreases* in the face of suggestibility, research on children's reluctance to disclose abuse suggests that the probative value of delay and denial in *disproving* abuse *decreases* in the face of reluctance.

Evidence that abused children often delay and deny abuse has been misunderstood. When the term "child sexual abuse accommodation syndrome" (Summit, 1983) was coined in the 1980s to explain the dynamics of sexual abuse, particularly incest, some prosecutors assumed that delay and denial were evidence that the child had been abused, and presented evidence on accommodation as such (Summit, 1993). But the reader will recall that for delay and denial to be evidence of abuse, the percentage of abused children who delay and deny abuse must be higher than the percentage of non-abused children who delay and deny abuse. The problem with this logic is especially apparent with respect to denial. Since children who are directly questioned about abuse either deny or acknowledge abuse, the prosecutors' assumption flies in the face of logic: If denying abuse increases the likelihood of abuse, then *acknowledging* abuse *decreases* the likelihood of abuse.

Contemporary courts recognize the limited purpose that expert testimony about delay and denial play in sexual abuse trials. In California, for example, expert testimony on accommodation is admissible only after the child's credibility has been attacked by questions about the child's behaviour that the defence argues are inconsistent with abuse. Without commenting on the child's case, the prosecution's expert serves to rehabilitate the child by rebutting the defence's claims (*California v. Munch*, 2020). The expert explains the factors that lead many abused children to delay and deny abuse. The expert never testifies that the behaviours increase the likelihood of abuse, and jury instructions emphasize that testimony about accommodation is not evidence of abuse but describes "a pattern of behavior that *may be present* in child sexual abuse cases" (Judicial Council of California, 2024; emphasis added).

There is thus a parallel between arguments for suggestibility and arguments for reluctance. Many experts familiar with the suggestibility literature argue that a worrisome percentage of non-abused children will allege abuse if suggestively questioned, reducing the probative value of disclosure (Bruck & Ceci, 2013). They focus on the denominator of the likelihood ratio for disclosures and discuss the factors that increase the likelihood that non-abused children make false allegations. Experts familiar with the literature on reluctance argue that abused children often delay disclosing and deny abuse at some point in time, reducing the probative value of delay and denial (Lyon et al., 2020). They focus on the denominator of the likelihood ratio for delay and denial and discuss the factors that increase the likelihood that abused children delay and deny.

Avoiding fallacies in reasoning about probabilities

The legal system's initial difficulty in understanding accommodation evidence is symptomatic of a more general flaw in reasoning about evidence. The fact that a behaviour is common among abused children does not mean that the behaviour increases the likelihood that abuse occurred. Some types of sexualized behaviour are common among abused children but are also almost as common among non-abused children, and as such are only very weak evidence of abuse (Lyon & Koehler, 1996). Conversely, the fact that a behaviour is uncommon among abused children does not mean that it decreases the likelihood that abuse occurred. Indeed, behaviours that are uncommon among abused children are often strong evidence of abuse. For example, pregnancy is extremely rare in sexually abused children, and yet has substantial value in proving that abuse occurred.

Although it can be helpful to discuss percentages and probabilities when assessing the probative value of children's behaviours, numbers can also lead to confusion. A common fallacy in reasoning about percentages and probabilities is the inverse error. The probability of A given B is not the same as the probability of B given A. One way to avoid the error is to keep in mind examples that make the error obvious. The probability an animal has four legs, given that it is a dog (very high), is not the same as the probability that an animal is a dog, given that it has four legs (not very high). The probability that a person speaks Spanish, given that they live in Peru (very high), is not the same probability that a person lives in Peru, given that they speak Spanish (quite low; Royal Statistical Society Statistics and the Law Section, 2022).

The inverse error has led courts to misunderstand the evidentiary value of evidence in sexual abuse cases. For example, in *Pennsylvania v. Dunkle* (1992), the Pennsylvania Supreme Court reasoned that behaviours relevant to proving abuse must occur in more than half of abused children. The court argued that if certain behaviours occur in less than 50% of abuse cases, they cannot make abuse more likely than not. However, this reasoning confused the likelihood of a behaviour given abuse with the likelihood of abuse given the behaviour. Furthermore, it also misconstrued the standard for relevant evidence, which only requires that the evidence increase the likelihood of abuse, not that it makes abuse more likely than not.

Errors in reasoning are particularly likely to occur when evidence is offered to rehabilitate an alleged victim; that is, when the evidence is not offered to prove that abuse occurred, but to rebut claims that a specific behaviour is inconsistent with abuse. In *New Jersey v. J.L.G.* (2018), the New Jersey Supreme Court considered the admissibility of expert testimony on delays, denials, and other elements of child sexual abuse accommodation syndrome. The Court held that scientific evidence (as reflected by a consensus among experts) supports expert testimony explaining to jurors why abused children delay disclosing, because most abused children delay disclosing. However, the court held that experts could no longer explain denial and recantation in sexual abuse trials because experts do not agree about the percentage of abused children who deny and recant.

During oral argument in the case, the justices discussed a study finding that 23% of children substantiated by social services as sexually abused recanted at some point during the investigation and adjudication of abuse (Malloy et al., 2007). One of the justices argued that this statistic meant that only 23% of recantations were true cases of abuse, and the prosecutor was unable to explain why this wasn't so (Oral argument in *New Jersey v. J.L.G.*, 2018). This is an example of the inverse error: The justice was confusing the likelihood of recantation given abuse with the likelihood of abuse given recantation. What wasn't discussed (in oral argument or in the court's opinion) was the fact that the study found that children were more likely to recant when the suspect was a parent figure and the non-offending parent was unsupportive. These are the same factors that experts routinely discuss when explaining why abused children delay disclosure and sometimes deny abuse. The court's opinion also struggled with probabilities, misinterpreting rates of denial as rates of delayed disclosure, and confusing the probability of abuse given medical evidence with the probability of medical evidence given abuse (*New Jersey v. J.L.G.*, 2018, pp. 459–460; Lyon et al., 2020, p. 644 n. 1). We return to a discussion of the opinion below, after we explain other methodological problems in estimating delay and denial.

Case characteristics that influence the likelihood of delay and denial in abused children

There are some qualities of sexual abuse that make it inherently difficult to disclose. For example, a common explanation by survey respondents for why they never disclosed childhood abuse is that they were embarrassed (Anderson et al., 1993; Fleming, 1997). Nevertheless, there are also case factors that make sexual abuse victims particularly reluctant to disclose, and which increase the likelihood of delay and denial. There are several sources of evidence identifying those case factors. These include population surveys, clinical studies of children questioned about abuse, and clinical studies of admitted sexual abuse offenders questioned about grooming and their modus operandi. In reviewing the research, it is important to be mindful of ground truth: Whether one can distinguish between true and false reports. Furthermore, one must be mindful of selection biases that can lead to misestimation of reluctance and the effects it has on the correlates of delay and denial.

Closeness to the suspect

The closer the child is to the suspect, the greater the reluctance to disclose. Closeness can be defined in different ways, and this can complicate the relation between closeness and reluctance (Azzopardi et al., 2019). But some distinctions are universally understood: Strangers are on one end of the spectrum and caretaking parents are on the other end. Several literature reviews concluded that closer relationships increase children's reluctance to disclose (Alaggia et al., 2019; London et al., 2008; Lyon, 2009; McElvaney, 2015; Paine & Hansen, 2002; but see Latiff et al., 2024).

Population surveys

One line of evidence supporting the relation between closeness and reluctance comes from population surveys asking respondents if they were abused as children, and if so, if they ever disclosed. This work dates back to the middle of the twentieth century. Kinsey's large-scale survey of American women, which included questions about child sexual abuse, found that single assaults by a stranger were most likely to be disclosed (Gagnon, 1965, p. 183). More recently, six representative population surveys of adults asked respondents about child abuse and disclosure; five found that the relationship mattered, with closer relationships leading to longer delays or lower rates of prior disclosure (Anderson et al., 1993; Hébert et al., 2009; Kogan, 2004; Smith et al., 2000; Wyatt & Newcomb, 1990; but see Fleming, 1997). Four of these studies utilized a multivariate design allowing for assessment of the effects of relationship controlling for other factors (Hébert et al., 2009; Kogan, 2004; Smith et al., 2000; Wyatt & Newcomb, 1990). Moreover, a study examining the same sample as Smith and colleagues found that reporting to the police was more likely when the suspect was a stranger (Hanson et al., 1999).

A methodological concern with survey evidence is ground truth. There may be both false positives (survey respondents falsely reporting that they were abused) and false negatives (survey respondents falsely denying that they were abused). Some of the respondents might be repeating false reports that were the product of suggestive questioning or recovered memory therapy. However, there are reasons to think that only a small percentage of the reports of abuse could be due to suggestion. The surveys consistently found that only about 10–15% of the abuse reported to the surveyor was known to authorities (Miller & London, 2020), which means that few could be cases in which children were suggestively questioned in anticipation of and during an investigation. Even smaller percentages of abuse reported by survey respondents were recalled with the assistance of recovered memory therapy, which reduces the chances that the reports were false memories (Wilsnack et al., 2002).

With respect to false negatives, respondents who were abused may fail to tell the surveyor. This will lead to underestimates of delay and denial if respondents are consistent in their disclosure, that is, if reluctant victims are also reluctant survey respondents. Delayed disclosure will be underestimated because survey respondents who fail to report abuse are still delaying. Of course, because disclosures can be delayed until late in adulthood, the younger the survey respondents, the more likely it is that survey reluctance will underestimate delay. Indeed, surveys with younger respondents have often reported lower rates of abuse, less non-disclosure, and less delay (Lyon, 2009). Moreover, this can distort the relation between closeness to the suspect and prior disclosure. If survey respondents are particularly likely to withhold information about abuse by suspects that are close to them, then undisclosed abuse by close suspects will be underestimated. We will return to this point below, when we discuss conflicting evidence on the relation between child–suspect closeness and disclosure.

Proving that population surveys include false denials is obviously difficult. However, a classic finding is that substantial percentages of officially recognized cases of victimization (based on police reports, hospital records, and court records) will go unreported if the victims are later surveyed (e.g. one-third of rape cases known to police were not reported to surveyors when questioned within one year; Turner, 1972). With respect to child maltreatment, Hardt and Rutter's (2004) review of the literature noted that "the universal finding [is] that, even with well-documented serious abuse or neglect, about a third of individuals do not report its occurrence when specifically asked about it in adult life" (p. 240). Because documentation of child abuse is often dependent on childhood disclosure, these are disproportionately likely to have been cases in which the respondent disclosed at the time the abuse was documented, which makes these percentages conservative estimates of the likelihood of false denials in surveys.

Child interviews

There is also evidence from clinical studies of children questioned about abuse that closeness to the offender influences the likelihood of delay and denial. For example, reviewing the child clinical studies, London and colleagues (2008) noted that "a number of studies indicate that closer relationships are associated with longer delays and lower disclosure rates" (p. 37). In one of the largest studies, Hershkowitz (2006) analysed 26,000 disclosures of physical and sexual abuse elicited with the NICHD structured protocol. Whereas 91% of allegations against parents were delayed, 70% of allegations against other familiar suspects were delayed, as were 22% of allegations against strangers (see also Pipe et al., 2007; Wallis & Woodworth, 2020). A similarly large study by Hershkowitz and colleagues (2005) examined denial in over 26,000 NICHD Protocol interviews; for sexual abuse, disclosure rates were 21% against parents and 89% against non-parents. Three studies have examined the relation between child–suspect closeness and recantations of sexual abuse; all three found that recantations are more likely when the suspects were family members, parents, or parent figures (Baía et al., 2021; Celik, et al., 2017; Malloy et al., 2007).

As with survey evidence, a methodological concern in the child interview studies is ground truth. Parents might be more likely than non-parents to be falsely accused of abuse, and that could contribute to higher delay and denial rates when parental abuse is alleged. Therefore, it is important to identify cases that are more likely to be true. Consistent relations between child-suspect closeness and delayed disclosure have been found in prosecution samples (Goodman-Brown et al., 2003; Sas et al., 1993, 1995), which are particularly likely to include corroborating evidence, and in one study in which all of the suspects had confessed (Sjöberg & Lindblad, 2002). Furthermore, the magnitude of the differences in denial rates reported by Hershkowitz and colleagues (2005) (21% versus 89%) makes it unlikely that false suspicions are driving the difference in disclosure rates between parent and non-parent suspects. With respect to false positives and recantations, two of the three studies focused on substantiated cases; Malloy and colleagues (2007) examined substantiated cases for which allegations were filed in dependency court (and noted that recantation rates were not significantly lower among cases with corroboration), and Baía and colleagues (2021) examined criminal cases with corroboration.

With respect to false negatives, delay and denial will be underestimated to the extent to which children have yet to disclose (Finkelhor, 1994; Okur et al., 2020). If children are particularly likely to delay and deny abuse by close suspects, the underestimation of delay and denial will be greatest for those suspects. Similarly, focusing on substantiated cases when examining recantations underestimates recantations, because recantations reduce the likelihood of substantiation (Block et al., 2023). Substantial percentages of children recant at the time that formal investigation is initiated (DeVoe & Faller, 1999 [30%]; DiPietro et al., 1997 [28%]; Gordon & Jaudes, 1996 [16%]; Keary & Fitzpatrick, 1994 [14%]), but because these children fail to disclose formally, the allegations are presumed false (London et al., 2005). Again, to the extent that recantation occurs more often when suspects are close to the child, these cases are disproportionately likely to be overlooked in research.

Victims' explanations

Another line of research relevant to understanding the relation between closeness to the suspect and reluctance asks participants to explain why they failed to disclose abuse. Closeness suggests attachment to the suspect, which induces both love and fear. Several reviews of the literature have noted that participants who report having failed to disclose abuse attributed their failure to positive feelings for the suspect and fears of negative effects of disclosure on the suspect (Lemaigre et al., 2017; Morrison et al., 2018). In one of the few population surveys asking respondents why they failed to disclose, Anderson and colleagues (1993) found that a primary reason was a wish to protect the suspect. Conversely, suspects close to the child are also in a better position to punish the child for disclosure, and both a review of the literature (Alaggia et al., 2019) and a population survey (Anderson et al., 1993) identified fears of the suspect and concerns about the child's own safety as reasons for non-disclosure. Suspects who are close to the child are likely to be close to the child's family (e.g. a stepfather is close to the child's mother and siblings), and reviews have also noted that participants sometimes explained that they were deterred from disclosing because of the negative effects it would have on their families (Alaggia et al., 2019; Lemaigre et al., 2017). Some studies have shown a relation between subjective fears and delay; both Goodman-Brown and colleagues (2003) and Malloy and colleagues (2011) showed that delayed disclosure was more common when the child mentioned concerns about the consequences of disclosure for others, though Goodman-Brown and colleagues (2003) did not find such a relation for fears of the negative effects of disclosure on the suspect.

Conflicting evidence

Two literature reviews failed to find a consistent relation between closeness and disclosure (Azzopardi et al., 2019; Latiff et al., 2024). Examining disclosure rates in child interview studies, Azzopardi and colleagues' (2019) meta-analysis failed to find a relation between closeness and disclosure, with closeness defined as the distinction between intrafamilial and extrafamilial abuse. However, the authors cautioned:

> In light of discrepancies in how intrafamilial versus extrafamilial relationships were defined across studies and missing data due to the absence of identity disclosure, this unexpected result should be interpreted as preliminary and requires further analysis when more studies become available.
>
> (Azzopardi et al., 2019, pp. 300–301)

(See also Lippert et al., 2009, p. 103 [referring to "variability within the categories of 'intrafamilial' and 'extrafamilial'"].)

Examining surveys and clinical samples of interviews, Latiff and colleagues (2024) acknowledged that several studies examining child interviews found that victim-suspect closeness decreased disclosure (Hershkowitz et al., 2005 [26,446 interviews]; Lippert et al. 2009 [987 interviews]), but referred to "seemingly contradictory" findings from three studies (p. 9; citing McElvaney et al., 2020; Okur et al., 2020; Velloza et al., 2022). Two of the three studies essentially found null effects. McElvaney and colleagues (2020) found a significant relation between familial-extrafamilial abuse and delayed disclosure in a sample of 273 children questioned about sexual abuse but emphasized that they could not identify any group "contributing to the relationship to the extent that could be considered significant" (p. 5). Velloza et al. (2022) surveyed over 5,000 male and female 13- to 24-year-olds in Namibia regarding childhood sexual violence. However, the survey was not focused on child abuse, but included sexual violence perpetrated by a romantic partner or spouse. There was no relation between closeness and disclosure for females, and males were less inclined to disclose violence by their *romantic partners* than intrafamilial abuse; in most cases they explained that they failed to disclose because they did "not view … the experience as a problem" (p. 8).

Truly contradictory results came from the third study. Okur and colleagues (2020) surveyed 3,697 Dutch youth from 18 to 25 years of age about child sexual abuse. Among those reporting abuse to the surveyor, respondents were four times *less* likely to have disclosed sexual abuse by a stranger (48%) than by a family member (78%). One explanation for the anomalous finding was that respondents remained reluctant to disclose intrafamilial abuse. Noting survey literature that "30% to 80% of victims of CSA only disclose their experiences years later in adulthood", the authors emphasized the possibility "that respondents who were not ready to talk about what happened, or did not want to talk about it, will also have chosen not to do so during this survey" (p. 5271). Indeed, only 35 of the 3,697 respondents reported sexual abuse by a family member, and three times that many reported abuse by a stranger.

Researchers have long recognized that younger survey respondents may be less likely to disclose abuse. Reviewing five population surveys conducted from 1983 to 1990, Finkelhor (1994) noted that they showed slightly lower rates of abuse among the youngest age group. This might suggest that abuse had decreased over time, but Wyatt and colleagues' (1999) longitudinal examination showed no evidence of a decline from 1984 to 1994. Instead, Finkelhor noted that "[t]he youngest women may not yet have enough distance from childhood events to feel comfortable talking about them" (p. 44). (The evidence for declining rates of abuse in the 1990s relies on a different methodology that doesn't confound the age of the respondent with the timing of the abuse; Finkelhor & Jones, 2006).

More direct evidence for youthful underreporting comes from Fergusson and colleagues' surveys questioning the same respondents over time. Fergusson and colleagues (1996) conducted a population survey of 18-year-olds, and found relatively low prevalence rates, leading them to worry that many respondents were not ready to disclose. Three years later, Fergusson and colleagues questioned the same subjects when they were 21 (Fergusson et al., 2000). Almost half of those who reported sexual abuse had failed to disclose at 18, but the 21-year-olds showed evidence of continuing ambivalence about disclosure: Just over half of those who reported abuse at 18 failed to disclose at 21. The inconsistencies could not be attributed to uncertainty over whether the behaviour was abuse, because respondents were, if anything, less consistent in their reports of more serious abuse (Fergusson et al., 2000). Hence, because of persistent delays in disclosing abuse, more accurate understanding of respondent's childhood abuse experiences is probably available only after many more years have passed.

Induced closeness: grooming

Children naturally grow close to their parents through cohabitation and caretaking, and parents can take advantage of their special access and inherent authority to both abuse and silence the child. Other familiar adults in the child's life can build upon their pre-existing relationship (Leclerc et al., 2005). More distant adults may induce closeness through grooming. Grooming refers to the methods by which suspects obtain access to children, build trust, obtain compliance, and maintain secrecy (Craven et al.,

2006; Leclerc et al., 2009). Experts who testify about the dynamics of abuse disclosure often describe the grooming process (*US v. Halamek*, 2021).

In this century, strangers appear to be playing a larger role in grooming children. With the advent of the internet, strangers are able to ingratiate themselves into children's lives (Whittle et al., 2013; Korkman & Joleby, Chapter 7, this volume). In commercial sexual exploitation, sex traffickers pose as boyfriends and protectors, often taking advantage of children who were removed from their home or have run away (Quas et al., Chapter 3, this volume; Winters et al., 2022). When grooming succeeds, the usual differences between intrafamilial and extrafamilial abuse are blurred.

Based on children's reports, Sas et al. (1995) observed in their sample of criminal cases that when there was evidence of grooming, children were more likely to have delayed disclosure. Based on interviewers' observations and other evidence, Hershkowitz (2006) found that children more often delayed disclosure if they had been "cooperative" with the abuse (as opposed to "passive" or "resistant"), though the presence or absence of "grooming" was not related to delay. Similarly, in the only study of which we are aware in which incarcerated adult sex offenders were asked about disclosure, Leclerc and Wortley (2015) found in a multivariate analysis that disclosure was less likely if the child failed to resist. Interestingly, living with the offender and being related to the offender predicted *more* disclosure in the bivariate analysis, but these variables were unrelated to disclosure in the multivariate analysis.

With a few exceptions, the research on grooming methods has been based on interviews with offenders who admitted abuse. Of course, self-reports can lead to underestimation of behaviours that offenders were disinclined to report (Christiansen & Blake, 1990). Offenders often choose children on the basis of their vulnerability and the likelihood that they will comply and keep the abuse a secret (Beauregard et al., 2007; Conte et al., 1989). Offenders describe spending time with the child (Christiansen & Blake, 1990; Smallbone & Wortley, 2001) and giving the child gifts (Budin & Johnson, 1989; Christiansen & Blake, 1990). Children disclosing grooming add that suspects express interest in the child's life (Katz & Barnetz, 2016). When the offender is the child's parent (or parent figure), the extra attention paid to the child not only has the effect of making the child feel special but also isolates the child and the offender from other family members (Christiansen & Blake, 1990). When the suspect is outside the family, they attempt to build rapport with the family, often by offering assistance (Katz & Barnetz, 2016).

Offenders desensitize the child to sexual touch through progressively more invasive touch and talk (Elliott et al., 1995; Kaufman et al., 1998). The offender tests the child's acquiescence to abuse (Christiansen & Blake, 1990) and the likelihood that the child will disclose (Kaufman et al., 1998). If the child discloses at an early stage of the process, the offender can claim that the touch was merely affectionate, accidental, or otherwise nonsexual (Lang & Frenzel, 1988). As the abuse progresses, the offender assures the child of the harmlessness and morality of the behaviour (Christiansen & Blake, 1990). In part because of careful victim selection and preparation, initiation of overtly sexual acts need not involve violent force. Moreover, much of the persuasive power comes from the offender's status as an authoritative adult (Kaufman et al., 1998). Once the abuse has begun, offenders make an effort to keep the abuse a secret. Overt threats to induce secrecy may not be necessary. The child's acquiescence leads the child to blame themselves and to anticipate that disclosure will lead others to blame them as well. Moreover, the offenders' closeness to the family increases the likelihood that the child will anticipate disbelief and a lack of support from the family if they disclose. The offender may overtly threaten the child with harm, but more often the threats concern harms to the offender (whom the child wants to protect) (Smallbone & Wortley, 2001) and harms to the family if the abuse is disclosed (Lang & Frenzel, 1988).

Familial support

Delay and denial are more likely if the child's family is unsupportive, particularly the mother. Research has found that children are more likely to delay disclosing when the parents are unsupportive (Hershkowitz et al., 2007; Wallis & Woodworth, 2021). Family unsupportiveness reducing the likelihood of disclosure has been noted by both a review of the literature (Latiff et al., 2024) and studies examining children questioned about suspected abuse (Azzopardi et al., 2014; Elliott & Briere, 1994; Lippert et al., 2009). Addressing the ground truth problem, Lawson and Chaffin (1992) reviewed cases of children with sexually transmitted illness and found that the disclosure rate was much higher (63% versus 17%) when the parents acknowledged the possibility that their child had been abused.

Familial support is also related to the likelihood that the child will recant their allegation. Malloy and colleagues (2007) found that the odds of recantation more than doubled if the non-offending parent (almost always the mother) was unsupportive, with unsupportiveness usually reflected by a statement by the parent that they did not believe the child. Other research has similarly found a relation between familial disbelief and recantation (Baía et al., 2021 [caregivers and family members]; Elliott & Briere, 1994 [mothers], Malloy et al., 2016 [family members]). Because suspects who are close to the child are more likely close to the family, a close child–suspect relationship is likely to lead to less supportive familial reactions to disclosure, complicating analyses. Malloy and colleagues (2007, 2016) took a multivariate approach and found that the child–suspect relationship and familial support independently influenced the likelihood of recantation.

Children refer to familial disbelief as a reason for non-disclosure. This has been confirmed by several reviews of the literature (Lemaigre et al., 2017; Morrison et al., 2018) and by the two population surveys that asked respondents what deterred them from disclosing (Anderson et al., 1993; Fleming, 1997). The literature reviews also mentioned children's self-blame and fears of being blamed and punished as deterrents (Alaggia et al., 2019; Lemaigre et al., 2017). In their prosecution sample, Goodman-Brown and colleagues (2003) found that greater self-blame led to more delays in disclosing, and Hershkowitz and colleagues (2007) found that children who reported shame or fear of their parents' reaction were more likely to delay.

Interview characteristics that influence the likelihood of denial

Prior disclosure

Disclosure is less likely if the child has not previously disclosed. This has been noted by several reviews of the literature (Azzopardi et al., 2019; London et al., 2005, 2008), and child interview studies (Bailey et al., 2017; DeVoe & Faller, 1999; DiPietro et al., 1997; Gries et al., 1996; Keary & Fitzpatrick, 1994; Lippert et al., 2009). In their review London and colleagues (2008) found that "only 7 to 40% of children who made no prior disclosure disclosed at a later interview" (pp. 39–40), whereas children who had previously disclosed re-disclosed 74% to 93% of the time.

A major difficulty in interpreting these percentages is ground truth. As London and colleagues noted, the "lower rates of disclosure likely reflect a combination of unfounded cases as well as children who deny valid abuse cases" (p. 40). Of course, to the extent that false disclosures occur, the higher rates among children who had previously disclosed and disclosed again also reflect a combination of true and false cases.

A second problem with the percentages is that the relevant question for understanding disclosures and denials is not whether abused children *ultimately* disclose, but whether they *initially* and *consistently* disclose. Abused children who have never disclosed rarely appear in court (Block et al., 2023), and experts who explain the dynamics of abuse disclosure to jurors discuss how children sometimes delay and deny. Similarly, suggestibility experts cast doubt on cases in which children initially deny but then ultimately disclose. Many of the child interview studies credited as methodologically superior (London et al., 2005, 2008) examined the ultimate disclosure rate, rather than the initial disclosure rate (DeVoe & Faller, 1999 [two interviews]; Elliott & Briere, 1994 [up to three interviews]; Keary & Fitzpatrick, 1994 [up to three interviews]).

To account for these problems, it is important to consider cases with evidence of abuse other than disclosure to address ground truth and to examine children's disclosures when first officially interviewed. Hershkowitz and colleagues (2014) questioned 426 children aged from 4 to 13 years about alleged intrafamilial physical and sexual abuse with either the NICHD Structured Protocol or the Revised Protocol. In all cases there was external evidence, "including suspects' admissions, disinterested eyewitness testimony, medical evidence (including observable physical injuries), and material evidence" (p. 339). These were the first formal interviews (I. Hershkowitz 2024, personal communication). If the child had never previously disclosed, 48% disclosed in the interview. If the child had previously disclosed, 71% re-disclosed. Hence, the odds of disclosing were over two times as high if the child had previously disclosed.

One reason that prior disclosures lead to re-disclosures is that they reflect the child's willingness to disclose. Children who had not previously disclosed abuse were either concealing abuse or might have denied abuse when questioned. Hence, prior disclosers would be less reluctant to disclose than prior non-disclosers. Another reason concerns the kinds of questions that interviewers can ask prior disclosers, which we discuss below.

Initial questioning

Disclosure is less likely the first time the child is questioned about abuse. Experts testifying about the dynamics of abuse disclosure often testify in cases in which denials occurred before a formal forensic interview was conducted. Children may initially deny abuse when questioned by family members who suspect abuse (e.g. *California v. Croft*, 2016 [mother]; *California v. Elwood*, 2017 [father]; *California v. Sanchez*, 2016 [grandmother]). Furthermore, children are often not referred for a forensic interview when abuse is first suspected, but are initially questioned by medical personnel, social workers, and law enforcement, and may initially deny to them as well (e.g. *California v. Davis*, 2017 [emergency response social worker]; *California v. Rush*, 2017 [police detective]; *California v. Valdez*, 2019 [doctor]).

These cases arouse the greatest concern among suggestibility experts. Parents and frontline professionals are unlikely to use the latest research-based methods for questioning children. If initial denials evolve into allegations at the time of formal evaluation, the initial contacts with parents and others may have suggested information that was incorporated into the child's report, leading to a false allegation. On the other hand, if abused children are likely to have denied abuse when informally questioned, then reluctance is an alternative explanation for initial denial.

Because of selection biases, children's initial responses to questioning are likely to be missed by child interview studies. Children are not routinely screened for sexual abuse. Instead, child interview studies question children when suspicions of abuse have arisen. Indeed, most children in child interview studies have previously disclosed abuse (Azzopardi et al., 2019). Disclosure is the usual means by which abused children become recognized cases of abuse. If an abused child's denial allays a parent's concern, then the parent is less likely to seek formal intervention. If an abused child denies abuse when questioned by a medical provider, the medical provider is less likely to make a child abuse report. And if an abused child denies abuse when questioned by a social worker or law enforcement, the professional is less likely to substantiate the abuse allegation. Denial systematically excludes abused children from child interview samples.

To accurately assess the likelihood that abused children will disclose or deny abuse when first questioned, one must identify samples of children whose abuse can be confirmed without relying on the child's disclosure. Ground truth is addressed through evidence other than disclosure, which can be called non-disclosure evidence. But the selection bias problem requires more. Disclosure can't be the reason that abuse was suspected, and disclosure can't be the reason that non-disclosure evidence of abuse was discovered. The first researchers to recognize this problem were Lawson and Chaffin (1992), who identified a small number of children with sexually transmitted illnesses who were old enough to be interviewed about abuse, not old enough to consent to sex with agemates, and whose abuse was not suspected until after their illnesses were diagnosed. Interviewing the children with anatomically correct dolls, an approach that would now be viewed as unduly suggestive (Poole & Bruck, 2012), hospital social workers were able to obtain disclosures from 43% of the children. As we noted above, if the caretakers were unsupportive, the disclosure rate was 17%.

We've reviewed research identifying samples of children for whom disclosure was neither the precipitating event for suspicion, questioning, or a search for non-disclosure evidence, and found an average disclosure rate of 43% (Lyon et al., in press). Researchers often noted that several interviews were required, because disclosure rates were particularly low when children were first questioned. Initial disclosures in the emergency room ranged from 5 to 15% (Farrell et al., 1981; Ingram, 1994; Shapiro et al., 1993).

Investigators should take note of the fact that if children are questioned about abuse when it is first suspected, they are likely to be highly reluctant. Researchers should be careful to note when children in their samples were being questioned for the first time about abuse, because this can explain greater reluctance. For example, the high rates of reluctance among commercially sexually exploited adolescents (Henderson et al., 2021) may have less to do with age differences in reluctance and more to do with the fact that sexual exploitation is usually discovered prior to any disclosure by the victim (Farrell & Pfeffer 2014; see also Chapters 3 and 7, this volume).

When 10- to 17-year-olds' reluctance in sexual abuse interviews was assessed with the same measure (Nogalska et al., 2023), they showed far less reluctance than sexually exploited adolescents, and reluctance didn't vary from early to late adolescence. Virtually all adolescents had disclosed prior to their interview.

Support and question type

The extent to which the interviewer provides support to the child is likely to influence the disclosure rate. With respect to support, two studies have shown that the Revised NICHD Structured Protocol elicits higher rates of disclosures of physical and sexual abuse than the standard protocol (Hershkowitz et al., 2014; Hershkowitz & Lamb, 2020). Addressing ground truth concerns, Hershkowitz and colleagues (2014) focused on cases for which there was non-disclosure evidence of abuse: 50% of children disclosed in response to the standard protocol, whereas 60% did so in response to the Revised Protocol The Revised Protocol enhances supportiveness in a number of ways, including verbal and nonverbal encouragement; expressions of care and interest in the child; exploration, acknowledgement, and echoing of the child's expressed emotions; positive reinforcement of the child's efforts; and specific advice for encouraging the child when they expressed reluctance (see Hershkowitz et al., Chapter 9, this volume). Furthermore, the Revised Protocol recommends that if the child is extremely reluctant during the pre-substantive phases of the interview, the interviewer terminate questioning and schedule a follow-up interview, at which point many children disclose (Blasbalg et al., 2021).

Another factor is the questions the interviewer asks the child. The questions available to the interviewer are case-dependent. If the child has previously disclosed, this enables the trained interviewer to encourage re-disclosure without specifically asking about abuse. For example, the NICHD structured protocol recommends first asking the child the reason for the interview (e.g. "tell me what you came to talk to me about"), and a large percentage of children who disclose do so in response to this question (Lamb et al., 2018). Children questioned for the first time about abuse may not know the answer to this question. Children who previously disclosed are more likely to be aware of the purpose of the interview, as well as children whose abuse has been exposed through other means. If this question isn't effective, the subsequent questions remind children of prior disclosure recipients, or refer to non-disclosure evidence (Lamb et al., 2018). Of course, if the child has never disclosed, and non-disclosure evidence doesn't exist (or hasn't yet been discovered), these questions will be unavailable.

Practitioners are given little advice with respect to questioning when the child has never disclosed (Talwar et al., 2024), and untrained interviewers are unlikely to recognize the virtues of referring indirectly to prior disclosures (Brady et al., 1999). Allegation questions are frequently yes/no questions, which encourage unelaborated responses, and often include the words "any" and "ever", which suggest a "no" (Szojka et al., 2023). These include "Has anyone ever touched your private part?" (Gallion et al., 2016), "Has anyone ever touched you?" (Brady et al., 1999), and the question recommended by the American Academy of Pediatrics: "Is anything bothering you?" (Jenny et al., 2013). In assessing a child's early denials of abuse, an important issue is the questions the interviewer asked that elicited a denial, and whether the child's denial was simply a series of "no" responses.

The New Jersey Supreme Court's approach to denial in *J.L.G.*

In our view, the research reviewed here supports expert testimony designed to rehabilitate child witnesses whose credibility has been attacked by the defence on the grounds that the child delayed disclosing or at some point denied abuse. As noted above, 41 of the 50 states in the United States allow this type of expert testimony (*California v. Munch*, 2020). However, it is contrary to the New Jersey Supreme Court's holding in *New Jersey v. J.L.G.* (2018), and the court's opinion has been cited by lower courts (and some state supreme court justices) as supporting reconsideration of their jurisdiction's approval of expert testimony (e.g. *Michigan v. Jackson*, 2024).

The court in *J.L.G.* did not address the factors that increase reluctance in abused children. Had it done so, it might have recognized the evidence that closeness to the suspect and familial support affect disclosure rates, and the evidence that abused children are most likely to deny abuse when abuse is first suspected. Instead, it assessed overall rates of delay, denial, and recantation. It approved of expert testimony on delay in limited cases because experts agree that most abused children delay disclosing. It rejected expert testimony on denial and recantation because experts fail to agree about the percentage of abused children who deny or recant abuse.

The court also failed to acknowledge, let alone address, the selection biases that exclude the most reluctant children from child interview studies. Instead, it endorsed the approach of the expert witnesses for the defence who argued that in the "methodologically superior" studies disclosure rates approach 100% if one examines the "substantiated" subsamples (Bruck, 2017; see London et al., 2005, 2008).

Because substantiation is highly dependent on disclosure, the proponents of this approach acknowledged that their logic is "circular" (London et al., 2005, p. 210; London et al., 2021, p. 285) and their process "tautological" (London et al. 2008, p. 39). Nevertheless, they have consistently reiterated (Ceci & Bruck, 2013; London & Kulkofsky, 2009) and defended the approach (London et al., 2021), arguing that "some effort must be made to distinguish true and false cases or else the rates simply reflect disclosure among all children interviewed" (p. 286).

As we have argued in this chapter, a better approach is to focus on cases for which there was non-disclosure evidence. Doing so reveals much lower disclosure rates (Lyon et al., 2020, in press). Indeed, in their first pass at reviewing the literature London and colleagues (2005) acknowledged the virtues of examining non-disclosure evidence of abuse (p. 217). However, they mistakenly claimed that subsamples with non-disclosure evidence usually led to the same high disclosure rates (London et al., 2005; see discussion in Lyon et al., 2020), and confronted with research identifying low disclosure rates in children with non-disclosure evidence of abuse (including two of the "methodologically superior" studies; Dubowitz et al., 1992 [43%]; Gordon & Jaudes, 1996 [43%]), they then criticized the approach, noting that only a small percentage of abused children present with non-disclosure evidence, and arguing that children with non-disclosure evidence of abuse are *demographically* unrepresentative of abused children. For example, they pointed out that many of the studies examining childhood gonorrhoea were conducted at large urban hospitals serving predominantly low income African-Americans (London et al., 2008). The New Jersey Supreme Court also endorsed the representativeness concerns.

Neither the experts nor the court considered whether the demographic differences could explain the lower disclosure rates in the cases with non-disclosure evidence. There is little evidence for statistically significant demographic differences in disclosure and denial (Azzopardi et al., 2019), let alone differences that would explain dramatically lower rates of disclosure in samples with non-disclosure evidence of abuse. As London and colleagues argued, "it is not individual differences but rather methodological features, specifically the sampling methods used, that account for the largest differences" in disclosure rates (p. 38).

The bigger problem is that if we ignore the cases with non-disclosure evidence of abuse on the basis that they are unrepresentative, and limit our examination to the remaining substantiated cases, we are left with the cases for which the evidence of abuse was disclosure. The circularity becomes absolute: 100% of children disclose abuse in cases for which disclosure is the only evidence of abuse.

Conclusion

We've discussed the contrasting interpretations of delay and denial in children suspected of being sexually abused. Delay and denial may arouse suspicions that children's allegations are false, but they could also reflect reluctance. In order to assess the significance of children's behaviour, we should consider how both abused and non-abused children are likely to behave. Suggestibility reduces the probative value of disclosures to the extent that non-abused children make false disclosures. Suggestibility experts inform jurors of the factors that increase the likelihood children will make false reports. Reluctance reduces the probative value of delay and denial to the extent that abused children delay and deny. Reluctance experts inform jurors of the factors that increase the likelihood abused children will delay and deny.

We reviewed the factors that explain abused children's reluctance to disclose abuse in population surveys, child interview studies, and interviews with admitted offenders. We showed that closeness to the suspect and a lack of family support increase reluctance. Whenever possible, we identified research that addressed the ground truth problem by focusing on cases for which there was non-disclosure evidence strongly supporting the conclusion that abuse occurred. We also highlighted the importance of avoiding selection biases that systematically exclude abused children who deny abuse from research.

We also discussed interview factors that are important in understanding disclosure, and these include whether the child previously disclosed, whether the child was being questioned for the first time about abuse, and qualities of the interview, including supportiveness and the questions that were asked. Here too we focused on cases for which there was non-disclosure evidence and discussed how to avoid selection biases. We showed that children are quite likely to deny abuse when they are first questioned about abuse, even when the interview is state-of-the-art and the interviewer is supportive, and especially when the abuse is first suspected and the child is questioned by parents and professionals with limited training. These factors are important to investigators and factfinders when assessing the likelihood that abuse occurred and are factors that experts can explain to juries when children's credibility is attacked because of delay and denial.

Plenty more can be said about abused children's reluctance to disclose abuse. Although we focused on cases in which children deny that any abuse occurred, a great deal of work has explored children's reluctance short of denial, including their reluctance to describe certain aspects of the abuse (e.g. Allard-Gaudreau et al., 2021). It is of course important to better understand the factors that underlie this reluctance as well as the best means for interviewers to address it. Another important question concerns the role that experimental work on children's disclosure of wrongdoing can play in helping us understand abused children's delay and denial (e.g. Lytle et al., 2019). The New Jersey Supreme Court gave short shrift to that research because broken toys are not a "perfect analogy to sexual abuse" (p. 462) The Court's reaction is ironic; taking it seriously would force us to jettison suggestibility research in assessing the likelihood that non-abused children make false allegations of sexual abuse. In our view, experimental work has value for understanding both suggestibility and reluctance, though researchers might be more modest in their claims. Finally, we ignored the obviously important role that age might play in understanding delay and denial. We did so because of the added complexities, such as the selection bias problems in questioning respondents of different ages, a point we touched on above, and age differences in children's ability to recall and date specific events (Wandrey et al., 2012) which affects estimates of delay. We look forward to the third edition of this volume!

Acknowledgements

Preparation of this chapter was supported by Eunice Kennedy Shriver National Institute of Child Health and Human Development Grant HD101617.

References

Alaggia, R., Collin-Vézina, D., & Lateef, R. (2019). Facilitators and barriers to child sexual abuse (CSA) disclosures: A research update (2000–2016). *Trauma, Violence, & Abuse*, *20*(2), 260–283. https://doi.org/10.1177/1524838017697312

Allard-Gaudreau, N., Laforest, M., & Cyr, M. (2021). Les modalités du non-dévoilement dans les récits d'enfants victimes d'agression sexuelle: une étude de l'ellipse narrative. [Patterns of non-disclosure in the narratives of child sexual abuse victims: A study of narrative ellipsis.] *Travaux Neuchâtelois de Linguistique*, (75), 1–19. https://doi.org/10.26034/tranel.2021.3002

Anderson, J., Martin, J., Mullen, P., Romans, S., & Herbison, P. (1993). Prevalence of childhood sexual abuse experiences in a community sample of women. *Journal of the American Academy of Child & Adolescent Psychiatry*, *32*(5), 911–919. https://doi.org/10.1097/00004583-199309000-00004

Azzopardi, C., Eirich, R., Rash, C. L., MacDonald, S., & Madigan, S. (2019). A meta-analysis of the prevalence of child sexual abuse disclosure in forensic settings. *Child Abuse & Neglect*, *93*, 291–304. https://doi.org/10.1016/j.chiabu.2018.11.020

Azzopardi, C., Madigan, S., & Kirkland-Burke, M. (2014). Sexual abuse forensic evaluation with young children: Program outcomes and predictors of disclosure. *Journal of Child Custody*, *11*(4), 304–324. https://doi.org/10.1080/15379418.2014.988901

Baía, P. A. D., Alberto, I. M. M., & Dell'Aglio, D. D. (2021). Predictors of recantation after child sexual abuse disclosure among a Brazilian sample. *Child Abuse & Neglect*, *115*, 105006. https://doi.org/10.1016/j.chiabu.2021.105006

Bailey, C., Powell, M., & Brubacher, S. (2017). The attrition of indigenous and non-indigenous child sexual abuse cases in two Australian jurisdictions. *Psychology, Public Policy, and Law*, *23*(2), 178–190. https://doi.org/10.1037/law0000119.

Beauregard, E., Rossmo, D. K., & Proulx, J. (2007). A descriptive model of the hunting process of serial sex offenders: A rational choice perspective. *Journal of Family Violence*, *22*(6), 449–463. https://doi.org/10.1007/s10896-007-9101-3

Blasbalg, U., Hershkowitz, I., Lamb, M. E., & Karni-Visel, Y. (2021). Adherence to the Revised NICHD Protocol recommendations for conducting repeated supportive interviews is associated with the likelihood that children will allege abuse. *Psychology, Public Policy, and Law*, *27*(2), 209–220. https://doi.org/10.1037/law0000295

Block, S. D., Johnson, H. M., Williams, L. M., Shockley, K. L., Wang, E., & Widaman, K. F. (2023). Predictors of prosecutorial decisions in reports of child sexual abuse. *Child Maltreatment*, *28*(3), 488–499. https://doi.org/10.1177/10775595221074375

Boals, E. I. (2023). Is it science or storytime? Expert testimony evaluating child witness credibility in sexual assault cases. *American University Law Review*, *73*(1), 1–66.

Brady, M. S., Poole, D. A., Warren, A. R., & Jones, H. R. (1999). Young children's responses to yes–no questions: Patterns and problems. *Applied Developmental Science*, *3*(1), 47–57. https://doi.org/10.1207/s1532480xads0301_6

Brown, T. R., Murphy, E. R., & Coles, M. (2023). Brief for John Monahan, David Faigman, Christopher Slobogin, Edward Imwinkelried, Jennifer Mnookin, Roger Park, Paul Rothstein, and 15 other Evidence Professors as Amici Curiae Supporting Respondent. Diaz v. United States (U.S. Supreme Court, No. 23-14). https://www.uclawsf.edu/wp-content/uploads/2024/02/diaz-evidence-law-amicus-brief.pdf

Bruck M. (2017). Psychological Report, State of New Jersey v. J.L.G. Author.

Bruck, M., Ceci, S. J., & Hembrooke, H. (2002). The nature of children's true and false narratives. *Developmental Review*, *22*(3), 520–554. https://doi.org/10.1016/S0273-2297(02)00006-0

Bruck. M. & Ceci, S. J. (2013). Expert testimony in a child sex abuse case: Translating memory development research, *Memory*, *21*(5), 556–565. https://doi.org/10.1080/09658211.2013.769606

Budin, L. E., & Johnson, C. F. (1989). Sex abuse prevention programs: Offenders' attitudes about their efficacy. *Child Abuse & Neglect*, *13*(1), 77–87. https://doi.org/10.1016/0145-2134(89)90031-8

California v. Croft, 2016 WL 1735006 (Ct. App. 2016)

California v. Davis, 2017 WL 4675078 (Ct. App. 2017)

California v. Elwood, 2017 WL 4640131 (Ct. App. 2017)

California v. Julian, 34 Cal.App.5th 878 (Ct. App. 2019)

California v. Munch, 52 Cal.App.5th 464 (Ct. App. 2020)

California v. Rush, 2017 WL 4324853 (Ct. App. 2017)

California v. Sanchez, 2016 WL 270367 (Ct. App. 2016)

California v. Valdez, 2019 WL 2206724 (Ct. App. 2019)

Ceci, S. J., & Bruck, M. (2013). Loftus's Lineage in developmental forensic research: Six scientific misconceptions about children's suggestibility. In M. Garry & H. Hayne (eds), *Do justice and let the sky fall: Elizabeth F. Loftus and her contributions to science, law, and academic freedom* (pp. 65–77). Psychology Press.

Ceci, S. J., & Friedman, R. D. (2000). The suggestibility of children: Scientific research and legal Implications, *Cornell Law Review*, *86*(1), 33–108.

Celik, G., Tahiroğlu, A., Yoruldu, B., Varmiş, D., Çekin, N., Avci, A., Evliyaoğlu, N., & Nasiroğlu, S. (2018). Recantation of sexual abuse disclosure among child victims: Accommodation syndrome. *Journal of Child Sexual Abuse*, *27*(6), 612–621. https://doi.org/10.1080/10538712.2018.1477216

Christiansen, J. R., & Blake, R. H. (1990). The grooming process in father-daughter incest. In A. L. Horton, B. L. Johnson, L. M. Roundy, & D. Williams (eds), *The incest perpetrator: A family member no one wants to treat* (pp. 88–98). Sage

Conte, J. R., Wolf, S., & Smith, T. (1989). What sexual offenders tell us about prevention strategies. *Child Abuse & Neglect*, *13*(2), 293–301. https://doi.org/10.1016/0145-2134(89)90016-1

Craven, S., Brown, S., & Gilchrist, E. (2006). Sexual grooming of children: Review of literature and theoretical considerations. *Journal of Sexual Aggression*, *12*(3), 287–299. https://doi.org/10.1080/13552600601069414

DeVoe, E. R., & Faller, K. C. (1999). The characteristics of disclosure among children who may have been sexually abused. *Child Maltreatment*, *4*(3), 217–227. https://doi.org/10.1177/1077559599004003003

DiPietro, E. K., Runyan, D. K., & Fredrickson, D. D. (1997). Predictors of disclosure during medical evaluation for suspected sexual abuse. *Journal of Child Sexual Abuse*, *6*(1), 133–142. https://doi.org/10.1300/J070v06n01_09

Dubowitz, H., Black, M., & Harrington, D. (1992). The diagnosis of child sexual abuse. *American Journal of Diseases of Children*, *146*(6), 688–693. https://doi.org/10.1001/archpedi.1992.02160180046015

Elliott, D. M., & Briere, J. (1994). Forensic sexual abuse evaluations of older children: Disclosures and symptomatology. *Behavioral Sciences & the Law*, *12*(3), 261–277. https://doi.org/10.1002/bsl.2370120306

Elliott, M., Browne, K., & Kilcoyne, J. (1995). Child sexual abuse prevention: What offenders tell us. *Child Abuse & Neglect*, *19*(5), 579–594. https://doi.org/10.1016/0145-2134(95)00017-3

Farrell, A., & Pfeffer, R. (2014). Policing human trafficking: Cultural blinders and organizational barriers. *The Annals of the American Academy of Political and Social Science*, *653*(1), 46–64. https://doi.org/10.1177/0002716213515835

Farrell, M. K., Billmire, M. E., Shamroy, J. A., & Hammond, J. G. (1981). Prepubertal gonorrhea: a multidisciplinary approach. *Pediatrics*, *67*(1), 151–153.

Fergusson, D. M., Horwood, L. J., & Lynskey, M. T. (1996). Childhood sexual abuse and psychiatric disorder in young adulthood: II. Psychiatric outcomes of childhood sexual abuse. *Journal of the American Academy of Child and Adolescent Psychiatry*, *35*(10), 1365–1374. https://doi.org/10.1097/00004583-199610000-00024

Fergusson, D. M., Horwood, L. J., & Woodward, L. J. (2000). The stability of child abuse reports: a longitudinal study of the reporting behaviour of young adults. *Psychological Medicine*, *30*(3), 529–544. https://doi.org/10.1017/s0033291799002111

Finkelhor D. (1994). Current information on the scope and nature of child sexual abuse. *The Future of Children*, *4*(2), 31–53.

Finkelhor, D., & Jones, L. (2006). Why have child maltreatment and child victimization declined? *Journal of Social Issues*, *62*(4), 685–716. https://doi.org/10.1111/j.1540-4560.2006.00483.x

Fleming, J. M. (1997). Prevalence of childhood sexual abuse in a community sample of Australian women. *Medical Journal of Australia*, *166*, 65–68.

Gagnon, J. H. (1965). Female child victims of sex offenses. *Social Problems*, *13*(2), 176–192. https://doi.org/10.1525/sp.1965.13.2.03a00070

Gallion, H. R., Milam, L. J., & Littrell, L. L. (2016). Genital findings in cases of child sexual abuse: genital vs vaginal penetration. *Journal of Pediatric and Adolescent Gynecology*, *29*(6), 604–611. https://doi.org/10.1016/j.jpag.2016.05.001

Goodman-Brown, T. B., Edelstein, R. S., Goodman, G. S., Jones, D. P., & Gordon, D. S. (2003). Why children tell: a model of children's disclosure of sexual abuse. *Child Abuse & Neglect*, *27*(5), 525–540. https://doi.org/10.1016/s0145-2134(03)00037-1

Gordon, S., & Jaudes, P. K. (1996). Sexual abuse evaluations in the emergency department: Is the history reliable? *Child Abuse & Neglect*, *20*(4), 315–322. https://doi.org/10.1016/0145-2134(96)88716-3

Gries, L. T., Goh, D. S., & Cavanaugh, J. (1996). Factors associated with disclosure during child sexual abuse assessment. *Journal of Child Sexual Abuse*, *5*(3), 1–20. https://doi.org/10.1300/J070v05n03_01

Hanson, R. F., Resnick, H. S., Saunders, B. E., Kilpatrick, D. G., & Best, C. (1999). Factors related to the reporting of childhood rape. *Child Abuse & Neglect*, *23*(6), 559–569. https://doi.org/10.1016/S0145-2134(99)00028-9.

Hardt, J., & Rutter, M. (2004). Validity of adult retrospective reports of adverse childhood experiences: Review of the evidence. *Journal of Child Psychology and Psychiatry*, *4*(2), 260–273.vhttps://doi.org/10.1111/j.1469-7610.2004.00218.x

Hébert, M., Tourigny, M., Cyr, M., McDuff, P., & Joly, J. (2009). Prevalence of childhood sexual abuse and timing of disclosure in a representative sample of adults from Quebec. *The Canadian Journal of Psychiatry*, *54*(9), 631–636. https://doi.org/10.1177/070674370905400908

Henderson, H. M., Cho, S. J., Nogalska, A. M., & Lyon, T. D. (2021). Identifying novel forms of reluctance in commercially sexually exploited adolescents. *Child Abuse & Neglect*, *115*, 104994. https://doi.org/10.1016/j.chiabu.2021

Hershkowitz, I. (2006). Delayed disclosure of alleged child abuse victims in Israel. *American Journal of Orthopsychiatry*, *76*(4), 444–450. https://doi.org/10.1037/0002-9432.76.4.444

Hershkowitz, I., & Lamb, M. E. (2020). The effects of the NICHD Revised Protocol on allegation rates and credibility assessment in child abuse cases. *Psychology, Public Policy, and Law*, *26*(2), 176–184. https://doi.org/10.1037/law0000230

Hershkowitz, I., Horowitz, D., & Lamb, M. E. (2005). Trends in children's disclosure of abuse in Israel: A national study. *Child Abuse & Neglect*, *29*(11), 1203–1214. https://doi.org/10.1016/j.chiabu.2005.04.008

Hershkowitz, I., Lamb, M. E., & Katz, C. (2014). Allegation rates in forensic child abuse investigations: Comparing the revised and standard NICHD protocols. *Psychology, Public Policy, and Law*, *20*(3), 336–344. https://doi.org/10.1037/a0037391

Hershkowitz, I., Lanes, O., & Lamb, M. E. (2007). Exploring the disclosure of child sexual abuse with alleged victims and their parents. *Child Abuse & Neglect*, *31*(2), 111–124. https://doi.org/10.1016/j.chiabu.2006.09.004.

Horan, J., & Goodman-Delahunty, J. (2020). Expert evidence to counteract jury misconceptions about consent in sexual assault cases. *University of New South Wales Law Journal*, *43*(2), 707–737. https://doi.org/10.53637/FDBI9255

Ingram D. L. (1994). Neisseria gonorrhoeae in children. *Pediatric Annals*, *23*(7), 341–345. https://doi.org/10.3928/0090-4481-19940701-07

Jenny, C., Crawford-Jakubiak, J. E., & Committee on Child Abuse and Neglect (2013). The evaluation of children in the primary care setting when sexual abuse is suspected. *Pediatrics*, *132*(2), 558–567. https://doi.org/10.1542/peds.2013-1741

Judicial Council of California (2024). *California Criminal Jury Instructions*. Author.

Katz, C., & Barnetz, Z. (2016). Children's narratives of alleged child sexual abuse offender behaviors and the manipulation process. *Psychology of Violence*, *6*(2), 223–232. https://doi-org.libproxy1.usc.edu/10.1037/a0039023

Kaufman, K. L., Holmberg, J. K., Orts, K. A., McCrady, F. E., Rotzien, A. L., Daleiden, E. L., & Hilliker, D. R. (1998). Factors influencing sexual offenders' modus operandi: An examination of victim–offender relatedness and age. *Child Maltreatment*, *3*(4), 349–361. https://doi.org/10.1177/1077559598003004007

Keary, K., & Fitzpatrick, C. (1994). Children's disclosure of sexual abuse during formal investigation. *Child Abuse & Neglect*, *18*(7), 543–548. https://doi.org/10.1016/0145-2134(94)90080-9

Kogan, S. M. (2004). Disclosing unwanted sexual experiences: Results from a national sample of adolescent women. *Child Abuse & Neglect*, *28*(2), 147–165. https://doi.org/10.1016/j.chiabu.2003.09.014

Lamb, M. E., Brown, D. A., Hershkowitz, I., Orbach, Y., & Esplin, P. W. (2018). *Tell me what happened: Structured investigative interviews of child victims and witnesses* (2nd ed.). John Wiley & Sons.

Lang, R. A., & Frenzel, R. R. (1988). How sex offenders lure children. *Annals of Sex Research*, *1*(2), 303–317. https://doi.org/10.1007/BF00852802

Latiff, M. A., Fang, L., Goh, D. A., & Tan, L. J. (2024). A systematic review of factors associated with disclosure of child sexual abuse. *Child Abuse & Neglect*, *147*, 106564. https://doi.org/10.1016/j.chiabu.2023.106564

Lawson, L., & Chaffin, M. (1992). False negatives in sexual abuse disclosure interviews: Incidence and influence of caretaker's belief in abuse in cases of accidental abuse discovery by diagnosis of STD. *Journal of Interpersonal Violence*, *7*(4), 532–542. https://doi.org/10.1177/088626092007004008

Leclerc, B., & Wortley, R. (2015). Predictors of victim disclosure in child sexual abuse: Additional evidence from a sample of incarcerated adult sex offenders. *Child Abuse & Neglect*, *43*, 104–111. https://doi.org/10.1016/j.chiabu.2015.03.003

Leclerc, B., Proulx, J., & Beauregard, E. (2009). Examining the modus operandi of sexual offenders against children and its practical implications. *Aggression and Violent Behavior*, *14*(1), 5–12. https://doi.org/10.1016/j.avb.2008.08.001

Leclerc, B., Proulx, J., & McKibben, A. (2005). Modus operandi of sexual offenders working or doing voluntary work with children and adolescents. *Journal of Sexual Aggression, 11*(2), 187–195. https://doi.org/10.1080/13552600412331321314

Lemaigre, C., Taylor, E. P., & Gittoes, C. (2017). Barriers and facilitators to disclosing sexual abuse in childhood and adolescence: A systematic review. *Child Abuse & Neglect, 70*, 39–52. https://doi.org/10.1016/j.chiabu.2017.05.009

Lempert, R. O. (1977). Modeling relevance. *Michigan Law Review, 75*(5), 1021–1057. https://doi.org/10.2307/1288024

Lippert, T., Cross, T. P., Jones, L., & Walsh, W. (2009). Telling interviewers about sexual abuse: Predictors of child disclosure at forensic interviews. *Child Maltreatment, 14*(1), 100–113. https://doi.org/10.1177/1077559508318398

London, K., & Kulfofsky, S. (2009). Factors affecting the reliability of children's forensic reports. In G. M. Davies & D. B. Wright (eds), *Current issues in applied memory research* (pp. 119–141). Psychology Press.

London, K., Bruck, M., Ceci, S.J., & Shuman, D.W. (2005). Disclosure of child sexual abuse: What does the research tell us about the ways that children tell? *Psychology, Public Policy, and Law, 11*(1), 194–226. https://doi.org/10.1037/1076-8971.11.1.194

London, K., Bruck, M., Miller, Q. C., & Ceci, S. J. (2020). Analyzing the scientific foundation of Child Sexual Abuse Accommodation Syndrome: A reply to Lyon et al. *Behavioral Sciences & the Law, 38*(6), 648–653. https://doi.org/10.1002/bsl.2489

London, K., Bruck, M., Wright, D. B., & Ceci, S. J. (2008). Review of the contemporary literature on how children report sexual abuse to others: Findings, methodological issues, and implications for forensic interviewers. *Memory, 16*(1), 29–47. https://doi.org/10.1080/09658210701725732

London, K., Kulkofsky, S., & Perez, C. O. (2021). Factors affecting the reliability of children's forensic reports: An updated review. In J. Rummel (ed.), *Current issues in memory: Memory research in the public interest* (pp. 272–295). Routledge.

Lyon, T. D. (2009). Abuse disclosure: What adults can tell. In B. Bottoms, C. Najdowski, & G. Goodman (eds), *Children as victims, witnesses, and offenders: Psychological science and the law* (pp. 19–35). Guilford.

Lyon, T. D. (2023) Child maltreatment, the law, and two types of error. *Child Maltreatment, 28*(3), 403–406. https://doi.org/10.1177/10775595231176454

Lyon, T. D., & Koehler, J. J. (1996). The relevance ratio: Evaluating the probative value of expert testimony in child sexual abuse cases. *Cornell Law Review, 82*, 43–78. https://scholarship.law.cornell.edu/cgi/viewcontent.cgi?article=2671&context=clr

Lyon, T. D., Williams, S., Stolzenberg, S. N. (2020). Understanding expert testimony on child sexual abuse denial after New Jersey v. J.L.G.: Ground truth, disclosure suspicion bias, and disclosure substantiation bias. *Behavioral Sciences & the Law, 38*, 630–647. https://doi.org/10.1002/bsl.2490

Lyon, T. D., Wylie, B.E., & Szojka, Z.A. (in press). Initial denial of sexual abuse: Reluctance or Suggestibility. In G. S. Goodman, T. D. Lyon, S. D. Hobbs, and R.

Enriquez (eds), *The Handbook of Child Witnesses: Improving Psychological Science and Legal Practice*. American Psychological Association.

Lytle, N. E., Dickinson, J. J., & Poole, D. A. (2019). Techniques for interviewing reluctant witnesses. In J. J. Dickinson, N. S. Compo, R. N. Carol, B. L. Schwartz, & M. R. McCauley (eds), *Evidence-based investigative interviewing: Applying cognitive principles* (pp. 193–215). Routledge. https://doi.org/10.4324/9781315160276-11

Malloy, L. C., Brubacher, S. P., & Lamb, M. E. (2011). Expected consequences of disclosure revealed in investigative interviews with suspected victims of child sexual abuse. *Applied Developmental Science*, *15*(1), 8–19. https://doi.org/10.1080/10888691.2011.538616

Malloy, L. C., Lyon, T. D., & Quas, J. A. (2007). Filial dependency and recantation of child sexual abuse allegations. *Journal of the American Academy of Child and Adolescent Psychiatry*, *46*(2), 162–170. https://doi.org/10.1097/01.chi.0000246067.77953.f7

Malloy, L. C., Mugno, A. P., Rivard, J. R., Lyon, T. D., & Quas, J. A. (2016). Familial influences on recantation in substantiated child sexual abuse cases. *Child Maltreatment*, *21*(3), 256–261. https://doi.org/10.1177/1077559516650936

McElvaney, R. (2015). Disclosure of child sexual abuse: Delays, non-disclosure and partial disclosure. What the research tells us and implications for practice. *Child Abuse Review*, *24*(3), 159–169. https://doi.org/10.1002/car.2280

McElvaney, R., Moore, K., O'Reilly, K., Turner, R., Walsh, B., & Guerin, S. (2020). Child sexual abuse disclosures: Does age make a difference?. *Child Abuse & Neglect*, *99*, 104121. https://doi.org/10.1016/j.chiabu.2019.104121

Michigan v. Jackson, 11 N.W.3d 515 (2024).

Miller, Q. C., & London, K. (2020). Forensic implications of delayed reports from child witnesses. In J. Pozzulo, E. Pica, & C. Sheahan (eds), *Memory and sexual misconduct* (pp. 100–131). Routledge.

Morrison, S. E., Bruce, C., & Wilson, S. (2018). Children's disclosure of sexual abuse: A systematic review of qualitative research exploring barriers and facilitators. *Journal of Child Sexual Abuse*, *27*(2), 176–194. https://doi.org/10.1080/10538712.2018.1425943

Mueller, C. B., Kirkpatrick, L. C., & Richter, L. L. (2018). *Evidence* (6th ed.). Aspen.

New Jersey v. J.L.G., 190 A.3d 442 (2018).

Nogalska, A.M., Henderson, H.M., Cho, S.J., & Lyon, T.D. (2023). Novel forms of reluctance among suspected child sexual abuse victims in adolescence. *Child Maltreatment*, *28*(2), 275–285. https://doi.org/10.1177/10775595221104828

Okur, P., van der Knaap, L. M., & Bogaerts, S. (2020). A quantitative study on gender differences in disclosing child sexual abuse and reasons for nondisclosure. *Journal of Interpersonal Violence*, *35*(23–24), 5255–5275. https://doi.org/10.1177/0886260517720732

Paine, M. L., & Hansen, D. J. (2002). Factors influencing children to self-disclose sexual abuse. *Clinical Psychology Review*, *22*(2), 271–295. https://doi.org/10.1016/s0272-7358(01)00091-5

Pennsylvania v. Dunkle, 602 A.2d 830 (Pa. 1992).

Pennsylvania v. McGinnis, 305 A.3d 547 (2023).

Pipe, M. E., Lamb, M. E., Orbach, Y., Stewart, H., Sternberg, K., & Esplin, P. (2007). Factors associated with nondisclosure of suspected abuse during forensic interviews. In Pipe, M. E., Lamb, M. E., Orbach, Y., & Cederborg A. C. (eds). *Child sexual abuse: Disclosure, delay, and denial* (pp. 77–96). Psychology Press.

Poole, D. A., & Bruck, M. (2012). Divining testimony? The impact of interviewing props on children's reports of touching. *Developmental Review*, *32*(3), 165–180. https://doi.org/10.1016/j.dr.2012.06.007

Poole, D. A., Brubacher, S. P., & Dickinson, J. J. (2015). Children as witnesses. In B. L. Cutler & P. A. Zapf (eds), *APA handbook of forensic psychology, Vol. 2. Criminal investigation, adjudication, and sentencing outcomes* (pp. 3–31). American Psychological Association. https://doi.org/10.1037/14462-001

Principe, G. F., & London, K. (2022). How parents can shape what children remember: Implications for the testimony of young witnesses. *Journal of Applied Research in Memory and Cognition*, *11*(3), 289–302. https://doi.org/10.1037/mac0000059

Royal Statistical Society Statistics and the Law Section (2022). *Healthcare serial killer or coincidence? Statistical issues in investigation of suspected medical misconduct.* Author Report_Healthcare_serial_killer_or_coincidence_statistical_issues_in_investigation_of_suspected_medical_misconduct_Sept_2022_FINAL.pdf

Sas L., Hurley P., Hatch A., Malla S., Dick T. (1993). *Three years after the verdict: A longitudinal study of the social and psychological adjustment of child witnesses referred to the Child Witness Project.* London Family Court Clinic.

Sas, L. D., Cunningham, A. H., Hurley, P., Dick, T., & Farnsworth, A. (1995). *Tipping the balance to tell the secret: Public discovery of child sexual abuse.* London Family Court Clinic.

Shapiro, R. A., Schubert, C. J., & Myers, P. A. (1993). Vaginal discharge as an indicator of gonorrhea and Chlamydia infection in girls under 12 years old. *Pediatric Emergency Care*, *9*(6), 341–345. https://doi.org/10.1097/00006565-199312000-00004

Sjöberg, R. L., & Lindblad, F. (2002). Delayed disclosure and disrupted communication during forensic investigation of child sexual abuse: A study of 47 corroborated cases. *Acta Paediatrica*, *91*(12), 1391–1396. https://doi.org/10.1111/j.1651-2227.2002.tb02839.x

Smallbone, S. W., & Wortley, R. K. (2001). Child sexual abuse: Offender characteristics and modus operandi. *Trends and Issues in Criminal Justice*, *193*, 1–6.

Smith, D. W., Letourneau, E. J., Saunders, B. E., Kilpatrick, D. G., Resnick, H. S., & Best, C. L. (2000). Delay in disclosure of childhood rape: Results from a national survey. *Child Abuse & Neglect*, *24*(2), 273–287. https://doi.org/10.1016/S0145-2134(99)00130-1

Stolzenberg, S. N., & Lyon, T. D. (2014). How attorneys question children about the dynamics of sexual abuse and disclosure in criminal trials. *Psychology, Public Policy, and Law*, *20*(1), 19–30. doi:10.1037/a0035000

Summit, R. C. (1983). The child sexual abuse accomodation syndrome. *Child Abuse & Neglect*, *7*(2), 177–193. https://doi.org/10.1016/0145-2134(83)90070-4

Summit, R. C. (1993). Abuse of the child sexual abuse accommodation syndrome. *Journal of Child Sexual Abuse*, *1*(4), 153–164. https://doi.org/10.1300/J070v01n04_13

Szojka, Z. A., Henderson, H. M., Hur, J., Siepmann, H., & Lyon, T. D. (2023). Elaborations and denials in children's responses to yes–no any/some questions in forensic interviews. *Child Maltreatment*, *28*(3), 407–416. https://doi.org/10.1177/10775595231154552

Talwar, V., Crossman, A. M., Block, S., Brubacher, S., Dianiska, R., Espinosa Becerra, A. K., Goodman, G., Huffman, M. L., Lamb, M., London, K., La Rooy, D., Lyon, T. D., Malloy, L., Maltby, L., Nguyen Greco, V. P., Powell, M., Quas, J., Rood, C. J., Spyksma, S., Steele, L. C., Szojka, Z., Wu, Y., & Wylie, B. (2024). Urgent issues and prospects on investigative interviews with children and adolescents. *Legal and Criminological Psychology*. Advance online publication. https://doi.org/10.1111/lcrp.12269

Turner, A. (1972). *San Jose Methods Test of Known Crime Victims*. U.S. Department of Justice, Law Enforcement Assistance Administration, National Institute of Law Enforcement and Criminal Justice.

United States v. Halamek, 5 F.4th 1081 (9th Cir. 2021).

Velloza, J., Davies, L., Ensminger, A., Theofelus, F. M., Andjamba, H., Kamuingona, R., Nakuta, J., Uiras, W., Massetti, G., Coomer, R., Wolkon, A., Forster, N., & O'Malley, G. (2022). Disclosure and help-seeking behaviors related to sexual and physical violence in childhood and adolescence: Results from the Namibia Violence Against Children and Youth Survey. *Child Abuse & Neglect*, *128*, 105624. https://doi.org/10.1016/j.chiabu.2022.105624

Wallis, C. R., & Woodworth, M. (2021). Non-offending caregiver support in cases of child sexual abuse: An examination of the impact of support on formal disclosures. *Child Abuse & Neglect*, *113*, 104929. https://doi.org/10.1016/j.chiabu.2021.104929

Wallis, C. R., & Woodworth, M. D. (2020). Child sexual abuse: An examination of individual and abuse characteristics that may impact delays of disclosure. *Child Abuse & Neglect*, *107*, 104604. https://doi.org/10.1016/j.chiabu.2020.104604

Wandrey, L., Lyon, T. D., Quas, J. A., & Friedman, W. J. (2012). Maltreated children's ability to estimate temporal location and numerosity of placement changes and court visits. *Psychology, Public Policy, and Law*, *18*(1), 79–104. https://doi:10.1037/a0024812

Whittle, H., Hamilton-Giachritsis, C., Beech, A., & Collings, G. (2013). A review of online grooming: Characteristics and concerns. *Aggression and Violent Behavior*, *18*(1), 62–70. https://doi.org/10.1016/j.avb.2012.09.003

Wilsnack, S. C., Wonderlich, S. A., Kristjanson, A. F., Vogeltanz-Holm, N. D., & Wilsnack, R. W. (2002). Self-reports of forgetting and remembering childhood sexual abuse in a nationally representative sample of US women. *Child Abuse & Neglect*, *26*(2), 139–147. https://doi.org/10.1016/S0145-2134(01)00313-1

Winters, G. M., Schaaf, S., Grydehøj, R. F., Allan, C., Lin, A., & Jeglic, E. L. (2022). The sexual grooming model of child sex trafficking. *Victims & Offenders*, *17*(1), 60–77. https://doi.org/10.1080/15564886.2021.1926031

Wood, J. M. (1996). Weighing evidence in sexual abuse evaluations: An introduction to Bayes's Theorem. *Child Maltreatment*, *1*(1), 25–36. https://doi.org/10.1177/1077559596001001004

Wyatt, G. E., & Newcomb, M. D. (1990). Internal and external mediators of women's sexual abuse in childhood. *Journal of Consulting and Clinical Psychology*, *58*(6), 758–767. https://doi.org/10.1037/0022-006X.58.6.758

Wyatt, G. E., Loeb, T. B., Solis, B., Carmona, J. V., & Romero, G. (1999). The prevalence and circumstances of child sexual abuse: Changes across a decade. *Child Abuse & Neglect*, *23*(1), 45–60. https://doi.org/10.1016/S0145-2134(98)00110-0

Zajac, R., Garry, M., London, K., Goodyear-Smith, F., & Hayne, H. (2013). Misconceptions about childhood sexual abuse and child witnesses: Implications for psychological experts in the courtroom. *Memory*, *21*(5), 608–617. https://doi.org/10.1080/09658211.2013.778287

3

Challenges to identification and interviewing of suspected youth victims of commercial sexual exploitation and trafficking

Jodi A. Quas, Emma Simpson, and Sarah C. Kim

Challenges to identification and interviewing of

Since the early 2000s, attention towards the problem of commercial sexual exploitation and sex trafficking, especially of minors, has grown dramatically (Franchino-Olsen et al., 2022; Logan et al., 2009). The increased attention is reflected not only in campaigns and workshops regarding the basics of trafficking for laypersons and wide ranges of professionals, but also in federal and international laws and treaties designed to prevent its occurrence, protect victims, and prosecute perpetrators (United Nations, 2000; Faulkner, 2023; 18 U.S.C. §1591, 2022). A core assumption is that the growing efforts have led to significant increases in the number of victims being identified, services being provided, and traffickers being imprisoned.

Yet, considerable challenges remain with regard to victim identification and intervention. That is, evidence suggests that large numbers of victims are still not identified, services for victims are under-utilized, and prosecutorial success in trafficking cases is lower than it is for cases involving other types of sex crimes against minors (Farrell et al., 2014, 2016; Quas et al., 2024). Challenges arise in part because of a lack of understanding among laypersons and professionals as to what trafficking victims are like and hence how best to identify them and in part from victims' distrust of and reluctance to disclose their experiences to or seek assistance from professionals (Clawson & Dutch, 2008; Farrell et al., 2010; Gozdziak, 2010). When victims are not identified and details concerning their experiences are not known, interventions cannot be provided and criminal investigations and prosecutions are hampered. The overarching goal of the current chapter is to review literature relevant to these challenges and suggest possible remedies. Our review focuses on three overlapping literatures. First, we describe research concerning common characteristics of trafficking victims. Knowledge of these characteristics provides context for

DOI: 10.4324/9781003427155-3

understanding why victims are particularly and perhaps uniquely difficult to identify and interview. Second, we discuss studies evaluating what laypersons and professionals know about trafficked minors, including why this knowledge matters for victim identification. Third, we review a newer body of work focused on interviewing suspected minor victims of trafficking. This work has examined how interviews are conducted, how victims respond, and how interviews might be improved to enhance victim disclosure. We close by highlighting remaining questions regarding how best to identify and intervene on behalf of minor victims of trafficking and prosecute perpetrators of this heinous crime.

Before turning to our review, it is useful to provide definitions of what we mean by sex trafficking, distinguishing it from human trafficking and commercial sexual exploitation of children (CSEC). All terms are at times used interchangeably, but there are subtle differences. Sex trafficking is a form of human trafficking, which itself refers to any unlawful transporting, coercing, or manipulating people into providing some form of work, most often sex or labour. Sex trafficking of minors and CSEC both involve exploitation specifically of youth under age 18, that is, the age of legal consent. However, CSEC is slightly broader, including any form of sexual activity with a minor done for economic or material gain. CSEC includes sex trafficking or prostitution of children, but also child pornography, child sex tourism, and forced marriages. The Institute of Medicine defines sex trafficking of a minor specifically as recruiting, enticing, harboring, transporting, providing, obtaining, and/or maintaining, a minor for the purposes of sexual exploitation or prostitution. (Institute of Medicine & National Research Council, 2013). Note that this definition does not include explicit mention of force or coercion. With minor victims, force, coercion, or manipulation is not required for the crime to have occurred, although the exact requirements vary across counties and states.

Our chapter focuses primarily on sex trafficking of minors, including the challenges associated with identifying minor victims, interviewing them about their experiences, and prosecuting traffickers. Our chapter emphasizes adolescent- rather than child-age victims. Although children can be CSEC victims and trafficked, most minor victims of trafficking are adolescents, that is, between 12 and 17 years, when they are identified (Clawson et al., 2009; Greenbaum, 2014; Hardy et al., 2013; Reid, 2016; Smith et al., 2009). Thus, in our review, we include some mention of hallmark characteristics of adolescent development that can shape minors' reactions to being questioned by professionals and professionals' perceptions of and responses to the adolescents' behaviours and disclosures (Lavoie et al., 2019).

Characteristics of trafficked minors

Knowledge concerning how best to question suspected minor victims of trafficking needs to begin with a clear understanding of what victims are like. This includes knowledge of characteristics that place youth at risk for trafficking and characteristics of youth's experiences while being trafficked. Both affect how easily victims are identified, their reactions to others who attempt to intervene, and their disclosures in interview settings.

First, with regard to victim history, perhaps one of the most common features is victims having previously suffered some form of child maltreatment (Franchino-Olsen, 2021; Goldberg et al., 2017; Hershberger et al., 2018; Reid et al., 2017). High percentages of trafficked minors have experienced child sexual abuse, most often by a family member, with many also experiencing physical abuse and neglect (De Vries & Goggin, 2020). For a majority of these youth, the maltreatment was sufficiently serious to warrant their removal from home and placement into some type of out-of-home care, such as with a foster family or in congregate care. Many victims report having bounced around different foster placements or having been returned to home only to be re-removed again later (Dierkhising et al., 2022; Latzman et al., 2019). Given these experiences, it is not surprising many have run away from their placements, often repeatedly, resulting in them being homeless and at times using sex to survive (Kaestle, 2012; Tyler & Johnson, 2006; Warf et al., 2013). Other characteristics commonly reported by trafficked minors include drug and alcohol use, mental health symptoms, delinquent behaviour, and gang affiliation (Choi, 2015; Countryman-Roswurm & Bolin, 2013; Herman, 2003; Mitchell et al., 2010). Some of these characteristics (e.g. drug and alcohol use) are likely consequences of youth's earlier exposure to maltreatment and could reflect forms of the youth's coping with or responses to prior violence. Others, such as gang affiliation, may afford victims protection, shelter, or the provision of basic needs when other placements are not believed to be an option.

The aforementioned experiences not only contribute to significant levels of trauma in victims but also lay a foundation for some of the reasons why identifying, engaging with, and ultimately interviewing these victims is likely challenging. Specifically, severe maltreatment, living with foster families, congregate care, or residential facilities, and contact with the justice system due to delinquency all involve repeated encounters with social services, law enforcement, and legal professionals. These encounters may be stressful and perceived as highly negative (Baugerud & Melinder, 2012; Bejinarui et al., 2021; Heyman et al., 2020). The youth may blame professionals for removing them from their parents' custody or for placing them in unfamiliar or poorly fitting foster families. They may have been interrogated as suspects by law enforcement officers who have no knowledge of their potential status as victims. Even if the officers have some knowledge, they may see the youth as prostitutes and not victims, continuing to interrogate rather than interview them (Halter, 2010; McMahon-Howard, 2017). Victims may, as a result, be highly distrusting of authorities (Helpingstine et al., 2021; Phillips, 2015; Sabina et al., 2012) even those who purport to want to help. This distrust may be expressed in victims' general unwillingness to engage with authorities, attempts to escape (Farrell et al., 2019), or not showing up for interviews or trial when summoned (Quas et al., 2023); but also in victims interviews or while testifying, with victims refusing to answer questions, denying victimization, or responding in evasive, sassy, and largely unhelpful ways (Cho et al., in press; Henderson et al., 2021a).

Second, regarding victims' experiences while being trafficked, there are several reasons why these may lead to additional challenges in interview settings. These include most notably victims' relationships with their traffickers and how they were manipulated into trafficking. Some traffickers exploit their victims, particularly those who are homeless or who have drug or alcohol addictions, by providing basic needs (e.g. food, shelter), material goods (e.g. clothes, phone) or alcohol or drugs, the latter of which could serve to fuel addiction further (Reid & Piquero, 2014; Reid & Jones, 2011). Victims are unlikely to willingly disclose their experiences or name their trafficker if they believe doing so could compromise their survival and support or get them in trouble. Traffickers may also manipulate victims into believing that they are in a romantic relationship (Anderson et al., 2014; Reid, 2016) and guilt or threaten victims not to tell. Victims, out of a desire to protect their boyfriends, may not tell. Moreover, adolescents in general often feel that they have the right to make their own decisions, including about with whom they form relationships (Daddis, 2011; Kansky et al., 2017), and adolescents may perceive any questions about their romantic relationships as implying that they are not able to make decisions on their own. Finally, traffickers may threaten or use violence to control victims, leading to fear-induced non-disclosure. Of note, many traffickers use multiple forms of manipulation at the same time, such as stressing a romantic relationship but also threatening victims if they do not comply (Baird & Connolly, 2023; Quas et al., 2023), leading to considerable pressure on victims not to engage with or disclose to professionals, especially when victims feel that professionals have disrupted their lives repeatedly in the past.

In summary, minor victims of trafficking have a history of adversity that precedes and likely contributes to their ultimate risk for trafficking. This history includes maltreatment and perceived negative contact with social services and the juvenile justice systems, including the dependency and delinquency branches, all of which may have fostered considerable distrust of authorities. Traffickers may exploit this history when recruiting victims, feigning love and romance to youth with tumultuous and violent home lives; providing basic needs, material goods, drugs, and alcohol; or threatening minors with harm if they do not comply. The extent to which adults are aware of victims' histories and experiences likely affects how adults interact with victims during encounters and how victims respond. Thus, we next turn to how much adults know about victims' history and trafficking.

Adults' knowledge of trafficking victims

A wide range of adults may be involved directly and indirectly in victim identification and intervention. Laypersons, for instance, may encounter victims in public locations (e.g. beaches, restaurants, parks) and have opportunities to contact authorities when concerns arise. Laypersons also serve as jurors in trials and make decisions based on their interpretation of evidence, which can include the victims' demeanour in court, statements provided in court or in interviews, and descriptions of how victims became involved in trafficking or why victims might have been in a gang or delinquent (Quas et al., 2023). Diverse groups of professionals also encounter victims. This includes law enforcement, child protection workers, and legal professionals, all of whom may question minors because of suspected exploitation. The same professionals question minors about their home life, delinquency, crime, and prostitution, presenting an opportunity for trafficking to be discovered indirectly. Professionals in school (e.g. teachers, counsellors) and healthcare (e.g. nurses, therapists) settings or in service industries (e.g. motel, nail salons) also encounter victims. Sizeable numbers of victims, for example, report attending school while being trafficked (Goldberg et al., 2017), and nearly 90% of victims report having visited a health clinic while being exploited (Baldwin et al., 2011; Chisolm-Straker et al., 2016; Lederer & Wetzel, 2014). In order for these individuals – laypersons and professionals – to be effective at victim identification, they need to possess sufficient knowledge of common characteristics of victims, particularly adolescent-age victims, why victims might behave or interact with others in particular ways, and how to engage minor victims who are reluctant to disclose and highly mistrusting of adults.

Layperson perceptions

Most research on layperson perceptions has focused on whether laypersons are aware of human trafficking and whether their beliefs conform to stereotypes of trafficking victims depicted in popular media, advertisements, movies, television shows, and sensationalized stories. In these, the victims are presented as scared, often white, women and girls who are physically restrained, threatened, and violently forced to engage in sexual activity. Regarding awareness, evidence indicates that laypersons are aware that sex trafficking does occur, including in first-world countries like the United States (Cunningham & Cromer, 2016), and that trafficking is a problem

(Strohacker et al., 2021). Thus, public awareness campaigns are working to some extent. Regarding beliefs about trafficking and victims, however, evidence reveals numerous incorrect beliefs in laypersons, which could undermine their ability to identify victims, assess responsibility, and render decisions in criminal cases (Digidiki & Baka, 2022). For example, laypersons tend to believe that trafficking only refers to situations in which victims are physically held against their will (Strohacker et al., 2023), suggesting that, when laypersons learn that an individual (minor or adult) was not restrained and did not actively attempt to escape, the individual is not a victim. Laypersons also incorrectly assume that a person, including a minor, who knowingly solicits commercial sex cannot be a victim of trafficking (Bouché et al., 2018). In a study of laypersons' perceptions of a vignette describing a sexual encounter between an adult and minor that was highly suggestive of trafficking, Winks et al. (2023) found that, although two thirds of respondents correctly reported that the sexual activity (67%) in the scenario was illegal, only 5% correctly labelled it trafficking. Some laypersons instead reported that the vignette described prostitution. Further, some respondents attributed responsibility for the situation to the minor because she was a prostitute, similar, in part, to laypersons at times blaming women for having been raped (Cunningham & Cromer, 2016).

The vignette in Winks et al.'s study was very brief and did not mention any of the aforementioned characteristics or history common to trafficked minors, such as their maltreatment history, delinquent behaviour, or perceived romantic relationship with their trafficker. Had these characteristics been mentioned, laypersons might have interpreted the situation differently, though not necessarily in ways that improved their ability to detect trafficking. As an example, when victims' past delinquent behaviour or their general scepticism and distrust of authorities is described, laypersons could be even less likely to see the minor as a victim, instead seeing the minor as problematic and choosing prostitution. Such a pattern was observed in an investigation by Kim et al. (2024) who presented laypersons with vignettes highly suggestive of trafficking that varied the minor victim's delinquent behaviour and cooperativeness with authorities. Laypersons' perceptions of the victims' responsibility for her situation increased when delinquency was mentioned. Similar victim blaming has been observed in laypersons' perceptions of adolescent sexual abuse victims, such as when they are described as having been in age-inappropriate locations (Back & Lips, 1998; Franklin & Menaker, 2015; Rogers et al., 2007).

In summary, without accurate or detailed knowledge of how trafficking occurs and how minors especially might be manipulated, laypersons may well overlook many cues to trafficking and fail to identify victims in places they might frequent. In court, if a trafficked minor does not behave in a way that laypersons think victims should act, for instance, if the minor has a history of problematic behaviour and is evasive when questioned, laypersons may see the minor as partly responsible for what happened rather than seeing the defendant as solely culpable.

Professional perceptions

Professionals' ability to recognize potential victims and respond partly hinges on their knowledge not only about trafficking risk and victim characteristics but also about how to ask questions when those risk factors are present. Some studies have surveyed professionals regarding their perceptions of trafficking, perceived need for training in trafficking, and knowledge of victims and victim disclosures (Farrell & Pfeffer, 2014; Gonzalez-Pons et al., 2020; Halter, 2010; Hartinger-Saunders et al., 2017; Litam & Lam, 2021; O'Brien, 2019; Wilson & Dalton, 2008). Other studies have presented vignettes that depict trafficking situations tailored to the types of encounters that specific professional groups might experience and assessed whether professionals in those groups recognize trafficking and how they report they would respond (e.g. Baker et al., 2024; Luna et al., 2023; Winks et al., 2023). Finally, a few studies have directly asked professionals, most often law enforcement, about interviewing trafficking victims, including what challenges arise while doing so and what they do to combat those challenges (Dianiska et al., 2023; Farrell et al., 2019). Results paint a complicated picture of professionals' knowledge of and ability to identify and question suspected minor victims.

It is useful to distinguish non-legal (i.e. healthcare professionals, mandated reporters, school professionals) and legally relevant professionals (i.e. forensic interviewers, law enforcement, attorneys, judges), given that the types of encounters and consequences of those encounters diverge between the groups in important ways. Non-legal professionals do not interview victims for legal purposes, but they may still encounter and engage with victims in their jobs and hence need to talk to (that is, question) the victims. Such questioning is often framed as history taking, building rapport, or conducting a needs assessment. Regardless of what the questioning approach is called, the professionals nonetheless need to ask minors questions to find out about their experiences, perceptions, needs, and well-being. Given that children, adolescents, and adults, including those considered high risk, are often quite trusting of non-legal professionals, especially healthcare workers, such professional may be in an ideal position to be able to elicit disclosures from minor victims. Such professionals will only be able to capitalize on this opportunity if they recognize common characteristics and risks in victims and know how to ask the minors questions about those risks.

When considering how much non-legal professionals know about trafficking, most recognize that commercial exploitation and trafficking of minors are problems (Balasa et al., 2024) and report that they need training on identification and intervention (Havig & Mahapatra, 2021; O'Brien et al., 2022). For example, clinic healthcare workers, fire and emergency service first responders, victim advocates, child welfare workers, and social service case management workers all see trafficking as a problem in their state of practice and in communities they serve (Coppola et al., 2019; O'Brien, 2019; Varma et al., 2015). A wide range of professionals also recognize limitations in their knowledge, stating that they feel ill equipped to handle trafficking situations because their organizations lack clear policies or procedures or that they need additional training (Winks et al., 2023). Of note, Fraley et al. (2018) found that school nurses did not consider minor sexual exploitation (the broader term was included in the survey) to be a major problem in the United States, but the nurses still indicated that they need to be trained on its occurrence and should be screening for it in schools.

Despite evidence suggesting broad awareness about trafficking among non-legal professionals, when probed further about what characteristics or behaviours are indicative of trafficking, limitations in their knowledge emerge. Non-legal professionals correctly identify some historical and experiential risk factors for trafficking, such as prior child abuse, threats and mistreatment within the family, and forceful sexual encounters (Goldberg et al., 2017; Schwarz et al., 2020; Titchen et al., 2017) but fail to see connections between other characteristics (e.g. delinquency, evasiveness) and trafficking. In a survey of medical students and physicians in the United States, for instance, only about 20% correctly recognized homelessness as a risk factor for trafficking (Titchen et al., 2017). Similarly, some school professionals in the United States and Canada do not know that minors engaging in survival sex while living on the streets is a form of exploitation (Baker et al., 2024).

Evidence also reveals that non-legal professionals often endorse stereotypes similar to those endorsed by laypersons, such as that force, fraud, and coercion are necessary for trafficking to have occurred (Gonzalez-Pons et al., 2020; O'Brien, 2019) and that adolescent females who choose to prostitute themselves are not victims (Hartinger-Saunders et al., 2017). Healthcare professionals also mislabel trafficked youth as child abuse victims or prostitutes (Beck et al., 2015; Winks et al., 2023). Even though majorities of school professionals recognize that victims may incorrectly think that they are in a romantic relationship with their trafficker (Baker et al., 2024), such professionals still mislabel vignettes that describe trafficking situations as consensual risky sexual behaviour. Health care first-responders evidence similar limitations, often failing to recognize trafficking when presented in vignettes, even when they acknowledge that the situations might be risky for adolescents (Winks et al., 2023).

One other study, specifically a survey of knowledge of trafficking among mandated reporters is worth mentioning. Although all of these respondents, by virtue of their designation as a mandated reporter, must encounter youth in some capacity, the range of ages of youth with whom they might interact likely varies considerably. They may not have any training in adolescent development or in risk factors that might place children or youth at risk for specific forms of harm, and certainly may not have ever been exposed to training in exploitation or trafficking. Their knowledge, perhaps unsurprising, was limited. When asked about minors' behaviour, 57% indicated that many victims willingly choose to prostitute themselves; 25% indicated sex trafficking does not happen in their own community; 21% incorrectly indicated that most trafficking victims come into the United States from other nations; and 10% expressed their belief that sex trafficking is "blown out of proportion" in the United States (Hartinger-Saunders et al., 2017). Such perceptions may well lead to under-identification, with many mandated reporters simply failing to recognize and hence report concerns about suspected victims.

Overall, variability in non-legal professionals' knowledge, combined with their seemingly limited ability to identify trafficking when presented with scenarios highly suggestive of trafficking, reveal that sizable numbers of professionals lack the skills, training, or protocols to enable effective responses. Moreover, even if professionals recognize signs of trafficking, it is not clear that they have the requisite knowledge to know what to ask or how to respond, given surveys sometimes revealing low rates of understanding of best practice approaches to interviewing (or history taking or background assessments) to elicit complete and accurate details (Baker et al., 2024; Winks et al., 2023). It may be highly valuable for professionals to have some requisite general training in adolescent development, which could help the professionals identify and understand age-normative changes in adolescents' broad disclosure tendencies regarding personal information, need for autonomy, and scepticism in adults' motives (Dianiska et al., 2024a; Smetana et al., 2006). Such broad training, when combined with specific information about trafficking and minors' risk, could improve how professionals identify, engage with, and ultimately question and respond to potential adolescent victims in the most effective and supportive manner possible.

Legally relevant professionals, such as police, forensic interviewers, and attorneys, must directly question suspected minor victims to ascertain their prior and future risk, document details of a crime, identify perpetrators, and collect evidence for juvenile or criminal court. These professionals' knowledge of sex trafficking of minors and of questioning suspected adolescent victims are both crucial. Surveys of law enforcement and legal professionals suggest substantial improvements in knowledge over the past two decades, along with a few notable gaps. For instance, in the mid 2000s, only a minority of law enforcement (4%) believed human trafficking was prevalent in their communities (Farrell, 2009). In a more recent survey conducted in the 2020s, nearly two thirds of law enforcement professionals believed it was serious (Dianiska et al., 2023), perhaps due to increases in officer training about trafficking. Law enforcement no longer view highly sensationalized or stereotypical versions of trafficking as being the norm (e.g. kidnapped and chained children being auctioned off to the highest bidder; Rodríguez-López, 2018; Uy, 2011). Instead, they increasingly recognize realistic depictions as the most prevalent types of cases (e.g. domestically based, at-risk minors; victims exchanging sex for basic needs or material goods; Gerassi et al., 2021; Renzetti et al., 2017).

Surveys also reveal that law enforcement are aware of several characteristics of victims that make interviewing them difficult (Farrell et al., 2010, 2014; Dianiska et al., 2023), such as victims' relationship to their trafficker and prior encounters with authorities. For example, Dianiska et al. (2023) conducted a national survey of law enforcement professionals' perceptions of and encounters with suspected minor victims. Professionals identified a number of challenges to these encounters. For example, they estimated that about two-thirds of victims do not disclose in their first formal interview and repeated interviews are needed to elicit disclosures (Dianiska et al., 2023). Other challenges identified by professionals included victims' evasiveness, lack of trust in authorities, and uncooperativeness, as well as their financial dependence on traffickers and perceived romantic involvement with their trafficker. Thus, law enforcement recognized characteristics that can make victims vulnerable and directly linked these characteristics to interviewing challenges. Finally, in a separate part of the same survey, law enforcement read and answered questions about vignettes describing forensic interviews with suspected victims displaying varying degrees of cooperativeness. When asked how they would conduct interviews, law enforcement endorsed more witness-focused questioning tactics than suspect interrogation tactics, suggesting that they recognize the need to approach victims in supportive manners and the need to avoid highly suggestive questioning (Luna et al., 2023).

In summary, with relatively few exceptions, diverse groups of professionals recognize that trafficking exists and that additional training on trafficking characteristics and intervention would be valuable. Yet, for non-legal professionals, their accurate knowledge largely stopped there. Many incorrectly endorsed stereotypical depictions of what victims are like, suggesting that the professionals are likely failing to identify victims and hence missing an important opportunity for early intervention and support. Legal professionals, on the other hand, displayed more impressive levels of knowledge of risk factors in trafficked minors, including how those risk factors might affect victims' disclosures. Of course, knowing about risk factors and interviewing challenges is not the same as knowing how to overcome those challenges when actually questioning minor victims. Next, we describe emerging research analysing forensic interviews with suspected minor victims of trafficking.

Forensic interviews with suspected minor victims

A new wave of studies has begun to document how law enforcement and attorneys question suspected victims of sex trafficking and how victims respond (Dianiska et al., 2024b; Henderson et al., 2021a, 2021b; Lindholm et al., 2015). Some of these studies have further compared attorney questions and victim responses in trafficking cases to those in child sexual abuse cases, at times matching victim age to ensure that broader age-related changes in questioning strategies (e.g. children versus adolescents) do not account for evident group differences. Of interest is whether the questioning approaches are similar between the two types of victims, given that both can be reluctant to disclose (Alaggia et al., 2019; Henderson et al., 2021a; Nogalska et al., 2023; Schönbucher et al., 2012; Morrison et al., 2018; Manay & Collin-Vezina, 2021; see also Chapter 2, this volume).

How investigators question victims

In two early but particularly important studies, Lindholm and colleagues (2014, 2015) analysed police interviews of suspected adolescent victims of sex trafficking in Sweden. First, in a qualitative analysis, Lindholm et al. (2014) identified two themes in the interviews that were important for understanding how the interviews unfolded and the content of victims' disclosures. One concerned victims' combined sense of agency and identity as victims. The victims' language suggested they were taking some responsibility for their experiences (e.g. referring to themselves as prostitutes) while acknowledging that they had been manipulated. The second was victim evasiveness when discussing sexual behaviour. For example, one victim used vague terminology rather than concrete language to describe her experiences, reporting that money was paid "because we were with them". It was only when police pressed the victim that she acknowledged that money was exchanged for sex. Second, in a quantitative study, Lindholm et al. (2015) evaluated 24 Swedish police interviews with victims aged 13–17 years of age when they were exploited in the sex trade. Perhaps the most significant finding was the seeming effectiveness of closed-ended and suggestive questions in eliciting victim disclosures. Open-ended questions, in contrast, were associated with evasive responses from victims, especially when the questions asked about crime-specific sexual activities.

Other studies have since reported similar trends. Nogalska et al. (2023), for instance, analysed police interviews in the United States with eight victims trafficked by the same perpetrator and found that open-ended questions led to more reluctant responding from victims than closed-ended questions did. Dykstra et al. (2024) reported a similar trend in a larger sample that included the original eight interviews plus forty more. Dykstra et al. also found that closed-ended questions were quite prevalent in trafficking interviews, or at least more prevalent than is typically observed in interviews with suspected victims of child sexual abuse. In the trafficking interviews, over 30% of the questions were closed-ended, whereas just under 40% of the questions were open-ended, and 23% were suggestive. In studies of child sexual abuse interviews, the percentages of closed-ended and suggestive questions are often substantially lower, as best practice interviewing strategies promote the use of open-ended questions that encourage elaborated responses (Brown et al., 2015; Fernandes et al., 2024; Goodman & Melinder, 2007; Lamb et al., 2018). What is worth exploring in subsequent research is the consequences of such questions on trafficking victims' perceived credibility. Concerns about false reports, for instance, commonly emerge when interviews with suspected child sexual abuse victims contain high proportions of closed-ended and suggestive questions (Ceci & Bruck, 1993; Ceci & Friedman, 2000; Korkman et al., 2024). It would be of interest to ascertain if and how often concerns about false reports arise in trafficking cases (see Quas et al., 2023, for some discussion of this issue).

Other recent studies have focused on law enforcement behaviour in interviews with suspected minor victims of trafficking. For example, in light of law enforcement explicitly citing rapport and support as being effective at reducing evasiveness and eliciting disclosures in trafficking victims (Dianiska et al., 2023) and in light of consistent evidence showing benefits of rapport and support on children's reporting completeness and accuracy (Brubacher et al., 2015; Saywitz et al., 2019), Dianiska et al. (2024b) evaluated forensic interviews with trafficked minors for the use of rapport and support. Rapport use by interviewers was variable. Some, particularly those who report having received prior training in forensic interviewing of children, utilized a wide range of rapport tactics early in the interview. These included providing introductions, explaining the purpose of the interview, asking about the suspected victim's personal history, acknowledging the interviewers' potential for errors, and beginning with initial open-ended prompts that allow victims to report what they know and guide the initial part of the interview (Dianiska et al., 2024d). All of the behaviours are consistent with those shown in field and analogue studies to enhance child sexual abuse victims' disclosures and report completeness (Brubacher et al., 2015; Henderson et al., 2022; Price et al., 2016; Yi & Lamb, 2018). Yet, when general support throughout the interview, which has also been shown to improve children's reporting (Hershkowitz & Lamb, 2020; Saywitz et al., 2019), was considered, its use was extremely rare. Thus, although trained interviewers were using what one could argue are some beneficial approaches at the outset of interviews, they did not appear to continue their use of these throughout.

In another investigation of interviewer behaviour, Henderson et al. (2021b) found that local police often rely on tactics common to interrogations rather than best practices common in child forensic interviews. The team coded the police interviews of eight victims mentioned above for manipulative questioning tactics, finding evidence for both maximization (e.g. one officer accused a victim of lying and another confronted the victim) and minimization (e.g. one officer feigned empathy, and another gave the victim justification for her participation). The police also alluded to their expertise on trafficking by using trafficking slang terms in the questions, perhaps in an attempt to find common ground with victims and elicit disclosures. The police's use of interrogative tactics is unsurprising first because police training often contains a heavy emphasis on suspect interrogation and second because the victims themselves may have been identified initially for delinquent or problematic behaviour. Yet, the use of interrogation tactics may also have undermined the victims' trust and, hence, willingness to participate, which was already likely low.

In an extension of the prior work, Dianiska et al. (under review) analysed how two attorneys, a prosecutor and a defence attorney, questioned suspected minor victims during a criminal trial. Of interest was whether the attorneys built rapport and what types of questions they asked. The analysis was also unique because all of the victims who testified in the trial were male, ranging in age from 12 to 19 at the time of their testimony. The crimes included trafficking and pandering, but also pornography and sexual abuse of the boys. Multiple defendants were also involved, with all ultimately being found guilty. Rapport building by the attorneys was very rare; when it did occur, its use tended to be with the younger boy victims and only by the prosecutor, as one might expect. In addition, and consistent with forensic interviewer behaviour with trafficking victims, neither attorney provided support throughout the boys' testimony. Finally, both attorneys relied primarily on closed-ended questions, consistent with how attorneys tend to question other child victims of sexual offences (Ahern et al., 2015; Andrews et al., 2015; Stolzenberg & Lyon, 2014). The defence attorney relied heavily on leading questions, especially as the boys got older. Whether similar patterns would emerge in trials with older girl victims, nonbinary youth, or LGBTQ youth, the latter two groups of whom are at increased risk for multiple forms of victimization, including trafficking (Georges, 2023; Hogan & Roe-Sepowitz, 2023; Mitchell et al., 2023; Scheer et al., 2021), is worth exploring. What this initial qualitative case study demonstrates is that attorneys are likely strategic in how they question boy victims. The uniqueness of that strategy, such as whether it is specific to younger v. older boys, to trafficked minors, or their combination, awaits further investigation.

How victims respond

As previously mentioned, both law enforcement and prosecutors repeatedly cite victim uncooperativeness as a key challenge to effective interviewing of trafficking victims and prosecution of perpetrators (Farrell et al., 2014; Dianiska et al., 2023; Lavoie et al., 2019), prompting several investigations of how uncooperativeness might manifest itself. At a broad level, uncooperative victims might not appear for scheduled interviews or at trial. When this occurs, cases cannot be filed, or if they are, prosecutors might have to drop the case or offer a better plea arrangement to the defendant. Perhaps more savvy prosecutors know of these risks and, as a result, rely more heavily on other forms of evidence, such as videotaped statements, advertisements (e.g. social media posts), receipts (e.g. motel), or expert testimony (Quas et al., 2023; Reid, 2013; Serano, 2017). Regardless, when victims are broadly uncooperative, the ability of law enforcement and the justice system to collect evidence and prosecute cases are compromised.

When considering the interview context itself, more direct forms of uncooperativeness may emerge in terms of how victims respond to an interviewer's questions. In a series of investigations, Henderson, Lyon, and colleagues have begun to document how trafficking victims express uncooperativeness or reluctance in interviews, with follow up work then comparing these modes of expressions to those of adolescent victims of sexual abuse, who are at risk for non-disclosure of sexual abuse and as a result might be reluctant to tell (Henderson et al., 2021a; Nogalska et al., 2023). Overt and covert expressions of reluctance emerged. Victims sometimes failed to respond, explicitly refused to answer, or sidetracked when asked questions. Others critiqued or corrected the questioner, used profanity when answering, or answered in a completely uninformative manner (e.g. Q: "Who was with you?" A: "People". Q: "What people?" A: "People I know"). When Henderson et al. (2021a) analysed the police interviews of the eight trafficking victims, 26% of their responses contained at least one of the aforementioned forms of reluctance. When these same victims' testimony at trial was evaluated, the percent of reluctant responses was lower (5.5%) but still notable.

Other researchers have now used the same coding system to examine reluctance in other data sets, finding rates of between 11–15% of trafficking victims' utterances in interviews and at trials. These percentages are higher than those observed in interviews with suspected adolescent victims of sexual abuse (Nogalska et al., 2023). Moreover, and of interest, reluctance in trafficking victims is higher when they are answering open- rather than closed-ended questions, perhaps because the open-ended nature of the question allows for a wider range of answers. Whether a similar pattern (i.e. higher reluctance to open-ended versus closed-ended questions) is evident when adolescent sexual abuse victims express reluctance would be worth exploring, as would whether the topic of the questions (e.g. on details of sexual activity) interact with the open-ended phrasing to influence victim reluctance.

Summary

Although the number of studies examining forensic interviews and legal testimony of trafficking victims remains relatively small, findings suggest that, despite best intentions and sometimes extensive general knowledge about trafficking, interviewers do not regularly or consistently employ optimal interviewing strategies. More promising behaviours, namely rapport building, are evident to some extent in well-trained interviewers, but the use of supportive strategies throughout and open-ended questions are less common. Perhaps interviewers heavier reliance on closed-ended questions could be a result of interviewers' knowledge that the often recommended open-ended questions are ineffective with trafficking victims, a possibility in need of more direct analysis. As might be expected based on victims' history, many are sceptical and likely distrusting of law enforcement and legal professionals, leading to general uncooperativeness and reluctance in interviews. Reluctance is also evident in interviews with adolescent victims of other types of sex crimes, but at a lower rate, suggesting that at least some of the evident reluctance could have roots in adolescent development.

Conclusions

Although research on experiences, interviewing, and disclosures among trafficked minors is still in a relatively early phase, several recommendations are already emerging as important for enhancing both identification and intervention. For one, both laypersons and professionals need more accurate knowledge about adolescent risk, trafficking, and disclosure. This need includes training for professionals who may not see themselves as "interviewers", but who nonetheless regularly interact with and question youth and, hence, may be in positions to collect information from vulnerable or high-risk youth. Many such professionals, such as healthcare workers, teachers, and school counsellors, are often more trusted by adolescents than are law enforcement, meaning that, if they possess adequate knowledge, they could play a significant role in earlier identification. Some training programs have shown promise at increasing knowledge around trafficking among healthcare professionals (Arceneaux et al., 2023; Berishaj et al., 2019; Fraley et al., 2020; Lee et al., 2021), and states are adding trafficking prevention training programs to school curricula (Salas & Didier, 2020). Research is needed, though, to ensure that these programs are evidence-based and are improving actual identification of victims, rather than just general knowledge.

Second, law enforcement would benefit from ongoing training regarding effective interviewing approaches for witnesses in general, as these approaches often include instructions on building rapport, asking open-ended questions, and eliciting narratives. Law enforcement are often knowledgeable at a general level about such approaches, but training may need to be directed towards translating knowledge into actual interviewing practices. When victims are reluctant or challenging, as may well be the case with trafficked minors, law enforcement may resort to interrogative tactics. Research, therefore, needs to focus on ensuring that law enforcement, even in the face of resistance, maintain best practice approaches, but also on strategic methods of interviewing reluctant victims. The latter could include developing novel approaches to build rapport that expand on effective techniques for child sexual abuse victims (Lavoie et al., 2019) to take into account adolescents' developmental needs (e.g. Dianiska et al., 2024c) and testing approaches that ensure adolescents' autonomy and independence are respected while they are being questioned (Deck et al., 2024). Results would be highly valuable in continuing to improve how suspected minor victims are questioned, the quality of information they provide, and the provision of services when needed.

In closing, commercial sexual exploitation and sex trafficking, especially of minors, is now widely recognized as a significant problem in society. Yet, identifying and intervening on behalf of victims remain challenging. Trauma and delinquency backgrounds among victims may lead them to turn to sex for survival or obtain material goods; increase their risk of being manipulated by traffickers; and make them particularly sceptical of professionals, even those who purport to or can help. Victims are often uncooperative and reluctant, making it difficult for professionals to obtain detailed disclosures to intervene and help victims and prosecute traffickers. Lack of knowledge on the part of professionals about the aforementioned risk characteristics can further undermine efforts to identify victims. As research continues to elucidate what questioning approaches work best with adolescent-aged victims of trafficking, and as effective training programs are developed and implemented, broader improvements in identification and interventions will follow, as will successful prosecutions of traffickers.

References

18 U.S.C. §1591 (2022). Retrieved from www.govinfo.gov/content/pkg/USCODE-2011-title18/pdf/USCODE-2011-title18.pdf

Ahern, E. C., Stolzenberg, S. N., & Lyon, T. D. (2015). Do prosecutors use interview instructions or build rapport with child witnesses? Behavioral Sciences & the Law, 33(4), 476–492. https://doi.org/10.1002/bsl.2183

Alaggia, R., Collin-Vézina, D., & Lateef, R. (2019). Facilitators and barriers to child sexual abuse (CSA) disclosures: A research update (2000–2016). *Trauma, Violence, & Abuse*, *20*(2), 260–283. 10.1177/1524838017697312

Anderson P. M., Coyle K. K., Johnson A., Denner J. (2014). An exploratory study of adolescent pimping relationships. *Journal of Primary Prevention*, *35*(2), 113–117. 10.1007/s10935-014-0338-3

Andrews, S. J., Lamb, M. E., & Lyon, T. D. (2015). The effects of question repetition on responses when prosecutors and defense attorneys question children alleging sexual abuse in court. *Law and Human Behavior*, *39*(6), 559. 10.1037/lhb0000152

Arceneaux, S. P. (2023). Education improves emergency department providers' knowledge of human trafficking. *Advanced Emergency Nursing Journal*, *45*(2), 138–144. 10.1097/TME.0000000000000455

Back, S., & Lips, H. M. (1998). Child sexual abuse: Victim age, victim gender, and observer gender as factors contributing to attributions of responsibility1. *Child Abuse & Neglect*, *22*(12), 1239–1252. https://doi.org/10.1016/S0145-2134(98)00098-2

Baird, K., & Connolly, J. (2023). Recruitment and Entrapment Pathways of Minors into Sex Trafficking in Canada and the United States: A Systematic Review. Trauma, Violence, & Abuse, 24(1), 189–202. https://doi.org/10.1177/15248380211025241

Baker, M., Winks, K. M. H., Rood, C. J., Quas, J. A., & Williams, S. (2024). Improving the value of school professionals as partners in efforts to enhance recognition of and responses to youth sex trafficking. *Journal of School Psychology*, *61*(9), 3785–3811. https://doi.org/10.1002/pits.23250

Balasa, R., Khan, M., Gesink, D., Forman, L., & Perez-Brumer, A. (2024). Experiences of child sex trafficking identification among Ontario pediatric emergency department healthcare providers: a qualitative study. *Child Abuse & Neglect*, *153*, 106852. https://doi.org/10.1016/j.chiabu.2024.106852

Baldwin S.B., Eisenman D.P., Sayles J.N., Ryan G., & Chuang K.S. (2011). Identification of human trafficking victims in health care settings. *Health & Human Rights*, *13*(1), 36–49.

Baugerud, G. A., & Melinder, A. (2012). Maltreated children's memory of stressful removals from their biological parents. *Applied Cognitive Psychology*, *26*(2), 261–270. https://doi.org/10.1002/acp.1817

Beck, M. E., Lineer, M. M., Melzer-Lange, M., Simpson, P., Nugent, M., & Rabbitt, A. (2015). Medical providers' understanding of sex trafficking and their experience with at-risk patients. *Pediatrics*, *135*(4), e895–e902. 10.1542/peds.2014-2814

Bejinariu, A., Kennedy, M. A., & Cimino, A. N. (2021). "They said they were going to help us get through this …": documenting interactions between police and commercially sexually exploited youth. *Journal of Crime and Justice*, *44*(3), 241–257. 10.1080/0735648X.2020.1807389

Berishaj, K., Buch, C., & Glembocki, M. M. (2019). The impact of an educational intervention on the knowledge and beliefs of registered nurses regarding human trafficking. *Journal of Continuing Education in Nursing*, *50*(6), 269–274. 10.3928/00220124–20190516-07

Bouché, V., Farrell, A., & Wittmer-Wolfe, D. E. (2018). Challenging the dominant frame: The moderating impact of exposure and knowledge on perceptions of sex trafficking victimization. *Social Science Quarterly*, *99*(4), 1283–1302. 10.1111/ssqu.12492

Brown, D. A., & Lamb, M. E. (2015). Can children be useful witnesses? It depends how they are questioned. *Child Development Perspectives*, *9*(4), 250255. https://doi.org/10.1111/cdep.12142

Brubacher, S. P., Poole, D. A., & Dickinson, J. J. (2015). The use of ground rules in investigative interviews with children: A synthesis and call for research. *Developmental Review*, 36, 15–33. https://doi.org/10.1016/j.dr.2015.01.001

Ceci, S. J., & Bruck, M. (1993). Suggestibility of the child witness: A historical review and synthesis. *Psychological Bulletin*, *113*(3), 403–439. https://doi.org/10.1037/0033-2909.113.3.403

Ceci, S. J., & Friedman, R. D. (2000). The suggestibility of children: Scientific research and legal implications. *Cornell Law Review*, *86*, 33–108.

Chisolm-Straker, M., Baldwin, S., Gaïgbé-Togbé, B., Ndukwe, N., Johnson, P.N., & Richardson, L.D. (2016). Health care and human trafficking: We are seeing the unseen. *Journal of Health Care for the Poor and Underserved 27*(3), 1220–1233. https://doi.org/10.1353/hpu.2016.0131.

Cho, S., Henderson, H., Nogalska, A., Siepmann, H., & Lyon, T. (2024). Detecting subtle forms of reluctance in courtroom testimony with commercially sexually exploited adolescents. Manuscript under review.

Choi, K. R. (2015). Risk Factors for Domestic Minor Sex Trafficking in the United States: A Literature Review. *Journal of Forensic Nursing*, *11*(2), 66. https://doi.org/10.1097/JFN.0000000000000072

Clawson, H. J., & Dutch, N. (2008). *Identifying victims of human trafficking: Inherent challenges and promising strategies from the field*. Washington, DC: US Department of Health and Human Services. https://aspe.hhs.gov/reports/identifying-victims-human-trafficking-inherent-challenges-promising-strategies-field-0

Clawson, H. J., Dutch, N., Solomon, A., & Goldblatt Grace, L. (2009, August 29). *Human trafficking into and within the United States: A review of the literature*. Washington DC: US Department of Health and Human Services. https://aspe.hhs.gov/reports/human-trafficking-within-united-states-review-literature-0

Coppola, J. S., Cantwell, E. R., Kushary, D., & Ayres, C. (2019). Human trafficking: Knowledge and awareness in nursing practice. *Journal of Nursing Practice Applications & Reviews of Research*, *9*(1), 40–49. 10.13178/jnparr.2019.0901.0907

Countryman-Roswurm, K., & Bolin, B. L. (2014). Domestic minor sex trafficking: Assessing and reducing risk. *Child and Adolescent Social Work Journal*, *31*(6), 521–538. https://doi.org/10.1007/s10560-014-0336-6

Cunningham, K. C., & Cromer, L. D. (2016). Attitudes about human trafficking: Individual differences related to belief and victim blame. *Journal of Interpersonal Violence*, *31*(2), 228–244. https://doi.org/10.1177/0886260514555369

Daddis, C. (2011), Desire for increased autonomy and adolescents' perceptions of peer autonomy: "Everyone else can; Why can't I?". *Child Development, 82*, 1310–1326. https://doi.org/10.1111/j.1467-8624.2011.01587.x

Deck, S., Quas, J. A., & Powell, M. (2024). Unique considerations for forensic interviews with adolescents: An exploration of expert interviewers' perspectives. *Child Maltreatment*. https://doi.org/10.1177/10775595241270046

De Vries, I., & Goggin, K. E. (2020). The impact of childhood abuse on the commercial sexual exploitation of youth: A systematic review and meta-analysis. *Trauma, Violence, & Abuse, 21*(5), 886–903. https://doi.org/10.1177/1524838018801332

Dianiska, R. E., Luna, S., Winks, K. M., Quas, J. A., & Redlich, A. D. (2023). Current investigator practices and beliefs on interviewing trafficked minors. *Psychology, Public Policy, and Law, 29*(1), 32. https://doi.org/10.1037/law0000378

Dianiska, R. E., Quas, J. A., & Lyon, T. D. (2024a). Using rapport building to improve information yield when interviewing adolescents: A systematic review and call for research. *Child Abuse & Neglect, 154*, 106898. https://doi.org/10.1016/j.chiabu.2024.106898

Dianiska, R. E., Simpson, E., & Quas, J. A. (2024c). Rapport building with adolescents to enhance reporting and disclosure. *Journal of Experimental Child Psychology, 238*, 105799. https://doi.org/10.1016/j.jecp.2023.105799

Dianiska, R. E., Simpson, E., Kim, S., Lyon, T. D., & Quas, J. A. (2024b). Building rapport in interviews with adolescent trafficking victims. *Child Abuse Review, 33*(2), e2864. https://doi.org/10.1002/car.2864

Dianiska, R. E., Winks, K. M. H., Brown, D., & Quas, J. A. (2024d). Developmental differences in rapport building and questioning of sexually exploited boys in court. Manuscript under review.

Dierkhising, C. B., Eastman, A. L., & Walker Brown, K. (2022). Examining housing instability among females who are system-involved: Comparing females with and without histories of commercial sexual exploitation. *Child Maltreatment, 27*(4), 637–646. 10.1177/10775595211039463

Digidiki, V., & Baka, A. (2022). Who's to blame in the sex trafficking of women: Situational and individual factors that define a "deserving victim". *Journal of Human Trafficking, 8*(4), 353–366. 10.1177/10775595211039463

Dykstra, V. W., Dianiska, R. E., Lyon, T. D., & Quas, J. A. (2024, June). Question type and reluctant responding in trafficked adolescents. Paper presented at the International Investigative Interviewing Research Group Conference, Ottawa, ON, Canada.

Farrell, A., & Pfeffer, R. (2014). Policing human trafficking: Cultural blinders and organizational barriers. *ANNALS of the American Academy of Political and Social Science, 653*(1), 46–64. https://doi.org/10.1177/0002716213515835

Farrell, A. (2009). State and local law enforcement responses to human trafficking: Explaining why so few trafficking cases are identified in the United States. *Sociology of Crime Law and Deviance, 13*, 243–259. 10.1108/S1521–6136(2009)0000013016.

Farrell, A., Dank, M., de Vries, I., Kafafian, M., Hughes, A., & Lockwood, S. (2019). Failing victims? Challenges of the police response to human trafficking. *Criminology & Public Policy, 18*(3), 649–673. https://doi.org/10.1111/1745-9133.12456

Farrell, A., DeLateur, M. J., Owens, C., & Fahy, S. (2016). The prosecution of state-level human trafficking cases in the United States. *Anti-Trafficking Review*, *6*, 48–70. https://doi.org/10.14197/atr.20121664

Farrell, A., McDevitt, J., & Fahy, S. (2010). Where are all the victims? Understanding the determinants of official identification of human trafficking incidents. *Criminology & Public Policy*, *9*(2), 201–233. https://doi.org/10.1111/j.1745-9133.2010.00621.x

Farrell, A., Owens, C., & McDevitt, J. (2014). New laws but few cases: Understanding the challenges to the investigation and prosecution of human trafficking cases. *Crime, Law and Social Change*, *61*, 139–168. 10.1007/s10611-013-9442-1

Fernandes, D., Gomes, J. P., Albuquerque, P. B., & Matos, M. (2024). Forensic interview techniques in child sexual abuse cases: a scoping review. *Trauma, Violence, & Abuse*, *25*(2), 1382–1396. 10.1177/15248380231177317

Fraley, H. E., Aronowitz, T., & Jones, E. J. (2018). School nurses' awareness and attitudes toward commercial sexual exploitation of children. *Advances in Nursing Science*, *41*(2), 118–136. 10.1097/ANS.0000000000000197

Fraley, H. E, Aronowitz, T., & Stoklosa, H. M. (2020). Systematic review of human trafficking educational interventions for health care providers. *Western Journal of Nursing Research*, *42*(2), 131–142. 10.1177/0193945919837366

Franchino-Olsen, H. (2021). Vulnerabilities relevant for commercial sexual exploitation of children/domestic minor sex trafficking: A systematic review of risk factors. *Trauma, Violence, & Abuse*, *22*(1), 99–111. https://doi.org/10.1177/1524838018821956

Franchino-Olsen, H., Chesworth, B. R., Boyle, C., Rizo, C. F., Martin, S. L., Jordan, B., … & Stevens, L. (2022). The prevalence of sex trafficking of children and adolescents in the United States: A scoping review. *Trauma, Violence, & Abuse*, *23*(1), 182–195. 10.1177/1524838020933873

Franklin, C. A., & Menaker, T. A. (2015). The impact of observer characteristics on blame assessments of prostituted female youth. *Feminist Criminology*, *10*(2), 140–164. https://doi.org/10.1177/1557085114535234

Georges, E. (2023). Review of the Literature on the Intersection of LGBTQ Youth and CSEC: More Than a Monolith. *Current Pediatrics Reports*, *11*(4), 105–115.

Gerassi, L. B., Cheng, S. Y., Muentner, L., & Benson, M. (2021). Prevalence and associated characteristics of youth who trade sex in a representative sample of high school students. *Journal of Adolescence*, *93*, 1–9. 10.1016/j.adolescence.2021.09.008

Goldberg, A. P., Moore, J. L., Houck, C., Kaplan, D. M., & Barron, C. E. (2017). Domestic minor sex trafficking patients: A retrospective analysis of medical presentation. *Journal of Pediatric and Adolescent Gynecology*, *30*(1), 109–115. https://doi.org/10.1016/j.jpag.2016.08.010

Gonzalez-Pons, K. M., Gezinski, L., Morzenti, H., Hendrix, E., & Graves, S. (2020). Exploring the relationship between domestic minor sex trafficking myths, victim identification, and service provision. *Child Abuse & Neglect*, *100*, 104093. https://doi.org/10.1016/j.chiabu.2019.104093

Goodman, G. S., & Melinder, A. (2007). Child witness research and forensic interviews of young children: A review. *Legal and Criminological Psychology*, *12*(1), 1–19. https://doi.org/10.1348/135532506X156620

Gozdziak, E. M. (2010). Identifying child victims of trafficking: Toward solutions and resolutions. *Criminology & Public Policy*, *9*(2), 245. 10.1111/j.1745-9133.2010.00623.x

Greenbaum, V. J. (2014). Commercial sexual exploitation and sex trafficking of children in the United States. *Current Problems in Pediatric and Adolescent Health Care*, *44*(9), 245–269. https://doi.org/10.1016/j.cppeds.2014.07.001

Halter, S. (2010). Factors that influence police conceptualizations of girls involved in prostitution in six U.S. cities: Child sexual exploitation victims or delinquents? *Child Maltreatment*, *15*(2), 152–160. https://doi.org/10.1177/1077559509355315

Hardy, V. L., Compton, K. D., & McPhatter, V. S. (2013). Domestic minor sex trafficking: Practice implications for mental health professionals. *Affilia*, *28*(1), 8–18. https://doi.org/10.1177/0886109912475172

Hartinger-Saunders, R. M., Trouteaud, A. R., & Matos Johnson, J. (2017). Mandated reporters' perceptions of and encounters with domestic minor sex trafficking of adolescent females in the United States. *American Journal of Orthopsychiatry*, *87*(3), 195–205. https://doi.org/10.1037/ort0000151

Havig, K., & Mahapatra, N. (2020). Health-care providers' knowledge of human trafficking: Implications for building service capacity in a frontier state. *Journal of Human Trafficking*, *7*(4), 366–383. https://doi.org/10.1080/23322705.2020.1747011

Helpingstine, C. E., Stephens, D. P., Kenny, M. C., & Eaton, A. A. (2021). Adolescent girls with a history of Commercial Sexual Exploitation (CSE): Perceptions and characteristics of social networks. *Child Abuse & Neglect*, *115*, 105015. https://doi.org/10.1016/j.chiabu.2021.105015

Henderson, H. M., Konovalov, H., Williams, S., & Lyon, T. D. (2022). The utility of the birthday prompt in narrative practice with maltreated and non-maltreated 4- to 9-year-old children. *Applied Developmental Science*, *26*(4), 679–688. https://doi.org/10.1080/10888691.2021.1963729

Henderson, H. M., Cho, S. J., & Lyon, T. D. (2021b). Police interviewing behaviors and commercially sexually exploited adolescents' reluctance. *Psychology, Public Policy, and Law*, *27*(3), 328–340. https://doi.org/10.1037/law0000315

Henderson, H. M., Cho, S. J., Nogalska, A. M., & Lyon, T. D. (2021a). Identifying novel forms of reluctance in commercially sexually exploited adolescents. *Child Abuse & Neglect*, *115*, 104994. https://doi.org/10.1016/j.chiabu.2021.104994

Herman, J. L. (2003). Hidden in plain sight: Clinical observations on prostitution. In M. Farley (Ed.), *Prostitution, trafficking, and traumatic stress* (pp. 1–13). Binghamton, NY: The Haworth Press.

Hershberger, A. R., Sanders, J., Chick, C., Jessup, M., Hanlin, H., & Cyders, M. A. (2018). Predicting running away in girls who are victims of commercial sexual exploitation. *Child Abuse & Neglect*, *79*, 269–278. https://doi.org/10.1016/j.chiabu.2018.02.023

Hershkowitz, I., & Lamb, M. E. (2020). Allegation rates and credibility assessment in forensic interviews of alleged child abuse victims: Comparing the revised and standard NICHD protocols. *Psychology, Public Policy, and Law*, *26*(2), 176–184. https://doi.org/10.1037/law0000230

Heyman, J. C., White-Ryan, L., Kelly, P., Farmer, G. L., Leaman, T. L., & Davis, H. J. (2020). Voices about foster care: The value of trust. *Children and Youth Services Review*, *113*, 104991. https://doi.org/10.1016/j.childyouth.2020.104991

Hogan, K. A., & Roe-Sepowitz, D. (2023). LGBTQ+ homeless young adults and sex trafficking vulnerability. *Journal of Human Trafficking*, *9*(1), 63–78. 10.1080/23322705.2020.1841985

Institute of Medicine & National Research Council. (2013). *Confronting commercial sexual exploitation and sex trafficking of minors in the United States.* The National Academies Press. https://doi.org/10.17226/18358

Kaestle, C.E. (2012). Selling and buying Sex: A longitudinal study of risk and protective factors in adolescence. *Prevention Science*, *13*, 314–322. https://doi.org/10.1007/s11121-011-0268-8

Kansky, J., Ruzek, E., & Allen, J. (2017). Observing adolescent relationships: Autonomy processes in parent, peer, and romantic partner interactions. In *Autonomy in adolescent development* (pp. 33–52). Psychology Press.

Kim, S., Dianiska, R.E., Simpson, E., & Quas, J.A. (2024, March). Laypersons' perceptions on sex trafficking victimization and attribution of blame. Paper presented at the American Psychology-Law Society Conference, Los Angeles, California, United States.

Korkman, J., Otgaar, H., Geven, L. M., Bull, R., Cyr, M., Hershkowitz, I … Volbert, R. (2024). White paper on forensic child interviewing: research-based recommendations by the European Association of Psychology and Law. *Psychology, Crime & Law*, 1–24. https://doi.org/10.1080/1068316X.2024.2324098

Lamb, M. E., Brown, D. A., Hershkowitz, I., Orbach, Y., & Esplin, P. W. (2018). *Tell me what happened: Questioning children about abuse.* John Wiley & Sons.

Latzman N. E., Gibbs D. A., Feinberg R., Kluckman M. N., Aboul-Hosn S. (2019). Human trafficking victimization among youth who run away from foster care. *Child and Youth Services Review*, *98*, 113–124. https://doi.org/10.1016/j.childyouth.2018.12.022.

Lavoie, J., Dickerson, K. L., Redlich, A. D., & Quas, J. A. (2019). Overcoming disclosure reluctance in youth victims of sex trafficking: New directions for research, policy, and practice. *Psychology, Public Policy, and Law*, *25*(4), 225–238. https://doi.org/10.1037/law0000205

Lederer, L. J., & Wetzel, C. A. (2014). The health consequences of sex trafficking and their implications for identifying victims in healthcare facilities. *Annals of Health Law*, *23*(1), 61–91.

Lee, H., Geynisman-Tan, J., Hofer, S., Anderson, E., Caravan, S., & Titchen, K. (2021). The impact of human trafficking training on healthcare professionals' knowledge and attitudes. *Journal of Medical Education and Curricular Development*, *8*. https://doi.org/10.1177/23821205211016523

Lindholm, J., Börjesson, M., & Cederborg, A. C. (2014). "What happened when you came to Sweden?": Attributing responsibility in police interviews with alleged adolescent human trafficking victims. *Narrative Inquiry*, *24*(2), 181–199. 10.1075/ni.24.2.01lin

Lindholm, J., Cederborg, A. C., & Alm, C. (2015). Adolescent girls exploited in the sex trade: Informativeness and evasiveness in investigative interviews. *Police Practice and Research*, *16*(3), 197–210. https://doi.org/10.1080/15614263.2014.880839

Litam, S. D. A., & Lam, E. T. C. (2021). Sex trafficking beliefs in counselors: Establishing the need for human trafficking training in counselor education programs. *International Journal for the Advancement of Counselling*, *43*(1), 1–18. https://doi.org/10.1007/s10447-020-09408-8

Logan, T. K., Walker, R., & Hunt, G. (2009). Understanding human trafficking in the United States. *Trauma, Violence, & Abuse*, *10*(1), 3–30. 10.1177/1524838008327262

Luna, S., Dianiska, R. E., Winks, K. M., Redlich, A. D., & Quas, J. A. (2023). Examining investigator strategies for questioning suspected minor victims of sex trafficking. *Journal of Police and Criminal Psychology*, *38*(4), 813–825. 10.1007/s11896-022-09568-w

Manay, N., & Collin-Vézina, D. (2021). Recipients of children's and adolescents' disclosures of childhood sexual abuse: A systematic review. *Child Abuse & Neglect*, *116*, 104192. 10.1016/j.chiabu.2019.104192

McMahon-Howard, J. (2017). Youth involved in prostitution (YIP) exploring possible changes in interactions with police and social service agencies and narratives of victimization. *Criminal Justice Review*, *42*(2), 119–145. https://doi.org/10.1177/0734016817702194

Mitchell, K. J., Finkelhor, D., & Wolak, J. (2010). Conceptualizing juvenile prostitution as child maltreatment: Findings from the National Juvenile Prostitution Study. *Child Maltreatment*, *15*(1), 18–36. doi:10.1177/1077559509349443

Mitchell, K. J., Ybarra, M. L., Goodman, K. L., & Strøm, I. F. (2023). Polyvictimization among sexual and gender minority youth. *American Journal of Preventive Medicine*, *65*(2), 182–191. 10.1016/j.amepre.2023.01.045

Morrison, S. E., Bruce, C., & Wilson, S. (2018). Children's disclosure of sexual abuse: A systematic review of qualitative research exploring barriers and facilitators. *Journal of Child Sexual Abuse*, *27*(2), 176–194. 10.1080/10538712.2018.1425943.

Nogalska, A. M., Henderson, H. M., Cho, S. J., & Lyon, T. D. (2023). Novel forms of reluctance among suspected child sexual abuse victims in adolescence. *Child Maltreatment*, *28*(2), 275–285. 10.1177/10775595221104828

O'Brien, J. E. (2019). "What does it matter how We define it?": Exploring definitions of DMST among service providers and victims/survivors. *Journal of Human Trafficking*, *5*(2), 91–108. https://doi.org/10.1080/23322705.2017.1410415

O'Brien, J. E., DellaPenna, R., Gonzalez-Pons, K., & Mitchell, K. (2022). Medical first responders and child sexual exploitation: Needs, efforts, and next steps. *Journal of Human Trafficking*, 1–11. https://doi.org/10.1080/23322705.2022.2061280

Phillips, J. (2015). Black girls and the (im)possibilities of a victim trope: The intersectional failures of legal and advocacy interventions in the commercial sexual exploitation of minors in the United States. *UCLA Law Review*, *62*(6), 1642–1675.

Price, E. A., Ahern, E. C., & Lamb, M. E. (2016). Rapport-building in investigative interviews of alleged child sexual abuse victims. *Applied Cognitive Psychology*, *30*(5). https://doi.org/10.1002/acp.3249

Quas, J. A., Luna, S., Wilson, D. B., & Redlich, A. (2024). Human trafficking and the passage of the 2000 TVPA: A comparative analysis of prosecution of sex trafficking, child pornography, and sexual abuse cases. *Journal of Human Trafficking*, 1–21. 10.1080/23322705.2024.2331943

Quas, J. A., Mukhopadhyay, S., Winks, K. M. H., Dianiska, R. E., & Lyon, T. D. (2023). Successful criminal prosecutions of sex trafficking and sexual abuse of minors: A comparative analysis. *Child Maltreatment*, *28*(3), 500–516. https://doi.org/10.1177/10775595231176432

Reid, J. A. (2013). Rapid assessment exploring impediments to successful prosecutions of sex traffickers of US minors. *Journal of Police and Criminal Psychology*, *28*, 75–89. https://doi.org/10.1007/s11896-012-9106-6

Reid, J. A. (2016). Entrapment and enmeshment schemes used by sex traffickers. *Sexual Abuse*, *28*(6), 491–511. https://doi.org/10.1177/1079063214544334

Reid, J. A., Baglivio, M. T., Piquero, A. R., Greenwald, M. A., & Epps, N. (2017). Human trafficking of minors and childhood adversity in Florida. *American Journal of Public Health*, *107*(2), 306–311. https://doi.org/10.2105/AJPH.2016.303564

Reid J. A., & Jones S. (2011). Exploited vulnerability: Legal and psychological perspectives on child sex trafficking victims. *Victims & Offenders*, *6*, 207–231. https://doi.org/10.1080/15564886.2011.557327

Reid, J. A., & Piquero, A. R. (2014). On the relationships between commercial sexual exploitation/prostitution, substance dependency, and delinquency in youthful offenders. *Child Maltreatment*, *19*(3–4), 247–260. https://doi.org/10.1177/1077559514539752

Renzetti, C. M., Bush, A., Castellanos, M., & Hunt, G. (2017). Does training make a difference? An evaluation of a specialized human trafficking training module for law enforcement officers. In J. Reid (Ed.), Human Trafficking (pp. 56–72). New York: Routledge.

Rodríguez-López, S. (2018). (De)constructing stereotypes: Media representations, social perceptions, and legal responses to human trafficking. *Journal of Human Trafficking*, *4*(1), 61–72. https://doi.org/10.1080/23322705.2018.1423447

Rogers, P., Josey, N., & Davies, M. (2007). Victim age, attractiveness and, abuse history as factors in the perception of a hypothetical child sexual abuse case. *Journal of Sexual Aggression*, *13*(2), 121–137. https://doi.org/10.1080/13552600701644835

Sabina, C., Cuevas, C. A., & Schally, J. L. (2012). Help-seeking in a national sample of victimized latino women: The influence of victimization types. *Journal of Interpersonal Violence*, *27*(1), 40–61. https://doi.org/10.1177/0886260511416460

Salas, R.G. & Didier, K.A. (2020) California adds human trafficking prevention training to its 7–12 grade curriculum: Should other states follow? *Journal of Educational Strategies*, *93*, 12–18. DOI: 10.1080/00098655.2019.1677546

Saywitz, K. J., Wells, C. R., Larson, R. P., & Hobbs, S. D. (2019). Effects of interviewer support on children's memory and suggestibility: Systematic review and meta-analyses of experimental research. *Trauma, Violence, & Abuse*, *20*(1), 22–39. https://doi.org/10.1177/1524838016683457

Scheer, J. R., Edwards, K. M., Helminen, E. C., & Watson, R. J. (2021). Victimization typologies among a large national sample of sexual and gender minority adolescents. *LGBT health*, *8*(8), 507–518. 10.1089/lgbt.2021.0024

Schönbucher, V., Maier, T., Mohler-Kuo, M., Schnyder, U., & Landolt, M. A. (2012). Disclosure of child sexual abuse by adolescents: A qualitative in-depth study. *Journal of Interpersonal Violence*, *27*(17), 3486–3513. 10.1177/0886260512445380

Schwarz, C., Xing, C., Daugherty, R., Watt, S., & Britton, H. E. (2020). Frontline workers' perceptions of human trafficking: Warning signs and risks in the Midwest. *Journal of Human Trafficking*, *6*(1), 61–78. https://doi.org/10.1080/23322705.2018.1562316

Serano, A. P. (2017). Evidence considerations in proving sex trafficking cases without a testifying victim. *US Attorney's Bulletin*, *65*, 115.

Smetana, J. G., Metzger, A., Gettman, D. C., & Campione-Barr, N. (2006). Disclosure and secrecy in adolescent–parent relationships. *Child Development*, *77*(1), 201–217. https://doi.org/10.1111/j.1467-8624.2006.00865.x

Smith, L. A., Vardaman, S. H., & Snow, M. A. (2009). *The national report on domestic minor sex trafficking: America's prostituted children*. Vancouver, WA: Shared Hope International.

Stolzenberg, S. N., & Lyon, T. D. (2014). *How attorneys question children about the dynamics of sexual abuse and disclosure in criminal trials. Psychology, Public Policy, and Law*, *20*(1), 19–30. 10.1037/a0035000

Strohacker, E., Gibbs, J. C., & Woolford, S. (2021). Pennsylvanians' perceptions of the nature and extent of human trafficking. *Journal of Human Trafficking*, *9*(2), 212–228. https://doi.org/10.1080/23322705.2021.1898249

Strohacker, E., Gibbs, J. C., & Woolford, S. (2023). Pennsylvanians' Perceptions of the Nature and Extent of Human Trafficking. *Journal of Human Trafficking*, *9*(2), 212–228. https://doi.org/10.1080/23322705.2021.1898249

Titchen, K. E., Loo, D., Berdan, E., Rysavy, M. B., Ng, J. J., & Sharif, I. (2017). Domestic sex trafficking of minors: Medical student and physician awareness. *Journal of Pediatric and Adolescent Gynecology*, *30*(1), 102–108. 10.1016/j.jpag.2015.05.006

Tyler, K. A., & Johnson, K. A. (2006). Trading sex: Voluntary or coerced? The experiences of homeless youth. *The Journal of Sex Research*, *43*(3), 208–216. https://doi.org/10.1080/00224490609552319

United Nations. (2000). Protocol to prevent, suppress and punish trafficking in persons,especially women and children, supplementing the United Nations convention against transnational crime. Retrieved October 21, 2024. Retrieved from www.ohchr.org/sites/default/files/ProtocolonTrafficking.pdf

Uy, R. (2011). Blinded by red lights: Why trafficking discourse should shift away from sex and the perfect victim paradigm. *Berkeley Journal of Gender Law & Justice*, *26*, 204–219.

Varma, S., Gillespie, S., McCracken, C., & Greenbaum, V. J. (2015). Characteristics of child commercial sexual exploitation and sex trafficking victims presenting for medical care in the United States. *Child Abuse & Neglect*, *44*, 98–105. 10.1016/j.chiabu.2015.04.004

Warf, C. W., Clark, L. F., Desai, M., Rabinovitz, S. J., Agahi, G., Calvo, R., & Hoffmann, J. (2013). Coming of age on the streets: Survival sex among homeless young women in Hollywood. *Journal of Adolescence*, *36*(6), 1205–1213. 10.1016/j.adolescence.2013.08.013

Wilson, J. M., & Dalton, E. (2008). Human trafficking in the heartland: Variation in law enforcement awareness and response. *Journal of Contemporary Criminal Justice*, *24*(3), 296–313. https://doi.org/10.1177/1043986208318227

Winks, K. M. H., Cerda, F., Rood, C. J., & Quas, J. A. (2023). Frontline medical professionals' ability to recognize and respond to suspected youth sex trafficking. *Pediatric Emergency Care*, *39*(4), 219. https://doi.org/10.1097/PEC.0000000000002892

Yi, M., & Lamb, M. E. (2018). The effects of narrative practice on children's testimony and disclosure of secrets. *Applied Cognitive Psychology*, *32*(3). http://doi.org/10.1002/acp.3385

Truths and lies

Making sense of denials and recantations in sexual abuse cases

Victoria Talwar and Angela Crossman

One of the most challenging issues surrounding child witnesses has been how to elicit robust and accurate reports, consistently, from alleged victims of abuse. As the pendulum has swung historically between more and less intensive questioning practices, towards evidence-based approaches, concerns about some children's tendency to delay, deny or recant truthful allegations persist. Indeed, despite their self-protective goals, countervailing motivations may lead youths away from truthful reporting towards concealment or lie-telling. The current chapter aims to explore lying and truth-telling in childhood and adolescence to help make sense of why denial and recantation by children of various ages persist.

To gain a better understanding of false denials and recantations of true allegations, it is essential to first consider the development of children's lying and truth-telling throughout childhood and adolescence. Hence, we start by examining the development of children's conceptual and moral understanding of lying, as well as the development of their lie-telling abilities for different motivations. This understanding can provide insights into why children of different ages may deny or recant reports under certain conditions. We then discuss motivations particular to child witness situations that might affect children's disclosure. Finally, we discuss approaches practitioners working with alleged victims might find useful to facilitate children's truth-telling in situations where they might be tempted, encouraged or otherwise compelled to deny or recant allegations of their own victimization.

What is lying? Conceptual and moral understanding

At its most basic level, lying occurs when one makes a statement with the intent to mislead another into believing something to be true that the lie-teller knows to be false (e.g. Bok, 1999 [1978]; Lee, 2013). That is, there is a discrepancy between what the lie-teller communicates and what the lie-teller knows to be true. Though lie-telling emerges at an early age, children's understanding of what it means to lie, as well as their moral

DOI: 10.4324/9781003427155-4

evaluation of lie-telling, evolve somewhat in tandem with age, experience and socialization.

Children's conceptual understanding of truth and lies emerges early in the preschool years, shifting from a concrete, literal conceptualization of a dichotomy to an abstract, nuanced set of constructs over time (e.g. Bussey, 1992; Peterson et al., 1983; Piaget, 1965 [1932]; Strichartz & Burton, 1990). Children are able to reliably understand the differences between truths and lies based upon factuality between 3½ and 4 years of age (Lyon et al., 2013; Strichartz & Burton, 1990). However, children's understanding of truths versus lies seems to develop unevenly. Lyon et al. (2013) found that 3- to 5-year-olds were better at identifying truths than lies, while Bussey (1992) found that 8- and 11-year-olds were more accurate at identifying lies than 5-year-olds. Thus, it appears that children's conceptual knowledge of lies emerges in the preschool years based initially upon the factuality of a statement. With age, children come to understand that lies are knowingly false statements made with the intention to deceive. This is consistent with studies showing that children understand that lies are false before they understand that lies are intentionally false; the latter understanding develops in the school years (Peterson et al., 1983; Piaget, 1965 [1932]; Strichartz & Burton, 1990; Wimmer et al., 1984).

As with their conceptual understanding, children's early moral evaluations of truths and lies are broad. They seem initially to include all good verbal statements and behaviours in their concept of truth and all negative or bad words (e.g. swear words) and acts in their concept of a lie (e.g. labelling an honest confession of a bad act as a lie), coming to distinguish between honesty and valence of word or deed across the preschool years (Wandrey et al., 2012). Even very young children rate lie-telling as a negative behaviour, particularly for self-serving lies, and recommend that story characters tell the truth (e.g. Bussey, 1992, 1999; Wagland & Bussey, 2005). However, some children as young as 4 years differentially evaluate lies told with different intentions (e.g. to harm or protect another; Bussey, 1992, 1999; Siegal & Peterson, 1996), showing nuance in their evaluations.

Experience and socialization further hone children's evaluations and definitions of lying. Children are increasingly likely to evaluate lies told to benefit others less negatively with age (e.g. Popliger et al., 2011). In fact, Lee and Ross (1997) found that adolescents (ages 12 to 14 years) and college students were less inclined to classify untruthful statements as lies when told with the intent to help another individual than when told to harm. Thus, children's conceptual and moral understanding of lies increasingly differentiate with age. As they develop an appreciation for speakers' beliefs and intentions, they discriminate lies from honest mistakes, guesses, exaggerations, jokes, and eventually sarcasm and irony (Andrews et al., 1986; Creusere, 2000; Rothermich et al., 2020). Older children begin to appreciate that beliefs can be false (mistakes) and false statements can be uttered without the intention to deceive (jokes, sarcasm), both of which narrow the definition of a lie. Children also gradually take into consideration the social context in which lies are told, refining both their definitions and moral evaluations of lies. Overall, by early adolescence, children's conceptual and moral understanding of lying and truth-telling becomes comparable to that of adults.

Development of lying and lying maintenance

Although children begin to understand the concepts and morality of lies and truths from an early age, this understanding does not necessarily predict honesty (e.g. Lyon et al., 2008). Research has shown that children begin to lie from an early age, typically to conceal their own misdeeds (Newton et al., 2000; Talwar & Lee, 2002). Both parent-report and experimental studies have found that children's lie-telling emerges in the preschool years and develops rapidly through the school years. For instance, in laboratory studies, less than half of 3-year-olds tell lies to conceal a transgression (Evans & Lee, 2013; Leduc et al., 2017; Talwar & Lee, 2002), while the majority of children between 4 and 7 years of age lie about their transgressions (Talwar & Lee, 2002, 2008). Older children also tell such lies, though the rate of telling them may decline in early adolescence (Evans & Lee, 2010; Talwar, Gordon, & Lee, 2007).

However, young children are *not* skilled lie-tellers. To be successful, lie-tellers must control both their verbal and nonverbal behaviours to avoid arousing suspicion. This behavioural control must be exerted not only during the initial lie statement, but also throughout all subsequent conversations about the topic. This is no simple task, particularly for children. In terms of nonverbal control, while children may show a few non-verbal signs of their deception, there are no non-verbal cues that reliably distinguish between lie-tellers and truth-tellers (Lewis et al., 1989; Talwar & Lee, 2002; Talwar, Murphy, & Lee, 2007) and this has been well-established with adults (e.g. Denault et al., 2024; Luke, 2019), though recent studies have begun to explore potential alternative strategies for their elicitation and use with children, such as collective interviewing, use of a virtual agent and automatic decoding (e.g. Bruer et al., 2020; Şen & Küntay, 2019; Serras Pereira et al., 2018).

In terms of verbal control, preschool children struggle to verbally sustain their lies (Talwar, Gordon, & Lee, 2007; Talwar & Lee, 2002, 2008). For instance, younger children in one study (ages 3–5 years) were overwhelmingly likely to reveal incriminating information in subsequent statements after falsely denying a transgression, while approximately half of 6- and 7-year-olds were able to conceal and maintain their lies when answering follow-up questions (Talwar & Lee, 2002). When adults were asked to judge and detect which children were lying based on transcriptions of the children's verbal reports, they easily detected false denials among children who verbally revealed incriminating information (more commonly 3- to 5-year-olds). They did not detect them among children who maintained their lies (typically 6- to 7-year-olds), who were indistinguishable from children who told the truth. Subsequent studies have found similar developmental patterns in that children's ability to maintain lies in subsequent statements improves with age through childhood and adolescence (Debey et al., 2015; Evans & Lee, 2013; Talwar, Gordon, & Lee, 2007; Talwar & Lee, 2008).

Thus, preschool-aged children (ages 3–5 years) are generally limited in their skills at maintaining lies and consequently are often not effective lie-tellers. With age, however, they become more sophisticated at concealing their lies verbally. Furthermore, adults find older children's statements more credible and experience greater difficulty differentiating between true and deceptive statements as children's skills improve (Leach et al., 2004; Talwar et al., 2006). In other words, the older one becomes, the more likely one is able to convincingly deceive others.

How lie-telling behaviour relates to cognition

The creation and maintenance of a lie is a relatively complex task that requires a sophisticated level of cognitive development. A successful liar must take into account another individual's knowledge, construct a false statement that differs from their own true beliefs, remember the false information they are providing, ensure it remains consistent over time, and readily adapt or manipulate their non-verbal and verbal expressions to remain convincing. Thus, lying requires cognitive skills such as the ability to understand that others have beliefs, desires, and perspectives different from their own, or theory-of-mind, which is essential for producing effective lies. It also requires executive functioning skills, including self-regulation, inhibitory control, planning, attentional flexibility, and working memory.

Children's lie-telling skills emerge and evolve throughout their first decade of life and improvements appear to be related to significant advancements in their cognitive abilities (Talwar & Lee, 2008). In particular, theory-of-mind and executive functioning skills support children's maturing ability to lie. Young children tell only rudimentary lies that involve simple false denials and lack the skills to maintain their lies. As theory-of-mind and executive functioning skills (i.e. inhibitory control, working memory, planning, and cognitive flexibility) develop, they are able to tell more elaborate lies and to maintain those lies when questioned further. In this sense, early lying is the result of a positive development of cognition in children (e.g. Ding et al., 2014; Lavoie & Talwar, 2020; Ma et al., 2015; Talwar, Crossman, & Wyman, 2017; Williams et al., 2016). It also comports with evidence that lie-telling proficiency seems to peak in young adulthood and worsen through adulthood, along with inhibitory control (Debey et al., 2015). Furthermore, children with deficits in these mentalizing cognitive abilities, such those with autism spectrum disorder, tend to show delays in their lie-telling abilities (e.g. Li et al., 2011; Talwar et al., 2012). Thus, deception is considered to be a hallmark of cognitive maturity that emerges once children begin to understand another's mental states and consciously control their own behaviours (Talwar & Crossman, 2011).

Detection of children's lies

In line with children's growing cognitive abilities, and despite the fact that preschool-aged children tend to be less skilled liars, adults are poor at accurately detecting deception in children, with studies reporting that they perform slightly above chance levels (Domagalski et al., 2020; Edelstein et al., 2006; Gongola et al., 2017; Talwar et al., 2009; Wyman et al., 2018). One meta-analysis of adults' ability to detect deception in children found that accuracy was around 47.5% (Gongola et al., 2017). Adults tend to exhibit a truth bias, taking reports at face value and believing child senders (Bond & DePaulo, 2006; Domagalski et al., 2020).

Note, however, that research on credibility in CSA cases suggests that biases vary as a function of what is being assessed (e.g. accuracy versus truthfulness) and of case factors (e.g. gender, witness age). A truth bias does not seem to be present for older children (e.g. age 10) and adolescents in CSA cases, who may be perceived as inherently more suspect and less truthful, which can undermine perceptions of perpetrator guilt (e.g. Sumampouw et al., 2022; Voogt et al., 2020). Moreover, given that CSA victims may show reluctance to disclose and/or deny or recant their allegations (e.g. Eisen et al., 2021; Hershkowitz et al., 2021; Leander, 2010), any resulting inconsistencies could make them seem less credible, make their reports seem unreliable and lead to dismissal of their case (Bücken et al., 2023).

Unfortunately, detection of children's lies, whether they be true or false denials or recantations, becomes increasingly difficult with child age, as they become more skilled, but even more so when children are extensively coached to lie by adults (Talwar, Hubbard et al., 2018). Given that concerns about coaching may be raised in cases involving child witnesses (Bala & Schuman, 1999; Crossman et al., 2002), it is crucial for practitioners to bear in mind that, as with adults, it can be a challenge to detect when a child or adolescent is lying (Bond & DePaulo, 2006; Gongola et al., 2017). There are no consistent cues to deception (Denault, 2020). Thus, it is important to be aware of potential motivations that may lead children and adolescents to delay reporting, deny or recant abuse allegations, and essential to know evidence-based interview techniques focused on promoting and eliciting consistently honest reports.

Why lie? The motivations that can lead children to give false reports

Perhaps the most challenging, lasting, and frustrating question for researchers has been why children and adolescents would delay, deny or recant allegations of CSA, particularly when they themselves or a loved one have been victimized. Answers are complex. Generally speaking, lying occurs for a wide variety of reasons and children lie for similar reasons as adults (Newton et al., 2000), including to escape consequences or punishment, for personal gain, for impression management/reputational concerns, to appear in a positive light to others, to help or protect others, and to be polite.

As noted above, children's earliest lies tend to be self-serving, motivated most often by a desire to avoid immediate consequences, such as punishment (Newton et al., 2000). Other early lies are told for personal gain, and these may be motivated first by a desire for material benefits (i.e. a cookie from a forbidden cookie jar) and later by a desire for social rewards (e.g. self-presentation lies). For instance, a child may lie to their peers by falsely boasting about their athletic abilities to appear more impressive. Extrapolated to legal contexts, children may tell self-serving lies because they fear they have done something wrong and will get in trouble (e.g. feel shame about abuse) leading to denials of misdeeds, to avoid punishment (e.g. feign incompetence), for material/financial reasons or to gain something (e.g. to get disability benefits or accommodations), to please another person (e.g. custodial parent) or to be seen as important or credible by adults (Evans & Lyon, 2012).

Yet, children also lie for the sake or benefit of others, sometimes at personal cost, increasingly with age because they learn social norms around politeness, prosocial behaviours and secret-keeping (Crossman & Talwar, in press; Talwar & Crossman, 2011). For example, lies may be told to be polite, such as claiming to love a gift that is actually disliked. Politeness lies are often told to prevent hurt feelings and to smooth social relations and tend not to be judged harshly by others (Ning & Crossman, 2007). However, other-oriented lies can also be told to conceal another's transgression, perhaps for their protection. For instance, an adolescent might lie to help a peer get out of trouble (e.g. lying for a friend), a lie that does benefit another, but would not be perceived as socially acceptable.

Note that lying for oneself or for the sake of others can take different forms, alone or in combination. For instance, children may conceal information, such as not revealing the identity of a perpetrator or withholding information about one's own or another's misdeeds. This may be referred to as concealment, a lie of omission, or as secret-keeping (Ekman, 1985; Williams et al., 2020; see Crossman & Talwar, in press, for a more thorough discussion of the related constructs of secrecy and deception in children). Lying could also involve providing explicitly false information, such as offering a false denial or making a false allegation, sometimes called falsification or a lie of commission (Ekman, 1985). Because lie detection is poor (e.g. Domagalski et al., 2020), lying in any of these manners can be irreparably harmful in CSA cases. If a child lies, the lie may be believed and could lead to charges being laid where there is no case of abuse or cases of actual abuse not being pursued.

Children's use of such lie-telling strategies to achieve their interpersonal goals (e.g. to get something, to protect someone, to avoid negative consequences) is based on a cost–benefit analysis. Factors like immediate concerns, interpersonal costs of lying, and long-term considerations can influence their decision of whether to lie or reveal the truth (Popliger et al., 2011; Talwar et al., 2015). The familiarity and perceived authority of the person being lied to can influence that decision (Bücken et al., 2023; Williams et al., 2013). Children may be more comfortable lying to certain individuals based upon their relationship and status.

At the same time, developmental factors play an important role in children's decisions. Whereas external factors like punishments or social rewards may be more salient for younger children, older children are better able to consider both immediate benefits and long-term consequences of lying when making a decision. This reflects cognitive maturation as well as socialization, through which children internalize moral standards from parents and society (Talwar, Lavoie, et al., 2017; Tong & Talwar, 2021). For younger children, experiential factors such as parental guidance, punishments and social rewards shape their behaviours. With age, children begin to internalize moral standards to direct their own behaviour. They are also affected by developing empathy, perspective-taking and understanding of social norms and expectations, which influence their decision-making regarding telling the truth or lying. Moreover, as children internalize social-cultural, moral standards, they are influenced by internal factors, including their own situational assessments (Bandura, 1986). Older children and adolescents are more aware of the context and the implications of their reports, which may influence their decision to conceal or disclose.

There are two types of motivational contexts that are uniquely important to consider when interviewing child witnesses and victims. The first is the potential for direct coaching to push a child into concealing or lying about their experiences. The second is when children experience outside influence, pressure, or motivation that makes them feel like they must delay, deny, or recant their reports.

Coaching

Of particular concern for investigators are instances where children disclose transgressions committed by someone else. Fears include that children might be coached to lie about the events and threatened with negative consequences if they tell the truth. For instance, it may be claimed that a child fabricated an abuse allegation against one parent during a custody dispute at the behest of the other parent (Bala & Schuman, 1999; Crossman et al., 2002). Alternatively, in many abuse cases children are testifying about transgressions involving an interaction between themselves and an adult. At times, that adult may have asked the child to keep parts of the event secret and lie to protect the adult (Lyon et al., 2008; Talwar et al., 2004). In either instance, children may feel compelled to lie.

Talwar et al. (2004) examined experimentally whether 3- to 11-year-old children would, in fact, lie to conceal a parent's transgression (i.e. breaking a puppet while the experimenter was out of the room). Parents coached their child not to reveal the transgression because parents might get in trouble if the experimenter found out. Later, when children were interviewed about what happened, regardless of whether it was with or without their parent present, the majority of children told the truth and did not conceal their transgression. Notably, children were more likely to lie for their parent after it was clear that the child would not be blamed for breaking the puppet (Talwar et al., 2004). These results suggest that young children will lie for others, but might be motivated to do so only when that lie does not impinge on their own self-protection.

In another study conducted with 4- to 7-year-old children awaiting a court appearance in the Los Angeles County Dependency Court, Lyon et al. (2008) also found that children would lie to conceal an adult's transgression and that children would fabricate details about an event at their request. Similarly, Tye et al. (1999) examined the willingness of 6- to 10-year-olds to lie about a theft in a realistic scenario. After witnessing a research assistant steal a book and ask them to keep it secret, 81% of children truthfully revealed the theft. When it was their parent who stole the book, asking the child to keep it secret and suggesting they blame the research assistant if asked, 56% of children made the false allegation to protect their guilty parent. However, when a parent was falsely accused of the theft, and suggested that the child blame the research assistant, 69% children made the false accusation to protect their innocent parent. Together, these findings highlight the importance of understanding that coaching can influence children to conceal or to fabricate false events or event details to protect an adult. However, it should be noted that in many of these studies, the transgressions of interest were not directed at the child participants, as they would be in most abuse cases.

Given that lying is inherently challenging and the high stakes typically involved in legal contexts, one might wonder how difficult it is to coach children towards false reporting. Talwar and colleagues examined children's willingness to disclose or to conceal after receiving heavy versus light coaching. In this study, after 4- to 7-year-old children interacted at home with a researcher, a parent coached them to say they had played a game involving touching their body with stickers (i.e. making it more analogous to abuse reports). One week later, a second researcher interviewed the children about what they had done with the first researcher. While most children who received minimal coaching confessed or revealed the fabrication during the interview, the majority of children who received extensive parental coaching (45 minutes or more) were likely to maintain the fabrication during the interview and their fabrications resembled truthful reports (Talwar, Hubbard et al., 2018).

A similar result was found when the coach was a confederate who had broken a forbidden toy (Talwar, Yachison et al., 2018). After witnessing the transgression, 4- to 7-year-olds received no coaching, light coaching or extensive coaching. Younger children (5 and under) were not good at maintaining the false story, either fully or partially disclosing, except when they received extensive coaching by the confederate, which included help creating a cover story. These children were significantly better able to maintain the false story throughout the interview. For older children, even light coaching significantly improved their ability to maintain their false report (Talwar, Yachison, et al., 2018). These findings suggest that coaching can help children maintain false reports and make it harder to distinguish false from true reports. However, the impact of coaching may vary as a function of children's age and general abilities to give detailed reports.

Recent research also suggests that the types of questions used (e.g. free-recall vs close-ended questions) may differentially affect children's disclosures of another's transgression (e.g. Foster et al., 2022; Wyman et al., 2019). For instance, Foster and colleagues (2022) interviewed 7- to 13-year-olds after they witnessed a confederate commit a theft and ask them to lie about it. In response to a free recall question, 21% of children disclosed the crime and 9% more disclosed with repeated recall prompts. A further 15% disclosed in response to close-ended yes-no questions later (Foster et al., 2022). In a similar study by Wyman et al. (2019), children saw an experimenter find a stranger's wallet and were asked to make a false denial, false accusation, true denial, or true accusation about a theft from that wallet. In response to the free-recall question, older children (10- to 11-year-olds) and those telling the truth provided longer, more forthcoming and more detailed disclosures, while children under age 9 (6–7 and 8–9 years) and lie-tellers tended to disclose in response to closed-ended questions instead.

Despite concerns to the contrary, evidence suggests that false allegation of abuse or neglect and coaching children to protect or to target a stakeholder in a custody or support battle (Black et al., 2016; Trocmé & Bala, 2005) is quite uncommon. For example, although false allegations of child sexual abuse are estimated occur at rates between 2% and 5%, an overwhelming number of allegations are true. Instead, when child sexual abuse does occur, it is generally believed to be substantially underreported (O'Donohue et al., 2018; Olafson & Lederman, 2006). These low rates of disclosure and false allegations, combined with the popular belief that children's testimony cannot be trusted, makes children not only vulnerable to being disbelieved about such crimes, but can also make them more vulnerable to child sexual abusers who rely on this popular belief (Jones et al., 2021). Hence the importance of developing better questioning strategies for children.

Outside pressures: delay, denial, recantation

Discussions of coaching typically conjure concerns about false allegations. Yet children in sexual abuse cases can be responsive to a range of external influences beyond direct coaching. These influences may lead to lie-telling in the form of delayed disclosure, denial and recantation, undermining potential opportunities for protection.

Though delayed disclosure does not necessarily involve telling lies, it may involve concealment (sometimes called a lie of omission), a form of deception (Ekman, 1985). Goodman-Brown et al. (2003) found that children tended to delay disclosure longer when they were older, felt greater responsibility for the abuse, were afraid of negative consequences from disclosure and the abuse was perpetrated by a relative. Children's disclosure decisions were influenced both by their own feelings of responsibility as well as their expectations for the reactions of others. Delays can also reflect embarrassment, not recognizing their experiences as abuse and fear of outcomes following disclosure (Korkman et al., 2024).

Denials and recantations, on the other hand, are more likely to involve telling a lie about one's experiences. Either could reflect refusal to acknowledge or rescission of a false allegation or of a true report. If an allegation was initially in error, whether due to suggestion, coaching, intentional deception, or for some other reason, then subsequent denial or recantation would reflect an honest reversal of dishonesty or inaccuracy. When it was a true allegation, given many children's reluctance to disclose in the first place, it is perhaps unsurprising that some deny or reverse their allegations, possibly after consequences begin to arise (Katz, 2014). However, the existence of a false denial or recantation does not mean that an allegation is false (Bücken et al., 2023; Katz, 2014). For example, although is not yet clear how common recantations are, studies of children in substantiated sexual abuse cases have found recantation rates of 4%, 23%, and 25% (Eisen et al., 2021; Korkman et al., 2024; Malloy et al., 2007, 2016). While this suggests that recantations might not be rare, even in substantiated cases, limited research to date illuminates what predicts them.

A consistent factor associated with recantation is when disclosure recipients are unsupportive. Malloy et al. (2007) found evidence for a filial dependency model in which younger children, those with an offending parent figure and an unsupportive, non-offending caregiver were more likely to recant their allegations completely at least once, as were children who were initially sent to foster care placements (marginally). In an analogue experimental study, Malloy and Mugno (2016) coached mothers to react supportively or unsupportively to their 6- to 9-year-old child's disclosure of a transgression that they were asked to keep secret. Alarmingly, almost half of the children (46%) recanted their allegation when their mother reacted unsupportively, versus none of the children whose mothers were supportive. In a follow-up field study with matched controls (matched by child age, parent alleged offender and caregiver unsupportiveness), Malloy et al. (2016) showed that children in substantiated CSA cases were less likely to recant when a family member expressed belief in the allegations and marginally less when placed apart from siblings. They were more likely to recant when a family member expressed disbelief and when visits with the alleged perpetrator were recommended. Hence, external factors in the aftermath of disclosure, including the (un)supportive reactions of those around them are critical predictors of children's recantations (Korkman et al., 2024).

Reasons for unsupportive reactions seem to vary as well, from simple disbelief to material concerns. Because children are vulnerable to social influences and pressures from adults and other family members, they may seek to "undo" their reports, and the subsequent chaos, through their recantations (Katz, 2014). This may be further fuelled by feelings of guilt, fear, and a desire to avoid negative consequences. Cultural context may be relevant as well, at times fuelling children's desire to recant (Katz, 2014). Overall, then, children's disclosures can be influenced by a combination of factors and any child or adolescent's delay, denial or recantation will be unique based on their individual, familial, and cultural circumstances and is not necessarily diagnostic of the accuracy or inaccuracy of their reports (Korkman et al., 2024).

With regard to denials in particular, Eisen et al. (2021) found that among 3- to 16-year-old victims who were interviewed twice over a 5-day span, 39.2% denied substantiated sexual abuse and 55.6% denied substantiated physical abuse in one or both interviews. Leander (2010) also found 5- to 17-year-old CSA victims to be reluctant or avoidant reporters who sometimes denied documented abuse in police interviews. Denials were more common among children who had been victims of abuse that included intercourse (versus touching) and who had been abused over more than six months. Yet, children also generated significantly more sexual details in a second police interview compared to the first. Similarly, Hershkowitz et al. (2021) demonstrated that interviewer support of reluctant children in an initial interview predicted a dynamic of child cooperation and spontaneous allegations in a subsequent interview. This then supported enhanced use of open-ended questions by interviewers. Together, these field studies illustrate that social dynamics can be influential in forensic interviewing contexts as well, reinforcing the importance of allowing time and space to effectively develop rapport with reluctant children which can help facilitate their subsequent disclosure (Blasbalg et al., 2021).

Promoting children's truthful reports

Given the possibility of children concealing and lying, that we are poor at detecting lies, and the potential influence of coaching or risk of recantation, researchers have investigated techniques for promoting children's honesty. These techniques include methods such as reassuring children they will not get in trouble (Lyon et al., 2008), explicitly stating that the questioner would be happy if the child told the truth (external appeals for honesty: Talwar et al., 2015), suggesting to children that a co-transgressor wants them to tell the truth (putative confession: Lyon et al., 2014), punishment (Talwar & Lee, 2011; Talwar et al., 2015), reading moral stories about honesty (e.g. Lee et al., 2014; Talwar et al., 2016; Talwar, Yachison et al., 2018), modelling and praise for honesty (Engarhos et al., 2020; Sai et al., 2020), increasing self-awareness (Bender et al., 2018), and asking children to promise to tell the truth (e.g. Evans & Lee, 2010; Lyon & Dorado, 2008; Talwar et al., 2002).

To date, one of the most studied and effective honesty promotion techniques is promising to tell the truth (e.g. Bender et al., 2018; Bussey, 2010; Evans & Lee, 2010; Evans & Talwar, 2023; Heyman et al., 2015; Lyon & Dorado, 2008; Lyon et al., 2008; Quas et al., 2018; Talwar et al., 2002). For example, simply asking children to promise to tell the truth increased their truth-telling about their own misdeed (Talwar et al., 2002), decreased the likelihood they would lie for their parents (Talwar et al., 2004), and increased their truthful disclosure of an adult's transgression (Lyon et al., 2008). The word *promise* ostensibly creates a sense of obligation as it demonstrates a commitment or intention to act (Bussey, 2010). A host of studies that examined children's honesty after committing a transgression found that asking children 5 years of age and older to promise to tell the truth reduces lie-telling by approximately 20–30% though, importantly, many still lied. In contrast, promising to tell the truth does not successfully increase honesty with younger preschool aged children (Bender et al., 2018;

Evans & Talwar, 2023; Heyman et al., 2015; Quas et al., 2018; Talwar et al., 2002), perhaps due to younger children's limited understanding of the word "promise" (Lyon & Evans, 2014).

Further research has sought to understand the mechanisms underlying the effectiveness of truth-promoting appeals. According to Bandura's (1991) social cognitive theory of moral action, people's beliefs about outcomes expected for different types of conduct play a central role in determining their behaviour. Through socialization, children's behaviour is influenced by both external and internal factors (Bandura, 1986). Young children initially rely on guidance from others to shape their behaviours either through external physical factors (i.e. punishments) or external social factors (i.e. social rewards for pleasing another person) and as children internalize their culture's moral standards, they are also affected by internal social factors (i.e. pleasing oneself by doing the "right" thing). Along these lines, one study found that children were less likely to lie about a transgression when their "interrogators" appealed to either external or internal motivations to tell the truth, but not when external consequences were raised (Talwar et al., 2015).

In addition, Bandura's social learning theory (Bandura, 1991) suggests that social norms such as attitudes, values, and behaviours can be learned through observing others. Several studies have examined the influence of modelling truth- or lie-telling on children's own honesty (Engarhos et al., 2020; Hays & Carver, 2014; Ma et al., 2018), although the influence of modelling is often confounded with the consequences of truth- or lie-telling. For example, Engarhos and colleagues (2020) manipulated whether 5- to 8-year-olds observed a model who told a truth or a lie (about breaking someone's glasses) and whether the outcome was positive (thanked) or negative (upset reaction). Children who witnessed the experimenter tell the truth and receive a positive outcome were significantly more likely to disclose and tell the truth about their own misdeed compared to a control condition, significantly reducing lie-telling by approximately 30%. Children who saw the model lie with negative consequences were also more likely to disclose their misdeed (Engarhos et al., 2020). Similarly, if children experience more complex and possibly unexpected consequences of truth- versus lie-telling, their behaviour may shift. For instance, lack of support and/or blame from family members after disclosing abuse could invite or drive a child to lie and recant a truthful allegation (e.g. Malloy et al., 2016).

Modelling can also occur more formally, through reading moral stories to children. Stories have been used for centuries to pass on social norms and expectations. For example, Lee and colleagues (2014) examined whether reading classic moral stories to children influenced their honesty. Children were read one of four stories: *George Washington and the Cherry Tree* (praised for honesty), *The Boy Who Cries Wolf* (negative consequences of lie-telling), *Pinocchio* (both negative and positive consequences for lying and truth-telling), and *The Tortoise and the Hare* (control). Children who were read *George Washington and the Cherry Tree*, where modelling of truth-telling and praise for honesty were highlighted, were significantly more likely to tell the truth. These findings have been replicated examining children's willingness to lie to conceal someone else's transgression (Talwar et al., 2016), as well as after being coached to keep a secret (Talwar, Yachison et al., 2018). Stories that combined a story character modelling truth-telling with the resulting positive consequences for the character had the greatest impact on promoting children's honesty about their own transgressions (Evans & Talwar, 2023).

Notably, some studies suggest that truth-promotion techniques can increase honesty even when children are coached to lie, suggesting the effects of coaching may be ameliorated by some truth induction methods (Lyon et al., 2008; Talwar, Yachison et al., 2018). More research is needed to determine boundary conditions for the effectiveness of truth promotion techniques with children and adolescents. Yet, findings suggest that fostering their internal motivations for honesty could help bolster social incentives for truth-telling and remove competing social barriers to honesty.

Rapport-building

Successful investigative interviews with child and adolescent witnesses rely on effective rapport building and the provision of socio-emotional support throughout an interview. In theory, this is because supportive interviewers make children feel cared for and safe (Brubacher et al., 2019; Hershkowitz & Lamb, 2020; Lamb et al., 2018), while effective rapport-building helps establish a psychosocial context where children can overcome reluctance to disclose and feel comfortable discussing sensitive topics with a previously unknown interviewer (e.g. Hershkowitz et al., 2021; Saywitz et al., 2011). This is particularly important as children are more willing to lie to strangers than to individuals they know (Williams et al., 2013). Effective rapport-building establishes a sense of commonality, trust, and cooperation with the practitioner while countering possible feelings of pressure to lie or conceal information (Foster et al., 2022). Even with an effective initial interview, some children may recant in a subsequent interview, as a consequence of some of these pressures (Eisen et al., 2021; Katz, 2014), enhancing the importance of rapport-building with a skilled practitioner who allows sufficient time to effectively build rapport and offer social support (Hershkowitz et al., 2021).

Rapport-building typically refers to a stage at the start of an interview where the practitioner seeks to establish a connection (i.e. rapport) between themselves and the child interviewee. Many forensic interview guidelines (e.g. the NICHD standard and revised protocols) provide guidelines for doing so (e.g. use the child's name; respect the child's rhythm and silences; display positive, warm affect) and suggest that interviewers seek to adequately establish rapport at the beginning of an interview, before moving to a substantive phase in which they ask questions about suspected abuse, even if that requires a second interview (Korkman et al., 2024). This helps to ensure a supportive environment to increase children's comfort and competence to recall and disclose past events in detail, as research shows that effective rapport-building leads to more complete, accurate and credible event reports (Foster et al., 2022; Hershkowitz et al., 2021; Korkman et al., 2024).

At the same time, to be effective, rapport-building practices must be responsive to developmental and cultural issues. For instance, while young children might need more extensive narrative practice as a component of rapport-building (e.g. asking a child to describe a happy incident from their past), this might be perceived as infantilizing by an adolescent. On the other hand, older children and adolescents may be more responsive to practices that support their autonomy and reflect sharing of information. In one study, for instance, children witnessed a confederate steal money from a wallet and were then asked to lie about it. Foster et al. (2022) next engaged the children in investigative interviews, providing the 7- to 13-year-olds with either narrative practice or an interactional rapport-building task focused on the relational aspects of rapport-building (i.e. mutual attentiveness, positivity and coordination between child and interviewer). They found that the older children in the interactional condition were more likely to be truthful, they disclosed the transgression earlier, and they provided more details during the interviews. Nevertheless, much remains to be learned about developmental differences in the effectiveness of rapport-building. Similarly, cultural mores might require exceptional sensitivity when broaching the topic of sexual abuse, particularly where gender, ethnic, racial, linguistic or other differences between children and interviewers could be impactful (e.g. Hershkowitz & Lamb, 2020; Hershkowitz et al., 2021; Korkman et al., 2024; Lamb et al., 2018).

Truth–lie discussions: the link between conceptual understanding and behaviour

Child witnesses are typically asked about their understanding of truth and lies as a means of assessing their competence to testify (e.g. take an oath) or their commitment to tell the truth, whether in court or in investigative interviews (Bala et al., 2010; Lyon, 2013; Ministry of Justice, 2011; O'Connell et al., 2020). For instance, in the UK, the "Achieving Best Evidence in Criminal Proceedings" was created as a safeguard to protect vulnerable witnesses (Ministry of Justice, 2022) and this investigative protocol recommends that police officers end the rapport building phase of interviews with a truth–lies discussion (TLD) involving narratives, suited to a child's age. The aim of a TLD is to assess a child's conceptual understanding of the difference between truths and lies, to emphasize the importance of telling the truth, and to serve as a reminder of the consequences of lying (O'Connell et al., 2020). TLDs also help relay to the court that a child has been made aware of the importance of telling the truth. It is suggested that TLDs serve as a means of assessing children's competency to testify and the credibility of their statement (Lyon, 2011). An underlying assumption is that children who understand the difference between truths and lies, who appreciate the consequences of lying and recognize that lying is bad, will provide truthful and accurate statements (e.g. Bala et al., 2000). Yet, adults tell lies despite knowing that lie-telling is considered morally wrong under most circumstances (Batson & Thompson, 2001) and perjury laws exist to enforce truthfulness in court, as it cannot be assumed. Understanding the concept of lies does not ensure that a child's statements are true, nor does a lack of clear understanding imply a lack of commitment to honesty. In fact, children can tell the truth well before they can define it (Lyon, 2014).

Research has demonstrated the lack of relationship between children's understanding of (dis)honesty and their behaviour using questions that are typical of court procedures for assessing competency (Bala et al., 2010; Talwar et al., 2004). For instance, Talwar et al. (2002) did not find a relationship between children's conceptual understanding of truths and lies and their subsequent truth/lie-telling behaviour. Their conceptual and moral understanding of lies and truths does not seem to be diagnostic of honest behaviour. As a result, questioning children about the difference between truths and lies is not likely to be diagnostic of their ability or willingness to provide a truthful and/or accurate account in court. Hence, typical competency questioning, which asks about children's understanding of truth and lies to assess their likely truthfulness, is an unnecessary barrier to children's testimony in court. Such a practice might prevent children who are able to give truthful, accurate and useful testimony from testifying. In contrast, use of truth promotion techniques, such as asking children if they promise they will tell the truth, seems a more effective means for supporting children's accurate reporting in forensic contexts (e.g. Lyon et al., 2008; Quas et al., 2018; Talwar et al., 2002, 2004).

Summary

Overall, the development of children's lie-telling abilities is influenced by cognitive, social, and situational factors that change as children grow and mature. Adaptations in their lie-telling strategies reflect their understanding of consequences, social norms and their cognitive capabilities at different stages of development, which can have potentially important implications in legal and forensic settings. Investigators and courts are particularly concerned with the veracity of young children's testimony. Yet, research suggests that although children's lie-telling emerges in the preschool years, children are not skilled lie-tellers until the later elementary school years. The necessity of relatively sophisticated cognitive skills for elaborate lie-telling has implications for evaluating the reliability of child witness testimony. First, it suggests that children who struggle cognitively, either due to developmental delays or specific disorders, such as autism spectrum disorder, are less likely to be capable of generating or maintaining credible false reports. It also suggests that younger child witnesses are less capable of lying effectively when verbal elaboration is required.

Children can be coached to lie more effectively to help or protect others, although such lies do not come as early or as readily to children as lies to protect themselves. Children's decisions to lie are motivated by their evaluation of the potential consequences to self and a desire to minimize negative consequences. Thus, if a child believes that lying will protect them from such consequences, they may decide to conceal or fabricate information – or to deny or recant a previous disclosure.

Findings also demonstrate that, from an early age, escaping negative consequences is a powerful motivator. Child witnesses could be motivated to lie to conceal an event that they perceive to be a transgression or for which they anticipate punishment if they tell the truth. In such cases, younger children may be especially influenced by their perceptions of the possibility of punishment, highlighting the importance of reassurance to children when interviewing them. For instance, one study highlighted the impact that the fear of punishment can have on young children's lie-telling. Talwar and Lee (2011) investigated children's lying in two schools. In one school, a punitive, corporal punishment model was used to correct children's behaviour, while the other school did not use corporal punishment. They found that almost all the child participants in the punitive school were more likely to lie about their transgressions and were better at maintaining their lies in follow-up questioning than children from the non-punitive school. These children had learned that if they committed a transgression, they had nothing to lose by lying: they would be punished severely for the transgression if discovered, but if they lied successfully, they could possibly avoid punishment completely. Lying was a more adaptive choice than being honest in such an environment. Similarly, children seem more likely to lie for another when the costs or consequences to themselves are minimized. The weighting of various factors in such a cost/benefit analysis likely evolves and broadens with age. For instance, younger children may simply consider immediate concerns, such as the relative benefit or cost to themselves. Older children likely weigh both the immediate benefits of truth- versus lie-telling, as well as longer-term considerations, such as the interpersonal costs of getting caught in a lie (e.g. parental disappointment, peer rejection), as the adaptiveness of lie-telling as a strategy likely shifts with age as well. In attempting to elicit children's complete and honest reports (and potentially overcome inducements to lie), interviewers must therefore bear in mind the potential impact of this cost-benefit analysis and address children's perceptions of the consequences of lie- and truth-telling.

It is important to emphasize, however, that this research does not imply that children are more dishonest than adults. Research with adults finds that they commonly tell lies (DePaulo et al., 1996; Serota et al., 2010), and that children lie for the same reasons as adults. Yet, children's lies are less elaborate and they have difficulty sustaining them when questioned. Therefore, the risk of harm from children's lie-telling in court is, at worst, no greater than it is for adult witnesses.

Children's moral understanding and evaluation of lie-telling demonstrates clearly that children begin to understand the (im)morality of lying by age 2 to 3 years. Although children may initially over-generalize the concept of a lie, and seem to understand truths earlier than lies, they do recognize self-serving and hurtful lies as lies and perceive most lie-telling as a negative behaviour. However, as with adults, their conceptual and moral understanding of lies and truths does not seem to be diagnostic of honest behaviour. As a result, questioning children about the difference between truths and lies is not likely to be diagnostic of their ability or willingness to provide a truthful and/or accurate account in court. Hence, competency evaluations that rely on children's truth-lie knowledge or definitions are of little utility in ensuring that children offer truthful testimony or in helping the courts determine if a child is capable of testifying truthfully and accurately. At best, these assessments are ineffectual, as they are not diagnostic of children's honesty. At worst, they could contribute to a miscarriage of justice, if an otherwise competent child is barred from testifying. Moreover, they are often not developmentally appropriate. Asking about the intent of hypothetical honest or deceptive speakers, for example, might unnecessarily confound a young, but honest child witness. In addition, they may encourage children to lie in an effort to seem credible (e.g. "I have never lied"), undermining a potentially competent child's credibility. In these ways, they are likely to underestimate young children's competency. In contrast, lab-based research has found that promises to tell the truth influence children's honesty, suggesting that in actual cases, children who swear an oath or promise to tell the truth may be less likely to testify dishonestly in court.

Another implication of current research for the legal system is that novel procedures are needed to enhance and encourage children's motivations for truth-telling. Investigators must attempt to evaluate the motivations that might be driving children's behaviours in relation to the developmental level of the child, as well as their individual, familial, social, and cultural context, all of which could impact their willingness to disclose honestly. Reassuring children that their self-interests are served by truth-telling and reducing negative consequences for honesty would be beneficial as well. Finally, eliciting children's promises that they will tell the truth (or use of other truth induction techniques) may help to heighten the salience of honesty and shift children's motivations towards truth-telling. The goal for future researchers will be to continue identifying the developmental progression of children's lie-telling abilities and procedures for helping to ensure child witness testimony will be complete, accurate, and honest. In this way, we can hope to better protect children and adults from the impact of lies in the legal system.

Recommendations: implications for practitioners

When considering children's reports, it is critical to emphasize that children's testimony can be as trustworthy as that of adults. While many children do tell lies, they are not unique in this regard. Adults lie as well. Crucially, there is no evidence that there is greater risk of children making intentionally false allegations than adults. Children and adults may be motivated to lie or to conceal the truth for similar reasons. However, children may be less skilled at giving and maintaining plausible false reports – or at effectively concealing the truth. Also, while children may be influenced by adults to conceal or to recant truthful allegations, these influences are outside of the child. Children are not inherently unreliable, untrustworthy reporters.

Nevertheless, research on lying and truth-telling has important implications for clinicians and forensic interviewers working with alleged child and adolescent victims, seeking to understand denials and recantations. In light of the above reviewed literature, we offer the following recommendations:

- ***Understand children's developmental stages.*** Forensic interviewers should be aware of the role of developmental factors in children's lying and truth-telling. Cognitively, younger children are less able to inhibit behaviour, making them more likely to impulsively disclose, while older children and adolescents are better equipped to withhold information. Younger children are less skilled at lying and hence, less able to maintain false reports. Older children are better able to maintain consistency. Younger children may lie for immediate self-perceived benefit or protection, while older children and adolescents are more willing and able to weigh and appreciate both immediate and long-term consequences of lying and truth-telling. Socially, children become increasingly aware that lying and truth-telling can both harm and benefit others. They may lie for self-serving, protective reasons, but lies or concealment can also be altruistic and driven by compassion or loyalty to others.

- ***Recognize social influences.*** Children may be induced to lie by or for people they have close interpersonal relationships with, such as in maltreatment cases involving relatives, particularly when an allegation is disruptive and when they are not supported by a parent. Understanding the social context can help interviewers assess the motivations behind a child or adolescent's possible denial or recantation.
- ***Tailor interview strategies to developmental stage.*** Interviewers should be aware of the developmental stage of a child or adolescent and tailor their evidence-based questioning techniques accordingly. Younger children may need more cognitive supports, while adolescents may need more control over the conversation to support their autonomy. Understanding cognitive, social, and moral aspects of lying can also help interviewers create a supportive and conducive environment for children and adolescents to feel more safe and comfortable disclosing truths and help practitioners unpack potential reasons for denials or recantations.
- ***Promote truthful disclosures.*** Interviewers should create an environment that encourages truthful disclosure. Beyond reliance on open-ended questions and avoiding (mis)leading questions, this includes techniques such as sharing ground rules, requesting a promise to tell the truth, effectively building rapport, being warm and supportive and discussing the importance of truthful reports.
- ***Practice cultural sensitivity.*** Recognize that lying and truth-telling are social behaviours shaped by social and cultural norms and values. Cultural sensitivity may help practitioners seeking to understand factors that might drive a child or adolescent's denial or recantation.
- ***Enhance interviewer skills with evidence-based training.*** Continuous training and education based on research findings in developmental psychology, child behaviour and forensic interviewing can enhance forensic interviewers skills in assessing the truthfulness of children's statements.

Caution is invariably warranted when evaluating a child or adolescent's veracity, especially when they delay, deny or recant abuse. However, by incorporating these insights into their practices, interviewers can create a supportive and effective interviewing environment to encourage children to provide and maintain truthful disclosures.

References

Andrews, J., Rosenblatt, E., Malkus, U., & Gardner, H. (1986). Children's abilities to distinguish metaphoric and ironic utterances from mistakes and lies. *Communication Cognition*, *19*(3–4), 281–297.

Bala, N., Lee, K., Lindsay, R., & Talwar, V. (2000). A legal and psychological critique of the present approach to the assessment of the competence of child witnesses. *Osgoode Hall Law Journal*, 38, 409–451. https://doi.org/10.60082/2817-5069.1497

Bala, N., Lee, K., Lindsay, R. C. L., & Talwar, V. (2010). The competency of children to testify: Psychological research informing Canadian law reform. *International Journal of Children's Rights*, *18*, 53–77. https://doi.org/10.1163/157181809X458544

Bala, N., & Schuman, J. (1999). Allegations of sexual abuse when parents have separated. *Canadian Family Law Quarterly*, *17*(2), 191–243.

Bandura, A. (1986). Social foundations of thought and action. In D. F. Marks (ed.), *The health psychology reader*. Sage. https://doi.org/10.4135/9781446221129.n6

Bandura, A. (1991). Social cognitive theory of moral thought and action. In W. M. Kurtines & J. L. Gewirtz (eds), *Handbook of moral behavior and development* (vol. 1, pp. 45–103). Hillsdale, NJ: Lawrence Erlbaum Associates. https://doi.org/10.4324/9781315807294

Batson, C. D., & Thompson, E. R. (2001). Why don't moral people act morally? Motivational considerations. *Current Directions in Psychological Science*, *10*, 54–57. https://doi.org/10.1111/1467-8721.00114

Bender, J., O'Connor, A. M., & Evans, A. D. (2018). Mirror, mirror on the wall: Increasing young children's honesty through inducing self-awareness. *Journal of Experimental Child Psychology*, *167*, 414–422. https://doi.org/10.1016/j.jecp.2017.12.001

Black, T., Saini, M., Fallon, B., Deljavan, S., Theoduloz, R., & Wall, M. (2016). The intersection of child custody disputes and child protection investigations: Secondary data analysis of the Canadian incidence study of reported child abuse and neglect (CIS-2008). *International Journal of Child and Adolescent Resilience*, *4*(1), 143–157.

Blasbalg, U., Hershkowitz, I., Lamb, M. E., & Karni-Visel, Y. (2021). Adherence to the Revised NICHD Protocol recommendations for conducting repeated supportive interviews is associated with the likelihood that children will allege abuse. *Psychology, Public Policy, and Law*, *27*(2), 209–220. https://doi-org.ez.lib.jjay.cuny.edu/10.1037/law0000295

Bok, S. (1999 [1978]). *Lying: Moral choice in public and private life*. London: Quartet Books. https://doi.org/10.1086/292156

Bond, C. F. Jr., & DePaulo, B. M. (2006). Accuracy of deception judgments. *Personality and Social Psychology Review*, 10(3), 214–234. https://doi.org/10.1207/s15327957pspr1003_2

Brubacher, S. P., Poole, D. A., Dickinson, J. J., La Rooy, D., Szojka, Z. A., & Powell, M. B. (2019). Effects of interviewer familiarity and supportiveness on children's recall across repeated interviews. Law and Human Behavior, *43*(6), 507–516. https://doi.org/10.1037/lhb0000346

Bruer, K. C., Zanette, S., Ding, X. P., Lyon, T. D., & Lee, K. (2020). Identifying liars through automatic decoding of children's facial expressions. *Child Development*, *91*(4), e995–e1011. https://doi.org/10.1111/cdev.13336

Bücken, C. A., Otgaar, H., London, K., Riesthuis, P., Battista, F., & Mangiulli, I. (2023). "Nothing happened": Legal implications of false denials among abused children. *Child Abuse Review*, *32*(2), e2791. https://doi.org/10.1002/car.2791

Bussey, K. (1992). Lying and truthfulness: Children's definitions, standards, and evaluative reactions. *Child Development*, *63*, 129–137. https://doi.org/10.1111/j.1467-8624.1992.tb03601.x

Bussey, K. (1999). Children's categorization and evaluation of different types of lies and truths. *Child Development*, *70*, 1338–1347. https://doi.org/10.1111/1467-8624.00098

Bussey, K. (2010). The role of promises for children's trustworthiness and honesty. In K. J. Rotenberg (ed.), *Interpersonal trust during childhood and adolescence*, (155–176). Cambridge: Cambridge University Press.

Creusere, M. A. (2000). A developmental test of theoretical perspectives on the understanding of verbal irony: Children's recognition of allusion and pragmatic insincerity. *Metaphor and Symbol*, *15*(1–2), 29–45. https://doi.org/10.1207/S15327868MS151&2_3

Crossman, A. M., & Talwar, V. (in press). In G. Goodman, T. Lyon, S. Hobbs, & R. Enriquez (eds), In Mechanisms of denial: Children's deception and secrecy. *Handbook of child witnesses: Improving psychological science and legal practice.* American Psychological Association.

Crossman, A. M., Powell, M. B., Principe, G. F., & Ceci, S. J. (2002). Child testimony in custody cases. *Journal of Forensic Psychology Practice*, *2*(1), 1–31. https://doi.org/10.1300/J158v02n01_01

Debey, E., De Schryver, M., Logan, G. D., Suchotzki, K., & Verschuere, B. (2015). From junior to senior Pinocchio: A cross-sectional lifespan investigation of deception. *Acta Psychologica*, *160*, 58–68. https://doi.org/10.1016/j.actpsy.2015.06.007

Denault, V. (2020). Misconceptions about nonverbal cues to deception: A covert threat to the justice system? *Frontiers in Psychology*, *11*, 573460. https://doi.org/10.3389/fpsyg.2020.573460

Denault, V., Leclerc, C., & Talwar, V. (2024). The use of nonverbal communication when assessing witness credibility: A view from the bench. *Psychiatry, Psychology and Law*, *31*(1), 97–120. https://doi.org/10.1080/13218719.2023.2175068

DePaulo, B. M., Kashy, D. A., Kirkendol, S. E., Wyer, M. M., & Epstein, J. A. (1996). Lying in everyday life. *Journal of Personality and Social Psychology*, *70*(5), 979–995. https://doi.org/10.1037/0022-3514.70.5.979

Ding, X. P., Omrin, D. S., Evans, A. D., Fu, G., Chen, G., & Lee, K. (2014). Elementary school children's cheating behavior and its cognitive correlates. *Journal of Experimental Child Psychology*, *121*, 85–95. https://doi.org/10.1016/j.jecp.2013.12.005

Domagalski, K., Gongola, J., Lyon, T. D., Clark, S. E., & Quas, J. A. (2020). Detecting children's true and false denials of wrongdoing: Effects of question type and base rate knowledge. *Behavioral Sciences & the Law*, *38*(6), 612–629. https://doi.org/10.1002/bsl.2487

Edelstein, R. S., Luten, T. L., Ekman, P., & Goodman, G. S. (2006). Detecting lies in children and adults. *Law and Human Behavior*, *30*(1), 1–10. https://doi.org/10.1007/s10979-006-9031-2

Eisen, M. L., Goodman, G. S., Diep, J., Lacsamana, M., Ristrom, L. J., & Qin, J. J. (2021). Disclosures of sexual and physical abuse across repeated interviews. *Journal of Child Sexual Abuse, 30*(8), 932–952. https://doi.org/10.1080/10538712.2021.1960457

Ekman, P. (1985). *Telling lies: Clues to deceit in the marketplace, politics, and marriage*. Norton.

Engarhos, P., Shohoudi, A., Crossman, A., & Talwar, V. (2020). Learning through observing: Effects of modeling truth-and lie-telling on children's honesty. *Developmental Science, 23*, e12883. https://doi.org/10.1111/desc.12883

Evans, A. D., & Lee, K. (2010). Promising to tell the truth makes 8- to 16-year-olds more honest. *Behavioral Sciences & the Law, 28*, 801–811. https://doi.org/10.1002/bsl.960

Evans, A. D., & Lee, K. (2013). Emergence of lying in very young children. *Developmental Psychology, 49*(10), 1958. https://doi.org/10.1037/a0031409

Evans, A. D., & Lyon, T. D. (2012). Assessing children's competency to take the oath in court: The influence of question type on children's accuracy. *Law and Human Behavior, 36*(3), 195–205. https://doi.org/10.1037/h0093957.

Evans, A. D., & Talwar, V. (2023). Encouraging honesty: Developmental differences in the influence of honesty promotion techniques. *Developmental Psychology, 60*(3), 481–490. https://doi.org/10.1037/dev0001640

Foster, I., Talwar, V., & Crossman, A. (2022). The role of rapport in eliciting children's truthful reports. *Applied Developmental Science*. https://doi.org/10.1080/10888691.2022.2058507

Gongola, J., Scurich, N., & Quas, J. A. (2017). Detecting deception in children: A meta-analysis. *LAW AND HUMAN BEHAVIOR, 41*(1), 44. https://psycnet.apa.org/doi/10.1037/lhb0000211

Goodman-Brown, T. B., Edelstein, R. S., Goodman, G. S., Jones, D. P. H., & Gordon, D. S. (2003). Why children tell: A model of children's disclosure of sexual abuse. *Child Abuse & Neglect, 27*(5), 525–540. https://doi.org/10.1016/S0145-2134(03)00037-1

Hays, C., & Carver, L. J. (2014). Follow the liar: the effects of adult lies on children's honesty. *Developmental Science, 17*(6), 977–983.

Hershkowitz, I., & Lamb, M. E. (2020). Allegation rates and credibility assessment in forensic interviews of alleged child abuse victims: Comparing the Revised and Standard NICHD Protocols. *Psychology, Public Policy, and Law, 26*, 176–184. https://psycnet.apa.org/doi/10.1037/law0000230

Hershkowitz, I., Lamb, M. E., Blasbalg, U., & Karni-Visel, Y. (2021). The dynamics of two-session interviews with suspected victims of abuse who are reluctant to make allegations. *Development and Psychopathology, 33*(2), 739–747. https://doi.org/10.1017/S0954579420001820

Heyman, G. D., Fu, G., Lin, J., Qian, M. K., & Lee, K. (2015). Eliciting promises from children reduces cheating. *Journal of Experimental Child Psychology, 139*, 242–248. https://doi.org/10.1016/j.jecp.2015.04.013

Jones, T. M., Bottoms, B. L., Sachdev, K., Aniciete, J., & Gorak, K. (2021). Jurors' gender and their fear of false child sexual abuse accusations are related to their belief in child victims' allegations. *Journal of Child Sexual Abuse, 30*(7), 828–846. https://doi.org/10.1080/10538712.2021.1931612

Katz, C. (2014). "Please believe me; I am the biggest liar that exists": Characterising children's recantations during forensic investigations. *Children and Youth Services Review*, *43*, 160–166. https://doi.org/10.1016/j.childyouth.2014.05.020

Korkman, J., Otgaar, H., Geven, L. M., Bull, R., Cyr, M., Hershkowitz, I., ...Volbert, R. (2024). White paper on forensic child interviewing: Research-based recommendations by the European Association of Psychology and Law. *Psychology, Crime & Law*, ahead-of-print, 1–44. https://doi.org/10.1080/1068316X.2024.2324098

Lamb, M. E., Brown, D. A., Hershkowitz, I., Orbach, Y., & Esplin, P. W. (2018). *Tell me what happened: Questioning children about abuse* (2nd ed.). Chichester, UK: John Wiley. https://doi.org/10.1002/9781118881248

Lavoie, J., & Talwar, V. (2020). Care to share? Children's cognitive skills and concealing responses to a parent. *Topics in Cognitive Science*, *12*(2), 485–503. https://doi.org/10.1111/tops.12390

Leach, A., Talwar, V., Lee, K., Bala, N., & Lindsay, R. C. L. (2004). Intuitive lie detection of children's deception by law enforcement officials and university students. *Law and Human Behavior*, *28*, 661–685. https://doi.org/10.1007/s10979-004-0793-0

Leander, L. (2010). Police interviews with child sexual abuse victims: Patterns of reporting, avoidance and denial. *Child Abuse & Neglect*, *34*(3), 192–205. https://doi.org/10.1016/j.chiabu.2009.09.011

Leduc, K., Williams, S., Gomez-Garibello, C., & Talwar, V. (2017). The contributions of mental state understanding and executive functioning to preschool-aged children's lie-telling. *British Journal of Developmental Psychology*, *35*(2), 288–302. https://doi.org/10.1111/bjdp.12163

Lee, K. (2013). Little liars: Development of verbal deception in children. *Child Development Perspectives*, *7*(2), 91–96. https://doi.org/10.1111/cdep.12023

Lee, K., & Ross, H. J. (1997). The concept of lying in adolescents and young adults: Testing Sweetser's folkloristic model. *Merrill-Palmer Quarterly* 1982, 43, 255–270. www.jstor.org/stable/23092491

Lee, K., Talwar, V., McCarthy, A., Ross, I., Evans, A., & Arruda, C. (2014). Can classic moral stories promote honesty in children? *Psychological science*, *25*(8), 1630–1636. https://doi.org/10.1177/0956797614536401

Lewis, M., Stanger, C., & Sullivan, M. W. (1989). Deception in 3-year-olds. *Developmental Psychology*, *25(3)*, 439–443. https://doi.org/10.1037/0012-1649.25.3.439

Li, A. S., Kelley, E. A., Evans, A. D., & Lee, K. (2011). Exploring the ability to deceive in children with autism spectrum disorders. *Journal of Autism and Developmental Disorders*, *41*, 185–195.

Luke, T. J. (2019). Lessons from Pinocchio: Cues to deception may be highly exaggerated. *Perspectives on Psychological Science*, *14*(4), 646–671. https://doi.org/10.1177/1745691619838258

Lyon, T. D. (2011). Assessing the competency of child witnesses: Best practice informed by psychology and law. In M. E. Lamb, D. J. La Rooy, L. C. Malloy, & C. Katz (eds), *Children's testimony: A handbook of psychological research and forensic practice*. Hoboken: Wiley-Blackwell. https://doi.org/10.1002/9781119998495.ch4

Lyon, T. D. (2014). Interviewing children. *Annual Review of Law and Social Science, 10*, 73–89. https://doi.org/10.1146/annurev-lawsocsci-110413-030913

Lyon, T. D. & Evans, A.D. (2014) Young children's understanding that promising guarantees performance: The effects of age and maltreatment. *Law and Human Behavior, 38*, 162–169. https://doi.org/10.1037/lhb0000061

Lyon, T. D., Quas, J. A., & Carrick, N. (2013). Right and righteous: Children's incipient understanding and evaluation of true and false statements. *Journal of Cognition and Development, 14*(3), 437–454. https://doi.org/10.1080/15248372.2012.673187

Lyon, T. D., & Dorado, J. S. (2008). Truth induction in young maltreated children: The effects of oath-taking and reassurance on true and false disclosures. *Child Abuse & Neglect, 32*(7), 738–748. https://doi.org/10.1016/j.chiabu.2007.08.008

Lyon, T.D., Malloy, L.C., Quas, J.A., & Talwar, V. (2008). Coaching, truth induction, and young maltreated children's false allegations and false denials. *Child Development*, 79, 914–929. https://doi.org/10.1111/j.1467-8624.2008.01167.

Lyon, T. D., Wandrey, L., Licht, E. C. R., Sim, M. P. Y., Quas, J. A. (2014). Eliciting maltreated and non-maltreated children's transgression disclosures: Narrative practice rapport building and a putative confession. *Child Development, 85*(4), 1756–1769. https://doi.org/10.1111/cdev.12223

Ma, F., Evans, A. D., Liu, Y., Luo, X., & Xu, F. (2015). To lie or not to lie? The influence of parenting and theory-of-mind understanding on three-year-old children's honesty. *Journal of Moral Education, 44*(2), 198–212. https://doi.org/10.1080/03057240.2015.1023182

Ma, F., Heyman, G. D., Jing, C., Fu, Y., Compton, B. J., Xu, F., & Lee, K. (2018). Promoting honesty in young children through observational learning. *Journal of Experimental Child Psychology, 167*, 234–245. https://doi.org/10.1016/j.jecp.2017.11.003

Malloy L. C., Lyon T. D., & Quas J. A. (2007). Filial dependency and recantation of child sexual abuse allegations. *Journal of the American Academy of Child & Adolescent Psychiatry, 46*, 162–170. doi:10.1097/01.chi.0000246067.77953.f7

Malloy L. C., & Mugno A. P. (2016). Children's recantation of adult wrongdoing: An experimental investigation. *Journal of Experimental Child Psychology, 14*, 11–21. doi:10.1016/j.jecp.2015.12.003

Malloy, L. C., Mugno, A. P., Rivard, J. R., Lyon, T. D., & Quas, J. A. (2016). Familial influences on recantation in substantiated child sexual abuse cases. *Child Maltreatment, 21*(3), 256–261. https://doi.org/10.1177/1077559516650936

Ministry of Justice. (2022). *Achieving Best Evidence in Criminal Proceedings: Guidance on Interviewing Victims and Witnesses, and Guidance on Using Special Measures.* https://assets.publishing.service.gov.uk/government/uploads/system/uploads/attachment_data/file/1051269/achieving-best-evidence-criminal-proceedings.pdf

Newton, P., Reddy, V., & Bull, R. (2000). Children's everyday deception and performance on false-belief tasks. *British Journal of Developmental Psychology, 18*, 297–317. https://doi.org/10.1348/026151000165706

Ning, S. R., & Crossman, A. M. (2007). We believe in being honest: Examining subcultural differences in the acceptability of deception. *Journal of Applied Social Psychology*, *37*, 2130–2155. https://doi.org/10.1111/j.1559-1816.2007.00254.x

O'Connell, F., Cherryman, J., & Warmelink, L. (2020). Mock juror's perceptions of a child witness passing or failing a truth and lies discussion or promising to tell the truth. *Applied Cognitive Psychology*, *34*(1), 285–292. https://doi.org/10.1002/acp.3612

O'Donohue, W., Cummings, C., & Willis, B. (2018). The frequency of false allegations of child sexual abuse: A critical review. *Journal of Child Sexual Abuse*, *27*(5), 459–475. https://doi.org/10.1080/10538712.2018.1477224

Olafson, E., & Lederman, J. C. S. (2006). The state of the debate about children's disclosure patterns in child sexual abuse cases. *Juvenile and Family Court Journal*, *57*(1), 27–40. https://doi.org/10.1111/j.1755-6988.2006.tb00112.x

Peterson, C. C., Peterson, J. L., & Seeto, D. (1983). Developmental changes in ideas about lying. *Child Development*, *54*, 1529–1535. https://doi.org/10.2307/1129816

Piaget, J. (1965 [1932]). *The moral judgment of the child* (M. Gabain, trans.). New York: The Free Press. https://doi.org/10.2307/1416357

Popliger, M., Talwar, V., & Crossman, A. M. (2011). Predictors of children's prosocial lie-telling: Motivation, socialization variables, and moral understanding. *Journal of Experimental Child Psychology*, *110*(3), 373–392. https://doi.org/10.1016/j.jecp.2011.05.003

Quas, J. A., Stolzenberg, S. N., & Lyon, T. D. (2018). The effects of promising to tell the truth, the putative confession, and recall and recognition questions on maltreated and non-maltreated children's disclosure of a minor transgression. In *Journal of Experimental Child Psychology* 166, 266–279. https://doi.org/10.1016/j.jecp.2017.08.014

Rothermich, K., Caivano, O., Knoll, L. J., & Talwar, V. (2020). Do they really mean it? Children's inference of speaker intentions and the role of age and gender. *Language and Speech*, *63*(4), 689–712. https://doi.org/10.1177/0023830919878742

Sai, L., Liu, X., Li, H., Compton, B. J., & Heyman, G. D. (2020). Promoting honesty through overheard conversations. *Developmental Psychology*, *56*(6), 1073–1079. https://doi.org/10.1037/dev0000933

Saywitz, K. J., Lyon, T. D., & Goodman, G. S. (2011). Interviewing children. In J. E. B. Myers (ed.), *The APSAC handbook on child maltreatment* (3rd ed., pp. 337–360). Sage.

Şen, H. H., & Küntay, A. C. (2019). Nonverbal markers of lying during children's collective interviewing with friends. *Journal of Nonverbal Behavior*, *43*(1), 39–57. https://doi.org/10.1007/s10919-018-0287-2

Serota, K. B., Levine, T. R., & Boster, F. J. (2010). The prevalence of lying in America: Three studies of self-reported lies. *Human Communication Research*, *36*(1), 2–25. https://doi.org/10.1111/j.1468-2958.2009.01366.x

Serras Pereira, M., de Lange, J., Shahid, S., & Swerts, M. (2018). A perceptual and behavioral analysis of facial cues to deception in interactions between children and a virtual agent. *International Journal of Child-Computer Interaction*, *15*, 1–12. https://doi.org/10.1016/j.ijcci.2017.10.003

Siegal, M., & Peterson, C. C. (1996). Breaking the mold: A fresh look at children's understanding of questions about lies and mistakes. *Developmental Psychology*, *32*, 322–334. https://doi.org/10.1037/0012-1649.32.2.322

Strichartz, A. F., & Burton, R. V. (1990). Lies and the truth: A study of the development of the concept. *Child Development*, *61*, 211–220. https://doi.org/10.2307/1131060

Sumampouw, N. E. J., de Ruiter, C., & Otgaar, H. (2022). Potential for police investigator bias: The impact of child sexual abuse victims' background characteristics on perceived statement credibility, case outcome and quality of interview questions. *Police Practice & Research: An International Journal*, *23*(3), 370–387. https://doi.org/10.1080/15614263.2021.1952872

Talwar, V., Arruda, C., & Yachison, S. (2015). The effects of punishment and appeals for honesty on children's truth-telling behavior. *Journal of Experimental Child Psychology*, *130*, 209–217. https://doi.org/10.1016/j.jecp.2014.09.011

Talwar, V., & Crossman, A. (2011). From little white lies to filthy liars: The evolution of honesty and deception in young children. In J. Benson (ed.), *Advances in child development and behavior*, *vol. 40* (pp. 139–179). Burlington: Academic Press. https://doi.org/10.1016/b978-0-12-386491-8.00004-9

Talwar, V., Crossman, A. M., Gulmi, J., Renaud, S. J., & Williams, S. (2009). Pants on fire? Detecting children's lies. *Applied Developmental Science*, *13*(3), 119–129. https://doi.org/10.1080/10888690903041519

Talwar, V., Crossman, A., & Wyman, J. (2017). The role of executive functioning and theory of mind in children's lies for another and for themselves. *Early Childhood Research Quarterly*, *41*, 126–135. https://doi.org/10.1016/j.ecresq.2017.07.003

Talwar, V., Gordon, H., & Lee, K. (2007). Lying in the elementary school years: Verbal deception and its relation to second-order belief understanding. *Developmental Psychology*, *43*, 804–810. https://doi.org/10.1037/0012-1649.43.3.804

Talwar, V., Hubbard, K., Saykaly, C., Lee, K., Lindsay, R. C. L., & Bala, N. (2018). Does parental coaching affect children's false reports? Comparing verbal markers of deception. *Behavioral Sciences & the Law*, *36*(1), 84–97. https://doi.org/10.1002/bsl.2331

Talwar, V., Lavoie, J., Gomez-Garibello, C., & Crossman, A. M. (2017). Influence of social factors on the relation between lie-telling and children's cognitive abilities. *Journal of Experimental Child Psychology*, *159*, 185–198. https://doi.org/10.1016/j.jecp.2017.02.009

Talwar, V., & Lee, K. (2002). Development of lying to conceal a transgression: Children's control of expressive behaviour during verbal deception. *International Journal of Behavioral Development*, *26*, 436–444. https://doi.org/10.1080/01650250143000373

Talwar, V., & Lee, K. (2008) Socio-cognitive correlates of children's lying behavior: Conceptual understanding of lying, executive functioning, and false beliefs. *Child Development*, *79*, 866–881. https://doi.org/10.1111/j.1467-8624.2008.01164.x

Talwar, V., & Lee, K. (2011). A punitive environment fosters children's dishonesty: A natural experiment. *Child Development*, *82*, 1751–1758. https://doi.org/10.1111/j.1467-8624.2011.01663.x

Talwar, V., Lee, K., Bala, N., & Lindsay, R. C. L. (2002). Children's conceptual knowledge of lying and its relation to their actual behaviors: Implications for court competence examinations. *Law and Human Behavior*, *26*, 395–415. https://doi.org/10.1023/A:1016379104959

Talwar, V., Lee, K., Bala, N., & Lindsay, R. C. L. (2004). Children's lie-telling to conceal parents' transgressions: Legal implications. *Law and Human Behavior*, *28*, 411–435. https://doi.org/10.1023/B:LAHU.0000039333.51399.f6

Talwar, V., Lee, K., Bala, N., & Lindsay, R. C. L. (2006). Adults' judgments of children's coached reports. *Law and Human Behavior*, *30*, 561–570. https://doi.org/10.1007/s10979-006-9038-8

Talwar, V., Murphy, S., & Lee, K. (2007). White lie-telling in children for politeness purposes. *International Journal of Behavioral Development*, *31*, 1–11. https://doi.org/10.1177/0165025406073530

Talwar, V., Yachison, S., & Leduc, K. (2016). Promoting honesty: The influence of stories on children's lie-telling behaviours and moral understanding. *Infant and Child Development*, *25*(6), 484–501. https://doi.org/10.1002/icd.1949

Talwar, V., Yachison, S., Leduc, K., & Nagar, P. M. (2018). Practice makes perfect? The impact of coaching and moral stories on children's lie-telling. *International Journal of Behavioral Development*, *42*(4), 416–424. https://doi.org/10.1177/0165025417728583

Talwar, V., Zwaigenbaum, L., Goulden, K. J., Manji, S., Loomes, C., & Rasmussen, C. (2012). Lie-telling behavior in children with autism and its relation to false-belief understanding. *Focus on Autism and Other Developmental Disabilities*, *27*(2), 122–129. https://doi.org/10.1177/1088357612441828

Tong, D., & Talwar, V. (2021). Understanding the development of honesty in children through the domains-of-socialization approach. *Infant and Child Development*, *30*(6), e2268. https://doi.org/10.1002/icd.2268

Trocmé, N., & Bala, N. (2005). False allegations of abuse and neglect when parents separate. *Child Abuse & Neglect*, *29*(12), 1333–1345. https://doi.org/10.1016/j.chiabu.2004.06.016

Tye, M. C., Amato, S. L., Honts, C. R., Devitt, M. K., & Peters, D. (1999). The willingness of children to lie and the assessment of credibility in an ecologically relevant laboratory setting. *Applied Developmental Science*, *3*, 92–109. https://doi.org/10.1207/s1532480xads0302_4

Voogt, A., Klettke, B., Thomson, D., & Crossman, A. (2020). The impact of extralegal factors on perceived credibility of child victims of sexual assault. *Psychology, Crime & Law*, *26*, 823–848. https://doi.org/10.1080/1068316X.2020.1742336

Wagland, P., & Bussey, K. (2005) Factors that facilitate and undermine children's beliefs about truth telling. *Law and Human Behavior*, *29*, 639–655. https://doi.org/10.1007/s10979-005-7371-y

Wandrey, L., Quas, J. A., & Lyon, T. D. (2012). Does valence matter? Effects of negativity on children's early understanding of the truth and lies. *Journal of Experimental Child Psychology*, *113*(2), 295–303. https://doi.org/10.1016/j.jecp.2012.04.006

Williams, S. M., Kirmayer, M., Simon, T., & Talwar, V. (2013). Children's antisocial and prosocial lies to familiar and unfamiliar adults. *Infant and Child Development*, *22*(4), 430–438. https://doi.org/10.1002/icd.1802

Williams, S., McWilliams, K., & Lyon, T. (2020). Children's concealment of a minor transgression: The role of age, maltreatment, and executive functioning. *Journal of Experimental Child Psychology*, *191*, 104664. https://doi.org/10.1016/j.jecp.2019.104664

Williams, S., Moore, K., Crossman, A. M., & Talwar, V. (2016). The role of executive functions and theory of mind in children's prosocial lie-telling. *Journal of Experimental Child Psychology*, *141*, 256–266. https://doi.org/10.1016/j.jecp.2015.08.001

Wimmer, H., Gruber, S., & Perner, J. (1984). Young children's conception of lying: Lexical realism – moral subjectivism. *Journal of Experimental Child Psychology*, *37*(1), 1–30.

Wyman, J., Foster, I., Lavoie, J., Tong, D., & Talwar, V. (2018). Detecting children's false allegations and recantations of a crime. *Psychology, Crime & Law*, *24*(6), 652–671. https://doi.org/10.1080/1068316X.2017.1402018

Wyman, J., Foster, I., Crossman, A., Colwell, K., & Talwar, V. (2019). The efficacy of free-recall, cognitive load, and closed-ended questions when children are asked to falsely testify about a crime. *Applied Cognitive Psychology*, *33*(4), 544–560. https://doi.org/10.1002/acp.3494

5

Historical cases

Consequences of delayed disclosure on criminal prosecutions

Deborah A. Connolly and Heather L. Price

We begin by attempting to define the term *historical child sexual abuse* (HCSA). Newbury (2014) wrote "historical child sexual abuse' (or HCSA) is an informal, non-legal phrase that struggles for precise definition" (p. 43). Roberts (2017) wrote "in general, 'historic' has referred to events that are alleged to have occurred a number of years in the past, although how many years is often not specified" (p. 175). Given this lack of consensus on the definition of "historical", it is not surprising that it has been defined differently across reports. Connolly and Read (2003) defined "historical" as a delay of two or more years from the date of the last reported offence to a court date (see Roberts, 2017 for a similar definition). Cashmore, Taylor, and Parkinson (2017) defined it as an offence that occurred in childhood that was reported when the complainant was an adult (see also the National Society for the Prevention of Cruelty to children, cited in Nortje & du Toit, 2017). Others have used a delay of one year to define a case as historical (Hester & Lilley, 2017). Whatever the minimum length of delay used to qualify a report as historical, the average length of delay is substantial – in the range of decades (e.g. 13 years based on 2064 HCSA complaints heard in Canadian courts; Connolly & Read, 2006).

Since the early 2000s, several countries, including Australia, Canada, Ireland, United Kingdom, United States, and Scotland have conducted public inquiries into HCSA (Connolly, Coburn, & Chong, 2017). Although these inquiries focused, primarily, on institutional CSA, they served to shine a very bright light on the widespread problem of the sexual abuse of children alongside the disbelief of authorities and the indifference of the state and other entities responsible for protecting children. These inquiries also raised awareness of delayed disclosure and delayed prosecutions of CSA generally, not just CSA within institutions. Indeed, Connolly et al. (2017) reported that the vast majority of the 3,035 HCSA complaints they reviewed did not occur in the context of institutional care, these crimes were committed by parents, other relatives, family friends, or members of the community whose status gave them access to children (e.g. priests, teachers, sports coaches).

DOI: 10.4324/9781003427155-5

Prior to the early 2000s, much research and discussion on delayed reports of CSA focused on repressed/recovered memories (Connolly & Read, 2003). This sparked conversations (often heated) on recovered versus false memories and the debate continues today (Otgaar et al., 2022). We do not address this issue in the current chapter for two reasons. First it is a gnarly topic that has been the subject of many papers, books, and scholarly meetings. We could not do justice to the issues in this chapter. Second, most HCSA cases do not involve reports of recovered memory; in fact, it has been estimated that about 93% of HCSA prosecutions in Canada are cases in which the complainant reports to having always remembered the abuse (Connolly & Read, 2006).

The sociolegal context

As described throughout this volume, there has been a lot of excellent research on characteristics of the child, the abuse, and the relationship between the child and the alleged perpetrator to explain children's delayed disclosure of sexual abuse. This is critical work that helps us to understand some of the complexities of disclosure and to develop steps to reduce the delay and minimize its impact. It is unlikely that interventions will eliminate delayed reporting for all children and so this research explains why we continue to prosecute CSA cases long after the alleged offence occurred.

Ring (2017) argued that we must also consider the sociolegal zeitgeist when considering delayed disclosure and prosecution of CSA. Before the latter part of the twentieth century, it was virtually impossible to prosecute to conviction cases of sexual offences against children (van Tongeren Harvey & Dauns, 2001). If timely CSA cases could not be prosecuted to conviction, they could only proceed as HCSA cases, if at all. The improbability of a successful prosecution can be attributed to legal doctrines and social attitudes that had the effect of barring most cases: the Recent Complaint Doctrine, statutes of limitation, mandatory warnings, and a pervasive attitude that children's evidence is inherently unreliable. Although all of these barriers would have led to delayed prosecutions, the first two are a direct consequence of delayed disclosure and the latter two compelled delayed prosecutions even if a disclosure was timely.

Recent complaint doctrine

During the 1980s and early 1990s, this doctrine was abrogated in common-law jurisdictions around the world including: Australia, Canada, Ireland, New Zealand, United Kingdom, and United States (Lewis, 2006). The doctrine stated that if a victim of sexual assault, whether a child or adult, did not complain at the first opportunity after the assault, the trier of fact was *required* to infer that the allegation was false or that the complainant consented to having sex, unless there was evidence to the contrary. This doctrine probably dates back to the thirteenth century, when failure to report a sexual assault immediately was a full defence to rape (Cossins, 2002; Lewis, 2006). The Supreme Court of Canada provided the following archaic passage describing the doctrine:

> When therefore a virgin has been so deflowered and overpowered, against the peace of the lord the king, forthwith and while the act is fresh she ought to repair with hue and cry to the neighboring vills and there display to honest men the injury done to her, the blood and her dress stained with blood, and the tearing of her dress; and so she ought to go to the provost of the hundred and to the serjeant of the lord the king and to the coroners and to the viscount and make her appeal at the first county court.
>
> (Cited in *R. v. D. D.*, 2000, para. 60)

More recently, the Recent Complaint Doctrine was a *rebuttable presumption*, meaning that the prosecution could present evidence to displace the assumption. However, the Recent Complaint Doctrine was the starting point for courts and was a significant barrier to prosecuting allegations of sexual assault that were not reported immediately. As late as 1960, in *Kribs et al. v. The Queen*, the Supreme Court of Canada reasserted the doctrine in the following passage:

> The principle is one of necessity. It is founded on factual presumptions which, in the normal course of events, naturally attach to the subsequent conduct of the prosecutrix shortly after the occurrence of the alleged acts of violence. One of these presumptions is that she is expected to complain upon the first reasonable opportunity, and the other, consequential thereto, is that if she fails to do so, her silence may naturally be taken as a virtual self-contradiction of her story.

Based on the excellent research presented throughout this volume, we now know that most child victims of sexual assault do not complain immediately; in fact, up to two-thirds delay reporting and half of those don't report until adulthood (London et al., 2005). As such, most CSA cases could not have been prosecuted to conviction prior to the latter part of the twentieth century because the foreseeable delay resulted in a presumption that the offence had not occurred.

Statutory limitation periods

A statute of limitation has the effect of barring a case from proceeding if a specified period of time has elapsed following some triggering event (e.g. the harm was done, the complainant attained the age of majority, the injured party identified that he/she suffered harm). In most common-law jurisdictions, there are statutes of limitation on civil proceedings, but no statutes of limitation on serious criminal offences. An exception to this has been the United States (Lewis, 2006). Importantly, statutes of limitation on child sexual abuse in many US states have been abrogated and the trend seems to be continuing (Connolly et al., 2017). Thus, although statutes of limitation were a significant barrier to prosecuting CSA cases in the United States if there was a long delay to disclosure, their effect is diminishing.

Mandatory warnings

It was not until 1988 that the requirement that courts warn triers of fact of the dangers of convicting on the uncorroborated evidence of an unsworn child was abolished in Canada (Bala, 1999). This same rule was operative in other common-law jurisdictions through the 1980s when jurisdictions began to abrogate the rule (Bussey, 2009; Ceci & Bruck, 1995; Flin & Spencer, 1995; Goodman, 1984; Myers et al., 1999). This rule was strict and required acquittal in the absence of independent corroborating evidence to prove the allegation. Acquittal was required even if the trier of fact was convinced beyond a reasonable doubt that the assault had happened (Bala, 1999).

This rule would have been particularly oppressive for CSA victims because, often, in these cases children testify as unsworn witnesses and there is no corroborative evidence (Bala, 1999; Sas & Cunningham, 1995); the only evidence is the testimony of the child. In many CSA cases, then, the only evidence, the testimony of the child, was the subject of a strong judicial warning until the late 1980s through early 1990s. If a CSA victim wished to pursue a criminal prosecution, the only option would be to delay the official report until they were an adult. As discussed in this chapter, a long delay to prosecution brings with it several unique and thorny challenges for the legal system.

Attitudinal barrier

Finally, there was an attitudinal barrier to convicting on the basis of a child's testimony. Myers et al. (1999) reported that before 1975 very little was written about CSA in psychiatric, medical, psychological, sociological, and legal journals and what little was written was negative. That is, there was a pervasive belief that the evidence of children was inherently unreliable, particularly in allegations of sexual assault (see also Bala, 1999; Flin & Spencer, 1995). Consider this quote by respected jurist John Wigmore (recall that John Wigmore published the blistering cross-examination of Hugo Munsterberg's assertion that psychology can and should inform legal process):

> Modern psychiatrists have amply studied the behaviour of errant young girls and women coming before the courts in all sorts of cases. Their psychic complexes are multifarious, distorted partly by inherent defects, partly by diseased derangements or abnormal instincts, partly by bad social environment, partly by temporary physiological or emotional conditions. One form taken by these complexes is that of contriving false charges of sexual offenses by men.
>
> (Wigmore, 1940, cited in Bala, 1990, p. 15)

In summary, across most common-law countries, the late 1980s and early 1990s saw a rapid decline in unjust rules and stubborn attitudes that had the effect of making it "virtually impossible to prosecute to conviction" sexual crimes involving children (van Tongeren Harvey & Dauns, 2001, p. 148). Coincident with these changes was a substantial rise in HCSA prosecutions in Australia, Canada, England, Ireland, New Zealand, Scotland, United States (if a statute of limitations did not bar the prosecution), and Wales (Connolly et al., 2017; Lewis, 2006; Ring, 2017; Wells et al., 2014).

It is likely that some of the HCSA prosecutions that come forward shortly after these changes came into effect would have been prosecuted as CSA cases, had it been possible to do so at the time of the offence. This means that there was likely a backlog of cases involving sexual offences against children that had to proceed as HCSA prosecutions. Today, cases that can go forward as CSA cases, will not become future HCSA cases, suggesting an eventual decline in HCSA prosecutions (Connolly et al., 2017).

The magnitude of the eventual decline in HCSA prosecutions depends on reasons for the delay. If factors associated with the offence, the child, and the relationship between the child and the accused account for most delays, we can expect to continue to prosecute HCSA cases. If sociopolitical factors, described above, explain the delay for some complainants, the number of HCSA prosecutions will decline once the backlog is cleared. As discussed throughout this book, intrinsic factors are a significant cause of delay for many children. Thus, in the absence of new legal barriers to prosecuting HCSA cases, common-law jurisdictions can expect to continue to see many HCSA cases in criminal courts.

Before turning to a discussion of challenges associated with prosecuting HCSA cases, we want to personalize the cases by describing an average HCSA complainant. We do this to help the reader to imagine the individuals involved in these cases. Based on a review of 2064 HCSA criminal complaints in Canada, Connolly and Read wrote the following:

> The complainant is probably female. On average, she was 9 years old when the abuse began, 12 years old when it ended, and 26 years old at trial. She is unlikely to be reported to have been in therapy, and she is very likely to report continuous memory for the offence. Her abuser is more likely than not to be a male relative and he is, on average, 23 years older than her. On average, he was 33 years old when the abuse began, 36 years old when it ended, and 51 years old at trial. In the majority of cases, the complainant reports repeated abuse that was sustained over an average of almost 4 years. A threat is probably not reported to have accompanied the abuse, but if one is reported, it is likely to be against the complainant's or her family's physical safety.
>
> (Connolly & Read, 2006, p. 424)

Perhaps the most perplexing challenge in HCSA cases is assessing credibility.

Credibility

Whether a CSA prosecution is delayed or timely, successful adjudication often turns on an assessment of credibility of the complainant and the accused (e.g. Castelli et al., 2005; Goodman et al., 2002; Shead, 2014; Vallano et al., 2020). This assessment is more complex in delayed than timely prosecutions because the passage of time degrades evidence. Physical evidence that might have been available at the time of the offence may be lost, memories fade or become less reliable with time, witnesses can be hard to identify and locate, and corroboration may be unavailable (Flatman & Bagaric, 1997; Hughes & Jonas, 2015).

We often hear that these are "he said, she said" contests where the trier of fact must decide who to believe. This is not the case in criminal court. The onus is on the prosecution to prove all elements of the offence. It is not up to the defence to prove innocence. The effect of positioning this as a contest between two reports is to shift an onus onto the accused to prove his innocence – an outcome that could lead to a successful appeal. In *R. v. W. (D.)* (1991, para. 28) the Supreme Court of Canada provided the following test:

> First, if you believe the evidence of the accused, obviously you must acquit.
>
> Second, if you do not believe the testimony of the accused but you are left in reasonable doubt by it, you must acquit.

> Third, even if you are not left in doubt by the evidence of the accused, you must ask yourself whether, on the basis of the evidence which you do accept, you are convinced beyond a reasonable doubt by that evidence of the guilt of the accused.

This may be articulated differently in different jurisdictions, but the principle is consistent. The burden is on the prosecution to prove all elements of the offence beyond a reasonable doubt. The burden is not on the accused to prove his innocence. This is a high burden that, arguably, is harder to meet when there is a delay to trial.

A reasonably consistent conclusion in the literature is that delayed disclosure of a sexual assault has a negative effect on perceived credibility of the complainant (Balogh et al., 2003; Ellison & Munro, 2009; Miller et al., 2022; Thompson et al., 2021). That is, a complainant who does not come forward in a timely way is seen as less worthy of belief than a complainant who comes forward soon after the abuse. What is not clear from the literature is why a delay has this negative effect. Credibility is thought to be comprised of two factors: perceived honesty and perceived cognitive competence (Bottoms, 1993; Ross et al., 2003). Does a delay affect perceptions of honesty or cognitive competence or both? This is important because the reason for the effect will inform the remedy.

On the one hand, the negative effect of delay on perceived credibility could be viewed as an indicator of the complainant's dishonesty; a complainant who delays reporting their abuse is less honest than a complainant who discloses their abuse soon after it occurred. This suggests that the complainant is, in some way, complicit in causing the delay; perhaps because the alleged abuse did not happen or did not happen as reported (readers may hear echoes of the Recent Complaint Doctrine). If this accounts for the effect of delay on perceived credibility, there is hope. First, there is growing public awareness that children often delay disclosing their abuse for understandable reasons (Miller & London, 2020). We should not attribute the delay to a "choice" the child made. Second, Harvey et al. (submitted) found that when the reason for a delay is outside of the control of the witness (i.e. not a choice and the result of a delayed investigation process), delay did not have a negative effect on the perceived credibility of the witness. This latter observation related to witnessing a physical assault, and thus, the relations to sexual assault must still be examined.

On the other hand, it could be that delay is seen as having a negative effect on the complainant's ability to recall the abuse, leading to a report that is less reliable than one made shortly after the abuse occurred. Harvey et al. (submitted) found that while delay that was outside of the control of the witness did not affect perceptions of the witness' credibility, it did result in fewer guilty verdicts, perhaps because the witness' report following a delay were seen as less reliable. In these studies, the evidence was identical across conditions and so the effects could not be attributed to actual differences in case strength, although perceptions of case strength may have varied. Harvey et al. (submitted) continue to investigate the effect of reasons for delay on perceived credibility.

In summary, if the effect of delay on perceived credibility is explained by perceived honesty, the growing awareness that delay is not a choice the child makes should reduce the negative impact of delay on perceived credibility. If the effect is explained by perceptions of memory decay following a delay, educating legal practitioners and jurors on the forgetting curve (as discussed below, most forgetting occurs shortly after an event) may reduce the impact of delay on perceived credibility.

We now turn to a discussion of perceived honesty and perceived cognitive competence in the psychological and legal literatures and apply it to HCSA prosecutions. A conundrum arises when assessing perceived honesty and perceived cognitive competence when there is a long delay to trial (i.e. when an adult describes events that happened when she was a child). To understand this conundrum, we first discuss these two factors.

In law, two factors to be assessed when weighing a witness' evidence are credibility and reliability. Connolly et al. (2010) argued that credibility in law is roughly akin to honesty in the psychological literature. The equivalent of the legal definition of reliability is a bit trickier, but similar indices of reliability in law are reflected in the cognitive competence factor in the psychological literature. When all other factors are controlled and only age is varied, young children are seen as more honest and less cognitively competent than older children and adults (e.g. Goodman et al., 1987; Nunez et al., 2011).[1] Accordingly, when credibility rests more on honesty than cognitive competence, younger children are seen as more credible than older children and adults. This can occur in cases where the cognitive resources needed to encode, store, and retrieve details of a past event are within the abilities of a child (e.g. the offence was committed in a familiar environment, by a familiar person, and repeatedly – characteristics typically present in CSA cases). As long as the witness is being honest, the report is likely to be true. When credibility rests more on cognitive competence than honesty, older children and adults are seen as more credible than younger children. This may occur when the event is more difficult to encode, store and retrieve (e.g. a single unfamiliar event in an unfamiliar environment by an unfamiliar person).

Now for the conundrum that arises in HCSA cases. The complainant was a child when the alleged event occurred and an adult when testifying about it. What age should be the focus in the analysis of credibility? In *R.*

v. W. (R.) (1992) the Supreme Court of Canada considered this and ruled as follows:

> In general, where an adult is testifying as to events which occurred when she was a child, her credibility should be assessed according to criteria applicable to her as an adult witness. Yet with regard to her evidence pertaining to events which occurred in childhood, the presence of inconsistencies, particularly as to peripheral matters such as time and location, should be considered in the context of the age of the witness at the time of the events to which she is testifying.
>
> (*R. v. W. (R.)*, 1992, p. 134)

The Supreme Court of Canada held that when assessing credibility (akin to honesty), the age of the complainant at trial is most relevant. However, when assessing reliability (akin to cognitive competence), the age of the complainant at the time of the alleged offence is most relevant. Recall that children are seen as more honest and less cognitively competent than adults. So, when an HCSA case is adjudicated, honesty is assessed based on the complainant's age at trial (losing the child's advantage) and cognitive competence is assessed based on their age when the alleged offence occurred (losing the adult's advantage)!

Perceived honesty

When considering HCSA cases, honesty should be assessed based on the age of the complainant at trial. A 30-year-old reporting an event that happened when she was 5 should not be seen as more honest than a 30-year-old reporting an event that happened when she was 14 (although a 5-year-old is seen as more honest than a 14-year-old).

Connolly et al. (2010) coded 7,776 judicial comments concerning honesty and cognitive competence in 32 CSA and 32 HCSA bench trials. They selected cases such that approximately half of the cases in each category ended in convictions and half in acquittals. Consistent with the direction from the Supreme Court of Canada, age at trial appeared to be most relevant in judges' comments about honesty. That is, absent evidence of suggestive influences, children (CSA cases) were seen as more honest than adults (HCSA cases), even though all cases involved sexual offences against children.

Perceived cognitive competence

Perceived cognitive competence is more complex when considered in the context of adults testifying about events that happened in childhood. Recall that in law, this factor is roughly akin to reliability. Reliability in law is assessed based on the report itself, including factors such as completeness, clarity, consistency, corroboration, apparent accuracy, and ability to observe (Connolly et al., 2010). According to Ornstein et al. (1998), to understand what adults can recall about events that occurred in childhood, one must consider "age related differences in prior knowledge, in the strength and organization of underlying representations, [and] in the time course of forgetting" (p. 1031).

As this is not a chapter on children's memory, we provide only conclusions about each of these factors. Usually, children's memory is weaker and less well organized than adults' (Baker-Ward & Thomas, 2022; Ornstein & Haden, 2002). This is due, in part, to differences in knowledge structures and immature memory strategies. Age differences in memory sometimes disappear or even reverse when children have similar or superior knowledge structures to adults (Chi, 1978; for a review, see Goldfarb & Mindthoff, 2020). This is potentially important when one considers memory for salient childhood events that occur repeatedly and over a long period of time. Above, we described a typical HCSA complainant as reporting repeated abuse over a period of almost four years beginning when she was 9 years old. To our knowledge, no research on age differences in memory have tested differences under these peculiar (and unfortunate) circumstances. Children forget faster than adults (Brainerd & Reyna, 1995). Importantly, not all kinds of details follow the same forgetting trajectory. Next, we consider memory for central and peripheral details.

Central details

One can expect the central details of an event to be recalled with good accuracy even following a lengthy delay, particularly if the event was unique, startling, or unusual (Brainerd & Reyna, 1995; Brewin et al., 1993; Hardt & Rutter, 2004; Peterson, 2011; Peterson & Whalen, 2001). An excellent illustration of very long-term memory for central details is a study by Goldfarb et al. (2019). In their study, 30 adults, all of whom had undergone an in-patient medical examination that included an anogenital examination 20 years earlier, were interviewed about the experience. The interview included open-ended questions, closed-ended questions (e.g. "Did the doctor examine your genitals during the examination?"), and suggestive questions (e.g. "At the end, did the doctor kiss you?"). Across the entire interview, almost half of the respondents reported the genital touch that had occurred during the examination. Adults who were older at the time of the examination were more likely than adults who were younger at the time of the examination to report genital touch (28.6% of those who were 3 to 5 years old, 40% of those who were 6 to 10 years old, and 62.5% of those who were 11 to 15 years old).

As with all studies, several questions remain. All adults in the study had undergone an anogenital examination and so this study cannot address the possibility of false reports when the same questions are asked of adults who did not undergo an anogenital examination in childhood. It is possible that some adults who reported an anogenital examination recalled that they had undergone an in-patient assessment for possible sexual abuse and assumed they must have had an anogenital exam as part of the assessment, without having a memory for the genital examination. Notwithstanding these qualifications, it is striking that a sizable minority of participants were able to report an anogenital exam that occurred 20 years earlier as part of a longer and more complex investigation into child abuse.

It is noteworthy that a majority of participants did not report the genital exam. And less than one-third of the adults who were between 3 and 5 years old at the time of the exam reported it. It could be that they were reluctant to report it, for myriad reasons. It is also possible that they did not recall the genital exam, possibly because it was not experienced as remarkable. Howe (2013) wrote that children, particularly young children, may not experience non-intrusive sexual assaults (such as watching pornography and touching genitals) as stressful, painful, or traumatic and wondered how such benign memories would be recalled in adulthood as sexual assaults – or remembered at all.

One's ability to report just a few central details of a past sexual assault is probably insufficient to proceed with a criminal prosecution. Shead wrote, from a prosecutor's perspective:

> If all that the now adult victim can say upon complaint about the experiences of the offending against them is, for example, that an offender anally penetrated them on many occasions, without being able to specify a particular event or timeframe, there cannot be a charge.
>
> (Shead, 2014, p. 60)

An investigation is almost certainly going to involve attempts to elicit some details that may be considered peripheral to the event.

Peripheral details

Memory for peripheral details fades more quickly than memory for central details and may follow a power function. That is, most of the absolute amount of forgetting will occur within the first year after the event and relatively less forgetting occurs after that (Peterson, 2011; Rubin & Wenzel, 1996). Two important conclusions follow from this. First, the absolute amount of forgetting following a delay of decades may not be meaningfully different from the absolute amount of forgetting that occurs following a delay of a year. Second, the amount of forgetting of peripheral details could be substantial, even following a relatively short delay.

Memory researchers are not concerned or particularly alarmed that peripheral details fade quickly. Of course they do! However, in the context of investigating HCSA complaints, failure to provide context could be problematic. Wells et al. (2014) described a typical police interview with a hypothetical complainant of HCSA in the UK. Following a free recall account, the police officer would ask a series of question to gather (additional) information including details about location, who was present, the time, duration, clothing, weather, and what they thought at the time.

Contrast this with what one might expect an HCSA complainant to recall. Wells et al. (2014) studied 496 memories from participants who were instructed to report on the earliest positive and negative memories they were certain had occurred. The interview followed practices typically used by police in interviews with HCSA complainants. Reports were brief (about 5 details). Most reports included what happened, where it happened, and who was present. Only about half of the reports included details about the weather, their age at the time, and what they thought at the time, even when asked specifically about these details. Reports rarely contained details about duration, time of the event, or clothing. Thus, the details police may ask an HCSA complainant to recall may be the very details they are least likely to remember. The result of such an interview can be to elicit a report that is implausibly detailed or that includes a series of "I don't know" responses. Either result could make a complainant appear not credible and could lead the investigators to decline to proceed. Roberts (2017) concluded that interviewers of HCSA complainants need details, such as dates and time to help with the investigation. Some interviewers may use inappropriate techniques in an effort to secure a detailed report. It seems that detailed reports are important in the legal system!

Next, we turn to memory for when and how often the alleged abuse occurred. We address these specifically because this information is needed to charge an offence.

Dating events from the past

For many reasons, an investigator must obtain a date or range of dates within which the alleged acts occurred (Roberts, 2017). First, a prosecutor must be prepared to prove all elements of the offence that was in place at the time the act(s) occurred. If the name and offence elements changed between when the alleged act happened and when it was charged, the old offence must be charged (Shead, 2014). Second, if the complainant was around the age of consent at the time of the alleged acts, the charges will be different depending on whether she was below or above the age of consent. Third, the prosecutor must know if, at the time of the alleged crime, the accused was between the ages of 12 and 17 or older than 17 to identify if criminal responsibility attaches and, if it does, which Act applies.[2] Fourth, to be sufficiently particular, the accused must know when the alleged offence(s) occurred. Clearly, identifying a range of dates within which the alleged offence occurred is important.

A long delay can affect one's ability to estimate when the offence(s) occurred. Thompson (1998) stated that "there is no temporal trace in autobiographical memory … we believe that the location of personal [autobiographical] events in time is entirely reconstructed" (p. 36). The information used to reconstruct the date(s) of a past event may be non-central to the event itself (i.e. the grade one was in at school or the house one lived in at the time). These details might be considered peripheral. As discussed earlier, peripheral details tend to decay quickly. And, up to a certain point (recall the power function of forgetting), the longer the delay the less information that may be retrieved and the higher the likelihood that errors will occur (Connolly & Read, 2003). Dating errors are not completely random. In a phenomenon called *telescoping*, we remember past events as having occurred more recently than they actually did. And, as the delay between the event and recall increases, the telescoping effect becomes stronger (Wang et al., 2019).

Frequency

Investigators will attempt to obtain a frequency estimate to inform the number of charges to lay. This may be particularly difficult for HCSA complainants for at least two reasons. First, HCSA complainant are likely to report more frequent abuse than CSA complainants (Connolly et al., 2015). Second, for HCSA complainants, frequency estimates will be made long after the alleged offences occurred. Although we are not aware of research on frequency estimates following a very long delay, it seems plausible that it will become more difficult as the delay increases.

The need to gather frequency information implicates two issues: frequency estimates and memory for specific instances of repeated abuse. Memory for frequency is imprecise. There is a positive correlation between actual and estimated frequency such that a person who reports that abuse occurred 5 times probably experienced fewer instances than a person who reports that abuse occurred 20 times (Connolly et al., 1996). However, the precise number should not be relied on.

If a complainant reports that abuse occurred repeatedly, they will be asked to describe particular instances to satisfy the particularization principle in law. The particularization principle, articulated in *Brodie v. The King* (1936), p. 198 and affirmed in *R. v. B. (G.)* (1990) states, "the indictment must describe the offence so as to lift it from the general to the particular" (see Woiwod & Connolly, 2017 for a discussion of this principle across multiple jurisdictions). A predictable consequence of event repetition is that memory moves from the particular to the general. Isolating one instance from a series of similar incidents is incredibly difficult, even after a short delay (Woiwod et al., 2019). As discussed above, a more detailed report is also seen as more credible than a general report. In fact, a report that contains only a few central details may not be sufficiently particular to convince a prosecutor to proceed with the case (Roberts, 2017; Shead, 2014).

Challenges that arise at trial

The effect of delay on the accused

To this point, we have focussed on the effect of delay on the complainant. There is another party involved in these cases – the accused. The effect of the long delay is relevant at trial and, if convicted, it could be relevant at sentencing. Flatman and Bagaric (1997) highlight the difficulties accused persons have in defending against an alleged sexual act from the distant past:

> Human memory is such that we do not recall historical events which are unremarkable. Thus, the paradoxical situation that accused find themselves in when an old child sexual offense is alleged against them, is that the more likely it is that the act was innocent the less probable it is that they will be able to provide a detailed innocent explanation for the incident.
>
> (Flatman & Bagaric, 1997, p. 6)

If an accused is convicted, issues related to the long delay arise at the sentencing portion of the proceeding. As discussed next, several scholars have pondered whether delay should be a mitigating factor at sentencing in HCSA cases. The accused may be a very different person than he was at the time of the offences. He may be quite old, ill, and apparently reformed (Hughes & Jonas, 2015; Jülich, 2006; Nortje & du Toit, 2017). It is one thing to sentence a 25-year-old to a period of incarceration shortly after the crime was committed. It may be a different thing to sentence a 70-year-old who may have health problems, and has been (apparently) crime-free for 40 years to the same period of incarceration (Hughes & Jonas, 2015; Jülich, 2006).

Flatman and Bagaric (1997) also discussed principles of sentencing in the context of HCSA cases. There are five principles that inform sentencing decisions: deterring others from committing a similar offence (general deterrence); deterring the perpetrator from committing the offence again (specific deterrence); rehabilitation of the perpetrator; protecting the public from the perpetrator; and retribution for the offence. When the convicted individual is elderly, the relevance of rehabilitation, specific deterrence, and protection of the community fade. This leaves only retribution and general deterrence as factors to consider in sentencing (Flatman & Bagaric, 1997).

We offer no opinion on the weight that should be attached to the age of the perpetrator at sentencing. However, it is a point of discussion in the literature and should be reflected in this chapter on HCSA prosecutions.

Joined versus severed trials

The question of joined versus severed trials arises whenever there are multiple complainants against a single accused. We discuss it briefly in this chapter because multiple complainants are likely to be more common in HCSA than CSA trials. This is because delayed disclosure may place other children at risk (e.g. Goodman-Brown et al. 2003; Sas & Cunningham, 1995), resulting in more complainants when the accused is finally charged.

Often, in HCSA cases, there are multiple complainants against the same accused (Lewis, 2006). Should all complainants be heard in the same trial (joined trial) or should there be a separate trial for each complainant (severed trials) (Shead, 2014)? The defence may argue that a joined trial will lead juries to believe that this accused is the type of person likely to commit this type of crime. This can result in an improper basis on which to convict; a conviction based on, in part, his character. The prosecution may argue that it is inefficient and unfair to complainants and witnesses to have multiple trials in which they may have to testify. It is also difficult for the trier of fact to hear the entire narrative if only details related to an individual complaint can be presented in a single trial. Furthermore, it is costly to hold multiple trials for the same accused.

Defence concerns that an accused is more likely to be convicted in a joined trial than a single-complainant trial has some empirical support. A small body of research on the *joinder effect* finds that accused persons are more likely to be convicted when there are between two and four complainants joined in a single trial than when there is a single complainant (Bordens & Horowitz, 1983, 1986; Greene & Loftus, 1985; Tanford & Penrod, 1984; Tanford et al., 1985). Possible explanations for the joinder effect include social and cognitive factors. Cognitive factors have focused on evidence interference: that is, remembering inculpatory evidence from one complainant as relating to a different complainant to support a conviction (Bordens & Horowitz, 1983; Horowitz & Bordens, 2000; Tanford & Penrod, 1984; Tanford et al., 1985). When a trial is joined, typically, the trier of fact is directed to consider each complainant independent of the other complainants (*R. v. P.E.C.*, 2005). That is, when deliberating on a charge related to one complainant, only evidence related to that complainant should be considered.

Social explanations concern character evidence. When multiple reports of sexual abuse are presented in the same trial, the accused may be seen as the type of person who would commit such a crime (Bordens & Horowitz, 1986; Greene & Loftus, 1985; Tanford & Penrod, 1984; Tanford et al., 1985). Typically, this type of evidence, called character evidence, is inadmissible because it is prejudicial and may displace the presumption of innocence (Lewis, 2006). A person ought not to be convicted based on his character. A conviction should be supported by admissible evidence that the accused committed that crime.

Future research

Chenier and colleagues noted, "[T] there is little practical consideration and research on childhood sexual abuse interviews with adult reporters in historical cases" (Chenier et al., 2022, p. 4). It is clear that there is a lot of work to be done in this field. In our view, the most pressing issue for researchers is to provide guidance on how to interview a person when the alleged event happened a long time ago. This issue is pressing because the way in which an interview is conducted can have a tremendous influence on the resulting report and the amount and type of details that are reported (e.g. Lamb et al., 2007). In a recent call for research on interviewing witnesses about events from long ago, Price and colleagues (Price et al., in press) noted that though there are volumes of research on how to effectively elicit information from witnesses reporting timely experiences, there is a stark dearth of research that considers the special circumstances associated with eliciting memories from long ago. This dearth of research is even more pressing in HCSA cases, given the reliance on witness reports and the increased complexities the sexual abuse complaints bring to witness statements.

At the time of abuse, the reporter was a child who was probably abused repeatedly. In HCSA cases, at the time of reporting, a long period of time has elapsed and the reporter's cognitive, verbal, and social capacities have likely changed considerably. What is the effect of these potentially opposing forces: degradation of the memory trace due to the elapsing of time and opportunities for interference in memory, contrasted with enhanced ability to report experiences as a function of maturation and social development processes? What can we expect a 26-year-old to remember about an event that occurred 17 years earlier when she was only 9 years old? What information is expected to be absent from her report? What are the factors that may render a complainant's memory so unreliable that they should be barred from testifying? How can such factors be identified?

It is also important to consider the context of adult disclosures of childhood abuse. What factors increase the likelihood that an adult will make a formal complaint of CSA? How can this formal complaint be elicited in a way that respects the complainant's experience, and also maximizes the likelihood that reliable, detailed evidence will be obtained? Finally, an important legal question is raised in cases with multiple historical complaints. What is the impact of having multiple complainants in a single trial? Under what conditions does joining complaints increase a just case outcome? There are so many unknowns in delayed sexual abuse cases, but these cases are continuously being decided by the courts. The need for research to better inform legal decisions is urgent.

Summary

Delayed disclosure of child sexual abuse is common. Factors associated with the complainant, the accused, the nature of the abuse, the relationship between the accused and the complainant contribute to delays, and sociolegal factors add to delays. If the delay is long (years or decades), the case will proceed, if it proceeds at all, as HCSA. HCSA cases present myriad challenges including interviewing complainants, assessing credibility, dating events, and complications that arise when the reported abuse occurred repeatedly. The accused is in a position of having to respond to reported events from the distant past. If the case goes to trial and if there are multiple complainants, a judge must decide whether to sever or to join counts. If the trial results in a conviction, the sentencing judge must decide if age and delay are mitigating factors. Many of these issues are or should continue to be the subject of psychological inquiry. As jurisdictions are faced with increasing numbers of HCSA cases, will there be more reliance on experts to assist with the cases (e.g. Connolly, Price, & Read, 2006)? Howe (2013) wrote "It is because the hallmark of these cases is adult recall of early childhood events that memory expertise is sorely needed" (pp. 578–579).

Notes

1 In two field studies involving 1,563 (Melkman et al., 2014) and 4,775 (Hershkowitz et al., 2018) assessments of credibility made by child forensic interviewers, older children were judged to be more credible than younger

children. It is likely that reports of older children were more coherent and complete than reports of younger children. Completeness and coherence may be a stronger indicator of perceived credibility than age. In this section, we are concerned with age differences, independent of other factors that may vary with age.

2 In Canada, a person younger than 12 years old cannot be held criminally responsible. A person between the ages of 12 and 17 years old will be prosecuted as a young offender, even if the charge is laid when he is an adult. At the age of 18, full criminal responsibility attaches.

References

Baker-Ward, L. E., & Thomas, T. E. (2021). Children's reports of personal experiences: From the laboratory to the doctor's office to the courtroom. In L. E. Baker-Ward, D. F. Bjorklund, & J. L. Coffman (eds), *The development of children's memory: The scientific contributions of Peter A. Ornstein* (pp. 93–114). Cambridge University Press. https://doi.org/10.1017/9781108871105.010

Bala, N. (1990). Double victims: Child sexual abuse and the Canadian criminal justice system. *Queen's Law Journal, 15*, 3–32.

Bala, N. (1999). Child witnesses in the Canadian criminal courts: Recognizing their capacities and needs. *Psychology, Public Policy, and Law, 5*, 323–354. https://doi.org/10.1037/1076-8971.5.2.323

Balogh, D. W., Kite, M. E., Pickel, K. L., Canel, D., & Schroeder, J. (2003). The effects of delayed report and motive for reporting on perceptions of sexual harassment. *Sex Roles, 48*, 337–348. https://doi.org/10.1023/A:1022990530657

Bordens, K. S., & Horowitz, I. A. (1983). Information processing in joined and severed trials. *Journal of Applied Social Psychology, 13*(4), 351–370. https://doi.org/10.1111/j.1559-1816.1983.tb01745.x

Bordens, K. S., & Horowitz, I. A. (1986). Prejudicial joinder of multiple offenses: Relative effects of cognitive processing and criminal schema. *Basic and Applied Social Psychology, 7*(4), 243–258. https://doi.org/10.1207/s15324834basp0704_

Bottoms, B. L. (1993). Individual differences in perceptions of child sexual assault victims. In G. S Goodman, & B. L. Bottoms, *Child victims, child witnesses: Understanding and improving testimony* (pp. 229–261). New York: Guilford Press.

Brainerd, C. J. & Reyna, V. F. (1995). Learning rate, learning opportunities, and the development of forgetting. *Developmental Psychology, 31*, 251–262. https://doi.org/10.1037/0012-1649.31.2.251.

Brewin, C. R., Andrews, B., & Gotlib, I. H. (1993). Psychopathology and early experiences: A reappraisal of retrospective reports. *Psychological Bulletin, 113*, 82–98. https://doi.org/10.1037/0033-2909.113.1.82

Brodie v. The King, [1936] S.C.R. 188.

Bussey, K. (2009). An international perspective on child witnesses. In B. L. Bottoms, C. J. Najdowski, & G. S. Goodman (eds), *Children as victims, witnesses, and offenders: Psychological science and the law* (pp. 209–232). New York: Guilford Press.

Cashmore, J., Taylor, A., & Parkinson, P. (2017). The characteristics of reports to the police of child sexual abuse and the likelihood of cases proceeding to prosecution after delays in reporting. *Child Abuse & Neglect*, *74*, 49–61. https://doi.org/10.1016/j.chiabu.2017.07.006

Castelli, P., Goodman, G. S., & Ghetti, S. (2005). Effects of interview style and witness age on perceptions of children's credibility in sexual abuse cases. *Journal of Applied Social Psychology*, *35*, 297–319. https://doi.org/10.1111/j.1559-1816.2005.tb02122.x

Ceci, S. J., & Bruck, M. (1995). *Jeopardy in the courtroom: A scientific analysis of children's testimony*. American Psychological Association. https://doi.org/10.1037/10180-000

Chenier, K., Shawyer, A., Milne, R., & Williams, A. (2022). Police interviews with adult reporters of historical child sexual abuse: Exploring the link between verbal rapport and information obtained. *Child Abuse & Neglect*, *134*, 1–13. https://doi.org./10.1016/j.chiabu.2022.105943

Chi, M. T. H. (1978). Knowledge structures and memory development. In R. S. Siegler (ed.), *Children's thinking: What develops?* (pp 73–96). Hillsdale, NJ: Erlbaum.

Connolly, D. A., Coburn, P. I., & Chong, K. (2017). Twenty-six years prosecuting historic child sexual abuse: Has anything changed? *Psychology, Public Policy, and Law*, *23*, 166–177. https://doi.org.10.1037/law0000121

Connolly, D. A., Chong, K., Coburn, P. I., & Lutgens, D. (2015). Factors associated with delays of days to decades to criminal prosecutions of child sexual abuse. *Behavioral Sciences and the Law*, *33*, 546–560. https://doi.org/:10.1002/bsl.2185

Connolly, D.A., Hockley, W.E., & Pratt, M.W. (1996). A developmental evaluation of frequency memory for actions presented in lists, scripts, and stories. *Memory*, *4*, 243–263. https://doi.org/10.1080/096582196388942

Connolly, D. A., Price, H. L., & Gordon. H. M. (2010). Judicial decision-making in timely and delayed prosecutions of child sexual abuse: A study of honesty and cognitive ability in assessments of credibility. *Psychology, Public Policy, and Law*, *16*, 177–199. https://doi.org/10.1037/a0019050

Connolly, D.A., Price, H. L., & Read, J.D. (2006). Predicting expert testimony in criminal prosecutions of historic child sexual abuse. *Legal and Criminological Psychology*, *11*, 55–74. https://doi.org/10.1348/135532505X50312

Connolly, D.A. & Read, J.D. (2003). Remembering historical child sexual abuse. *Criminal Law Quarterly*, *47*, 438–480.

Connolly, D. A. & Read, D. J. (2006). Delayed prosecutions of historic child sexual abuse: Analyses of 2064 Canadian criminal complaints. *Law and Human Behavior*, *30*, 409–434. https://doi.org/10.1007/s10979-006-9011-6

Connolly, D. A., Price, H. L., & Gordon, H. M. (2009). Judging the credibility of historic child sexual abuse complainants: How judges describe their decisions. *Psychology, Public Policy, and Law*, *15*(2), 102–123. https://doi.org/10.1037/a0015339

Cossins, A. (2002). The hearsay rule and delayed complaints of child sexual abuse: The law and the evidence. *Psychiatry, Psychology and Law*, *9*(2), 163–176. https://doi.org/10.1375/13218710260612055

Ellison, L. & Munro, V. E. (2009). Reacting to rape: Exploring mock jurors' assessments of complainant credibility. *British Journal of Criminology*, *49*, 202–219. https://doi.org/10.1093/bjc/azn077

Flatman, G., & Bagaric, M. (1997). Problems in prosecuting cases involving historic child sexual abuse: The Victorian experience. *Deakin Law Review*, *4*(1), 1–20. www4.austlii.edu.au

Flin, R., & Spencer, J. R. (1995). Children as witnesses – Legal and psychological perspectives. *Child Psychology & Psychiatry & Allied Disciplines*, *36*, 171–189. https://doi.org/10.1111/j.1469-7610.1995.tb01819.x

Goldfarb, D., Goodman, G. S., Larson, R. P., Eisen, M. L., & Qin, J. (2019). Long-term memory in adults exposed to childhood violence: Remembering genital contact nearly 20 years later. *Clinical Psychological Science*, *7*, 381–396. https://doi.org/10.1177/2167702618805742

Goldfarb, D., & Mindthoff, A. (2020). Often but not always: When does age at the time of event predict memory for sexual violence? In J. Pozzulo, E. Pica, & C. Sheahan (eds), *Memory and sexual misconduct: Psychological research for criminal justice*. (pp. 71–99). Routledge. https://doi.org/10.4324/9780429027857-4

Goodman, G. S. (1984). Children's testimony in historical perspective. *Journal of Social Issues*, *40*, 9–31. https://doi.org/10.1111/j.1540-4560.1984.tb01091.x

Goodman, G. S., Batterman-Faunce, J. M., Schaaf, J. M., & Kenney, R. (2002). Nearly 4 years after an event: Children's eyewitness memory and adults' perceptions of children's accuracy. *Child Abuse & Neglect*, *26*(8), 849–884. https://doi-org/10.1016/S0145-2134(02)00354-X

Goodman, G. S., Golding, J. M., Helgeson, V. S., Haith, M. M., & Michelli, J. (1987). When a child takes the stand: Jurors' perceptions of children's eyewitness testimony. *Law and Human Behavior*, *11*(1), 27–40. https://doi.org/10.1007/BF01044837

Goodman-Brown, T. B., Edelstein, R. S., Goodman, G. S., Jones, D. P. H., & Gordon, D. S. (2003). Why children tell: A model of children's disclosure of sexual abuse. *Child Abuse & Neglect*, *27*, 525–540. https://doi.org/10.1016/S0145-2134(03)00037-1

Greene, E. & Loftus, E. F. (1985). When crimes are joined at trial. *Law and Human Behavior*, *9*, 193–207. https://doi.org/10.1007/BF01067051

Hardt, J., & Rutter, M. (2004). Validity of adult retrospective reports of adverse childhood experiences: review of the evidence. *Journal of Child Psychology and Psychiatry*, *45*(2), 260–273. https://doi.org/10.1111/j.1469-7610.2004.00218.x

Harvey, M. B., Price, H. L., & Connolly, D. A. (registered report resubmitted). Differential impacts of investigative and witness delays on perceptions of witness credibility.

Hershkowitz, I., Melkman, E. P., & Zur, R. (2018). When is a child's forensic statement deemed credible? A comparison of physical and sexual abuse cases. *Child Maltreatment*, *23*(2), 196–206. https://doi.org/10.1177/1077559517734059

Hester, M., & Lilley, S. (2017). Rape investigation and attrition in acquaintance, domestic violence and historical rape cases. *Journal of Investigative Psychology and Offender Profiling*, *14*, 175–188. https://doi.org/10.1002/jip.1469

Horowitz, I. A., & Bordens, K. S. (2000). The consolidation of plaintiffs: The effects of number of plaintiffs on jurors' liability decisions, damage awards, and cognitive processing of evidence. *Journal of Applied Psychology*, *8*, 909–918. https://doi.org/10.1037/0021-9010.85.6.909

Howe, M. L. (2013). Memory lessons from the court room: Reflections on being a memory expert on the witness stand. *Memory*, *21*, 576–583. https://doi.org/10.1080/09658211.2012.725735

Hughes, J., & Jonas, M. (2015). Time and crime: Which cold case investigations should be reheated? *Criminal Justice Ethics*, *34*(1), 18–41. https://doi.org/10.1080/0731129X.2015.1025505

Jülich, S. (2006). Views of justice among survivors of historical child sexual abuse: Implications for restorative justice in New Zealand. *Theoretical Criminology*, *10*(1), 125–138. https://doi.org/10.1177/1362480606059988

Kribs et al. v. The Queen [1960] SCR 400.

Lamb, M. E., Orbach, Y., Hershkowitz, I., Esplin, P.W., Horowitz, D. (2007). A structured forensic interview protocol improves the quality and informativeness of investigative interviews with children: A review of research using the NICHD Investigative Interview Protocol. *Child Abuse & Neglect*, *31*, 1201–1231. https://doi.org/10.1016/j.chiabu.2007.03.021

Lewis, P. (2006). *Delayed prosecution for childhood sexual abuse*. New York: Oxford University Press. https://doi.org/10.1093/acprof.oso/9780199282289.001.0001

London, K., Bruck, M., Ceci, S. J., & Shuman, D. W. (2005). Disclosure of child sexual abuse: What does the research tell us about the ways that children tell? *Psychology, Public Policy, and Law*, *11*, 194–226. https://doi.org/10.1037/1076-8971.11.1.194

Melkman, E. P., Hershkowitz, I., & Zur, R. (2017). Credibility assessment in child sexual abuse investigations: A descriptive analysis. *Child Abuse & Neglect*, *67*, 76–85. https://doi.org/10.1016/j.chiabu.2017.01.027

Miller, Q. C., Call, A. A., & London, K. (2022). Mock jurors' perceptions of child sexual abuse cases: Investigating the role of delayed disclosure and relationship to the perpetrator. *Journal of Interpersonal Violence*, *37*(23–24), NP23374–NP23396. https://doi.org/ 10.1177/08862605221078812

Miller, Q. C., & London, K. (2020). Forensic implications of delayed reports from child witnesses. In J. Pozzulo, E. Pica, & C. Sheahan (eds), *Memory and sexual misconduct: Psychological research for criminal justice* (pp. 100–131). Routledge. https://doi.org/10.4324/9780429027857-5

Myers, J. E. B., Diedrich, S., Lee, D., Fincher, K., & Stern, R. (1999). Professional writing on child sexual abuse from 1900 to 1975: Dominant themes and impact on prosecution. *Child Maltreatment*, *4*, 201–216. https://doi.org/10.1177/1077559599004003002

Newbury, M. (2014). Historic child sexual abuse investigations: A case for law reform. *Current Issues in Criminal Justice*, *26*(1), 43–54. https://doi.org/10.1080/10345329.2014.12036006

Nortje, W., & du Toit, P. (2017). A fresh perspective on historic sexual abuse: The case of Hewitt v S 2017. *Potchefstroom Electronic Law Journal*. https://doi.org/10.17159/1727-3781/2017/v20i0a2229

Nunez, N., Kehn, A., & Wright, D. B. (2011). When children are witnesses: The effects of context, age and gender on adults' perceptions of cognitive ability and honesty. *Applied Cognitive Psychology*, *25*, 460–468. https://doi.org/10.1002/acp.1713

Ornstein, P. A., Ceci, S. J., & Loftus, E. F. (1998). Adults' recollections of childhood abuse: Cognitive and developmental perspectives. *Psychology, Public Policy and Law*, *4*, 1025–1051. https://doi.org/10.1037/1076-8971.4.4.1025.

Ornstein, P. A., & Haden, C. A. (2002). The development of memory: Toward an understanding of children's testimony. In M. L. Eisen, J. A. Quas, & G. S. Goodman (eds), *Memory and suggestibility in the forensic interview*. (pp. 29–61). Lawrence Erlbaum Associates Publishers.

Otgaar, H., Howe, M. L., & Patihis, L. (2022). What science tells us about false and repressed memories. *Memory*, *30*, 16–21. https://doi.org/10.1080/09658211.2020.1870699

Peterson, C. (2011). Children's memory reports over time: Getting both better and worse. *Journal of Experimental Child Psychology*, *109*, 275–293. https://doi.org/10.1016/j.jecp.2011.01.009

Peterson, C., & Whalen, N. (2001). Five years later: Children's memory for medical emergencies. *Applied Cognitive Psychology*, *15*(7), S7–S24. https://doi.org/10.1002/acp.832

Price, H. L., Luther, K., Thomas, W., Gabbert, F., & Hope, L. (in press). Extracting witness evidence in "cold case" investigations: What we know and what we need to learn. *Journal of Police and Criminal Psychology*. https://doi.org/10.1007/s11896-024-09666-x

R. v. B.(G.), [1990] 2 S.C.R. 3.

R. v. D.D. [2000] S. C. J. No. R. 275.

R. v. P. E. C. [2005] 1 S.C R. 290.

R. v. R. (J.W.) [2001] 151 C. C. C. (3d) 236

R. v. R.E.M., 2004 BCSC 1596 (CanLII).

R. v. W. (D.), [1991] 1 S. C. R. 742

R. v. W. (R.), [1992] 2 S.C.R. 122

Ring, S. (2017). The victim of historical child sexual abuse in the Irish courts 1999–2006. *Social and Legal Studies*, *26*(5), 562–580. https://doi.org/10.1177/0964663917694706

Ross, D. F., Jurden, F. H., Lindsay, R. C. L., and Keeney, J. M. (2003). Replication and limitations of a two-factor model of child witness credibility. *Journal of Applied Social Psychology*, *33*, 418–431. https://doi.org/10.1111/j.1559-1816.2003.tb01903.x

Roberts, K. A. (2017). Police interviews with survivors of historic child sexual abuse: Challenges and solutions. In N. L. Asquith, I. Bartkowiak-Theron and K. A. Roberts (eds), *Policing Encounters with Vulnerability*, (pp. 175–198). Switzerland: Springer International). https://doi.org/10.1007/978-3-319-51228-0_8.

Rubin, D. C. & Wenzel, A. E. (1996). One hundred years of forgetting: A quantitative description of retention. *Psychological Review*, *4*, 734–760. https://doi.org/10.1037/0033-295X.103.4.734

Sas, L. D., & Cunningham, A. H. (1995). *Tipping the balance to tell the secret: The public discovery of child sexual abuse.* London, Ontario, Canada: London Family Court Clinic.

Shead, K. (2014). Responding to historical child sexual abuse: a prosecution perspective on current challenges and future directions. *Current Issues in Criminal Justice, 26*, 55–73. https://doi.org/10.1080/10345329.2014.12036007

Tanford, S., & Penrod, S. (1984). Social inference processes in juror judgments of multiple-offense trials. *Journal of Personality and Social Psychology, 47*(4), 749–765. https://doi.org/10.1037/0022-3514.47.4.749

Tanford, S., Penrod, S., & Collins, R. (1985). Decision making in joined criminal trials: The influence of charge similarity, evidence similarity, and limiting instructions. *Law and Human Behavior, 9*(4), 319–337. https://doi.org/10.1007/BF01044474

Thompson, C. P. (1998). The bounty of everyday memory. In C. P. Thompson, D. J. Herrmann, D. Bruce, J. D. Read, D. G. Payne, & M. P. Toglia (eds), *Autobiographical memory: Theoretical and applied perspectives* (pp. 29–44). Lawrence Erlbaum Associates Publishers.

Thompson, L. E., Pica, E., & Pozzulo, J. (2021). Jurors' decision making in a sexual assault trial: The influence of victim age, delayed reporting, and multiple allegations, *American Journal of Forensic Psychology, 39*, 19–46.

Vallano, J. P., Pickel, K. L., & Shambaugh, L. J. (2020). Legal Perspectives on Historical Misconduct Cases: Issues with Civil and Criminal Cases. In *Memory and Sexual Misconduct* (pp. 175–197). Routledge. https://doi.org/10.4324/9780429027857-7

van Tongeren Harvey, W., & Dauns, P. E. (2001). *Sexual offences against children and the criminal process* (2nd ed.). Toronto, Ontario, Canada: Butterworths.

Wang, Q., Peterson, C., Khuu, A., Reid, C. P., Maxwell, K. L., & Vincent, J. M. (2019). Looking at the past through a telescope: Adults postdated their earliest childhood memories. *Memory, 27*, 19–27. https://doi.org/10.1080/09658211.2017.1414268

Wells, C., Morrison, C., & Conway, M. (2014). Adult recollections of childhood memories: What details can be recalled? *The Quarterly Journal of Experimental Psychology, 67(7)*, 1249–1261.doi.org/10.1080/174070218.2013.856451

Woiwod, D. M., Fitzgerald, R. J., Sheahan, C. L., Price, H. L., & Connolly, D. A. (2019). A meta-analysis of differences in children's reports of single and repeated events. *Law and Human Behavior, 43*, 99–116. https://doi.org/10.1037/lhb0000312

Woiwod, D. M., & Connolly, D. A. (2017). Continuous child sexual abuse: Balancing defendants' rights and victims' capabilities to particularize individual acts of repeated abuse. *Criminal Justice Review, 42*, 206–225. https://doi.org/10.1177/0734016817704700

6

When allegations of child sexual abuse are false

Ros Burnett and Carolyn Hoyle

Introduction

The value of showing victims of sexual abuse, particularly child victims, that they are believed when they make allegations, and throughout the criminal process that follows, is clear to criminal justice professionals and activists. Given the typical absence of forensic evidence to prove an offence occurred, especially when there has been a long delay before the complaint is made, there is a need to rely on complainants' claims and to reassure them that they will be supported. In line with this approach, consensus emerged – in public discourse, research articles, official reports and services working with victims and survivors – that false allegations of sexual abuse are rare. While estimates of prevalence rates can be unreliable (Migliavaca et al., 2020; Shah, 2020; see Chapter 2, this volume), an increase in *false* allegations of child sexual abuse, alongside true ones, may be an unintended consequence of child-safeguarding with mandatory reporting of suspicions, and victim-centred policies encouraging reporting, including of historical cases, irrespective of the length of delay.

This chapter begins with a brief overview of what is known about the prevalence of false allegations, bearing in mind the limitations of research. It does so within a broad definition of "false allegations of child sexual abuse". This includes those made erroneously as well those made intentionally, and incorporates false allegations made by adults of "historical", non-recent child sexual abuse in their childhood. It reviews the research on causal or contributing factors, touching on the confounding issue of false retractions, before considering cultural and sociolegal developments that have encouraged reporting of abuse. While of benefit to victims who hitherto have been inhibited from seeking justice, these developments have potentially also increased the risk of false allegations. The chapter finally outlines findings from the authors' own research on the impact of false allegations on those wrongly accused of abuse (Hoyle et al., 2016; Burnett, 2016; Burnett et al., 2017; Speechley & Burnett, 2022), and factors affecting the review process for appealing against wrongful convictions (Hoyle & Sato, 2019).

DOI: 10.4324/9781003427155-6

Conceptualizing false allegations of child sexual abuse

Saunders rightly observes that "criminal justice professionals and researchers and commentators do not subscribe to the same definition of the false allegation …" (2012, p. 1153). There is a "bewildering array" of related terms and meanings (Rumney & McCarten, 2017), some of which are limited to malicious false claims while others refer primarily to erroneous or unsubstantiated reports. While the concept of "false allegation" (or "false accusation") is commonly applied in reference to offences of sexual and domestic abuse, there is no established legal definition.

Though it is not in itself a crime to make a false allegation, those who make *knowingly false* allegations could face legal consequences. In the UK, they may be charged with "perverting the course of justice" if "a person deliberately makes a false allegation about an offence in order to have a person arrested".[1] The same legislation specifies that "It is an offence to cause a wasteful employment of the police by knowingly making a false report – either orally or in writing – to the police or anyone else". In the US, "making a false report" is a misdemeanour or a felony in many states (Turvey et al., 2018).

In contrast to knowingly false allegations are complaints made in good faith but based on an incorrect belief (including misinterpretation of benign events or a child's ambiguous utterances; incorrect recollection of experiences when the complainant was intoxicated; or distorted memories of childhood experiences) or on mistaken identification of the perpetrator. Vulnerability to false memories may be greatest in cases of historical (non-recent) abuse (Pendergrast, 2017; see also Chapter 5, this volume).

There is understandable anger among victims and their supporters when suspects accuse them of lying. Indeed, those who respond to allegations of sexual abuse – whether they are police, prosecutors or those working in victim support services – are trained to resist the key "rape myths" about women and girls lying about sexual abuse (Lonsway & Fitzgerald, 1994; Suarez & Gadalla, 2010). But a more nuanced understanding of the concept of lies might be helpful (see also Chapter 4, this volume, for a detailed discussion of lies).

Of course, the distinction between lying and telling the truth may be reductionist. In considering the content of claims of sexual abuse made by children, or by adults on their behalf, it is appropriate to distinguish between false reports which are "factually inaccurate due to conscious lies on the part of the child" and false reports due to "unconscious assimilation of false suggestions and pressures made by those … who have access to the child" (Hirtz et al., 2015, p. 4). Turvey et al. (2018) point to the significance of exaggeration, omissions and half-truths which commonly characterize statements, as well as sources of contamination. Such features of otherwise true statements may tip them over into incriminating others.

Burnett (2016) used the alternative concept of "*wrongful* allegations" to move beyond the pejorative insinuation that false allegations are always made by liars, and to focus on the harms done to people wrongly accused of such offences, irrespective of whether the complaint was mistakenly believed or was knowingly false. For our present purposes, the more inclusive definition of "false allegations" is applied in order to consider the implications of both intentionally false and erroneously false allegations.

In the absence of a clear, internationally applied definition of "false allegations" within the context of child sexual offences, it is appropriate to consider how police services distinguish between true and false allegations when recording cases. The International Association of Chiefs of Police (IACP) rule for counting and recording false allegations of sexual assault by police services maintains that, "The determination that a report of sexual assault is false can be made only if the evidence establishes that no crime was committed or attempted" (International Association of Chiefs of Police, 2005). Such evidence may be difficult to produce as proving something did not happen can be even more challenging than proving it did. In consequence, such cases are recorded as unsubstantiated, as distinct from "unfounded" or "baseless", concepts sometimes used synonymously with "false". This is pertinent for the studies of the prevalence of false allegations discussed below, which have mainly been based on police records.

Counting false allegations of child sexual abuse

In contrast to several national and international surveys of the prevalence of child sexual abuse (e.g. Stoltenborgh et al., 2011), there are relatively few surveys on the prevalence of *false* allegations, and the more methodologically robust among these have combined false allegations of child sexual abuse with false allegations of sexual offences against adults. Notwithstanding methodological disparities, the received view is that false allegations of sexual offences are relatively rare (Ferguson & Malouff, 2016; Rumney, 2006). Indeed, the consensus seems to be that many true cases are never reported so the accurate rate of child abuse may be much higher than recorded data suggest. Of course, it is also likely that false accusations may be more prevalent than assumed given that they are not a recognized crime and so are not recorded.

With specific regard to the prevalence of false allegations of child sexual abuse, Korkman et al. (2019) conducted the first population-based prevalence survey of unfounded allegations. Based in Finland, with large samples of adolescents and adults, they found that 1.5% of adolescents and 1.9% of adults had been the subject of unfounded suspicions (e.g. someone falsely believing abuse had taken place). A careful and thorough review of past studies of cases accessed via family courts was conducted by O'Donohue,

Cummings, and Willis (2018). Notwithstanding caveats about contextual and methodological differences between the studies, they found that most allegations of child sexual abuse are true: "no study reported a majority or even a sizeable minority of claims to be false". However, they also found that "false allegations do occur at a non-negligible rate"; in some studies, "nearly a third of children made false claims of touching" (O'Donohue et al., 2018, p. 471). The authors cautiously concluded: "Thus, it seems that false allegations of [child sexual abuse] do occur and thus ideologies such as 'believe the children' which may be construed to mean 'always believe every child' need to be tempered by this information" (O'Donohue et al., 2018, p. 473).

Two substantial surveys of high-quality prevalence studies of false allegations of sexual offences, while not distinguishing child victims from adult victims, are helpful for shedding light on claims that false allegations are rare. Ferguson and Malouff (2016) identified seven high quality surveys "focused on determining the frequency of confirmed false allegations of sexual assault made to police" (p. 1185). All were based on police records, and therefore on the IACP rule for counting false allegations of sexual assault which limits the recording of false allegations to those where there is evidence that "no crime was committed or attempted" by the accused (see above). As such, they are likely to underestimate false allegations. Yet their meta-analysis found the prevalence rate to be 5%.

Nankivell and Papadimitriou (2023) revisited the same seven surveys and agreed that the most common estimates are that approximately 5% or between 2% and 10% of reports are false. However, based on their detailed analysis of the categories and decision points used by the police as well as methods used by the researchers, they suggest that these should be seen as "lower bound" estimates, explaining that:

> the rules followed by the studies to determine whether to classify a report as "false" exclude many false and potentially false reports. Their estimates are premised on there being no false allegations among the many equivocal or ambiguous cases classified as having insufficient evidence, or where the alleged victim withdrew their complaint, or where the accused was tried but acquitted.
>
> (Nankivell & Papadimitriou, 2023, p. 1)

Reviewing the attrition points at which potential false allegations were not investigated, and applying estimates based on "more realistic but still modest assumptions about the share of false reports in these categories", Nankivell and Papadimitrioiu proposed that the actual prevalence rate could be materially greater. While they reached the measured conclusion that "nothing we have found challenges the view that the majority of sexual assault reports are true" (Nankivell & Papadimitriou, 2023, p. 16), their analysis led them to observe that:

> it is an extreme and unjustifiable assumption to presume that no unproven accusation is false. And it is potentially misleading to promulgate prevalence estimates based on that assumption, as the high-quality studies effectively do, at least without properly communicating that assumption and its ramifications.
>
> (Nankivell & Papadimitriou, 2023, p. 17)

A case in point is the misuse of statistics drawn from the Crown Prosecution Service analysis of cases charged for "perverting the course of justice" (Levitt, 2013). The Levitt Report found that over a 17-month period there were 5,651 prosecutions for rape of adults and children and 35 (0.6%) prosecutions for "perverting the course of justice". This extremely small prevalence rate is often cited in the media as authoritative evidence to validate assertions that false allegations of sexual offences against adults and children are too few to matter. However, such reports do not make sufficiently clear that the data were limited to the narrow subsection of all purported false allegations where evidence emerged of deliberate falsehoods and a decision was made to prosecute the accuser, which is rare. Few complainants who give evidence against an alleged perpetrator who is nonetheless acquitted will be charged with perverting the course of justice, and the same applies to alleged victims whose evidence did lead to a conviction later quashed at an appeal. It may well be that the very few cases that result in prosecutions for perverting the course of justice are but a fraction of a wider population.

An important source of data to substantiate concerns that false allegations of sexual offences may be more frequent than is typically recognized can be found in the records of exonerations for wrongful conviction in sexual offence cases. In the United States, the National Registry of Exonerations maintains detailed records.[2] Figures as of March 2024 show that, from a total of 3492 exonerations, there have been 323 exonerations for "child sexual abuse" since 1989, and identify contributing factors to these wrongful convictions, including "false allegations" and/or "perjury" in 273 (85%) cases.[3]

Understanding false allegations of child sexual abuse

The important question of what would cause a child or an adult to make a false allegation of child abuse cannot be answered with a simple reference to motives. That is especially so under a broad definition of false allegations, including those that are unintentionally and accidentally false. Explanatory factors are varied and interactive and may have developed over time in episodic memories, revisited, shaped and clarified in conversations with others (Korkman et al., 2014, 2024; Principe & London, 2022). Even the distinction between knowingly and unknowingly made false allegations can be blurred in cases where an initial lie comes to be regarded by the complainant as true, after repetition and expansion in discussion with others, particularly following validation by significant others. Furthermore, people apart from the child are often involved in interpreting what exactly took place (Korkman et al., 2014), which in turn can affect the child's understanding and impact on the development of claims (Principe & London, 2022; Korkman et al., 2024). An adult looking back on incidents in childhood is likely to have rehearsed the details in their mind, perhaps filling in gaps with later understanding, knowledge and interpretations supplied by others (Rose, 2016; Smith, 2016a), or confabulating distorted memories of a shared reality (French, Garry, & Loftus, 2009).

Useful typologies have been developed to distinguish different motives and explanatory factors for false allegations of child sexual abuse. O'Donohue et al. (2016) suggested the following causal pathways: lies made by the child; suggestive influences by parents or by investigators; misinterpretation of benign events; confabulation of different but benign experiences; distortion guided by having a stake in the outcome; or certain child or adult pathology. Goodyear-Smith (2016), reviewing numerous cases of false allegations of sexual assault, identified the following types of motives and explanatory factors: providing an alibi; obtaining sympathy and attention; seeking revenge or retribution; financial/claiming compensation; parental alienation during custody disputes; factitious disorder and Munchausen syndrome by proxy; or investigation-pressured false confessions. While most of the evidence she drew on focused on adult sexual abuse, it included references to cases of child sexual abuse and some of the explanatory categories – especially custody disputes – are particularly pertinent to such cases.

False and recovered memories of child sexual abuse

An exception to the general scarcity of academic research on false allegations is the abundance of analogue studies on false memories of child sexual abuse within the field of cognitive psychology memory research. Interlinked areas of research concern the "misinformation effect" – how added suggestions, conversations and pictures can distort the memory of a recent event (Bruck & Ceci, 2013; Loftus & Klemfuss, 2024) – and the validity of recovered repressed memories of childhood abuse (Otgaar et al., 2022; Patihis et al., 2023).

With regard to reports of recent child sexual abuse, a corpus of laboratory-based analogue studies demonstrated that children's accounts of recent events can be influenced by verbal cues and non-verbal props: younger children especially are susceptible to suggestion by others (Bruck & Ceci, 2013; Korkman et al., 2024). Importantly, the first conversations they have about related events are typically with parents, teachers or child-protection services who may be biased towards a presumption that comments or behaviour by the child are symptomatic of sexual abuse (Bruck & Ceci, 2013; Principe & London, 2022). Also, their understanding of an event may be influenced by conversations with school friends (Principe & Ceci, 2002).

Once a case is referred to forensic interviewers, or specialists working with victims of child sexual abuse, their prior assumptions about the probability of sexual abuse can result in biased interviewing. It is well established that certain interviewing styles – for example, with leading, suggestive, and repeated questions, or with use of drawings and anatomically correct dolls – can cause children to agree with false reports of abuse (Ceci & Bruck, 1995; Lamb et al., 1994). While tremendous progress has been made in developing reliable protocols for interviewing children (Lamb et al., 1997, 2007; Korkman et al., 2024; see also Chapter 9, this volume), it remains the case that whoever has spoken to the child before may already have helped consolidate a belief that they were sexually abused. And "once a child's statement has been tainted, it may be impossible to untaint in subsequent interviews, regardless of the skill of the interviewer" (Bruck & Ceci, 2013, p. 559).

While the evidence suggests that false and unreliable evidence "is an unavoidable feature of witness testimony" (Radcliffe et al., 2016, p. 8) it may also engender confirmation bias in the process of investigating claims of child sexual abuse. Confirmation bias is:

> a type of selective thinking. Once a hypothesis has been formed, our inclination is to confirm rather than refute it. We tend to look for supporting information, interpret ambiguous information as consistent with our beliefs, and minimize any inconsistent evidence. … Confirmation bias can cause a detective to interpret information in a biased manner – evidence that supports the investigative theory.
>
> (Rossmo & Pollock, 2019, p. 814)

As O'Donohue and Cirlugea (2021, pp. 377–378) have observed, there needs to be more explicit recognition that confirmation bias is omnipresent and can impact on forensic interviews with children who may have been abused sexually (see also Zhang et al., 2022). In the absence of evidence beyond testimony, confirmation bias can result in "tunnel vision" throughout the prosecution process, identified as a common contributing factor towards wrongful convictions (MacFarlane & Cordner, 2008). It may be particularly difficult to remain impartial during the investigation process in cases of child sexual abuse, given the repulsion and anger such cases evoke (Ask & Granhag, 2007; Peace et al., 2012).

Increasing interest in repressed memories recovered in therapy, alongside the growth of psychotherapeutic counselling professions, was critical to the "discovery" around the 1980s of widespread incest and abuse in childhood, formerly a hidden issue. Encouragement to talk about their childhood no doubt enabled some clients to discuss undisclosed past abuse of which they had discontinuous memories, but national psychological societies concluded that, with methods such as hypnosis, role-play or free association, it was possible for adults to *recover* memories of childhood abuse of which they had no previous awareness. This claim, that repressed memories, of which the individual had no conscious knowledge, could be recalled in detail during therapy sessions – sometimes linked to a diagnosis of "multiple personality disorder" – engendered acrimonious debate.

Debates over the reliability of adult's memories of child sexual abuse "recovered" during therapy, and whether they could have been "implanted", became known as the "memory wars", and, though particularly fierce in the 1980s, the conflicts between therapists and memory researchers have continued (Pendergrast, 2017). Though scientific research has cast doubts on the likelihood that child sexual abuse could be completely repressed from consciousness, there continues to be substantial support for such by public, legal and mental health professionals (French & Ost, 2016; Radcliffe & Patihis, 2024).

Many of those accused following recovered memories, mostly fathers, were charged and convicted; there were also significant numbers of retractors, although such retractions could take decades. The validity and professional basis for therapies including "repressed memory therapy", subsequently relabelled "dissociative amnesia", has not been scientifically supported, and cases were successfully challenged by a series of lawsuits (Pendergrast, 2017; Barden, 2016). Memory experts had hoped the "memory wars" were over (Lynn et al., 2023) but therapists using similar methods (hypnosis, guided imagery, eye movement desensitization and reprocessing) and specializing in "dissociative amnesia" continue to practice; for example, in the Netherlands, France, and Germany (Niehaus & Krause, 2023; Shaw & Vredeveldt, 2019).[4]

Telling lies

In general discourse on allegations of sexual offences, false allegations tend to be equated with lies, but the terms "knowingly" or "unknowingly" false provide a distinction between deceit and error. A substantial body of empirical research indicates that most people tell lies sometimes, but a small proportion do so much more frequently than others (DePaulo et al., 1996) and teenagers are the most prolific liars (Levine et al., 2013). Debey and colleagues' (2015) large-scale study of age-related differences in lying found that lying *frequency* peaked in adolescence while lying *proficiency* improved during childhood and excelled in young adulthood. Other research indicates a link between impulsivity and lie-telling during late childhood and early adolescence: those with heightened impulsivity were more likely to lie for short-term benefits without considering the later consequences (Dykstra et al., 2023). Meanwhile, prolific liars are more inclined to use deception for personal gain (Lyon et al., 2020) and the Levitt report (2013) observed that "Some suspects admitted lying to provoke a reaction or divert attention from their own behaviour from their parents, partners, or friends" (Levitt, 2013, p. 26).

Teachers seem especially vulnerable to lies being told about them, though research on false allegations against teachers has proved particularly challenging (Sikes & Piper, 2010). One survey by the Association of Teachers and Lecturers (Rawlinson, 2015) of 685 of its members found that 22% of school and college staff had been the subject of a false allegation of (either sexual of physical) abuse by a pupil, driving some experienced staff out of teaching.[5] Teachers and childcare staff, especially men, increasingly feel that they should leave or avoid the profession in case they are falsely accused (Cruickshank, 2019; Leander et al., 2019).

Knowingly false allegations are sometimes made in family court disputes: a parent may lie or be accused of lying about the sexual abuse of their child in order to either gain custody, or to prevent the other parent having access to their child, sometimes causing "parental alienation" – one parent being excluded from contact with their children (Warshak, 2006). Of course, it may not be that a child who refuses contact with the estranged parent has always been lied to by the custodial parent. Bernet and Xu argued that the most common cause of parental alienation was "the child's indoctrination by the favoured parent to dislike or fear the alienated parent" though they conceded that another person – such as a grandparent or a therapist – may have "influenced the child to reject a parent" (2023, p. 3). In their review of studies analysing referrals to child protection services, Saini and colleagues concluded that while intentionally false allegations have been more frequent in cases involving custody disputes, "the rates of malicious allegations are nowhere near the reported rates originally presented with the theory of alienation by Gardner and others in the last century" (Saini et al., 2020, p. 428). Nevertheless, equal weight and sensitivity should be given to the possibility of preventing false negatives and false positives (Faller & Everson, 2012).

To question whether compensation can be a motive for filing a false retrospective allegation is held by some to be provocative. Carl Beech, the main police informant in "Operation Midland" who fabricated claims of historical abuse and murder by a number of high-profile people, went on to be interviewed on radio and on television under his pseudonym, Nick (Henriques, 2016). Before the police discovered that his claims were fraudulent, he was praised for his role in exposing individuals[6] for organized historical abuse and obtained compensation, though that was unlikely to be his only motive.

Anyone whose life has been blighted by childhood sexual abuse clearly deserves to take advantage of compensation. However, while it is well established that a high proportion of offenders, including those convicted of crimes of dishonesty, have been victims of abuse, they are likely to come into contact in custodial settings with others who were not but may be tempted to take advantage of compensation claims, should an opportunity to make one arise. This risk is especially likely if they realize that they spent time in a residential institution when a known child molester or paedophile was present. They may thus be tempted to join a class action. In some cases, the authors of false allegations made in such circumstances may have "real" memories of being abused themselves by persons unrelated to the compensation case. Adding to the risk is that personal injury solicitors sometimes provide reassurances that, once a non-recent crime has been reported to the police, it is unlikely that an alleged victim who joins class action litigation will be called as a witness when it comes to court, because the great majority of such cases are settled without a trial. This alone may encourage false claimants to think they have nothing to lose and much to gain from participation in the action.

"Corroboration by numbers" cases have on occasion been found to conceal a "bandwagon effect", whereby compensation has been advertised as an "inducement for giving false or exaggerated evidence during investigations of this kind" (HASC, 2002). Though exceptional, such cases have been recorded: in 2013, a former UK prisoner publicly admitted that he joined a "class action" for compensation against a member of staff at a school he had attended, after seeing an advert from a personal injury solicitor. He had afterwards decided to withdraw from the case because he did not believe the accused was guilty (Gunn, 2013). In another case, a football coach was acquitted after the complainant admitted to lying with a view to getting compensation (Cassidy, 2018).

One of the most widely reported scandals pertains to child sexual abuse in UK residential schools for children "in care", which resulted in multiple convictions for historical abuse but also multiple acquittals and some exonerations. The social historian, Richard Webster conducted an in-depth study of the children's home "panic" in 1990s North England and Wales (Webster, 1998, 2005). He provided an eloquent explanation of the process whereby an emotionally troubled and economically deprived background, behavioural problems including a habit of lying in order to survive, the need for recognition and love, the opportunity to be believed and treated as important and to receive other rewards, might all interact to persuade ex-residents to claim they were victims when invited by the police to look back to their time in an institution. However, he also pointed to the influence on false allegations of vivid media coverage and a "witch-hunt" atmosphere or moral panic about institutional abuse (Webster, 1998, 2005; see also Smith, 2016a).

False recantations

It would be remiss in a chapter about false allegations against innocent people not to mention their inverse, "false recantations" (also referred to in the literature as "false retractions"). As Denne and colleagues explained, "Recantation rates can be difficult to interpret as they point to one of two explanations: either the child was correcting an untrue statement or was making a false denial" (2021, p.1). Both "false allegations" and "false recantations" deny the truth but in opposite directions; the former can result in "false positives" in the determination of guilt, while false recantations are likely to result in "false negatives" that acquit a guilty person.

Similar pressures and motivations can explain both *false allegations* and *false recantations*: for example, persuasion or coercion by others regarding what actually happened; concern about the consequences for the claimant or for the accused; or because the false claim will bring closure or improve the complainant's situation in some way (Bücken et al, 2022; Malloy & Mugno, 2016). In a study of false recantations by adult survivors of sexual assault, Malouff and Schutte (2021) identified the following possible risk factors: being young and suggestible, feelings of shame, being fearful of the assailant, and having low social support at the time of interrogation. While focused on adults, the findings would seem to be germane for children.

Reviewing several studies, Ost (2017) emphasized the primacy of belief over memories: some people had no recollections of abuse that they believed had happened. He found that the more frequent reason given by retractors for withdrawing belief in their recollections of abuse was "external evidence", mainly in the form of media reports revealing that people can misremember sexual abuse. Clearly, it is important that "investigators and policy makers do not make the assumption that a withdrawn complaint equals a false complaint because the variety of reasons why a complaint might be withdrawn covers both true and false complaints" (Petherick, 2020, p. 445). That said, a substantial review of disclosure and recantation rates from 24 child clinic studies found that, while victims often delayed disclosure of child sexual abuse, subsequent recantations were rare (London et al., 2008).

The risk of false allegations of CSA

The shifting pendulum of credibility

The presumption of innocence places the burden of proof of a crime having been committed on the prosecution. It is therefore appropriate that complainants are questioned under oath so that magistrates, judges and juries can test the veracity of their claims. For a long time though, complainants were treated poorly by the defence, receiving inadequate protection by judges, particularly in sexual offence cases. This led some to argue that the trial was akin to a second rape (McGlynn, 2017). Mechanisms were put in place to make the experience of testifying in court less traumatic for all victims, but particularly vulnerable ones (Hoyle, 2012). Over time, in difficult cases concerning allegations of sexual abuse, there has been increasing disquiet that the pendulum of credibility has moved to a strong presumption in favour of the victim and with the attendant risk that even false allegations of child sexual abuse will be believed, thereby increasing the rate of both false and true allegations (Hebenton & Seddon, 2016).

This has been, in part, at least, a product of growing awareness of child sexual abuse, in families and in other institutional settings, primarily through high profile cases that led to state action. Government inquiries, safeguarding, policing operations, and new laws around child protection followed revelations of serial child sexual abuse in different contexts: pre-school daycare, local neighbourhoods, church communities, children's residential schools, as well as intrafamilial sexual abuse exposed through psychotherapy and counselling.

Cases of children abducted, raped and murdered led to eponymous laws for notifying the public about sex offenders living in the community,[7] and disclosure and barring services to prevent the employment of staff who could be a danger to children.[8] High profile scandals in the UK, notably the sexual exploitation of teenage girls by networks of men in numerous cities,[9] and the Jimmy Savile scandal (Smith, 2016b) served as a clarion call to police services and the Crown Prosecution Service. The Victims' Code for England and Wales, introduced in 2004, was developed to improve victims' experiences of the criminal justice process and to provide a framework for policy and practice (Ministry of Justice, 2024). Lifelong anonymity for victims of sexual offences was assured.[10] Police Services, reflecting on their past responses to complaints of sexual offences, acknowledged that they had in the past been remiss in failing to act on some serious complaints of child sexual abuse (HMIC, 2013). These were all reasonable measures to protect vulnerable victims and help the criminal process to deal more effectively with complaints of child sexual abuse.

That said, policing and prosecution policies may have inadvertently increased the risk of false allegations. The revised *Guidelines on Prosecuting Cases of Child Sexual Abuse* (Crown Prosecution Service, 2013) steered prosecutors away from questioning the credibility of the complainant, and toward challenging the "myths" surrounding the reporting of sexual crimes (para. 1) and specified that "prosecutors should guard against looking for 'corroboration' of the victim's account or using 'lack of corroboration' as a reason not to proceed with a case" (para. 55). A report by HM Inspectorate of Constabulary (HMIC, 2014) recommended that: "The presumption that the victim should *always* be believed should be institutionalised" (our emphasis). In March 2015, the Home Secretary announced the Independent Inquiry into Child Sexual Abuse (IICSA) in England and Wales to examine the handling of investigations into allegations of child sex abuse in the past (IICSA, 2022). Increasingly people came forward with retrospective claims of familial and institutional abuse. Similar national inquiries into CSA have been carried out in Northern Ireland, Ireland, and Australia, and are ongoing in Scotland and New Zealand.

While there were numerous claims about organized or systemic child sexual abuse by so-called "paedophile rings" in settings including day care, many of the accused and prisoners eventually were acquitted or exonerated. This is not to say that the Church and residential care homes for both young offenders and "looked after" children have not been sites of abuse, across various countries. Indeed, the UK Church's failure to address sexual abuse of children by John Smyth exposed children beyond the UK border to sexual violence, the recognition of which led to the resignation of the Archbishop of Canterbury (Savage, 2024). Furthermore, there is no doubt that Jimmy Savile abused a number of children. However, other investigations indicated that "moral panics" among parents and social workers had resulted in children being unnecessarily removed from their homes, and the number of offenders involved had been overstated (La Fontaine, 1994; HASC, 2002).

Furthermore, in the UK, the Waterhouse Report (2000) found that child abusers in residential schools had acted individually rather than in organized paedophile rings; policing methods of "trawling" for more complainants to name suspects were criticized as "over-zealous" (HASC, 2002; Rose, 2016); and a significant number of people who had been imprisoned for institutional historical abuse were successful in their appeals against conviction. The House of Commons Select Committee report, *The Conduct of Investigations into Past Cases of Abuse in Children's Homes* recognized the problem of false allegations and factors that might facilitate them:

> It has been suggested, and we believe it to be so, that a new genre of miscarriages of justice has arisen from the over-enthusiastic pursuit of these allegations … Set in the context of a growing compensation culture … the risks of effecting a miscarriages of justice in these cases are said to be unusually high.
>
> (HASC, 2002, para. 2, p. 5)

In addition to concerns about policing methods, this report looked into the risks associated with "corroboration by number", likely to be enabled by personal injury solicitors' callouts for witnesses. There is potential for personal injury solicitors to facilitate false corroborative evidence, especially via advertisements in prisons that are seen by former residents of residential schools for children who were young offenders (Gunn, 2013; Rose, 2016; Smith, 2016a).

While it is vital that the state responds with competence and sensitivity to complaints of child sexual abuse, those subjected to false allegations perceive that their due process protections have been disregarded (Burnett et al., 2017; Corteen & Steele, 2018; Greenwood, 2024; Jensen & Jensen, 2011). Policy and legal developments to enhance the credibility of complainants in the absence of forensic evidence have made it correspondingly harder for people falsely accused of sexual offences to defend themselves (Speechley & Burnett, 2022). With this in mind, the investigation by Sir Richard Henriques (2016) into the conduct of "Operation Midland" recommended that the instruction to police to believe a "victim's account" should end. He identified "unwarranted and disproportionate belief" and a concomitant failure to "investigate the facts objectively and impartially and with an open mind".

Shifting credibility in appeals against conviction

Those sentenced in England and Wales whose appeals against their conviction are not upheld can apply to the Criminal Cases Review Commission (CCRC) for their conviction to be reviewed with a view to it being referred back to the Court of Appeal for reconsideration. This only happens in a very small proportion of cases (typically less than five percent) when the CCRC decides that the evidence to support a referral meets the "real possibility test": there must be some new evidence or a fresh argument (not already considered at trial or an earlier appeal) to create a real possibility that the Court of Appeal will rule that a conviction is unsafe.

Hoyle and Sato (2019) found that until about 2017, the CCRC had resisted the political climate that was primarily concerned with wrongful acquittals. Even while legislation and policies in the last several decades focused on protecting complainants, the CCRC focused on how complainant credibility could be undermined in cases that appeared to present persuasive claims of false allegations. A range of "credibility checks" on the victims in sexual offence cases became standard CCRC policy. However, Hoyle and Sato found that the CCRC was not immune to the influence of growing enthusiasm for victim-centred justice.

Police and prosecutors had moved away from viewing complainants' vulnerability, such as a troubled upbringing, promiscuity, evidence of intoxication, or factors relating to the late reporting of a crime, as undermining their credibility. In turn, the Court of Appeal started to distinguish between vulnerability and credibility more clearly as society's focus shifted from a concern about wrongful convictions to wrongful acquittals. Eventually, the CCRC – influenced by the Court's narrowing position on what constitutes credibility – was persuaded to stop relying so heavily on perceptions about complainants' credibility unrelated to sexual abuse (e.g. previous false allegations of *physical* abuse) to discredit them. Hence, in 2017, the CCRC's revised policy on sexual offence cases removed the *requirement* for credibility checks in all such cases, though it remained an option. The criminal justice system has come a long way in improving the treatment of complainants and reducing wrongful acquittals, but today it may be more difficult for those people convicted on the basis of false allegations to find relief from the Court of Appeal (Hoyle & Sato, 2019).

Harms caused by false allegations of abuse: the Oxford Study

It does not take much imagination to appreciate the harms caused to innocent people arrested for child sexual abuse, suspended from their jobs, and sometimes having to defend themselves at trial, when such abuse is repellent to them. Once accused, the wheels of justice can be grindingly slow, and meanwhile they are compelled to live with the identity of a suspected sex offender, with all the stigma that entails. However, there has been little academic research on this matter. A study into the impact of being wrongly accused of abuse (in most cases, against a child) while working in occupations of trust aimed to understand the human costs of false allegations of abuse, exploring the structural, cultural and psychological harms suffered by the participants (Hoyle et al., 2016; Burnett et al., 2017). These 24 men and 6 women had ultimately been cleared and yet every aspect of their lives had been affected, and they had no prospect of restoring what they had lost.

The researchers took a stringent approach to selecting participants, recognizing that some claims to being falsely accused are also false. Those included in the study were current or past members of a long-standing voluntary organization that supports people wrongly accused of abuse in occupational contexts. They had either: not been charged with the alleged abuse for want of sufficient evidence (14 cases); had been charged but acquitted as there was insufficient evidence for a conviction (15 cases); or had their conviction overturned on appeal because of evidence of their innocence (1 case).

Most of the participants who were working at the time of the allegation were not able to return to the same occupations, either because they had lost their jobs while under investigation or because they had lost confidence in returning to the same kind of work. Police and employment records of employees who have been under suspicion and investigated were a barrier against applying for an alternative position to make a fresh start. Participants spoke about the frustration that they were no longer able to exercise their professional skills to help others and the loss of their professional identity. Considerable financial burdens accrued, impacting the financial security of partners and children. Participants lost earnings but also faced burdensome legal fees and reduced pensions from the need to take early retirement. A few lost their homes, and in some cases, their accommodation had been linked to their work.

Their mental and physical health was affected, in the immediate aftermath of being accused and also in the long term. Following the initial shock of being subject to a false allegation, a dominant theme recurrent in participants' accounts was periods of great despair, when they could not function properly. Eight participants reported suicidal thoughts. Most had experienced high anxiety levels, severe depression, ill health and associated symptoms of enduring trauma, and some endured permanent behavioural and personality changes. Partners and children too suffered with anxiety and depression.

The stigma attached to being accused of abuse was a prevalent theme; arising first from actions and comments from others, who judged and excluded them, causing them to feel shame and hurt; and second, from a feeling of being personally stained, even if they had been found unanimously not guilty, or even if they not been charged. While many participants had partners who believed and stood by them, the stigma of a false allegation is felt by the whole family and can lead to long-term resentment or unhappiness within the family, or permanently damaged relationships. Some had to abandon friendships and working relationships spanning decades, resulting in social withdrawal, panic, fear, anxiety and inability to trust others, with the inevitable costs on mental health. Measures taken to prevent the accused from discussing allegations with colleagues made it difficult for them to mount a defence and prevented them from drawing on support from co-workers. Several participants described themselves as resilient, able to fight the allegation knowing they were innocent; others revealed fear and emotional vulnerability, a sense of being worn down by accusations.

For those falsely accused but not prosecuted or convicted, there is no formal exoneration and many feared that some in their communities would remain convinced of their guilt. This made it difficult for them to put the matter behind them and move on with their lives. Hence, a common theme in accounts was that the "old", pre-allegation person had gone, replaced by a "new" individual who was wary and distrustful. A few referred to the experience as a bereavement, with frequent references to part of them having died. Over half described a permanent personality change, referring to their new selves as cynical and untrusting, wary of others' intentions. The majority reported permanent behavioural and personality changes.

Though these participants' cases had been dropped without charge or they had been acquitted during court proceedings, there were clear and irrevocable negative consequences, adversely affecting their health, finances, careers, family relationships and well-being.

Conclusion

The last two decades have seen an exponential growth in awareness of and concerns about the sexual abuse of children and the harms done by not believing their allegations. In accordance with this awareness, socio-legal developments have encouraged timely and unquestioning responses to reports of abuse, with perhaps too little attention to the attendant risks of false accusations, leading to wrongful convictions.

It remains very difficult to secure convictions in reported sexual offences cases that lack forensic evidence. Even with changes in police and prosecution policies and practices, as well as improvements in support for victims in seeking and obtaining justice, victims of child sexual abuse may not get justice for the trauma they have suffered. That said, a likely corollary of some policy shifts – not least, mandatory reporting of suspicions of child sexual abuse, and of inviting people to come forward to report their childhood experiences of abuse (as some lawyers now do) – is the risk that some allegations are untrue, whether knowingly or mistakenly so.

With due regard for those who work to reduce the incidence and harms of child sexual abuse, the research findings discussed above shine a light on the risks of placing too much reliance on either the honesty or the accuracy of complainants' reports of abuse, perhaps especially when adults have provided detailed accounts of children's abuse that have developed from initial and misleading comments by those children; and where adults report abuse in their own childhood in responses to a police operation or formal inquiry into institutional abuse or a class action.

While at present, prosecution guidelines and relevant policy documents specify that false allegations are rare, it may be time to include codes of practice to guard against the risk, and to assimilate such consideration into best practice for the treatment of complainants. Services dealing with victims and survivors of child sexual abuse should facilitate easily accessible mechanisms for complainants to retract false allegations before investigations proceed too far. If only considered from the perspective of police resources wasted on investigating false allegations of child sexual abuse,[11] more attention given to recognizing and deterring false allegations would improve policy and practice for both victims of abuse and innocent suspects.

Notes

1 Section 5(2) of the Criminal Law Act 1967.
2 The National Registry of Exonerations cumulative record is divided into five categories of offences including "child sexual abuse" and "sexual assault". See www.law.umich.edu/special/exoneration/Pages/mission.aspx (figures checked 28 March 2024).
3 In England & Wales, the Criminal Cases Review Commission does not include a similar breakdown.
4 Lynn et al. (2023, p. 726) note that, "In diagnostic terms, dissociative amnesia denotes the inability to recall important autobiographical information that is too extreme to be explained by ordinary forgetting" *Diagnostic and Statistical Manual of Mental Disorders, Fifth Edition* [*DSM-5*], American Psychiatric Association [APA], 2013.
5 The survey did not distinguish between cases of sexual and physical abuse.
6 Individuals who eventually received apologies and compensation from the police, some posthumously.
7 Megan's Law in the US, and Sarah's Law in the UK.
8 The 2002 murder of two schoolgirls by their school caretaker in Soham, Cambridgeshire led to an Inquiry (Bichard, 2004) and the Safeguarding Vulnerable Groups Act 2006. The Act provides a new vetting and barring scheme to replace the existing arrangements for safeguarding children and vulnerable adults from harm, or the risk of harm, by employees and volunteers whose work gives them significant access to these vulnerable groups.
9 Including Rotherham, which led to a government inquiry (Jay, 2014).
10 Complainer anonymity was established by s.1 of the Sexual Offences (Amendment) Act 1992.
11 Operation Midland, for example cost the Metropolitan Police £2.5 million (De Simone, 2016).

References

Ask, K. & Granhag, P. (2007) Hot cognition in investigative judgments: The differential influence of anger and sadness. *Law and Human Behavior*, *31*, 537–551. https://doi.org/10.1007/s10979-006-9075-3

Barden, R. C. (2016) Memory and reliability: developments and controversial issues. In Radcliffe, P., et al. (eds.). *Witness testimony in sexual cases: Evidential, investigative and scientific perspectives.* Oxford: Oxford University Press.

Bernet, W., & Xu, S. (2023). Scholarly rumors: Citation analysis of vast misinformation regarding parental alienation theory. *Behavioral Sciences & the Law*, *41*(5), 231–245. https://doi.org/10.1002/bsl.2605.

Bichard, M (2004) *The Bichard Inquiry report.* HC 653. London: The Stationery Office.

Bruck, M., & Ceci, S.J. (2013). Expert testimony in a child sex abuse case: Translating memory development research. *Memory*, *21*(5), 556–565. https://doi.org/10.1080/09658211.2013.769606

Bücken, C. A., Otgaar, H., London, K., Riesthuis, P., Battista, F., & Mangiulli, I. (2022). "Nothing happened": Legal implications of false denials among abused children. *Child Abuse Review*, *32*(2), e2791. https://doi.org/10.1002/car.2791

Burnett, R. (ed.) (2016) *Wrongful allegations of sexual and child abuse*. Oxford: Oxford University Press.

Burnett, R., Hoyle, C., & Speechley, N.-E. (2017). The context and impact of being wrongly accused of abuse in occupations of trust. *The Howard Journal of Crime and Justice*, *56*(2), 176–197. https://doi.org/10.1111/hojo.12199

Cassidy, R. (2018). Paisley footy coach accused of abusing young players CLEARED after alleged victim admitted lying to get a bigger compo payout. *The Scottish Sun*, 7 February. Retrieved from www.thescottishsun.co.uk/news/scottish-news/2200203/paisley-football-coach-kilmarnock-sheriff-court-abuse-victim-lied-compo

Ceci, S. J., & Bruck, M. (1995). *Jeopardy in the courtroom: A scientific analysis of children's testimony*. American Psychological Association.

Corteen, K., & Steele, R. (2018). A criminal injustice system? Sex offender suspects and defendants. *Liverpool Law Review*, *39*(3), 265–277. https://doi.org/10.1007/s10991-018-9219-9

Crown Prosecution Service. (2013) Guidelines on prosecuting cases of child sexual abuse. Retrieved from www.cps.gov.uk/legal/a_to_c/child_sexual_abuse/

Cruickshank, V. (2019). Male primary teachers' fear and uncertainty surrounding physical contact. *Education 3–13*, *47*(2), 247–257. https://doi.org/10.1080/03004279.2018.1434221

Debey, E., De Schryver, M., Logan, G. D., Suchotzki, K., & Verschuere, B. (2015). From junior to senior Pinocchio: A cross-sectional lifespan investigation of deception. *Acta Psychologica*, *160*, 58–68. https://doi.org/10.1016/j.actpsy.2015.06.007

Denne, E., Stolzenberg, S. N., & Neal, T. M. S. (2021). The effects of evidence-based expert testimony on perceptions of child sexual abuse involving recantation. *PLoS ONE*, 16(8), e0254961. https://doi.org/10.1371/journal.pone.0254961

DePaulo, B. M., Kashy, D. A., Kirkendol, S. E., Wyer, M. M., & Epstein, J. A. (1996). Lying in everyday life. *Journal of Personality and Social Psychology*, *70*(5), 979–995. https://doi.org/10.1037/0022-3514.70.5.979

De Simone, D. (2016). Operation Midland cost £2.5m, says Met Police. Retrieved from www.bbc.co.uk/news/uk-37027144

Dykstra, V. W., Turchio, V. M., Willoughby, T., & Evans, A. D. (2023). Longitudinal associations between impulsivity and lie-telling in childhood and adolescence. *Developmental Science*, *26*, e13370. https://doi.org/10.1111/desc.13370

Faller, K. C., & Everson, M. D. (2012). Contested Issues in the Evaluation of Child Sexual Abuse Allegations: Why Consensus on Best Practice Remains Elusive. *Journal of Child Sexual Abuse*, *21*(1), 3–18. https://doi.org/10.1080/10538712.2012.642944

Ferguson, C. E., & Malouff, J. M. (2016). Assessing police classifications of sexual assault reports: A meta-analysis of false reporting rates. *Archives of Sexual Behavior*, *45*, 1185–1193. https://ssrn.com/abstract=2924906

French, C. C., & Ost, J. (2016). Beliefs about memory, childhood abuse, and hypnosis among clinicians, legal professionals, and the general public. In R. Burnett (ed.), *Wrongful allegations of sexual and child abuse* (pp.143–154). Oxford: Oxford University Press.

French, L., Garry, M., & Loftus, E. (2009) False memories: A kind of confabulation in non-clinical subjects.In W. Hirstein (ed.), *Confabulation: Views from neuroscience, psychiatry, psychology, and philosophy* (pp. 33–66). Oxford: Oxford University Press.

Goodyear-Smith, F. (2016). Why and how false allegations of abuse occur: an overview. In: R. Burnett (ed.), *Wrongful allegations of sexual and child abuse* (pp. 99–117). Oxford: Oxford University Press.

Greenwood, H. (2024). Responding to the danger of wrongful conviction for historical sexual abuse: A case for resurrecting abuse of process for delay? *The International Journal of Evidence & Proof, 0*(0). https://doi.org/10.1177/13657127241237909

Gunn, B. (2013) The compensation carrot and false allegations of abuse. *FACT-ion, 4*(1), 10–12. *www.factuk.org/wp-content/uploads/2013/08/Vol4-1-corrected-100713.pdf*

Hebenton, B., & Seddon, T. (2016). Making accusations: Precautionary logic and embedded suspicion in an insecure and uncertain world. In R. Burnett (ed.), *Wrongful allegations of sexual and child abuse* (pp. 82–95). Oxford: Oxford University Press.

Henriques, R. (2016) *An independent review of the Metropolitan Police Service's handling of non-recent sexual offence investigations against persons of public prominence* (Online redacted report). Retrieved from http://news.met.police.uk/documents/report-independent-review-of-metropolitan-police-services-handling-ofnon-recent-sexual-offence-investigations-61510

Hirtz, A. C., Royer, C. E., Helm, R. K., Burd, K. A., Ojeda, K., & Ceci, S. J. (2015). Children's suggestibility research: Things to know before interviewing a child. *Anuario De Psicología Jurídica, 25*(1), 3–12.

HASC (Home Affairs Select Committee). (2002). The conduct of investigations into past cases of abuse in children's homes: Fourth report of Session 2001–02. Retrieved from https://publications.parliament.uk/pa/cm200102/cmselect/cmhaff/836/83602.htm

HMIC. (2013). Mistakes were made: Her Majesty's Inspector of Constabulary's review into allegations and intelligence material concerning Jimmy Savile between 1964 and 2012. Retrieved from www.justiceinspectorates.gov.uk/hmic/publications/mistakes-were-made/

HMIC. (2014). Crime recording: Making the victim count. Retrieved from www.justiceinspectorates.gov.uk/hmic/wp-content/uploads/crime-recordingmaking-the-victim-count.pdf

Hoyle, C. (2012). Victims, victimisation and criminal justice. In M. Maguire, R. Morgan, & R. Reiner (eds), *The Oxford handbook of criminology* (5th edn.). Oxford University Press.

Hoyle, C., & Sato, M. (2019). *Reasons to doubt: Wrongful convictions and the Criminal Cases Review Commission*. Oxford: Oxford University Press.

Hoyle, C., Speechley, N-E., & Burnett, R. (2016). The impact of being wrongly accused of abuse in occupations of trust: Victims' voices. Retrieved from www.law.ox.ac.uk/sites/files/oxlaw/the_impact_of_being_wrongly_accused_of_abuse_hoyle_speechley_burnett_final_26_may.pdf

IICSA. (2022). The report of the Independent Inquiry into Child Sexual Abuse. Retrieved from www.iicsa.org.uk/reports-recommendations/publications/inquiry/final-report.html

International Association of Chiefs of Police. (2005), *Investigating sexual assaults, concepts and issues paper*. Retrieved from www.enforcerapelaws.org/wp-content/uploads/2015/07/investigatingsexualassaultsconceptsissues.pdf

Jay, A. (2014). *Independent Inquiry into Child Sexual Exploitation in Rotherham (1997–2013)*. Rotherham: Rotherham Metropolitan Borough Council. Retrieved from www.rotherham.gov.uk/downloads/file/279/independent-inquiry-into-child-sexual-exploitation-in-rotherham

Jensen, G., & Jensen. I. (2011). *Presumed guilty: The plight of falsely accused and wrongly convicted carers and teachers*. FACT Briefing Document. Falsely Accused Carers and Teachers.

Korkman, J., Antfolk, J., Fagerlund, M., & Santtila, P. (2019). The prevalence of unfounded suspicions of child sexual abuse in Finland. *Nordic Psychology*, *71*(1), 39–50. https://doi.org/10.1080/19012276.2018.1470554

Korkman, J., Juusola. A., & Santtila, P. (2014). Who made the disclosure? Recorded discussions between children and caretakers suspecting child abuse. *Psychology, Crime & Law*, *20*(10), 994–1004. https://doi.org/10.1080/19012276.2018.1470554

Korkman, J., Otgaar, H., Geven, L.M., Bull, R., Cyr, M., Hershkowitz, I., Mäkelä, J.M., Mattison, M., Milne, R., Santtila, P., & van Koppen, P. (2024). White paper on forensic child interviewing: research-based recommendations by the European Association of Psychology and Law. *Psychology, Crime & Law*, 1–44. https://doi.org/10.1080/1068316X.2024.2324098

La Fontaine, J. S. (1994). *The extent and nature of organised and ritual abuse*. HMSO: London.

Lamb, M. E., Sternberg, K.J., and Esplin, P.W. (1994) Factors influencing the reliability and validity of statements made by young victim of sexual maltreatment. *Journal of Applied Developmental Psychology*, *15*(2), 255–280. https://doi.org/10.1016/0193-3973(94)90016-7

Lamb, M. E., Sternberg, K. J., Esplin, P. W., Hershkowitz, I., & Orbach, Y. (1997). Assessing the credibility of children's allegations of sexual abuse: A survey of recent research. *Learning and Individual Differences*, *9*(2) 175–194.

Lamb, M. E., Orbach, Y., Hershkowitz, I., Esplin, P. W., & Horowitz, D. (2007). Structured forensic interview protocols improve the quality and informativeness of investigative interviews with children: A review of research using the NICHD investigative interview protocol. *Child Abuse and Neglect*, *31*(11–12), 1201–1231. https://doi.org/10.1016/j.chiabu.2007.03.021

Leander, E. M., Pallesgaard Munk, K., & Lindsø Larsen, P., 2019. Guidelines for preventing child sexual abuse and wrongful allegations against staff at Danish childcare facilities. *Societies*, *9*(2), 42. https://doi.org/10.3390/soc9020042

Levine, T., Serota, K., Carey, F., & Messer, D. (2013). Teenagers lie a lot: A further investigation into the prevalence of lying. *Communication Research Reports*, 30(3), 211–220. https://doi.org/10.1080/08824096.2013.806254

Levitt, A. (2013) *Charging perverting the course of justice and wasting police time in cases involving allegedly false rape and domestic violence allegations.* London: Crown Prosecution Service. Retrieved from www.cps.gov.uk/sites/default/files/documents/legal_guidance/perverting-course-of-justice-march-2013.pdf

Loftus, E. F., & Klemfuss, J. Z. (2024). Misinformation – past, present, and future. *Psychology, Crime & Law.* Advance online publication. https://doi.org/10.1080/1068316X.2023.2219813

London, K., Bruck, M., Wright, D. B., & Ceci, S. J. (2008). Review of the contemporary literature on how children report sexual abuse to others: Findings, methodological issues, and implications for forensic interviewers. *Memory, 16*, 29–47. https://doi.org/10.1080/09658210701725732

Lonsway, K. A., & Fitzgerald, L. F. (1994). Rape myths: In review. *Psychology of Women Quarterly, 18*, 133–164. https://doi.org/10.1111/j.1471-6402.1994.tb00448

Lynn, S. J., McNally, R. J. & Loftus, E. F. (2023). The memory wars then and now: The contributions of Scott O. Lilienfeld. *Clinical Psychological Science, 11*(4), 725–743. https://doi.org/10.1177/21677026221133034

Lyon, T. D., Williams, S. & Stolzenberg, S. N. (2020). Understanding expert testimony on child sexual abuse denial after New Jersey v. JLG: Ground truth, disclosure suspicion bias, and disclosure substantiation bias. *Behavioral Sciences & the Law, 38*(6), 630–647. https://doi.org/10.1002/bsl.2490

MacFarlane, B. A. & Cordner, S. M. (2008). *Wrongful convictions: The effect of tunnel vision and predisposing circumstances in the criminal justice system.* Toronto: Government of Ontario.

Malloy, L. C. & Mugno, A. P., 2016. Children's recantation of adult wrongdoing: An experimental investigation. *Journal of Experimental Child Psychology, 145*, 11–21. https://doi.org/10.1016/j.jecp.2015.12.003

Malouff, J. M & Schutte, N. S. (2021) False recantations by adults of sexual assault allegations. Retrieved from https://blog.une.edu.au/usingpsychology/2021/01/19/false-recantations-by-adults-of-sexual-assault-allegations/

McGlynn, C. (2017). Rape trials and sexual history evidence: Reforming the law on third-party evidence. *The Journal of Criminal Law, 81*(5), 367–392. https://doi.org/10.1177/00220183177288

Migliavaca, C. B., Stein, C., Colpani, V., Munn, Z., & Falavigna, M., 2020. Quality assessment of prevalence studies: a systematic review. *Journal of Clinical Epidemiology, 127*, 59–68. https://doi.org/10.1016/j.jclinepi.2020.06.039

Ministry of Justice. (2024). Code of practice for victims of crime in England and Wales (Victims Code). Updated 10 June 2024. Retrieved from www.gov.uk/government/publications/the-code-of-practice-for-victims-of-crime/code-of-practice-for-victims-of-crime-in-england-and-wales-victims-code

Nankivell, T., & Papadimitriou, J. (2023) True or false, or somewhere between? Reviewing the high-quality studies on the prevalence of false sexual assault reports. Gander Research paper, May 2023. Retrieved from https://ganderresearch.org/wp-content/uploads/2023/08/GANDER-Prevalence-Studies-research-paper-4-April-23.pdf

Niehaus, S., & Krause, A., 2023. Threats to scientifically based standards in sex offense proceedings: Progress and the interests of alleged victims in jeopardy. *Monatsschrift für Kriminologie und Strafrechtsreform, 106*(3), 165–183. https://doi.org/10.1515/mks-2023-0018

O'Donohue, W. T., & Cirlugea, O. (2021). Controlling for confirmation bias in child sexual abuse interviews. *The Journal of the American Academy of Psychiatry and the Law*, 49(3), 371–380. doi: 10.29158/JAAPL.200109-20.

O'Donohue, W. T., Cirlugea, O., Bennett, N., & Benuto, L. T. (2016). Psychological and investigative pathways to untrue allegations of child sexual abuse. In W. T. O'Donohue & M. Fanetti (eds), *Forensic interviews regarding child sexual abuse* (pp. 257–273). Springer International Publishing.

O'Donohue, W. T., Cummings, C., & Willis, B. (2018). The frequency of false allegations of child sexual abuse: A critical review. *Journal of Child Sexual Abuse, 27*(5), 459–475. https://doi.org/10.1080/10538712.2018.1477224

Ost, J. (2017) Adults' retractions of childhood sexual abuse allegations: high-stakes and the (in)validation of recollection, *Memory, 25*(7), 900–909. https://doi.org/10.1080/09658211.2016.1187757

Otgaar, H., Howe, M. L., & Patihis, L., 2022. What science tells us about false and repressed memories. *Memory, 30*(1), 16–21. https://doi.org/10.1080/09658211.2020.1870699

Patihis, L., Otgaar, H., Lynn, S. J., Loftus, E. F. and McNally, R. J. (2023). The recovered memory debate: Wins, losses, and creating future open-minded skeptics. In *Toward a science of clinical psychology: A tribute to the life and works of Scott O. Lilienfeld* (pp. 377–394). Cham: Springer International Publishing.

Peace, K. A., Porter, S., & Almon, D. F. (2012). Side-tracked by emotion: Observers' ability to discriminate genuine and fabricated sexual assault allegations. *Legal and Criminological Psychology, 17*(2), 322–335. https://doi.org/10.1111/j.2044-8333.2011.02013.x

Pendergrast, M. (2017). *Memory warp: How the myth of repressed memory arose and refuses to die.* Vermont: Upper Access.

Petherick, W. A. (2020). Recantations and retractions in child sexual abuse. In I. Bryce, & W. Petherick (eds), *Child sexual abuse: Forensic issues in evidence, impact, and management* (pp. 435–443). Academic Press. https://doi.org/10.1016/B978-0-12-819434-8.00021-0

Principe, G. F., & Ceci, S. J. (2002). "I saw it with my own ears": The influence of peer conversations and suggestive questions on preschoolers' event memory. *Journal of Experimental Child Psychology, 83*(1), 1–25. https://doi.org/10.1016/S0022-0965(02)00120-0

Principe, G. F., & London, K. (2022). How parents can shape what children remember: Implications for the testimony of young witnesses. *Journal of Applied Research in Memory and Cognition, 11*(3), 289–302. https://doi.org/10.1037/mac0000059

Radcliffe, P., Gudjonnsson, G., Heaton-Armstrong, A., & Wolchover, D. (2016) *Witness testimony in sexual cases: Evidential, investigative and scientific perspectives.* Oxford: Oxford University Press.

Radcliffe, P. J. & Patihis, L. (2024). Judges and lawyers' beliefs in repression and dissociative amnesia may imperil justice: further guidance required. *Memory*, *32*(8), 1083–1099. https://doi.org/10.1080/09658211.2024.2383311

Rawlinson, K. (2015). One in five school staff victims of false claims, survey shows. *The Guardian*, 30 March. Retrieved from www.theguardian.com/education/2015/mar/30/one-in-five-school-staff-victims-of-false-claims-survey-shows

Rose, D. (2016). To catch a sex offender: police, trawls and personal injury solicitors. In R. Burnett (ed.), *Wrongful allegations of sexual and child abuse* (pp. 155–171). Oxford: Oxford University Press.

Rossmo, D., & Pollock, J. (2019). Confirmation bias and other systemic causes of wrongful convictions: A sentinel events perspective. *North Eastern University Law Review*, *11*(2), 790–835. http://dx.doi.org/10.2139/ssrn.3413922

Rumney, P. N. (2006). False allegations of rape. *The Cambridge Law Journal*, *65*(1), 128–158. https://doi.org/10.1017/S0008197306007069

Rumney, P. N., & McCartan, K. F. (2017). Purported false allegations of rape, child abuse and non-sexual violence: Nature, characteristics and implications. *The Journal of Criminal Law*, *81*(6), 497–520. https://doi.org/10.1177/00220183177467

Saini, M., Laajasalo, T., & Platt, S. (2020). Gatekeeping by allegations: An examination of verified, unfounded, and fabricated allegations of child maltreatment within the context of resist and refusal dynamics. *Family Court Review*, *58*(2), 417–431. https://doi.org/10.1111/fcre.12480

Saunders, C. L. (2012). The truth, the half-truth, and nothing like the truth: Reconceptualizing false allegations of rape. *British Journal of Criminology*, *52*(6), 1152–1171. www.jstor.org/stable/i40174394

Savage, R. (2024). Church of England "directly responsible" for John Smyth abuse in Zimbabwe, victim says. *The Guardian*, 16 November. Retrieved from www.theguardian.com/world/2024/nov/16/church-of-england-directly-responsible-for-john-smyth-abuse-in-zimbabwe-victim-says

Shah, H. A. (2020). The current prevalence of child sexual abuse worldwide: A systematic review and meta-analysis. *Competitive Social Science Research Journal*, *1*(3), 37–51. https://cssrjournal.com/index.php/cssrjournal/article/view/29/20

Shaw, J. and Vredeveldt, A., 2019. The recovered memory debate continues in Europe: Evidence from the United Kingdom, the Netherlands, France, and Germany. *Clinical Psychological Science*, *7*(1), 27–28. https://doi.org/10.1177/2167702618803649

Sikes, P. and Piper, H., 2009. *Researching sex and lies in the classroom: Allegations of sexual misconduct in schools*. London: Routledge.

Smith, M. (2016a) Telling stories? Adults' retrospective narratives of abuse in residential child case. In Burnett, R. (ed.) *Wrongful allegations of sexual and child abuse* (pp. 34–65). Oxford University Press.

Smith, D.J. (2016b). *The Jimmy Savile investigation report*. London: BBC.

Speechley, N. E., & Burnett, R. (2022) The plausibility of being wrongly convicted for a sexual offence: accounts from former prisoners. *Wrongful Convictions Law Review*, *3*(1), 1–33. https://doi.org/10.29173/wclawr59

Stoltenborgh, M., van IJzendoorn, M. H., Euser, E. M., & Bakermans-Kranenburg, M. J. (2011). A global perspective on child sexual abuse: Meta-analysis of prevalence around the world. *Child Maltreatment*, *16*, 79–101. https://doi.org/10.1177/1077559511140392

Suarez, E., & Gadalla, T. M. (2010). Stop blaming the victim: A meta-analysis on rape myths. *Journal of Interpersonal Violence*, *25*, 2010–2035. https://doi.org/10.1177/0886260509354

Turvey, B. E., Savino, J. O., & Mares, A. C. (2018) *False allegations: Investigative and forensic issues in fraudulent reports*. London: Academic Press.

Warshak, R. A., 2006. Social science and parental alienation: Examining the disputes and the evidence. In R. A. Gardner; R. S. Sauber, & D. Lorandos (eds), *The international handbook of parental alienation syndrome: conceptual, clinical and legal considerations* (pp. 352–371). Springfield, IL: Charles C Thomas.

Waterhouse, R. (2000) *Lost in care*. London: HMSO.

Webster, R. (1998) *The great children's home panic*. Oxford: Orwell Press.

Webster, R. (2005) *The secret of Bryn Estyn: The making of a modern witch hunt*. Oxford: Orwell Press.

Zhang, Y., Segal, A., Pompedda, F., Haginoya, S., & Santtila, P. (2022). Confirmation bias in simulated CSA interviews: How abuse assumption influences interviewing and decision-making processes? *Legal and Criminological Psychology*, *27*(2), 314–328. https://doi.org/10.1111/lcrp.12213

7

Disclosures and forensic interviews in the context of online child sexual abuse

Julia Korkman and Malin Joleby

Online child sexual abuse on the rise

Child sexual abuse (CSA) can be defined as follows:

> [T]he involvement of a child in sexual activity that he or she does not fully comprehend, is unable to give informed consent to, or for which the child is not developmentally prepared and cannot give consent, or that violates the laws or social taboos of society.
>
> (WHO, 1999, p. 15)

Online CSA does not refer to a completely new or different concept but is used widely when CSA involves "the use of information and communication technology as a means to sexually abuse children" (Greijer & Doek, 2016) and can be committed partly or completely through digital means (Hamilton-Giachritsis et al., 2020). Online CSA is thus a broad concept that can include a range of different acts, both directly and indirectly involving children.

Online CSA directly involving children includes grooming (e.g. Whittle et al., 2013), which is defined as "a process by which a person prepares a child, significant adults, and the environment for the abuse of this child" (Craven, Brown, & Gilchrist, 2006, p. 297), and involves using manipulative strategies to build trust, gain the child's compliance, and maintain secrecy to avoid disclosure. By using digital means for communication, an online perpetrator can incite children to engage in sexual activities such as *sexting*, defined as "sending/receiving/forwarding sexual images or sexual texts via cell phone and other electronic devices" (Klettke, Hallford & Mellor, 2014; Ligiero et al., 2019), or subject them to *sextortion*, defined as using threats to disseminate sexual or intimate images or other material without consent, typically with the aim of forcing the victim to produce additional sexual material (Greijer & Doek, 2016; Patchin & Hinduja, 2018) or engage in different sexual acts. Such acts can range from semi-nude

DOI: 10.4324/9781003427155-7

posing to painful penetration or involving siblings or pets in sexual activity (Joleby et al., 2021a). Both sexting and sextortion can, however, also involve only adults, and an umbrella term that is thus increasingly used when referring to the type of online abuse directly involving children is technology-assisted child sexual abuse (TA-CSA), which broadly encompasses child sexual abuse carried out via technology (Hamilton-Giachritsis et al., 2020). Additionally, digital technology can be used to organize sex trafficking of children (Gezinski & Gonzalez-Pons, 2024), or live-stream sexual abuse (Drejer et al., 2024), sometimes for an international audience of paying perpetrators directing the abuse.

More indirect forms of online CSA include the use and dissemination of child sexual abuse material (CSAM), which has increased drastically with the digital surge, especially on encrypted and anonymous Darknet forums where individuals with a sexual interest in children communicate and share CSAM (e.g. Huikuri & Insoll, 2022). CSAM can include everything from innocent pictures of children playing on the beach being misused for sexual purposes, covertly taken photos, self-produced images by young people, or documentation of severe sexual abuse that has occurred either online or offline (e.g. Quayle et al., 2018). A new trend resulting from AI technology is digitally generated CSAM either depicting entirely fictional children or sexually explicit images produced featuring real children (Krishna et al., 2024). In sum, CSA as a phenomenon is much older than the internet, but the online world facilitates and shapes the ways CSA is nowadays conducted (Quayle & Koukopoulos, 2019). This, in turn, might have implications for how children disclose online CSA.

Over the past decade, there has been a drastic increase in police reports regarding online CSA (e.g. Europol, 2023), reaching record highs in recent years. In Sweden, for example, there was a ten-fold increase in the number of police reports of online sexual exploitation of children during the course of ten years (World Childhood Foundation, 2022). A Finnish study (Hietajärvi, 2023) reported that almost 60% of the sex crimes against children reported to the police in 2022 had taken place partly or completely online. Cullen et al. (2020, p. 1) noted that creating and distributing CSAM is "one of the fastest growing illicit online industries in the United States". The US National Center for Missing and Exploited Children (NCMEC) has received over 100 million reports since the inception of CyberTipline in 1998, with the number of reports growing every year. In 2023 alone, they received more than 36 million reports (NCMEC, 2024).

A first global index based on data from 125 studies with representative samples from 57 countries indicated that around 1 in 8 children globally had been victims of different forms of online CSA in the past year (Childlight, 2024). This index included non-consensual taking, sharing, and exposure to sexual images and videos, non-consensual sexting, unwanted sexual questions, and unwanted sexual act requests. In the described data, however, it is not clear whether the child responded to the unwanted sexual questions or participated in the requested sexual acts, as many young people have successful strategies for warding off unwanted sexual requests (Lunde & Joleby, 2022). For example, a Spanish study on 2731 minors (aged 12–15, 51% females), found that 13% had received sexual solicitations, whereas 8% had actually engaged in sexual interactions (de Santisteban & Gámez-Guadix, 2018). The most common sexual interactions were maintaining a flirtatious relationship with an adult (4%), talking about sexual things (4%), and meeting the adult offline (4%), sending photos or videos of sexual content of themselves (1%), or meeting the adult offline with the expressed intention to have sexual contact (1%). A US study focusing on different forms of online CSA against children (Finkelhor et al., 2022) found that in a sample of 2639 individuals, 23% had experienced online solicitation, 10% had experienced threats or pressure to provide sexual images (regardless of whether they complied), 9% had engaged in sexual conversations or sharing sexual pictures/videos with a person 5+ years older voluntarily or involuntarily, 5% had experienced nonconsensual image sharing, 2% nonconsensual image taking, and around 1% online commercial exploitation. Evidently, online CSA encompasses a wide range of situations and incidents, and even though the most severe cases are the least common, they collectively result in a significant number of children worldwide being subjected to such crimes.

Initial research indicates that children falling victim to online CSA may face severe psychological consequences, such as feelings of embarrassment, shame, and self-blame, depression, post-traumatic stress disorder, self-harming, suicidal behaviour, disgust, hostility, trust deficits, panic attacks, and impaired relationships (Chauviré-Geib & Fegert, 2023; Finkelhor et al., 2023; Joleby et al., 2021a; Stänicke et al., 2024). There is a clear overlap between these consequences and symptoms observed in victims of offline abuse, and some studies have demonstrated that the emotional, psychological, and behavioural outcomes appear to be similar for online and offline abuse (Hamilton-Giachritsis et al., 2020, 2021; Jonsson et al., 2019). The impact of online CSA may, however, be accentuated by the existence of images or videos of the sexual acts, as fear of the perpetrator still having footage of the abuse, the risk that pictures will be circulated, or concern about being publicly recognized from the images can be an additional source of distress and anxiety (e.g. Jonsson et al., 2019; Schmidt et al., 2023; Stänicke et al., 2024).

Disclosure, delay, and denial of online child sexual abuse

While online CSA is fundamentally a form of CSA, it involves distinct characteristics that set it apart from offline CSA. It is important to consider how these differences might affect disclosure, delay, and denial. While the research on disclosure specifically for victims of online CSA is scarce, instances of such abuse frequently come to light through police investigations (Katz et al., 2021), or through one initial police report unveiling numerous additional victims, sometimes numbering in the tens or even over a hundred (B 1602–15, Borås District Court), who have all been victimized by the same perpetrator without reporting it. This strongly indicates that much like victims of offline CSA, children who experience online CSA face significant obstacles to disclosing their experiences (see, for instance, Katz et al., 2021; Save the Children, 2021). Research on online CSA disclosures remains scarce, but several qualitative studies offer valuable insights into factors likely to affect the disclosure process.

One study (Joleby et al., 2024) conducted in-depth interviews with seven young women (aged 17–24) with experiences of online CSA that started between ages 7 and 13. Only one of them had disclosed (to health care staff) while the abuse was ongoing, albeit after six years of ongoing abuse. Although the participants expressed a strong desire to have someone to share their experiences with, most delayed disclosing for several years, a few had never disclosed until the research interview, and none had self-disclosed to parents or the police although three had been contacted by the police and disclosed upon confrontation.

A second study (Katz et al., 2021) analysed 52 cases of probable online CSA (children aged 11–17). Only in three of these cases did a child disclose, the rest were revealed by a police investigation ($N = 31$), by a family member ($N = 13$), or by a peer ($N = 5$). The study revealed not only that it is uncommon for children to voluntarily disclose their experiences of online CSA, but also highlighted the challenges involved in recounting these experiences, even when prompted. Remarkably, twenty of the children initially refused to disclose anything, were reluctant to collaborate, or denied or concealed parts of their experiences, even when confronted with external evidence such as photographs and documentation of conversations.

That it is difficult to talk about CSA is well-known, as victims often experience intense feelings of shame, guilt, and fear (see Chapters 2 and 3). Disclosure is a multifaceted and complex process (McElvaney, 2015) wherein fragments of the experiences are gradually revealed and the response significantly affects the individual's comfort in fully disclosing (McElvaney & Culhane, 2017). As such, disclosure pertains not only to whether or not the child chooses to disclose but also to which and how many details of the abuse they share. A third study (Leander et al., 2008) of 68 young girls (aged 11–19), who were sexually abused both online and offline by the same perpetrator, compared forensic evidence in the form of chat logs with what the victims disclosed during forensic interviews. Victims generally disclosed most offline events, including sexual acts, but omitted or denied many online activities. They disclosed less about severe online acts (e.g. sending nude photos, webcam stripping) than less severe ones (e.g. sharing personal information or facial photographs, discussing meeting or sex). Specifically, 51% of the severe acts were omitted/denied compared to 28% of the less severe acts. Consistent with Katz et al. (2021), some victims denied documented online sexual acts, claiming "that's not me, it has to be a lookalike" upon confrontation with the documentation (Leander et al., 2008, p.1270). Knowing that children in general remember traumatic or stressful events (Lamb et al., 2018; Baugerud & Melinder, 2012), it is likely that psychosocial factors rather than vague memories affected their reporting.

Why it is difficult to disclose online child sexual abuse

In the study by Katz and colleagues (2021), social workers described the children as experiencing shame, guilt, and sadness. One reason given for the children's reluctance to disclose was their fear that the perpetrator would become angry and disseminate intimate images, videos, or conversations, or that their parents would become upset. The digital nature of the abuse, where the perpetrator is not physically present, requires the child's active participation in the acts (such as performing the penetration, recording the video, sending the image etc.), which can exacerbate feelings of responsibility, embarrassment, shame, and insecurities about the choices they had made (Schmidt et al., 2023). Victims of online CSA can feel responsible for the abuse and disgusted by their own active involvement (Joleby et al., 2020). A meta-synthesis summarizing 16 qualitative studies of online CSA (Stänicke et al., 2024) specifically identified self-blame as a predominant issue. Victims may fear that others will not understand the manipulation and therefore assume that they participated voluntarily, and blame them (Chauviré-Geib & Fegert, 2023). Studies have found that victims may never have heard of online CSA prior to their own victimization, and as their experiences lacked stereotypical elements of abuse, such as physical contact with the perpetrator, they did not initially recognize it as abuse and doubted that others would understand their experiences (Joleby et al., 2024; Schmidt et al., 2023). Moreover, the existence of digital evidence poses a risk of intensifying social shame upon disclosure (Stänicke et al., 2024), rendering it even more challenging to disclose. Additionally, the (perceived or actual) limited technological knowledge on the part of adult recipients of potential disclosures may contribute to the fear of not being understood (Gemara et al., 2023). This all taken together indicates that there are additional complexities at play when it comes to disclosing experiences of online CSA.

Another important aspect to consider in understanding the difficulty of disclosing is how the child fell victim to the abuse. Digital technology allows for constant contact with children regardless of their location, and perpetrators can deceive by fabricating identities, posing as peers, or, for instance, claiming affiliation with a modelling agency (Leander et al., 2008; Wolak & Finkelhor, 2016). Research has demonstrated that perpetrators are adept at manipulating their victims, employing grooming-like tactics involving flattery, expressions of love, feigning friendship, or in different ways exploiting the child's curiosity and desire to feel appreciated (Joleby et al., 2020, 2021b; Whittle et al., 2014). Some victims perceive the perpetrator as their boyfriend. For many victims, the abuse thus occurs within the context of natural sexual exploration. This in itself is typical of adolescence, but which youth might feel uncomfortable talking about, in particular with adults. In today's contemporary society, digital technology offers youth a new platform for such exploration, and the internet plays a notable role in many young people's sexual education, perception of sexuality, and development of intimacy and sexuality (e.g. Lykens et al., 2019; Razi et al., 2020). For instance, sharing sexually explicit images, videos, or messages is becoming a more widespread practice among youth (with 1 in 5 youth sending sexts, and 1 in 3 receiving sexts; Mori et al., 2022), and this can be exploited by adult perpetrators. In some cases, the young person understands the sexual intentions of the adult perpetrator and is willing to go along with them (Katz et al., 2021). However an engagement that initially made them feel valued and "seen" can gradually lead to feeling lured, tricked, or caught up in activities over which they have lost control (Stänicke et al., 2024). In such cases, feelings of shame and the perception that adults don't understand their digital world or sexual curiosity (Gemara et al., 2023), combined with a fear of being judged as reckless (Joleby et al., 2024), or losing privileges such as access to their phone (Gemara et al., 2022; Livingstone & Smith, 2014), might hinder them from disclosing. Furthermore, as many perpetrators develop a close and intimate bond with their victims, the victim often experiences conflicting feelings and dependency (Stänicke et al., 2024), which can be expressed as a desire to protect or please the perpetrator in order not to lose the relationship (e.g. Whittle et al., 2014). In other cases, the online perpetrators lie about their identity and pose as peers (Joleby et al., 2020), and the victims may not understand that they are being exploited and simply refrain from disclosing as they wish to keep their sexual exploration a secret.

For other victims, it is not a matter of sexual curiosity but rather their naivety and youth being exploited. A comprehensive review of all court cases in Sweden spanning one year uncovered that nearly one-tenth of victims were aged 7–9 years (Joleby et al., 2021a), and almost half of the self-generated sexual images reported to the ECPAT hotline depicted prepubescent children (ECPAT, 2020). Young children have less developed cognitive and problem-solving skills, and less sexual knowledge than older adolescents. This might render them more vulnerable to unwanted online exposure and solicitation (Ey & Cupit, 2011) as they might be incited to engage in acts they do not understand, such as pulling up their shirt or pulling down their pants, without consciously performing sexual posing (ECPAT, 2020). Another particularly vulnerable group is youth belonging to a sexual minority, who may face additional barriers to disclosing their experiences (e.g. see Kanefsky et al., 2024) as they may worry about their parents finding out about their sexual identity.

Digital technology has also created the opportunity for perpetrators to employ strategies different from those seen in traditional offline CSA. In addition to grooming, which is described as a slow process in which the perpetrator gradually gains the child's compliance and prepares the child for abuse (Craven et al., 2006), online perpetrators can adopt very aggressive approaches involving threats, promises of payment, or blackmail (Chiang & Grant, 2018; Kloess et al., 2019; Seymour-Smith & Kloess, 2021). Offline perpetrators have limited access to potential victims and must be cautious to avoid scaring them away. In contrast, online perpetrators can contact numerous children regardless of location, making it unnecessary to build trust. If a threatening strategy fails with one child, they can easily move on to others. This new approach, without initial grooming processes, results in a rapid progression from first contact to abuse - not uncommonly within the first initial contact (World Childhood Foundation, 2022). The threats may involve spreading rumours or images of the child, threatening to harm or kill their friends and family, or committing self-harm if sexual content is not provided. The child victim may believe that they have no other choice but to perform the sexual acts demanded. These threats may make the victim reluctant to defy the perpetrator's orders, and thus afraid to disclose (Katz et al., 2021). The perpetrators' significant control over the children becomes evident in the following quotes provided by affected children.

A 15-year-old girl who was forced to perform humiliating and painful sexual acts on herself described the perpetrator's power: "It's like I'm a puppet with strings that he just controls and makes me do things" (Wadbäck & Mehr, 2019). A 13-year-old girl who was frightened after having been coerced into engaging in sexual acts for three days said: "I am afraid of what you are going to make me do next time" and "Basically you are raping me" (Joleby et al., 2021a, p. 12).

Lastly, a phenomenon that has recently gained attention is how digital technology has created a new form of child sexual exploitation. Instead of seeking sexual images of children for their own gratification, perpetrators – often linked to organized crime – exploit this as a means of making money (ECPAT, 2023). They pose as a peer – often a young girl – and persuade the youth – often a young boy – to send sexual images. They then demand payment under the threat of spreading the images, often under severe time pressure. Since girls are typically the most common victims of sexual offences, the victimization of boys risks being overlooked (see Hietamäki et al., 2024). And due to the strong norm that boys are expected to be in control, victimized boys may be perceived as "unmanly" (ECPAT, 2023), creating barriers for them to disclose their experiences.

In sum, several potential factors in online CSA may affect the child's willingness to disclose. Professionals encountering these children need to understand this to increase the chances of disclosure. Stänicke et al. (2024) put forward the importance for professionals to openly and nonjudgmentally address online CSA, recognizing that it "can be related to exploration of relationship, intimacy, and sexuality" (p. 15), understanding the positive aspects that may accompany these relationships (such as feeling validated and supported), and how difficult it can be to end the relationship. Based on interviews with victims about the disclosure process of online CSA, Joleby et al. (2024) recommend fostering open dialogue on sensitive topics such as sexuality and abuse, providing children with an opportunity to tell, allowing them to be in control of the story and who learns about it, and helping to alleviate feelings of shame and blame. These facilitating factors are crucial for society and the adult world to be mindful of, and they are particularly important when exploring the experiences of child victims in the context of investigative interviews.

Encountering and interviewing children when investigating online child sexual abuse

The rapid advancement of digital technology and new methods of CSA present significant challenges for the judicial system and the police (Leclerc et al., 2022). These include heavy workloads (Wright et al., 2006), resource constraints, and a lack of standardized investigative procedures (Franqueira et al., 2018). Legal uncertainties arise as laws struggle to keep pace with online technologies (Cullen et al., 2020), certain online sexual offences have not yet been criminalized (Dushi, 2019), and the transnational nature of online CSA necessitates harmonizing legal frameworks (Witting, 2021). There is some evidence of significant room for improvement in recognizing and investigating online CSA by law enforcement officials, as well as a need for specialization (Hietajärvi, 2023; Leclerc et al., 2022).

Furthermore, cases of suspected online CSA often differ in important ways from those without online or digital elements, leading to a need for law enforcement agencies to adapt their investigation techniques accordingly. First, in offline cases, evidence of the abuse – other than the child's account – is often sparse (e.g. Herman, 2005), and the child interview is often the only or at least the main source of information in the case. In online CSA, on the other hand, there is more often evidence of the abuse in the form of images, videos, or chat logs. If there is clear evidence that a certain child has been abused by a certain adult, the child's testimony may not be as crucial to the criminal justice process or the child's future safety as in cases with no so-called "ground truth" (see Gemara et al., 2022).

Second, victims of online CSA may not be aware that they have been victimized, nor consider themselves to be victims of abuse (e.g. when the perpetrator has lied about his identity or when the child perceived the perpetrator as a romantic partner). While this may be true also for some offline cases, the perpetrators have ample opportunity to fake their identity in the online setting. Furthermore, children may be unaware that the abuse has been recorded and thus, the realization that the police have material depicting them nude and/or performing sexual activities can come as a shock to them (Joleby et al., 2020).

Another reason for specific guidance for investigative interviews in cases of suspected online CSA is the lack of insight into both the technicalities of online CSA and normative online behaviour of children and youth. The applications, games, and different online environments used by children, and thus also by perpetrators, change rapidly, and adult practitioners struggle to stay updated. In terms of judicial information, this implies that many crucial questions may remain unposed simply because the investigators lack the knowledge necessary to pose the right questions. A recent report (Mäenpää et al., 2022), published as part of a project focusing on ensuring child-friendly justice in Finland and financed by the Council of Europe, found that one of the core themes professionals investigating suspected crimes against children needed training in, was investigating online crimes against children. The police and other practitioners (forensic psychologists conducting investigations) noted that there was a lack of understanding about ICT (information and communications technology), social media, and investigating online crimes against children in general (Mäenpää et al., 2022).

Furthermore, as many cases of online CSA come to light through a police investigation rather than a disclosure (Katz et al., 2021), children may struggle to remember (particularly in less severe cases) if a lot of time has passed since the incident. Consequently, it might not be apparent to the child what the interviewer is referring to if the interviewer does not explain the context of the investigation to the child. Current interviewing guidelines may thus need to be specifically updated for the context of online CSA.

Practitioners have stressed the difficulty of confronting young victims with the reality that sexual material depicting them exists, especially when this information is only revealed at the police station. They stress the necessity of finding victim-sensitive approaches to providing this information. This notion echoes the experiences described by some victims. One girl, who at age 12 had engaged in sexual activities with someone whom she thought was a peer, described the sexual experience in positive terms ("It was super exciting! … but also … top secret"; Joleby et al., 2020, p. 5) and said that in the years following the experience she never really thought about it. A few years later, she was contacted by the police and learned that not only was this boy in fact an adult man who had sexually abused thirty other girls, the police also had a sexual video of her and all chat conversations from their contact. She described that "it was three to four years of pure shame about myself" (Joleby et al., 2020, p. 8), and that she "hadn't been genuinely happy for a long period since before the whole police interrogation thing" (Joleby et al., 2020, p. 7). Another girl described how she was affected by the first phone call from the police in which she was informed that they had found a picture of her on a suspect's computer:

> And I was like "Okay what kind of pictures?" And they were like "I think you know what kind of pictures," and I was like "Well okay yes I know." And then the world fell apart, I was extremely sad, I panicked.
>
> (Joleby et al., 2020, p. 8)

Other studies have found that if interviewers fail to confront young victims with evidence of their abuse in a sensitive and informed way, this can have a negative impact on the child's statement and indeed also on their well-being (Gemara et al., 2022; Katz, 2013). Consequently, not only does such "harsh" confrontation risk decreasing the quality of the investigative interview and the information provided, but it may also (re)traumatize the young victim.

In cases where the perpetrator has pretended to be a peer, it may only be during the criminal justice process that the victim discovers they have been deceived and that the person in fact was an adult (Gemara et al., 2022). A girl with previous experience of having been deceived online by an adult man posing as a peer described how, at age 14, to avoid it happening again, she took extra precautions by demanding a photo and address from the person she was communicating with. Nevertheless, the "same-age girl" that she had an online romantic and sexual relationship with for two years once again turned out to be an adult man. She blamed herself:

> I felt that *I* was so very stupid for having done this, like how can you trust someone you don't actually know whether you know? … I felt so very mad at myself for doing it, and often felt that if something happens now, it's still my fault to some extent. I've contributed to it, erm, so I guess I only have myself to blame.
>
> (Joleby et al., 2020, p. 8)

This bears resemblance to cases in which adult victims are lured in so-called love scams to, for instance, pay large sums of money to their "lovers" – who may turn out to be an organized group of criminals (Whitty, 2018; Whitty

& Buchanan, 2016). The sense of "having been foolish" may be a significant source of shame.

As noted by Vale et al. (2024), there are cases in which adolescents do not voluntarily disclose their sexual abuse experiences in response to open-ended questions. This finding is echoed also among young victims of sexual trafficking. Studies of Swedish police interviews of suspected young victims of sexual trafficking (Lindholm et al., 2014, 2015) showed that the victims in the trafficking cases avoided the core topics of the investigations such as selling sex and their relationships to the suspects, which led to the police to being all the more coercive. The interviews were highly suggestive and, according to the authors, had a character more similar to suspect interrogations rather than investigative interviews with presumed trafficking victims (see chapter 3 by Quas et al., this volume). And the more coercive techniques the police used, the less forthcoming the young victims were.

A similar pattern was found in a Swedish court case with 25 child victims who had been sexually abused online. The child interviews are described in the verdict as follows:

> The child interviews follow a pattern. The children are somewhat informed of what the interview is about but they do not know that the interviewer has access to the chat logs and photographs that in some cases have been sent during them. It is not uncommon for the children to initially deny their involvement in what at least for the perpetrator has had a sexual connotation. They often deny having sent photographs, in particular of a sexual nature, to the perpetrator. When the children realize that the interviewers have access to the chat logs and photographs, they react in different ways. Most become silent, some start to cry, and some break down.
>
> (B 10021-16, Stockholm District Court, p. 26; translation by the authors)

In a qualitative study of 20 interviews conducted with children aged 11 to 13 in cases of online CSA in Israel, Gemara et al. (2022) described how the children felt uncomfortable talking about the abusive incidents, stating that they did not want to talk about the matter. According to the authors, interviewers did not respect this request but exposed the children to the evidence at hand, depicting the sexual abuse they had experienced. The children in the study consistently expressed that they did not want to think or talk about the abuse but were pressured to do so by the interviewers. As Gemara et al. (2022, p. 4) wrote, they "were left with two options: deny the abuse or re-live it". The study includes heartbreaking examples such as the following:

I: Did anyone ask you to do anything sexual over the phone?

C: No, and even if they would, I would say no.

I: Look, many kids learn about relationships with boys over the phone. Did something like this happen to you?

C: Nothing happened to me. I never meet people who I do not know. I would never do such a thing.

I: I have information from the police that someone sent you a movie clip with an uncovered body part. Can you tell me about it?

The girl is quiet and starts to cry.

C: But I stopped it. I do not talk to anyone anymore.

(Gemara et al., 2022, p. 5)

And another child denied in a similar way:

I: Did someone hurt you using the phone?

C: No.

I: Did you have a sexual connection over the phone?

C: No. Not at all.

(Gemara et al., 2022, p. 5)

As noted by scholars, the reluctance of child victims should not be met with pressure (Vale et al., 2024, p. 20): "During the questioning stage, if the adolescent has not voluntarily disclosed the TFSA (technology-facilitated sexual abuse) in response to open-ended prompts and concrete evidence needs to be addressed, confrontation contradicts best practices and should be avoided". Investigators therefore need to carefully consider how they will inform the child about possibly existing material in an as sensitive way as possible, keeping in mind that the child victim may not be aware that images and videos exist and that the authorities may have them.

As mentioned previously, children belonging to a sexual minority need to be given special consideration, as they may be involved in the process at a moment when they do not feel ready to "be outed" or share their sexual identity with their parents. Kanefsky et al. (2024) state that victims should be properly informed about the confidentiality of their disclosure, based on their study population of young adults. Whether and how to contact the parents should be properly planned and the views of the child should also be taken into account to the extent possible.

In an example by Gemara et al. (2022), interviewers tried to get the child to verbally describe a picture that was sent (and that the police had in their possession). This was clearly unpleasant for the victim who said they had tried hard to forget the events and did not want to be reminded. In another case, the interviewer seemed determined to make the child – despite her forceful protests – verbally describe what was going on in a picture and refused to let her show the interviewer instead, as she had offered to do. Interviewers are trained to make children verbally describe their abusive experience, which in most offline cases is a requirement for a successful investigation where other evidence is lacking, and it is possible that interviewers struggle to change strategies in cases where there is in fact absolute evidence for the alleged events. For instance, Antila (2022) analysed Finnish cases of online CSA and noted that the "hard evidence" (for instance pictures and videos which were verified to depict the child and the suspect in the case) was at the core of the criminal justice process, with little evidentiary value added through the child's testimony in cases where the other evidence was definitive (i.e. there is a ground truth about the case). However, in many cases, the child's account may be crucial to the legal process or to getting a full understanding of the crime.

As pointed out by Gemara et al. (2022), adult investigators pressing or forcing adolescent children, in the midst of their sexual development, to discuss and view sexually explicit content in the company of adult strangers may be highly distressing in itself. It is quite possible, if not likely, that children would feel stressed already discussing positive sexual experiences in these circumstances!

Only a few studies have looked at forensic interviews and questioning styles in interviews with child victims of online CSA. In a scoping review, Vale et al. (2024) raised a concern about the lack of understanding of online abuse among professionals investigating and assessing cases, implying that some professionals are unprepared and ill-equipped to work on these cases. The authors underscored the urgent need to develop evidence-based practices to address the complexities of online CSA. The studies compiled by Vale et al. (2024) focusing on forensic interviews with child victims of online CSA included samples of interviews conducted using the NICHD Protocol (Gemara et al., 2022; Katz, 2013) and others that did not specify which protocol was followed.

The NICHD protocol is a widely used, research-based child interviewing protocol, implemented by police in numerous countries worldwide and currently the most researched child interviewing protocol (see, for instance Benia et al., 2015; La Rooy et al., 2015; Lamb et al., 2018). Vale et al. (2024) identified the need to "adjust and align the NICHD Protocol" with online CSA cases stressing the need for questions specifically tailored to this type of cases.

Enhancing disclosure in online child sexual abuse: suggesting a modification of the NICHD-R for online cases

The first version of the widely used and evidence-based NICHD protocol (Benia et al., 2015; La Rooy et al., 2015; Lamb et al., 2018), the Standard NICHD Protocol, focused mostly on cognitive factors associated with child interviewing, advising interviewers how to, in a non-suggestive way, help children remember. A new version, the Revised Protocol (NICHD-R) later put additional focus on strategies emphasizing rapport building, identification of reluctance, and providing supportive comments (Lamb et al., 2018). There is evidence that interviews based on the revised version of the NICHD are more likely to help children disclose and that children in the NICHD-R interviews are rated as more "credible" than children interviewed using the standard version of the NICHD (Hershkowitz & Lamb, 2020).

In response to the growing number of allegations of online CSA and the challenges related to these as described earlier, a group consisting of both researchers and practitioners[1] joined forces to develop a version of the NICHD protocol (NICHD-ROCSA) Revised for Online Child Sexual Abuse to address some of the needs raised. The NICHD-ROCSA was particularly developed for cases where there was evidence such as sexual/nude pictures, videos, or chat logs/messages, clearly indicating a particular child was participating. The aim was to suggest ways in which to address existing evidence of online CSA in as child-sensitive and non-suggestive ways as possible and to give examples of information/evidence that may help assess legal online abuse cases. Research is still needed to assess how well the protocol works in practice and to underpin further improvements of it. In general, the goal was to give the child enough information to understand the context of the interview (if otherwise not clear to them) and make informed decisions about whether or not to disclose.

The recommendations are in line with general interviewing recommendations on child forensic interviews (Korkman et al., 2024), with specific suggestions for addressing online elements. Interviewers are recommended to proceed as when using the regular NICHD-R, beginning with an introduction, rapport building, and ground rules, which should be explained in a way that the child can understand. Children are instructed to say if they do not understand, know or remember, and the importance of telling the truth is explained to them. In the practice interview, the interviewer aims to make the child familiar with the dynamics of a forensic interview – with the interviewer asking open-ended questions and the child providing most of the information – and further develop rapport with the child. At this point, if the child has not brought up any online activities, the interviewer may inquire about these, asking about what the child likes to do online or on devices the child uses. Interviewers are encouraged to follow up with cued invitations (i.e. open-ended questions that request the child to tell more about something already mentioned by the child). Examples of such questions could be:

- "You told me you play [Brawl stars]. Tell me about that."
- "You told me you like [TikTok]. Tell me more about that."
- "You told me you like to use [Snapchat]. I don't use that myself, so I don't know that much about it. Please tell me more about it."

As in investigative interviews generally, interviewers are advised to clarify terms used by the child. For example, the exact meaning of sexual terms, but also technical terms, may be of crucial importance in a possible trial. Interviewers are reminded to clarify the child's account, character, nickname, or username as well as how the child understands the terms and concepts addressed (for example "service", "nickname", "user").

The substantive phase: transition A (for suspicions with solid/strong evidence)

For the substantive phase, interviewers are advised to plan the interview well ahead, based on the information available. Where children come to the interview unaware of the reason behind it and do not have any concerns they want to raise themselves, the interviewer can for instance address the issues like this:

> The police are investigating a case where a certain user in [Snapchat, edit to fit the case] has been in contact with many children and [asked them to send pictures/sent them pictures/contacted children, edit to fit the case] and I want to ask you some questions about this. Tell me anything you know about this.
>
> This online-user has used this [nickname/username Mr Hoot; edit to fit the case]. Tell me everything about this [username].

When there is clearly identifiable evidence (for instance, photos or chat logs/messages written using the child´s user account) but the child seems unaware of the reason for the interview or does not reveal related information, the interviewer is advised to refer to the evidence quite early in this part of the interview, while still leaving as much opportunity as possible for the child to describe what happened in their own words. For example:

> The police have investigated devices (computer/phone) used by a certain [Mr Hoot, use the username of the perpetrator, as the child does not necessarily know their real name or identity or that the perpetrator is an adult] and found messages sent by him and pictures sent to him by children. Please tell me anything you know about this/Can you tell me anything about this/Mr Hoot?

Or:

> The police have found messages that Mr Hoot has sent to [Flowergirl13; use the child's username]. Please tell me about this.

Where the child is reluctant to talk and contradicts available evidence, the interviewer can support the child through emotional support, encouragements and other supportive strategies laid out in the NICHD-R as well as remind the child that they have a right not to talk:

> If there is something you don't want to tell me about, just say so. You have the right to not tell me about it. Just tell me you don't want to talk about it and I will respect that.

If the evidence recovered by the police *clearly shows* that the suspect has told the child not to tell anyone, this can be referred to as well:

> Mr Hoot has told some children not to talk about this with anyone. Please tell me everything you might know about that.

If there is strong evidence that Mr Hoot has asked the child to send nude pictures (etc.) or has sent the child pictures of himself, the interviewer may decide to refer to that. The interviewer may also decide to reveal the identity of the perpetrator to the child at this stage. However, this must be done with great consideration, as the child might be unaware that the perpetrator is an adult. This may be one of the most disturbing aspects of the interview for the child.

For example:

> The police have found out that Mr Hoot is actually not a child, but an older person (e.g. adult man) who has been in contact with several children. It is therefore important that we get all the information about him/her/them that we can. If you could tell us everything you know and remember about him/her, it would help the police very much to investigate the case better. Anything you know about him, any pieces of information you remember would be helpful to us.

The substantive phase: transition B (for suspicions with weaker evidence)

This alternative transition to the substantive phase is for cases where there is no ground truth for the case but the child has been identified as a possible victim and the police need to determine if the child was indeed involved. For instance:

> The police are investigating a case where a certain user in [e.g. Snapchat; edit to fit the case] has been in contact with many children and [asked them to send pictures/sent them pictures/contacted children; edit to

fit the case] and I want to ask you some questions about this. Tell me if there is anything you know about this.

The moderators/administrators of [e.g. Snapchat; edit to fit the case] have informed the police about this username, who we believe has been contacting children. Tell me everything you know about this username.

You told me that you use/play [service, platform, game; edit according to the case at hand]. Tell me about that [using that service, platform, playing that game]?

Use invitations or cued invitations.

If the child starts talking about the event or discloses any information, the interviewer follows the NICHD-R structure, collecting as much information as possible through active listening, open-ended questions and supporting the child's account. If the child *denies*, the interviewer is advised to refrain from asking any more direct questions and to consider discussing neutral topics, taking a break, or moving to close the interview. In such situations, a supportive approach by the interviewer can help reluctant children cope with negative emotions and hopefully overcome reluctance to disclose while simultaneously not increasing the risk of wrongful accounts by using closed questions or pressing interview techniques to push the child to talk (Lamb et al., 2018).

During the closure of the interview, the interviewer should thank the child for coming and say that it is understandable that the situation may have felt difficult for them, particularly if the child has struggled or refused to say anything.

The interviewer should end the interview on a positive note and if possible, say something about how the child could contact the interviewer later, should they want to.

Avoiding bias: alternative hypotheses and an investigative mindset

In cases where there is no absolute evidence (ground truth) of the child having been victimized, the fact that the child does not tell about abusive experiences may not necessarily signal reluctance – it might be that abuse did not occur, and that the allegation is based on a misinterpretation of something the child has said or done, or a false accusation. Interviewers thus need to think of alternative hypotheses based on available information and remain open to different explanations throughout the investigation. In online CSA cases with evidence of criminal actions committed against a child, the interviewer should be mindful that many facts may still be unknown. Investigators should thus keep an open mind or investigative mindset (O'Donohue & Cirlugea, 2021) and remember that there may be many things that are yet unknown to the investigator. Considering alternative explanations and maintaining an open investigative mind – recognizing that the information at hand may be lacking or misleading – decreases the risk of confirmation bias, which may otherwise lead to miscarriages of justice.

Existing evidence can also be wrongly linked to a particular child. Gemara et al. (2022) gave an example of a young girl who was exposed to severely distressing evidence that the police claimed depicted her behaviour, only to later discover the allegation was mistaken. Interviewers are thus advised to consider alternative explanations for the available evidence before the interview, as well as how to obtain information regarding these. In internet-based abuse online abuse cases, a central question may be who has actually been using an account or nickname related to the case at hand.

Currently, the modified protocol see Appendix is in its early stages and so far its effectiveness has not been evaluated. Feedback on its use and perceived strengths and weaknesses was collected initially when the protocol was first developed, and later in a number of training sessions for professionals, organized by the European Institute for Crime Prevention and Control, the Barnahus network (www.barnahus.eu/en), and the Finnish police college during 2023 and 2024. Currently, an interview study with experienced Finnish police officers, specialized in child interviewing and who have used the protocol in large cases of online CSA, is underway. However, research on the concrete effects of using the NICHD-ROCSA is needed, preferably comparing interviews where the NICHD-ROCSA protocol is used to comparable cases where the NICHD-R has been used.

A final remark

In view of the (albeit relatively few) existing studies on how children have been formally interviewed in investigations of online CSA, there is a need to carefully consider when and why it is necessary to interview a child. As noted by Gemara et al. (2022), when there is documented evidence of the sexual abuse of children whose consent is irrelevant (i.e. under the age of consent), the question of the ultimate purpose of a forensic child interview must be raised. As noted in this chapter, the interviews themselves may cause secondary traumatization or even feel more negative than the experiences they were intended to investigate (Gemara et al., 2022; Joleby et al., 2020; Katz et al., 2021). This risk must be taken seriously – the criminal justice system should not lead to unnecessary suffering among the victims it is designed to protect. Children should, however, be given the chance to make an informed choice as they do have the right to be heard in matters concerning them. And if they are interviewed, these interviews should be conducted by well-trained investigators who use well-known best practice guidelines included in the NICHD-R or similar protocols (see Lamb et al.,

2018 and Korkman et al., 2024), tailoring the interview to the context and child at hand and paying particular attention to introducing information about possibly existing evidence in a sensitive and well-planned way. As online sexual abuse cases may involve increased difficulty for children to disclose, an important task for the interviewer is to identify and manage reluctance through the kind of supportive approach advocated in the NICHD-R, tailored to the online cases. The modified interview protocol for cases of online CSA presented here aims to provide some assistance in doing this. It should be noted that this is still work in progress and further steps include gathering experiences of using the strategies presented among practitioners, and further refining them.

Acknowledgements

The first author would like to acknowledge that the work on which this chapter is based has been supported by the PROMISE Elpis Project, co-funded by the European Union. We wish to thank Senior Digital Information Librarian Muriel Wells from the National Child Advocacy Center for valuable support.

Note

1 Julia Korkman, Maria Hietajärvi, Malin Joleby, Michael Lamb and Irit Hershkowitz. The protocol was further developed in the EU-funded project ELPIS (2023–2025).

References

Antila (2022). Lasta seksualisoivan kuvan merkitys todisteena rikosasiassa. Retrieved from www.theseus.fi/bitstream/handle/10024/783978/YAMK_Antila.pdf?sequence=2&isAllowed=y

Baugerud, G. A., & Melinder, A. (2012). Maltreated children's memory of stressful removals from their biological parents. *Applied Cognitive Psychology*, *26*(2), 261–270. https://doi.org/10.1002/acp.1817

Benia, L. R., Hauck-Filho, N., Dillenburg, M., & Stein, L. M. (2015). The NICHD investigative interview protocol: A meta-analytic review. *Journal of Child Sexual Abuse*, *24*(3), 259–279. https://doi.org/10.1080/10538712.2015.1006749

Chauviré-Geib, K., & Fegert, J. M. (2023). Victims of technology-assisted child sexual abuse: A scoping review. *Trauma Violence Abuse*, 15248380231178754. https://doi.org/10.1177/15248380231178754

Chiang, E., & Grant, T. (2018). Deceptive identity performance: Offender moves and multiple identities in online child abuse conversations. Applied Linguistics, 1, 25. https://doi.org/10.1093/applin/amy007

Childlight. (2024). *Into the light: Index on child sexual exploitation and abuse globally: 2024 report.* Edinburgh: Childlight. https://childlight.org/sites/default/files/2024-05/into-the-light.pdf

Craven, S., Brown, S., & Gilchrist, E. (2006). Sexual grooming of children: Review of literature and theoretical considerations. Journal of Sexual Aggression, 12(3), 287–299. doi:10.1080/13552600601069414

Cullen, O., Ernst, K. Z., Dawes, N., Binford, W., & Dimitropoulos, G. (2020). "Our laws have not caught up with the technology": Understanding challenges and facilitators in investigating and prosecuting child sexual abuse materials in the United States. *Laws*, *9*(4), 28. https://doi.org/10.3390/laws9040028

de Santisteban, P., & Gámez-Guadix, M. (2018). Prevalence and risk factors among minors for online sexual solicitations and interactions with adults. *The Journal of Sex Research*, *55*(7), 939–950. https://doi.org/10.1080/00224499.2017.1386763

Drejer, C., Riegler, M. A., Halvorsen, P., Johnson, M. S., & Baugerud, G. A. (2024). Livestreaming technology and online child sexual exploitation and abuse: A scoping review. *Trauma, Violence, & Abuse*, *25*(1), 260–274. https://doi.org/10.1177/15248380221147564

Dushi, D. (2019). *The phenomenon of online live-streaming of child sexual abuse: Challenges and legal responses.* https://hdl.handle.net/10993/39916

ECPAT. (2020). *I början vart det lite läskigt men nu* är *det vardag: En rapport om yngre barn och egenproducerat material* [In the beginning it was a little scary but now it's everyday life: A report on younger children and self-produced material]. Stockholm: ECPAT Sverige.https://ecpat.se/wp-content/uploads/2021/04/ECPAT_HotlineRapport_2020.pdf

ECPAT. (2023). *Tjejer måste sluta skicka nakenbilder: En rapport om pojkar, nakenbilder, relationer och* åldersskillnader [Girls must stop sending nudes: A report on boys, nudes, relationships, and age differences]. Stockholm: ECPAT Sverige. https://ecpat.se/wp-content/uploads/2020/12/ECPAT-SVERIGE_Tjejer-borde-sluta-skicka_2022.pdf

Europol. (2023). *Internet organized crime threat assessment.* Retrieved from www.europol.europa.eu/cms/sites/default/files/documents/IOCTA%202023%20-%20EN_0.pdf (accessed 29April 2024).

Ey, L. A., & Cupit, C. G. (2011). Exploring young children's understanding of risks associated with Internet usage and their concepts of management strategies. *Journal of Early Childhood Research*, 9(1), 53–65. https://doi.org/10.1177/1476718X10367471

Finkelhor, D., Turner, H., & Colburn, D. (2022). Prevalence of online sexual offenses against children in the US. *JAMA Network Open*, *5*(10), e2234471. https://doi:10.1001/jamanetworkopen.2022.34471

Finkelhor, D., Turner, H., & Colburn, D. (2023). Which dynamics make online child sexual abuse and cyberstalking more emotionally impactful: Perpetrator identity and images? *Child Abuse & Neglect*, *137*, 106020. https://doi.org/10.1016/j.chiabu.2023.106020

Franqueira, V. N., Bryce, J., Al Mutawa, N., & Marrington, A. (2018). Investigation of indecent images of children cases: Challenges and suggestions collected from the trenches. *Digital Investigation*, *24*, 95–105. https://doi.org/10.1016/j.diin.2017.11.002

Gemara, N., Mishna, F., & Katz, C. (2023). "If my parents find out, I will not see my phone anymore": Who do children choose to disclose online sexual solicitation to? *Child & Family Social Work*. https://doi.org/10.1111/cfs.13069

Gemara, N., Cohen, N., & Katz, C. (2022). "I do not remember … You are reminding me now!": Children's difficult experiences during forensic interviews about online sexual solicitation. *Child Abuse & Neglect*, *134*, 105913. https://doi.org/10.1016/j.chiabu.2022.105913

Gezinski, L. B., & Gonzalez-Pons, K. M. (2024). Sex trafficking and technology: A systematic review of recruitment and exploitation. *Journal of Human Trafficking*, *10*(3), 497–511. https://doi.org/10.1080/23322705.2022.2034378

Greijer, S. & Doek, J. (2016). *Terminology Guidelines for the protection of children from sexual exploitation and sexual abuse*. ECPAT International. https://ecpat.org/wp-content/uploads/2021/05/Terminology-guidelines-396922-EN-1.pdf

Hamilton-Giachritsis, C., Hanson, E., Whittle, H., Alves-Costa, F., & Beech, A. (2020). Technology assisted child sexual abuse in the UK: Young people's views on the impact of online sexual abuse. *Children Youth Services Review*, 105451. https://doi.org/10.1016/j.childyouth.2020.105451

Hamilton-Giachritsis, C., Hanson, E., Whittle, H., Alves-Costa, F., Pintos, A., Metcalf, T., & Beech, A. (2021). Technology assisted child sexual abuse: professionals' perceptions of risk and impact on children and young people. *Child Abuse & Neglect*, *119*, 104651. https://doi.org/10.1016/j.chiabu.2020.104651

Herman, S. (2005). Improving decision making in forensic child sexual abuse evaluations. *Law and Human Behavior*, 29(1), 8. https://doi.org/10.1007/s10979-005-1400-8

Hershkowitz, I., Lamb, M. E., & Katz, C. (2014). Allegation rates in forensic child abuse investigations: Comparing the revised and standard NICHD protocols. *Psychology, Public Policy, and Law*, *20*(3), 336. https://doi.org/10.1037/a0037391

Hershkowitz, I., & Lamb, M. E. (2020). Allegation rates and credibility assessment in forensic interviews of alleged child abuse victims: Comparing the revised and standard NICHD protocols. *Psychology, Public Policy, and Law*, *26*(2), 176. https://doi.org/10.1037/law0000230

Hietajärvi, M. (2023). Online or offline? Online sexual crimes against children in 2022 police databases in Finland. The Police University College, Finland 11/2023. https://urn.fi/URN:NBN:fi:amk-2023120735101

Hietamäki, J., Husso, M., Arponen, T., & Lahtinen, H. M. (2024). Differences between girls and boys in the disclosure of sexual violence. *Journal of Interpersonal Violence*, *39*(11–12), 2629–2654. https://doi.org/10.1177/08862605231221283

Huikuri, S. & Insoll, T. (2022). Darknet online communities of child sexual abusers: Reinforcing and rationalising offending behaviour (Suojellaan Lapsia ry. 2022). Retrieved from www.suojellaanlapsia.fi/en/post/darknet-online-communities-of-child-sexual-abusers

Joleby, M., Landström, S., Lunde, C., & Jonsson, L. S. (2021a). Experiences and psychological health among children exposed to online child sexual abuse–a mixed methods study of court verdicts. *Psychology, Crime & Law*, *27*(2), 159–181. https://doi.org/10.1080/1068316X.2020.1781120

Joleby, M., Landström, S., Lunde, C., & Jonsson, L. S. (2024). "But I Wanted to Talk About it": Technology-Assisted Child Sexual Abuse Victims' Reasoning on Delayed Disclosure. *Child Protection and Practice*, 100062. https://doi.org/10.1016/j.chipro.2024.100062

Joleby, M., Lunde, C., Landström, S., & Jonsson, L. S. (2020). "All of me is completely different": Experiences and consequences among victims of technology-assisted child sexual abuse. *Frontiers in Psychology*, *11*, 606218. https://doi.org/10.3389/fpsyg.2020.606218

Joleby, M., Lunde, C., Landström, S., & Jonsson, L. S. (2021b). Offender strategies for engaging children in online sexual activity. *Child Abuse & Neglect*, *120*, 105214. https://doi.org/10.1016/j.chiabu.2021.105214

Jonsson, L. S., Fredlund, C., Priebe, G., Wadsby, M., & Svedin, C. G. (2019). Online sexual abuse of adolescents by a perpetrator met online: a cross-sectional study. *Child and Adolescent Psychiatry and Mental Health*, *13*(1), 32. https://doi.org/10.1186/s13034-019-0292-1

Kanefsky, R. Z., Newins, A. R., & Necaise, A. (2024). Sexual assault disclosure among sexual minority individuals: Associations with "outness", perceived stigma, community belonging, and perceptions of police. *Psychology of Sexual Orientation and Gender Diversity*, *11*(3), 498–507. https://doi.org/10.1037/sgd0000611

Katz, C. (2013). Internet-related child sexual abuse: What children tell us in their testimonies. Children and Youth Services Review, 35(9), 1536–1542. https://doi.org/10.1016/j.childyouth.2013.06.006

Katz, C., Piller, S., Glucklich, T., & Matty, D. E. (2021). "Stop waking the dead": Internet child sexual abuse and perspectives on its disclosure. *J Interpers Violence*, 886260518796526. https://doi.org/10.1177/0886260518796526

Klettke, B., Hallford, D. J., & Mellor, D. J. (2014). Sexting prevalence and correlates: A systematic literature review. *Clinical Psychology Review*, *34*(1), 44–53. https://doi.org/10.1016/j.cpr.2013.10.007

Kloess, J. A., Hamilton-Giachritsis, C. E., & Beech, A. R. (2019). Offense processes of online sexual grooming and abuse of children via Internet communication platforms. *Sexual Abuse*, 31(1), 73–96. https://doi.org/10.1177/1079063217720927

Korkman, J., et al. (2024). White Paper on Forensic Child Interviewing: Research-based recommendations by the European Association of Psychology and Law. *Psychology, Crime and Law*, online ahead of print. https://doi.org/10.1080/1068316X.2024 2324098

Krishna, S., Dubrosa, F., & Milanaik, R. (2024). Rising threats of AI-driven child sexual abuse material. *Pediatrics*, *153*(2). https://doi.org/10.1542/peds.2023-063954

Lamb, M. E., Brown, D. A., Hershkowitz, I., Orbach, Y., & Esplin, P. W. (2018). *Tell me what happened: Structured investigative interviews of child victims and witnesses.* Wiley.

La Rooy, D., Brubacher, S. P., Aromäki-Stratos, A., Cyr, M., Hershkowitz, I., Korkman, J., Myklebust, T., Naka, M., Peixoto, C. E., Roberts, K. P., Steward, H. & Lamb, M. E (2015). The NICHD protocol: A review of an internationally-used evidence-based tool for training child forensic interviewers.

Journal of Criminological Research, Policy and Practice, *1*(2), 76–89. http://doi.org/10.1108/JCRPP-01-2015-0001

Leander, L., Christianson, S. Å., & Granhag, P. A. (2008). Internet-initiated sexual abuse: adolescent victims' reports about On-and Off-line sexual activities. *Applied Cognitive Psychology*, *22*(9), 1260–1274. https://doi.org/10.1002/acp.1433

Leclerc, B., Cale, J., Holt, T., & Drew, J. (2022). Child sexual abuse material online: the perspective of online investigators on training and support. *Policing: A Journal of Policy and Practice*, *16*(4), 762–776. https://doi.org/10.1093/police/paac017

Ligiero, D., Hart, C., Fulu, E., Thomas, A., & Radford, L. (2019). What works to prevent sexual violence against children. Technical report, University of Lancashire.

Lindholm, Börjesson & Cederborg, A-C. (2014). "What happened when you came to Sweden?": Attributing responsibility in police interviews with alleged adolescent human trafficking victims. *Narrative Inquiry*, *24*. https://doi.org/10.1075/ni.24.2.01lin

Lindholm, J., Cederborg, A-C. & Alm, C. (2015) Adolescent girls exploited in the sex trade: informativeness and evasiveness in investigative interviews. *Police Practice and Research*, *16*(3), 197–210. https://doi.org/10.1080/15614263.2014.880839

Livingstone, S., & Smith, P. K. (2014). Annual research review: Harms experienced by child users of online and mobile technologies: The nature, prevalence and management of sexual and aggressive risks in the digital age. *Journal of Child Psychology and Psychiatry*, *55*(6), 635–654. https://doi.org/10.1111/jcpp.12197

Lunde, C., & Joleby, M. (2023). Being under pressure to sext: Adolescents' experiences, reactions, and counter-strategies. *Journal of Research on Adolescence*, *33*(1), 188–201. https://doi.org/10.1111/jora.12797

Lykens, J., Pilloton, M., Silva, C., Schlamm, E., Wilburn, K., & Pence, E. (2019). Google for sexual relationships: Mixed-methods study on digital flirting and online dating among adolescent youth and young adults. *JMIR Public Health and Surveillance*, *5*(2), e10695. doi:10.2196/10695

Mäenpää, M., Ovaska, A., Santtila, P. & Korkman, J. (2022). *Analysis of current practices and identification of training gaps and needs of target groups: Ensuring childfriendly justice through the effective operation of the Barnahus Units in Finland*. Finnish Institute for Health & Welfare.

McElvaney, R. (2015). Disclosure of child sexual abuse: Delays, non-disclosure and partial disclosure. What the research tells us and implications for practice. *Child Abuse Review*, *24*(3), 159–169. https://doi.org/10.1002/car.2280

McElvaney, R., & Culhane, M. (2017). A retrospective analysis of children's assessment reports: What helps children tell? *Child Abuse Review*, 26(2), 103–115. https://doi.org/10.1002/car.2390

Mori, C., Park, J., Temple, J. R., & Madigan, S. (2022). Are youth sexting rates still on the rise? A meta-analytic update. *Journal of Adolescent Health*, *70*(4), 531–539. https://doi.org/10.1016/j.jadohealth.2021.10.026

NCMEC. (2024). CyberTipline: By the numbers. Retrieved from www.missingkids.org/gethelpnow/cybertipline#bythenumbers (accessed 12 August 2024).

O'Donohue, W., & Cirlugea, O. (2021). Controlling for confirmation bias in child sexual abuse interviews. *The Journal of the American Academy of Psychiatry and the Law*, *49*(3), 371–380. https://doi.org/10.29158/JAAPL.200109-20

Patchin, J. W., & Hinduja, S. (2020). Sextortion among adolescents: Results from a national survey of US youth. Sexual Abuse, 32(1), 30–54. https://doi.org/10.1177/1079063218800469

Quayle, E., Jonsson, L. S., Cooper, K., Traynor, J., & Svedin, C. G. (2018). Children in identified sexual images – who are they? Self-and non-self-taken Images in the International Child Sexual Exploitation Image Database 2006–2015. *Child Abuse Review*, *27*(3), 223–238. https://doi.org/10.1002/car.2507

Quayle, E., & Koukopoulos, N. (2019). Deterrence of online child sexual abuse and exploitation. *Policing: A Journal of Policy and Practice*, *13*(3), 345–362. https://doi.org/10.1093/police/pay028.

Razi, A., Badillo-Urquiola, K., & Wisniewski, P. J. (2020, April). Let's talk about sext: How adolescents seek support and advice about their online sexual experiences. In *Proceedings of the 2020 CHI Conference on Human Factors in Computing Systems* (pp. 1–13). https://doi.org/10.1145/3313831.3376400

Save the Children Finland (2021). Grooming in the eyes of a child. https://pelastakaalapset.s3.eu-west-1.amazonaws.com/main/2021/08/03151159/grooming_in_the_eyes_of_a_child_2021.pdf

Schmidt, F., Varese, F., & Bucci, S. (2023). Understanding the prolonged impact of online sexual abuse occurring in childhood. *Frontiers in Psychology*, *14*, 1281996. https://doi.org/10.3389/fpsyg.2023.1281996

Seymour-Smith, S., & Kloess, J. A. (2021). A discursive analysis of compliance, resistance and escalation to threats in sexually exploitative interactions between offenders and male children. *British Journal of Social Psychology*. https://doi.org/10.1111/bjso.12437

Stänicke, L. I., Reiremo, G. K., Scheie, S. I., Jessen, R. S., & Jensen, T. K. (2024). Navigating, being tricked, and blaming oneself—A meta-synthesis of youth's experience of involvement in online child sexual abuse. *Child & Family Social Work*. https://doi.org/10.1111/cfs.13152

Vale, M., Gomes, J. P., & Matos, M. (2024). Forensic psychological procedures in cases of technology-facilitated sexual abuse among adolescents: A scoping review. *Behavioral Sciences & the Law*. https://doi.org/10.1002/bsl.2658

Wadbäck, P., & Mehr, D. (Producers). (2019). *Nätpedofilen i Husby* [The internet pedophile from Husby]. [Radio documentary]. Swedish Radio P3.

Whittle, H., Hamilton-Giachritsis, C., Beech, A., & Collings, G. (2013). A review of online grooming: Characteristics and concerns. *Aggression and Violent Behavior*, *18*(1), 62–70. https://doi.org/10.1016/j.avb.2012.09.003

Whittle, H. C., Hamilton-Giachritsis, C. E., & Beech, A. R. (2014). "Under His Spell": Victims' Perspectives of Being Groomed Online. *Social Sciences*, *3*(3), 404–426. https://doi.org/10.3390/socsci3030404

Whitty, M. T., & Buchanan, T. (2016). The online dating romance scam: The psychological impact on victims–both financial and non-financial. *Criminology & Criminal Justice*, *16*(2), 176–194. https://doi.org/10.1177/1748895815603773

Whitty, M. T. (2018). Do you love me? Psychological characteristics of romance scam victims. *Cyberpsychology, Behavior, and Social Networking*, *21*(2), 105–109. https://doi.org/10.1089/cyber.2016.0729

WHO. (1999). *Report of the consultation on child abuse prevention*. Geneva: World Health Organization.

Witting, S. K. (2021). Transnational by default: online child sexual abuse respects no borders. *The International Journal of Children's Rights*, *29*(3), 731–764. https://doi:10.1163/15718182-29030010

Wolak, J., & Finkelhor, D. (2016). *Sextortion: Findings from a survey of 1,631 victims*. Durham, NH: Crimes Against Children Research Center.

World Childhood Foundation. (2022). "It was a feeling that he was in the next room": A review of internet-related sexual abuse of children handled by Swedish district courts 2020–2021. https://childhood.se/wp-content/uploads/2022/10/childhood-stella-polaris-rapport-2022-internetrelaterade-sexuella-overgrepp-mot-barn-uppslag.pdf

Wright, R., Powell, M. B., & Ridge, D. (2006). Child abuse investigation: An in-depth analysis of how police officers perceive and cope with daily work challenges. *Policing: An International Journal of Police Strategies & Management*, 29(3), 498–512. https://doi:10.1108/13639510610684728

Appendix

NICHD-R for online cases

An adaptation of the NICHD-R interviewing protocol for investigating internet-related child sexual abuse[1]

This adaptation of the NICHD protocol is developed for use by ***trained child interviewers, familiar with the revised NICHD protocol.*** It is particularly developed for cases for which there is physical evidence or a strong suspicion of the existence of such evidence. That evidence could typically consist of:

- sexual **pictures, videos** or any other material clearly identifying the child
- **Online conversations**, where the child has demonstrably[2] been a participant.

The original NICHD protocol was developed for suspected cases of offline child abuse, which often entail little or no corroborating evidence. Cases of online CSA, however often entail strong technical evidence, wherefore there is a particular need to guide investigative interviewers in how to introduce the allegation and refer to possibly existing evidence. While it is still important to conduct the interview in a non-suggestive manner and build it around questions prompting for free recall, it may be necessary and ethical to be transparent with existing evidence early on in the interview in order to not blindside the child.

The aim of this modified interviewing protocol is this to suggest ways in which to address existing evidence of online abuse in as child-sensitive and non-suggestive a way as possible, and to give examples of information evidence that may be relevant to ask for the legal assessments of online abuse cases. Interviewers are encouraged to familiarise themselves with the revised NICHD protocol, in particular ways to support and encourage child interviewees. Literature on this is recommended at the end of this document, including relevant studies related to online abuse and its consequences for child victims.

In cases where the suspicion is not based on strong evidence for the particular child being victimised, using the regular NICHD-R is recommended.

However, the questions proposed in this adapted protocol may be used as reference on how to ask about issues that tend to be relevant to online cases. Before the interview, interviewers are encouraged to inform themselves about the social media platforms, applications or games that are related to the suspicion under investigation as well as how they operate.

Alternative hypotheses

Consider alternative explanations for the available evidence before the interview, as well as how to obtain information regarding these. In internet-based abuse cases, a central question may be who has actually been using an account or username related to the case at hand.

1.
2.
3.
...

PART 1. INTRODUCTION

My name is ________, I am a [profession] and my job is to talk to children about things that have happened to them. As you can see, we have a video camera here. It will record us talking so I can remember everything you tell me.

Check if the child is okay with all this and whether they have any questions.

PART 2: RAPPORT BUILDING

The purpose is to get the child to relax and settle into the situation as well as possible.

Make sure that the child feels as comfortable as possible: How are you feeling about being here to talk with me today? Do you have any concerns? Is there anything that I can do to help you feel more comfortable?

First, I would like to get to know you better. Tell me about things you like to do.

If the child does not answer, gives a short answer, or gets stuck, continue building rapport, asking the child open-ended questions about other things, for example: Tell me about things you like to do in your spare time?

Continue with the rapport building until the child seems to be at ease and provides detailed narrative responses. You can ask the child about their school, hobbies or other things that they like to do after school. Remember to give the child enough time to answer before asking new questions. You should also ask the child further invitations about things they have already mentioned, making sure the questions are open-ended. For example:

Tell me about [something the child has mentioned]. *Use various introductory questions to ask about different topics; one of those invitations should focus on internal contents: thoughts, feelings, sensations, or emotions. When the child mentions something, follow up on that with an open-ended prompt:* Tell me more about the time in the car. / You mentioned playing X, tell me about X". *These are cued follow up questions aimed to encourage the child to expand on topics they have mentioned.*

If the child seems nervous or hesitant to talk, you may address the issue by asking questions, such as: Tell me about your feelings right now?...

Support the child by thanking them: Thank you for sharing this this with me.

PART 3. GROUND RULES (RIGHTS AND RESPONSIBILITIES)

Explaining and practising ground rules (rights and responsibilities)

In accordance with the legislation at hand; explain who can/will see the interview and or/ the recording of it afterwards. You may want to stress that it will not be publicly available / available online or given out to other people than those concerned.

My co-workers will also be following this conversation from the room next door through that camera. They are there to help me, and they will remind me if I forget to ask you about something important. We will take a break at some point, and then I will ask them if there is anything else that I should ask you about.

Adjust the questions according to the child's developmental level.

There are certain ground rules related to this discussion, which I would like to tell you about next.

3.1 Understanding

It is important that we understand each other as well as possible. If I ask you a question that you don't understand, please tell me that you don't understand.

If I don't understand what you say, I'll ask you to explain.

And if I accidentally say something that is not true, you must tell me about it. Is that okay?

According to the child's age, practice these rules with some examples. The younger the child, the more they might need concrete examples to understand the concepts of the interview well. For example: "If I said that you are a ten-year old boy *(when the child is not)*, what should you answer?".

If the child does not get it right the first time, pose another practice question, for instance "You are wearing a grey jacket, what should you answer?" *or similar.*

Correct a wrong answer or reinforce the child if they give the right answer.

3.2 I don't know /I don't remember

If I ask you a question and you don't know the answer, just tell me: "I don't know."

So, if I ask you, [e.g. what did I have for breakfast today], what would you say? *If the child says: "I don't know", say:* Exactly. You don't know. *If the child offers a guess, ask:* Do you know what I had for breakfast today? *And continue:* No, you don't know me and [e.g., you weren't with me when I had my breakfast this morning], so you don't know. When you don't know the answer, please don't guess, just say that you don't know.

If the child does not get it right the first time, pose another practice question, for instance "What colour is my car / what is the name of my cat" *or similar.*

Correct a wrong answer or reinforce the child if she or he gives the right answer.

3.3 The right to decline

Part of my job is to talk to children and young people about things that have happened to them. I meet with lots of children and young people so that they can tell me the truth about things that have happened to them. It is very important that you tell me the truth today about things that have happened to you.

Here you might ask the child to promise to tell the truth or ask, "Can we agree that you will only tell the truth here when talking to me today?".

Legal rights or obligations relevant for the national context may be addressed in a similar way; making sure the child understands the situation as well as possible (if this has not already been done prior to the interview). Such obligations or rights may be, for example, the right not to incriminate a family member or the criminal liability for children over the age of 15 years. These need to be planned ahead of the interview, taking into account national legal requirements and the child's age, development and possible vulnerabilities.

The most important rule is that you must tell the truth. So if there is something you do not want to talk about, just tell me you don't want to talk about it. Is this okay with you?

4. PRACTISE INTERVIEW and building further rapport (Training in episodic memory)

Prior to the interview, please identify a recent, positive and meaningful event in which the child actively participated. The purpose is to ask the child to narrate something that has occurred and follow up on what the child has narrated similarly as with the suspected offence.

4.1 *Main invitation*

Before we talk about why you're here today, we're going to practise a bit. I would like for you to tell me as much as you can recall about an event or something that you have experienced. I understand that a few [days, weeks] ago there was [a holiday, birthday party, other event]? Tell me everything that happened [during the event], from the beginning to the end, as best as you can.

In case an event wasn't identified previously, ask: Has there recently been any special event that you could tell me about? / Have you done something out of the ordinary in your free time recently?

If the child doesn't identify a suitable event, say: So, tell me everything that happened [today, yesterday], from the time you woke up until you [got here / went to bed].

4.2 *Follow-up invitations*

Thank you, you have told me many things *[if they did*]. I want to ask you some more questions about what just you told me. *Repeat briefly, what the child has said and pair this with open-ended follow-up questions:* And then what happened? *Use this question as often as needed throughout this section until you have been given a full account of the event.*

Remember to support the child's account through active listening, nodding, showing interest, and thanking the child. Reinforce the child by providing supportive comments throughout in a way that feels natural to you and adapted to the development and context of the child, for instance: "Thank you [child] for telling me that. What you say is very clear and helps me understand what happened"/ Thank you for sharing that with me, it helps me get to know you.

4.3 *Time Segmenting invitations*

Try to use three times segmenting invitations, although you may adjust the quantity and type of

invitations to the child's capabilities and reactions, probing for information from different parts of the event described by the child.

Please tell me everything that happened from the moment [an activity the child mentioned] to the moment [a subsequent mentioned activity].

For example: You told me that you played inside before going to the market. Tell me everything that happened at home from the time you woke up until you left to go to the market".

Adjust to the child's developmental level, for example, asking simply "Tell me about the playing / going to the market" *if the child has difficulties understanding the longer instruction.*

4.4 *Cued invitations*

You should also aim to use some other questions probing for more detail. (About time, events, thoughts, emotions).

> Tell me more about [an activity, object]. / Earlier you spoke of [an activity, object]. Tell me all about that.

> Also ask the child about their thoughts and feelings.

> Earlier, you spoke about [thought, feeling]. Tell me more about that.

> If the child doesn't mention what they thought or felt, you can ask:

> You mentioned [X], tell me what did you think about that? / Tell me how did it make you feel?

4.5 *Discussing the topic of online activities*

If the child has not brought up any online activities (gaming, using Snapchat, TikTok, Instagram, Discord, Reddit, watching Youtube, streaming on Twitch, etc.) previously, you may also inquire about these, as openly as possible. This may be a good way to find out the child's general knowledge of online issues as well as how they describe them.

Examples of online-related questions:

Tell me about things you like to do online?

If the child doesn't understand the concept of "being online", you can ask:

Tell me about things you like to do on your phone? [/other devices]

Continue with cued invitations to ask the child for free narratives about issues they have already mentioned:

You told me that you are [*just scrolling around*], tell me more about that?

You told me you play [*Brawl stars*]. Tell me about that!

You told me you like [*TikTok*]. Tell me more about that!

You told me you like to use [*Snapchat*]. I'm new to the app myself, so I don't know that much about it. Could you please tell me more about it

You said that you are playing/online/chatting with your friends, what device do you use to do that?

You may also probe for more detail about different aspects of the online activities as well as the child's experiences, thoughts and emotions related to these.

You told me you play [*FIFA22*]. Tell me more about that game?

You told me about this online game [*Fortnite*] – tell me more. You said it has different characters. Tell me about the characters.

You told me you like to spend time on [*TikTok*]. Tell me about that. (*If the child doesn't give a descriptive response, you may ask:* What do you usually do there?)

You told me you usually play around 2 hours on a weeknight. Please tell me everything you can about that.

Tell me about using snapchat.

Tell me about the place you are in physically when [you play games/ use snapchat]? *(According to what the child has told about online activities. At home, at school, outside, in your room, at a friend's house, etc.)*

Tell me about other people who are present when you are gaming/ playing games? *(Physically in the same room / in the kitchen, in another room)*

You mentioned that your character has a nickname, tell me more about the nicknames?

You said you knew these things about these characters. Tell me how you know these things?

You said that you know these things because you've talked to them. Tell me more about talking with them?

Tell me about what happens when you are online? *(Pose follow up questions about how, where, whom / messages / chatting / on the phone / via video / webcam?)*

IMPORTANT: When a child tells you about events occurring in a digital space or a social media platform, always clarify the child's account, character, nickname, username or account name. Remember to clarify how the child understands the terms and concepts you are talking about, for example "service", "nickname", "user". For example: "Do you know what a username is? Can you tell me?" Can you tell me about usernames you use? *or* "You mentioned he DM'ed you, tell me about that?"

Remember to do this for all important terms used by the child, "You mentioned that you were scrolling your FYP, can you tell me what that means/ more about that?", "You said that the situation was bit sus, tell me what do you mean by that/more about that?", *also when you think you understand their meaning. For example, the exact meaning of sexual terms may be of crucial importance in a possible trial.*

5. THE SUBSTANTIVE PHASE (The alleged offence)

The interview proceeds to the suspected offence on a case-by-case basis, taking into account the individual characteristics (and hypotheses) of the incident, e.g. by referring to something the child has said, a doctor's appointment, someone's expressed worry about a child's internet contact or pictures or chat logs sent to the police or discovered by the child's guardians. Below are some example questions illustrating how you may address the issue. However, you must always plan them as appropriate.

5.1. *Transition to discussing the suspected offence*

Now (that we know each other a little better), I want to talk about why [you are, I am] here today. *Always plan how you'll proceed to the suspected offence on a case-by-case basis! As soon as the child begins to talk about the suspicion / offence, move to section 5.2.*

Do you know why you have come to see me today?

What did [*name of person escorting the child to the interview/mother/father...]* tell you when you came here?

Where online issues have been discussed during the interview, you can make a transition to the topic of the allegation for example like this: We have discussed some things you like to do online. Are there other things that you have experienced online that you would like to tell me about?

If the child doesn't seem to know why they are being interviewed or does not bring the subject up, there are two different scenarios of how to proceed according to the strength of the evidence already in the case.

It can be that the police have

5.1. A) strong evidence; photos, videos or other indisputable solid evidence such as messages, chat logs etc. that this child has been a victim of a crime or

5.1. B) suspicion / weaker evidence that this child has come up in the investigation as a possible victim and the police needs to know what the child knows about the perpetrator and possible abusive experiences.

Below are examples of possible ways to proceed with the interview in either scenario. Keep in mind that the child may not know why they are being interviewed. In this case, a gradual and careful provision of cues should follow so that the child is not forced to tell, and questions are as non-leading as possible. It is also possible that the child knows / thinks they know why the investigation is taking place and is reluctant to disclose due to feelings of responsibility, shame, fears of others' reactions or because they are in love with the perpetrator (or the person the perpetrator pretends to be) etc. In this case, the focus should be on continuous rapport building and support to reduce anxiety, to regulate emotions, to cope with internal conflicts and so.

5.1. TRANSITION A: For suspicions with solid/strong evidence; photos, videos or other indisputable solid evidence such as messages, chat logs etc. that this child has been a victim of a crime

The following example questions are created for situations where there is ***strong evidence*** *that the child has been a victim of online sexual abuse. This has to be judged on a case-by-case basis, depending on the available evidence. For example, pictures or video material of the child or proof of sexual conversations with the child have been delivered or reported to the police by the child's guardians, the internet service providers or other authorities.*

> The police are investigating a case where a user in [*Snapchat, edit to fit the case*] has contacted children and [*asked them to send pictures / sent them pictures, edit to fit the case]*. I want to ask you some questions about this. Tell me anything you know about this.
>
> This username is [*nickname / username Mr. Hoot, edit to fit the case*]. Tell me what you know about this *[username]*?
>
> *If appropriate (i.e., the child seems very reluctant or there is reason to believe they feel guilty themselves):* Sometimes children may experience confusing and unpleasant things online. Some children might think that they have done something wrong, but I just want you to know that this is not something you need to worry about now / we are not here because you have done something bad / forbidden.

Examples:

> The police have investigated devices (computer / phone) used by [*Mr. Hoot, use the username of the perpetrator, as the child does not necessarily know their real name or identity or that the perpetrator is an adult*] and found messages sent by their and pictures sent to them by children. Please tell me anything you know about this / Can you tell me anything about this / [*Mr Hoot*]?
>
> The police have found messages that Mr Hoot has sent to [*Flowergirl13, use the child's username*]. Can you tell me something more about this? *If the child doesn't answer:* Can you tell me about the username Flowergirl13?
>
> The police have found some photographs / videos when you are present. Can you tell me about these? (How have these photos ended up with Mr. Hoot?)

Where applicable: Again, please remember that we are not here because you would have done something wrong. The police are investigating what this person(s) (Mr. Hoot) has/have done.

The child is reluctant to talk

If the child contradicts available evidence, you can use one of the supportive statements, which refer specifically to the child.

[I am, people] are worried about you and I want to know if something may have happened to you. / If something has happened to you and you want it to stop, you can tell me about it. / Sometimes children think that if something happened to them, it's their fault, but children are not responsible if things happen to them.

If the child continues to contradict available evidence, remind the child that about it. Be supportive and encouraging.

If there is something you don't want to tell me about, just say so. You have the right to not tell me about it. Just tell me you don't want to talk about it, and I will respect that. / It's your choice if you want to tell me and it is my job to let you choose.

If the evidence recovered by the police clearly shows that the suspect has told the child not to tell anyone, this can be referred to as well;

I have seen messages sent to you by Mr. Hoot where he has told you not to talk about this with anyone, but you should know / I want you to know that you have the right to tell me anything you want / no one has the right to forbid you from telling about these things ...

If there is strong evidence that Mr. Hoot has asked the child to send naked pictures (etc.) or sent naked pictures of his own, you can refer to that;

The conversations we have seen seem to show that Mr. Hoot has *[asked children to send him pictures*] – tell me about that.

In some cases, it is possible to reveal the identity of the perpetrator to the child at this stage. However, consider carefully how to present this, as the child might be unaware that the perpetrator is an adult.

The police have found out that Mr. Hoot is actually not a child, but an older person (e.g., adult man), who has been in contact with several children. It is therefore important that we get all the information about him/her/them that we can. If you could tell us everything you know and remember about him/her, it would help the police very much to investigate the case better. Anything you know about him, any pieces of information you remember would be helpful to us.

5.1. TRANSITION B: Suspicion with weaker evidence. *The child has come up in the investigation as a possible victim and the police need to know what the child knows about the perpetrator and whether anything criminal has happened to her.*

The police are investigating a case where a certain user in [*Snapchat, edit to fit the case*] has contacted children and [*asked them to send pictures / sent them pictures edit to fit the case]* and I want to ask you some questions about this. Tell me if there is anything you know about this?

The moderators / administrators of [*Snapchat, edit to fit the case*] have informed the police about this username, who we believe has been contacting children. Please tell me everything you know about this username?

If the child doesn't seem to talk about the topic of the interview, here are some further examples:

You told me that you use [*service, platform, game – edit according to the case at hand*]. Tell me about that.

What is your username / account name / nickname on there?

Have you ever used other usernames?
Have you ever used the username [*Flowergirl13*]?
Tell me everything about that, on what sites / games / platforms have you used this username?

Have you ever interacted with the username [*Mr. Hoot*]? … "Tell me about that".
If the child denies, refrain from asking any more direct questions regarding this. You can address neutral support that doesn't imply something happened, example: Here kids can talk about good things and bad things that have happened to them. / If there is anything you want to tell me. / It's important for me to know/ listen. *Consider discussing neutral topics or taking a break or proceed towards closing the interview.*

Closure: In cases where the child has not disclosed anything; thank them for coming and say that it is understandable that the situation may feel difficult for them. Make sure to give the child contact details if they later feel there are things they would like to tell. Again, it is important to stress that the police don't think that the child has done anything wrong / bad (choose wording according to the child's age and the culture/context/language use at hand – and only for cases where there is no suspicion the child would have engaged in any criminal act themselves).

5.2 Exploring the incidents

If the child discloses any information, the interview is structured in accordance with the regular NICHD-R manual, using open questions to investigate what happened. It is also important to constantly give supportive comments to calm the child's possible anxiety, reduce reluctance and elicit detailed disclosures. Throughout the entire substantive part, it is important to preserve and enhance the rapport established with the child. Encourage and support the child in talking about what has happened.

If the child mentions a specific incident:

Explore eventual other applications.

If the child mentions several accounts, or several different episodes with the same perpetrator, thank the child for disclosing important information and investigate the situations one by one by referring back to what the child has previously said:

> You told me about someone who contacted you on Snapchat using the name X, tell me everything you can remember about them, from when they first contacted you until the last time you were in contact.

If the child mentions a number of incidents:

> You told me that [*briefly summarise the allegation the child has made*]. Tell me everything about [*the last/ first time/ at place/ at time/ specific incident]* from the beginning to the end.

You should aim to use the same expressions as used by the child (for example, "Tell me about the time your mother was raging about screen time.", "Tell me about the time Mr. Hoot got angry when you didn't put your camera on").
If the child gives a generic description and you cannot determine the number of incidents:

> You told me that you have been in touch with Mr. Hoot more than one time on [*WhatsApp, TikTok and Snapchat*]. Tell me everything about the first time you were in contact with him.

Let the child answer. And then what happened?

Tell me everything that has happened from the first contact with Mr. Hoot until the last one?

You told me that [*briefly summarise the allegation the child has made*]. Did that happen one time or more than one time?

You told me that Mr. Hoot sent you the first message on [*Instagram*]. Has he sent you messages there one time or more than once?

If the description is still generic, you can ask for examples:

You told me that Mr. Hoot asked for your *[TikTok*] username and then started to message you there. Tell me everything about that from beginning to end.

Please repeat the child's description of the action/occurrence that started the event. Then ask:

And then what happened?

You have told me many things and helped me understand what happened. Now,

I want to ask you more questions about [incident title]. Think back to that time [day, night] and please tell me everything that happened from the moment [an activity the child mentioned] to the moment [a subsequent activity the child mentioned].

Tell me more about [activity, object, feeling, thought].

You mentioned [activity, object, feeling, thought]. Tell me more about that.

You may also ask the child if they can show you the messages (either at this point or later in the interview)

5.3. Questions probing for more details (Directive questions)

The aim of this part of the interview is to elicit more information in narrative form using questions related to time, place, different internet site or applications

or games as well as feelings and thoughts. Always use as open-ended questions as possible and move onto more directive ones once you have collected as much information as possible using the open-ended ones. Make sure you test the relevant alternative hypotheses concerning the suspicion. Use further follow-up questions relevant to the child's account and the suspected incident.

Before ending the interview, take a short break or a moment to look at the checklist to ensure all relevant subjects have been discussed. Below are examples of online-related follow-up questions for different themes. You can use these as suitable for the case at hand or edit these examples according to the case, if answers to these questions have not already been answered by the child's previous disclosure.

General:

> Earlier you talked about [*activity, object, thought, feeling*] Tell me more about that.
>
> What do you mean when you say [*term used by the child*]?
>
> Earlier you talked about disturbing comments from Mr. Hoot. Tell me more about that.

First meeting:

> You told me that you have been in touch with Mr. Hoot on several different applications. Tell me everything about the very first time you were in contact?

Continued contact:

> You told me Mr. Hoot first messaged you on Instagram and then he continued to message you on Snapchat. Tell me how Mr. Hoot contacted you on Snapchat?
>
> You told me that you were talking on WhatsApp. Tell me more about that.
>
> You told me that you chatted (in the past) Mr. Hoot in TikTok? Tell me about the first / last time / tell me about how the contact ended?
>
> You told me about being in contact with Mr. Hoot, tell me about this? *If the time remains unclear, anchor what the child told you to a specific*

time (e.g. "Which grade were you in?", "Did this happen before or after Christmas?")

You told me that you used to message each other every week. Tell me about the last time you heard from him / you were in contact?

You said that you have been talking with Mr. Hoot, are you still in contact with him? / Do you think you might still hear from him (*if the child declines, you may ask them to expand – the child might for example have deleted the account or declined further contact)*

(*If the contact has ended*): You said the contact has ended. Tell me about that?

Investigating age / other facts

Tell me about what Mr. Hoot knows about you.

Tell me about the conversations you've had with Mr. Hoot. (What kinds of things did you talk about?)

You mentioned that Mr. Hoot knows your age. Can you explain how Mr. Hoot came to know these things about you? (*For example: Does the child's profile mention their age, is their profile public or private, does the profile show the child's age in the public information even if the rest of the profile is private, is the platform, for example Discord channel, made for children born a specific year, does the child's username include their year of birth or age etc.)* / Tell me did you talk with Mr. Hoot about your age? (*Remember that the suspects' knowledge of the age of the child may be crucial to the judicial context.)*

Tell me about when you've talked about your age with Mr. Hoot. (Where, when, how)

Tell me about what Mr. Hoot has shared with you about himself?

Is there anything else you know about Mr. Hoot?

Used apps / social media platforms / services

Tell me about the places or apps where you've talked with Mr. Hoot. (*You can ask the child to explain how the service/app/game works, how messages are sent etc;* Tell me how that app works / how you messaged etc*)*

Tell me about the different ways you communicated with Mr. Hoot.

How have you talked to / been in contact with Mr. Hoot? (*On a public chat -where-, sent private messages -where-, via WhatsApp, via e-mail, using a webcam, using Facetime, on the phone etc.)*

Actions

You told me about the time when Mr. Hoot turned weird. Tell me more about that. What happened next?

You told me that you responded, tell me about that.

You said that Mr. Hoot started asking weird questions. Tell me more about that.

You said that you used to send messages every night. Tell me about those messages?

Tell me where were you when this happened? (Both online and physically)

Tell me about who was around when this happened? (*Both online in the same game / server / chat and physically in the same room, home at the same time, where*)

Tell me how you were feeling or what you were thinking while this was happening?

Tell me about your feelings or thoughts afterwards / after it happened.

Taking / sending pictures

A) *In the case where it is not sure, whether there are photos of this victim:*

The police have information that Mr. Hoot has asked children to send him pictures of themselves. Can you tell me anything about this? / What do you know about this?

(Ask direct questions only if the child hasn't told you about this in response to open questions:)

Has Mr. Hoot asked you to send him pictures of yourself? (*If yes):* Tell me about this.

Has Mr. Hoot made you send him pictures? / Have you sent him pictures of yourself?

(If yes): What kind of pictures / videos have you sent him? (What happens in the pictures? What can be seen in the pictures?)

If the child confirms pictures, messages or videos have been exchanged that the police do not yet have access to, you may ask whether the child still have them on their device and if so, explain that these may be important for the police to investigate the actions of the suspect. The child may need reassurance that only adults who are looking into the issue professionally will be able to see the material, as they may feel embarrassed about it.

B) *If there is evidence of pictures of this particular child, but the child hasn't mentioned this:*

The police have found pictures of you from Mr. Hoot/Mr Hoot's computer. Can you tell me about this?

(Again, ask direct questions only if the child hasn't told you about this in response to open questions:)

Do you know how Mr. Hoot has these kinds of pictures? / How has Mr. Hoot gotten these pictures?

If the child says they sent the pictures themselves:

How did you take the pictures? (*also explore the device used)*

What happened to the pictures then?

→ Do you still have these pictures on your device (phone / pad / computer)?

What happened to the messages?

→ Do you still have messages between you and Mr. Hoot on your phone or your profile?

Other victims:

Tell me do you know anyone else who has sent messages to Mr. Hoot?

Tell me what do you know about them / the other children / that?

Meeting:

You said that you had talked about different kinds of things with Mr. Hoot. Tell me did you ever talk about meeting in real life with him?

(*if not clear from the open answer* - Who was the first one to suggest that?)

You said that you had talked about a lot of things. Tell me everything you think that you know about him.

5.5 What has the child disclosed about the incident to other people?

Explore the disclosure process, addressing the disclosure timing, circumstances, recipients, potential discussions of the event, and reactions to disclosure by both the child and recipients. Use open-ended questions whenever possible. For example:

Tell me about any person who knows about [Mr. Hoot]?

Tell me about any people Mr. Hoot introduced you to?

Can you tell me if there was anyone you introduced to Mr. Hoot? Tell me everything you remember about that situation?

Tell me about the people you've spoken to about what happened. Tell me everything you remember about those conversations?
Tell me more about your conversations with [person]. What did you talk about when it came to [sending pictures]? What do you remember saying?

Tell me about who might have seen the messages or pictures you sent to Mr. Hoot. Can you remember who, how they saw them, or where this happened?

If there are sexual pictures of the child circulating online, find out if the child is aware of this. Remember, that this can be very traumatising to the child and be prepared to direct him/her to relevant counselling /support groups after the interview. This needs to be planned ahead of the interview and adjusted to the child's level of development and understanding.

You told me before that Mr. Hoot had asked you to send him photos where you don't have your clothes on and that you had sent them to him. Tell me if you know what he needed them for? Tell me if you know what happened to these photos?

If the child doesn't seem to know about the distribution, try to talk about it as delicately as possible.

The police have found that Mr. Hoot has [*sent these photos further to someone / sold some photos further / posted some photos on xx, edit to fit the case*]. Your photo has been among these distributed materials. The police are doing the best we can to remove all your photos from the [*site / application / service*].

Make every effort to support the child and help them regulate their emotions, remind them that the responsibility is on the perpetrator, not on the child.

Do not confront the child with material unless absolutely necessary (or unless the child themselves want to see the material). For instance, to establish that it indeed is a certain child in a certain picture, you can show some of the background of the room or a piece of clothing or similar rather than the full material. Be mindful that sometimes material may be AI-generated.

Examine how the suspected incident has affected the child in an age-appropriate manner.

Tell me how you feel about talking with me today?

Tell me how do you feel about going home after this?
What do you wish to happen next?

F. *Ending the interview*

When closing the interview, it is good to ensure that the child has been able to tell everything that they have to say about the case. Thank the child and credit them for talking to you about their experiences.

Is there anything else you would like to tell me about?

Something I haven't come to think of to ask you about?

Is there anything you would like to ask me about? *For instance, does the child have questions about how the investigation will proceed?*

If you later come up with things that you haven't remembered to tell me, you can contact me (*tell the child how to best contact you, WhatsApp, text message or email for example*).

Remember, that you haven't done anything wrong here.

If you see something similar happening again in the future, to you or someone else, you can save the relevant information, for example by taking a screenshot, and send it to me (*or someone else, who?*).

It is important that the police know about these things, because the suspects are usually in contact with more than one child. The police need to know about these things, so the adults who do these things can be caught and stopped.

Talk with the child for a couple of minutes about a neutral topic. Also check that the child knows who to talk to / contact if he/she feels that he/she needs help related to the issue or if he/she later recalls something related to the discussed topic.

What are you going to do after we finish talking?

Thank the child for their time.

Notes

1 Modification by Dr Julia Korkman and Detective Sergeant Maria Rossi. Reviewed and commented by Dr Malin Joleby, Prof. Irit Hershkowitz, Prof. Michael E. Lamb, MEd, LPC Linda Cordisco Steele, Shawnna von Blixen-Finecke. Suggestions for further improvement can be sent to jkorkman(at)abo.fi and will be received with gratitude.

2 *demonstrably = the conversation or pictures have been saved on the child's own device or a device the child uses, or the nickname or account is known to be used by the child. This may be the case, for instance, when the child themself acknowledges using the account or username, or the information has been provided by the service provider based on registration- or log-in information, or when it is by other means clear.*

Further reading and resources:

Lamb., M.E., Brown, D.A., Hershkowitz, I., Orbach, Y. & Esplin, P.W. (2018). Tell me what happened: Questioning children about abuse, 2nd edition. Wiley.

Joleby, M., Lunde, C., Landström, S. & Jonsson, L.S. (2020). All of me is completely different: Experiences and consequences among victims of technology-assisted child sexual abuse. *Frontiers in Psychology,* doi: 10.3389/fpsyg.2020.606218

Korkman, J. & Joleby, M. (in press)

Disclosures and denials by young people suspected of sexual offences

Irit Hershkowitz, Tal Weissman Ben-Shahar, and Michael E. Lamb

Young people sometimes struggle to disclose abusive sexual experiences during forensic interviews. Truthful and detailed disclosures are the goal of forensic interviews, and these are often a prerequisite for access to justice and treatment regardless of whether the individuals are alleged victims, witnesses, or initiators of the sexual acts concerned. However, when children who are suspected of committing sexual acts are considered legally responsible, their disclosures and self-incrimination by admitting allegations made against them can result in legal proceedings. The inherent conflict among the desire to simultaneously safeguard the suspected children's rights, ensure their welfare along with the wellbeing of other children, and to understand possible offences illustrates the complexity of conducting forensic interviews with young suspects.

In this chapter we discuss denials, genuine disclosures or confessions, and possible false confessions by young suspects. Suspects, including young suspects, commonly deny suspected offences and are reluctant to disclose their wrongdoing, perhaps out of distrust, fear, or shame. Overcoming denial is important in order to reveal the truth and best serve the interests of justice and public safety. A child's denial can also be a barrier to treatment, not least because suspects who fail to take responsibility for their actions are less likely to be assigned to treatment programs and more likely to be subject to punitive measures.

However, when child suspects are pressured to admit the allegations against them in typical police investigations, they are more likely to incriminate themselves naively and involuntarily than adults are. Due to their immaturity, they are often unable to take advantage of legal protections against self-incrimination or to withstand coercive police pressure. Thus when subject to harsh interrogation tactics and psychological manipulations, young suspects may falsely admit offences they have not committed. Innocent young suspects may then be involved in unnecessary and harmful legal proceeding which have serious implications for their development and mental health.

DOI: 10.4324/9781003427155-8

The challenges for interviewers are thus to ensure that child suspects feel safe and confident, understand their rights and make voluntary decisions, and that they are interviewed using open, supportive and respectful methods without pressure. Although confessions provided in well-conducted interviews are desirable, those achieved in compromised interviews are inappropriate, unacceptable and risky. Of course, all children cannot be expected to fully understand the situation and make thoughtful and informed decisions that serve their best interests; even many adults struggle to navigate interrogations. Nevertheless, interviewers should strive to create the conditions that optimize children's functioning in forensic contexts.

This chapter provides an up-to-date review of the extant research, emphasizing the vulnerability of young suspects and discussing how they should best be interviewed. In that context, we describe a recent adaptation of the Revised NICHD protocol, the Revised Suspect Protocol (RSP), which involves developmentally appropriate and supportive strategies. Before doing so, however, we first describe the characteristics of children who engage in sexually harmful behaviour and the risk they pose to other children.

Who are these young suspects?

Although those children have been variably labelled, sometimes as child perpetrators or sexually abusive children, some researchers have suggested the adoption of less stigmatizing terminology, such as "children with harmful or problematic sexual behavior" (PBS; Campbell, Booth, Hackett, & Sutton, 2020; Silovsky, Letourneau & Bonner, 2020) in recognition of the fact that their behaviour is developmentally inappropriate and potentially harmful. Although some sexual behaviours are "normal" in childhood or adolescence, those become problematic when they involve much younger children and when they are aggressive or manipulative (Hackett, 2014). Children with PBS can be surprisingly young: a quarter of those so diagnosed are under 12 years of age (Puzzanchera, Sladky, & Kang, 2017), and prevalence rates peak between the ages of 12 and 14, after which they tend to drop or plateau (Dopp, Perrine, Parisi, Hill, & Caldwell, 2020; Finkelhor, Ormrod & Turner, 2009). Attempting to explain this surprising finding, Letourneau, Schaeffer, Bradshaw, Ruzicka, Assini-Meytin, Nair, and Thorne (2024) noted that early adolescence is commonly a time for exploring sexual relationships, which involve complex behaviours, rules and norms, as well as a time during which it is common to make mistakes and wrong decisions. Unfortunately, unclear messages from adults about developmentally normative sexual behaviour, sexual consent, and age of consent also abound.

Letourneau, Schaeffer, Bradshaw, and Feder (2017) described a multitude of risk factors associated with the development of PBS in the heterogeneous group of children involved (Chaffin et al., 2008). Recognized risk factors include exposure to pornography, poor knowledge about sex, experiences of abuse or neglect, inadequate supervision, negative peers, impulsivity, lack of boundaries, family problems, social problems, inappropriate parental discipline, and a history of trauma (Allen, 2017); of course, some of those factors characterize children with problematic non-sexual behaviours as well. Emphasizing the reversible risk factors that can be addressed by preventive programs, Letourneau et al. (2024) underscored these youth's poor understanding of child sexual abuse (CSA) and its definition, legal issues that pertain to CSA, sexual consent, and strategies to avoid, prevent, or address CSA. Others have identified poor self-control, judgement, and social environments (Ronis & Borduin, 2013) as risk factors, although again these are associated with non-sexual behaviour problems as well. Unfortunately, researchers have yet to identify risk factors associated only with sexual behaviour problems.

Children with PSB are amenable to treatment and are highly responsive to even low intensity behavioural management interventions, such as adaptations of Cognitive Behavioural Therapy (CBT), and represent little risk to other children following intervention (Chaffin, 2008; Letourneau, McCart, Asuzu, Mauro, & Sheidow, 2013; Letourneau, Henggeler, Borduin, Schewe, McCart, Chapman, & Saldan, 2009; Silovsky, Hunter, & Taylor, 2019). For example, Carpentier, Silovsky & Chaffin (2006) followed 12-year-old children with PBS for 10 years post CBT and reported a 2% rate of recidivism Similarly, Silovsky et al. (2019) reported significant decreases in PSB as well as internalizing, externalizing, and trauma symptoms for youth aged 10–14 following such an intervention. This is consistent with results of an earlier meta-analysis revealing that intervention was related to significant decreases in PSB (St. Amand, Bard, & Silovsky, 2008); such interventions included helping caregivers to manage child behaviour, sex education, abuse prevention, and the discussion of sexual behaviour rules. Even with youth displaying delinquent behaviours, low intensity treatment reduced externalizing behaviour problems (Jenkins, Grimm, Shier, van Dooren, Ciesar, & Reid-Quiñones, 2020). Thus, researchers have recommended that youth who have engaged in harmful sexual behaviour should be offered the least-restrictive intervention (Christiansen & Vincent, 2013). Unfortunately, however, most adolescents are referred to intensive and overly restrictive residential programs employing non-validated interventions (Chaffin, 2008; Kettrey, & Lipsey, 2018; Letourneau & Miner, 2005).

Research also shows that channeling children with any harmful behaviour into the juvenile legal system does not decrease recidivism and can even increase it (for a meta-analysis of research on children with non-sexual behaviour problems see Petrosino, Turpin-Petrosino, & Guckenburg, 2010). Moreover, juvenile court adjudications and criminal court convictions for children can have long-term effects on mental and physical health, education and employment opportunities, as well as subsequent juvenile and adult legal system involvement (Baker, Tazi, & Haney-Caron, 2023; Barnert et al., 2018; Jung, 2015; Powell, 2022). Overall, evidence-based interventions can improve outcomes for children with problematic sexual behaviour and avoidance of criminal sanctions is important for children in general.

What risk do these children pose to other children?

Although youth with PSB pose a very low risk to other children after they have been treated effectively, they may present a very serious risk if they have not. For example, Puzzanchera et al. (2017) suggested that more than one third of all offences against children, including very serious offences, such as rape or sexual assault with an object, were committed by other youth. Surprisingly, even very young suspects (those under 12) were involved in such serious crimes, representing as much as 23% of all young suspects. In another study (Finkelhor et al., 2009), US juvenile justice records suggested that 12- to 14-year-old adolescents were responsible for most juvenile offences against children under age 12, with similar figures found in the UK (Radford, Corral, Bradley, & Fisher, 2013) and Nordic countries (Kloppen, Haugland, Svedin, Mæhle, and Breivik, 2016). A later representative survey yielded the most concerning figure, with over 70% of CSA survivors in the US (76.7% for males and 70.1% for females) reportedly abused sexually by another child, most often a slightly older adolescent (Gewirtz-Meydan & Finkelhor, 2020). Perhaps such high estimates emerge from survivors' reports but not criminal justice records because alleged victims of other children delay disclosure and assume some responsibility for the abuse more than children alleging abuse by adults (Malloy et al., 2011).

In sum, sexually harmful behaviour by children and adolescents is clearly a serious social problem, affecting millions of child victims worldwide, with youth substantially contributing to persistently high CSA prevalence rates (Marcantonio et al., 2022; Letourneau et al., 2024). However, the treatment of these youths in the legal system is widely criticized on the grounds that it often fails to recognize developmental vulnerabilities and the youths' rights, compromising their access to justice.

Developmental vulnerability of youth during legal investigations

Despite the clear advantages of treatment over legal proceedings, youths who are suspected of committing sexual acts on other children are often referred to forensic investigators. The research reviewed below shows that they are not well equipped to participate effectively in forensic interviews, struggling to understand the rules of the investigation, to appreciate and invoke their rights, to withstand pressure exerted by interviewers, and to make legal decisions in their own best interests.

Cleary et al. (2017) reviewed the developmental factors likely to affect how youths behave when questioned, including a combination of reward sensitivity, self-regulation and future orientation. Supported by neurobiological evidence (Braams, Van Leijenhorst, & Crone, 2014; Luna, Padmanabhan, & Geier, 2014), developmental research suggests that adolescents, unlike adults and children, are particularly sensitive to reward (especially positive rewards; Casey, 2015), perhaps in response to hormonal processes (Shulman, Harden, Chein, & Steinberg, 2016), which may lead them to make hasty or false confessions in order to stop interviews (Malloy, Shulman, & Cauffman, 2014).

Reward sensitivity is especially influential in adolescence because self-regulation and cognitive control abilities, which can moderate this sensitivity, are still developing (Casey & Caudle, 2013; Steinberg, 2014). Adolescents tend to self-regulate poorly, especially under stressful and threatening conditions (Cohen et al., 2016) such as those that characterize forensic questioning which may involve multiple interviewers and prolonged pressure to confess (Malloy et al., 2014), lengthy interrogations (Davis & Leo, 2012), and social isolation in the absence of a parent or an attorney (Cleary, 2014; Feld, 2013). Under these threatening conditions, they are less able to control impulses, inhibit responses, and delay gratification, which may lead them to make poor legal decisions (Steinberg, 2008). Immature future orientation, including time perspective, anticipation of future events, and long-term planning (Steinberg, Cauffman, Woolard, Graham, & Banich, 2009), especially among delinquent youth (Cauffman, Steinberg, & Piquero, 2005), further strengthen youths' tendencies to prefer short term over long term rewards. Sharf, Rogers, and Williams (2017) reported that youths who only considered short-term consequences were 12 times more likely to waive their rights and confess. Thus, perceived threats derived from the interrogators' pressure and perceived rewards following promises of leniency may motivate youths' decision making and their tendencies to confess (Leo, 2012) during forensic interviews. Intriguingly, field studies suggest that interrogators employ high-pressure tactics with adolescents (Cleary, 2014; Feld, 2013), as well as techniques that intentionally increase the suspect's anxiety (Meyer & Reppucci, 2007), observations consistent with youths' self-reports (Arndorfer, Malloy, & Cauffman, 2015; Malloy et al., 2014). Police officers are trained to use the same techniques when questioning adults and youth (Cleary & Warner, 2016), and even when they report being aware that traditional interrogation practices may be problematic with youth, they do not make appropriate accommodations (Meyer & Reppucci, 2007).

Social development processes also render adolescents vulnerable to social influence and to power imbalances in the interview. Youths are more susceptible to influence than adults and are more likely to believe they need to obey authority, including police officers (Drury, 2003; Kassin et al., 2010; Meyer & Reppucci, 2007). Measures of intellectual functioning in adolescents predict suggestibility (McLachlan, Roesch, & Douglas, 2011), which in turn predicts false admission (Redlich & Goodman, 2003). In addition, interrogative suggestibility is negatively correlated with the comprehension of legal rights as well as with overall competence to stand trial (McLachlan et al., 2011; Redlich, Silverman, & Steiner, 2003). Adolescents are more likely than adults to change their statements in response to negative feedback (Redlich et al., 2003).

In addition to psycho-social and neurobiological factors, mental health factors may place young suspects at a disadvantage in forensic interviews. Many of the youth involved in the juvenile legal system have mental health problems (Fazel et al., 2008) and multiple psychiatric diagnoses (Copeland et al., 2007). These youth are likely to have experienced traumatic events and a substantial proportion of them are diagnosed with PTSD; among those with such a diagnosis, almost all report exposure to varied types of childhood trauma, and specifically to inter-personal violence (Abram et al., 2013; Dierkhising et al., 2013). Cleary et al. (2021) theorized that trauma predisposes young offenders to be susceptible to increased pressure from their interrogators and to making poor legal decisions. Correspondingly, psychopathology and negative life events increase interrogative suggestibility and promote false confession by young (Gudjonsson et al., 2009; Kassin, Drizin, Grisso, Gudjonsson, Leo, & Redlich, 2010) as well as adult (Drake, Gudjonsson, Sigfusdottir, & Sigurdsson, 2015) suspects. Cleary et al. (2021) also pointed to research that links trauma to reduced self-regulation, information processing and social judgment, skills that are essential for coping successfully in a high stress interview. Recognition of the developmental and clinical vulnerabilities that impede child suspects' performance in high pressure interviews has led researchers to suggest and assess ways to support their emotional and cognitive functioning.

The role of rapport and support when young suspects are interviewed

Many researchers have highlighted how rapport and an emotionally supportive environment can facilitate children's effective participation in interviews (Ahern, Sadler, Lamb, & Gariglietti, 2017; Collins et al., 2014; Saywitz, Larson, Hobbs, & Wells, 2015). As with young victims and witnesses, research shows that establishing rapport with suspects at the onset of the interview enhances their sense of wellbeing and trust in their interviewers, which in turn increases their cooperation and willingness to provide truthful statements. Because rapport is a powerful driver of disclosure, but in the case of child suspects, also of self-incrimination, it should be established with especially sensitive and neutral practices that enhance children's autonomy and avoid conveying any expectation that they should behave in certain ways to please the interviewer. Moreover, rapport should be seen as a component of the interview as a whole and be followed by open-ended and non-leading questioning and with non-suggestive support throughout the interview. Use of rapport in combination with pressure to waive rights and confess may strongly increase suggestibility and accompanying risks that the children might provide involuntary or even false accounts. Thus rapport building can have diverse effects and so must be employed very carefully in interviews with child suspects. Unfortunately, evidence shows that rapport is sometimes misused and is even used manipulatively to elicit confessions.

Rapport building has been extensively studied in interviews with adult criminal suspects and is widely considered to be a key component of humane approaches to reducing stress and enhancing trust and engagement. Although operational definitions vary, rapport in forensic interviews generally refers to the working relationship created by the interviewer to increase cooperation (Bettens, Cleary, & Bull, 2024; Beker Eck, 2022; Crough et al., 2022). Kelly et al. (2013) suggested that rapport is built and maintained through strategies like finding common ground with the interviewee, showing respect, or meeting the interviewee's basic needs. Other rapport-building practices include relationship-building tactics to promote personal connections, a demeanour-based approach to depicting the interviewer as friendly and available, and tactics that communicate interest in the suspect, including active listening and empathic responses (Gabbert, Hope, Luther, Wright, & Oxburgh, 2021; Meissner et al., 2021). Expert interviewers noted that rapport can be built with reluctant adolescents by paying attention to the interviewee's needs and providing appropriate support early in the interview (Gerryts, Deck, & Powell, 2024). Kaplan, Cutler, Leach, and Eastwood (2023) added that rapport is subjective in nature and reflects the interviewees' perceptions of the relationship with interviewers.

Humane approaches, which include rapport-building tactics, are associated with perceptions of the interrogation methods as fairer (Kebbell, Alison, & Hurren, 2008), self-reported cooperation and disclosure (Goodman-Delahunty, Martschuk, & Dhami, 2014; Snook, Brooks, & Bull, 2015), a higher likelihood of confession (Kebbell, Alison, Hurren, & Mazerolle, (2010), and with more reliable and critical information disclosure (Evans, Meissner, Ross, Houston, Russano, & Horgan, 2013). Indeed, a meta-analysis of laboratory-analogue studies showed that humane approaches were associated with more true confessions than were accusatorial approaches (Meissner et al., 2014). Emphasizing the subjective nature of relationships,

Bettens et al. (2024) recently showed that the use of humane strategies in forensic investigations predicted interrogation outcomes, confession, full cooperation and the disclosure of incriminating information. Increased subjective perceptions of rapport facilitated cooperation and information disclosure (Brimbal, Dianiska, Swanner, & Meissner, 2019; Brimbal et al., 2021; Deck, Quas, & Powell, 2024; Dianiska, Swanner, Brimbal, & Meissner, 2021; Gerryts et al., 2024; Goodman-Delahunty et al., 2014). Rapport between officers and suspects promoted cooperation and disclosure and was associated with more satisfactory case outcomes (Walsh & Bull, 2012). In addition, use of rapport strategies throughout the interview was more effective than just focusing on rapport-building early in the interview (Baker-Eck & Bull, 2022; Collins & Carthy, 2018). Alison, Alison, Noone, Elntib, and Christiansen (2013) showed that various rapport-building techniques were associated with positive interview outcomes, while Place and Meloy (2018) found that strategies involving empathy best overcame interviewee resistance, and Collins and Carthy (2019) reported that of three elements of rapport they analysed (attention, positivity, and coordination), coordination was positively correlated to information gain.

Interestingly, open questions facilitate rapport building and maintenance (Brubacher, Benson, Powell, Goodman-Delahunty, & Westera, 2020; Kelly & Valencia, 2021), and their co-occurrence in suspects' interviews is associated with higher cooperation from suspects (Kelly & Valencia, 2021). Indeed, Baker-Eck and Bull (2022) reported that the proportion of interviewers' questions that were open and the interviewers' empathy were associated with the amount of forensically relevant information provided. Lyon and Henderson (2021) emphasized the importance of having a balance between rapport-building and open-ended and wh- questions in order to gain more accurate information without eliciting false information.

Investigators have particular difficulty building rapport with older children and adolescents who are often reluctant to discuss embarrassing topics (Deck et al., 2024, Gerryts et al., 2024, Magnusson, Ernberg, Landström, & Akehurst, 2020). Although it is clear that they can provide more information about neutral topics than younger children can (Sauerland, Brackmann, & Otgaar, 2018), adolescents are more reluctant to share sensitive information like that discussed in forensic interviews (Augusti & Myhre, 2021; Dianiska, Luna, Winks, Quas, & Redlich, 2023) et al., 2023; Gerryts et al., 2024; McElvaney & Culhane, 2017). On the other hand, adolescents may especially benefit from rapport with interviewers: Sauerland et al. (2018) reported that adolescents who established rapport in a laboratory setting were more likely to be accurate than those who have not. Similarly, Dianiska, Simpson, and Quas (2024) found that, although rapport-building tactics differed in their impact, rapport with adolescents was generally associated with longer and more detailed narratives, especially from the youngest ones.

Interviewer support is not always distinguished from rapport building, with some researchers describing a supportive interviewer demeanour as one way to establish rapport (Gabbert, Hope, Luther, Wright, & Oxburgh, 2020). Others suggest that both rapport building and supportive behaviours are necessary aspects of a humane interviewing style (Alison et al., 2013; Clark & Milne, 2001; Dando & Oxburgh, 2016; Dando, Wilcock & Milne, 2008; Meissner, Redlich, Bhatt, & Brandon, 2012; Oxburgh & Ost, 2011). Yet others have focused on specific behaviours that can be considered supportive, such as empathy (Beker Eck & Bull, 2022). Supportive interviewing of reluctant young victims, witnesses and suspects is central to NICHD Protocol-guided interviews.

In a multi-year research project, Lamb, Hershkowitz and colleagues developed and implemented supportive interview techniques to cope with reluctance and reduce barriers to disclosure by victims of within-family abuse. They enhanced the developmentally attuned NICHD Protocol, which mostly focused on cognitive scaffolding, by adding more emphasis on socio-emotionally based practices, and particularly interviewer support, when devising the Revised NICHD Protocol (RP; Lamb, Brown, Hershkowitz, Orbach, & Esplin, 2018). Interviewers using the RP became more supportive and less insensitive to the reluctance of young alleged victims (Hershkowitz, Ahern, Lamb, Blasbalg, Karni-Visel, & Breitman, 2017), yielding decreased child reluctance and increased cooperativeness, increased emotional expression as well as improved informativeness, and increased disclosure rates in comparison to interviews conducted using the original or Standard Protocol (SP; Ahern, Hershkowitz, Lamb, Blasbalg, & Karni-Visel, 2019); Blasbalg, Hershkowitz, & Karni-Visel, 2018, Blasbalg, Hershkowitz, Lamb, Karni-Visel, & Ahern, 2019; Hershkowitz, Lamb, & Katz, 2014; Hershkowitz & Lamb, 2020; Karni-Visel, Hershkowitz, Lamb, & Blasbalg, 2019; Karni-Visel, Hershkowitz, Lamb, & Blasbalg, 2022). For a more detailed discussion of the RP, see Chapter 9 in this volume.

Hershkowitz and Lamb (2024) recently applied the lessons learned from use of the RP to interviews of youth who were suspected of sexually abusing children and were, like young suspected victims, reluctant to disclose or discuss their involvement in abusive events. The original NICHD Suspect Protocol (SSP) was altered to add a focus on the socio-emotional vulnerability of young suspects, resulting in the Revised Suspect Protocol (RSP). Interviewers using the RSP employed more supportive yet non-suggestive practices, established better rapport with the children, and obtained more complete and informative statements as discussed below.

Youths' comprehension of their legal rights

Like adults, young people need to be apprised of their legal rights before they are formally questioned in order for their statements to be admissible in court. Those rights (often referred to as Miranda rights in reference to the US Supreme Court decision that clarified those rights) include the right to remain silent and avoid self-incrimination, to speak to an attorney/parent/other adult before questioning, and to be advised by a lawyer if they so choose. A large body of research shows that many young people have difficulty understanding their rights and appreciating the long-term consequences of waiving those rights.

Unfortunately, the rights and associated warnings are often presented using unfamiliar words and complex syntax, which may impair recall of the information (Rogers, Steadham, Fiduccia, Drogin, & Robinson, 2014), undermine comprehension (Rogers, Hazelwood, Sewell, Harrison et al., 2008), and increase misunderstanding (Baker et al., 2023; Grisso, 1980; Zelle, Romaine, & Goldstein, 2015). Rogers and his colleagues (2014) have suggested that much of the relevant information delivered to youth may not be processed; after roughly 1 minute, youth had forgotten about two-thirds of what they were read, and even when they were presented using an additional modality (orally and in writing), youth recalled less than 50% of the key details (Rogers et al., 2016). Age and immaturity (Rogers, Blackwood, Fiduccia, Steadham, Drogin, & Rogstad, 2012; Rogers et al., 2014) as well as lower intelligence and academic performance (McLachlan et al., 2011) impair understanding of legal rights and make it more likely that young people will waive those rights and make valid or false confessions (Haney-Caron et al., 2018).

As far as comprehension is concerned, Woolard et al. (2008) found that 70% of young adolescents performed poorly on a standardized comprehension measure, and others reported that most youth did not understand one or more of the Miranda warnings (e.g. Grisso, 1980; Viljoen et al., 2007). Rates of impaired comprehension were even higher among youth in detention facilities, with 88% of them demonstrating comprehension deficits (Zelle et al., 2015). Beyond the uncommon language used to explain the rights, Rogers et al. (2016) suggested that the concepts are difficult for youth to understand and Palmer (2013) added that the anxiety-inducing nature of interrogations may further interfere with comprehension because stress inhibits cognitive performance.

Youths also appear to have difficulty grasping the consequences of waiving their rights. For example, over 40% of the youth in one study failed to understand that the waiver meant they would be formally questioned by the police (Abramovitch et al., 1993). Youth have particular difficulty appreciating that the right to remain silent (Goldstein et al., 2018; Viljoen et al., 2007) is fundamental and irrevocable rather than a conditional privilege that can be taken away (Goldstein et al., 2003, 2018), or that their silence could be used against them in court (Rogers et al., 2014).

Young people also tend to hold misconceptions about the nature and rules of interrogation, which may affect their decisions to waive or invoke their rights. For example, about half of youth (11- to 17- year-olds) in Woolard et al.'s (2008) study incorrectly believed that police must wait for parents to be present before questioning a minor, about half incorrectly believed that police are not allowed to lie to suspects, and one third did not know suspects can stop answering questions after having already started doing so. Zelle et al. (2015) also reported misunderstandings by youth about attorneys' roles and confusion between attorneys and other legal professionals such as social workers. Applying a formal measure of factual understanding of police interrogation practices among detained youth, Vidal et al. (2017) reported that, on average, the youths understood less than 60% of the relevant information.

Failure to describe their rights in a developmentally sensitive way may threaten comprehension by youth but police officers are not trained to adjust their techniques when questioning them (Cleary & Warner, 2016); many believe that the comprehension abilities of youth are similar to those of adults (Meyer & Reppucci, 2007). Some are aware that traditional interrogation practices may be problematic with youth, yet do not make appropriate accommodations (Meyer & Reppucci, 2007) although over 90% believe that officers are qualified and have been adequately trained to tell suspects of their legal rights (Time & Payne, 2002).

Observational studies suggest that officers often fail to present the legal rights in ways that are adjusted to youth capabilities and limitations. Although oral warnings are more difficult for suspects to comprehend, rights are typically administered orally (Chaulk et al., 2014; Kassin et al., 2007; McCardle et al., 2021) without use of an alternative (e.g. written) form to facilitate understanding (e.g. Eastwood & Snook, 2012; Hughes et al., 2013; Rogers et al., 2011). In addition, the rights are often presented in their entirety in a way that exceeds working memory capacity, rather than sentence by sentence as recommended (Fenner et al., 2002). Speech rate is not well suited for processing complex information (Rock, 2007; Sim & Lamb, 2018; Snook et al., 2010; Walsh & Bull, 2012) which may also compromise understanding. To check for understanding, officers may simply ask if the suspects understand their rights, without verifying that understanding (Walsh & Bull, 2012) or attempting to improve comprehension by providing complementary explanations (Eastwood et al., 2016; Snook et al., 2010, 2014), instead sometimes offering partial and even incorrect explanations (Clare et al., 1998; Sim & Lamb, 2018). Even when warnings were adapted for young people, they were sometimes too complicated for them to understand (Rogers et al., 2012), becoming very long, with added complexity and reduced comprehensibility. About half of the juvenile warnings examined by Rogers et al. (2012) were at least 225 words long, challenging recall and processing. Adjusted warnings used by some police jurisdictions were written at a higher reading level (Rogers, Hazelwood, Sewell, Shuman et al., 2008), were less readable (Kahn et al., 2006), and were sometimes more linguistically complex, further compromising comprehension (Goldstein et al., 2012; Rogers et al., 2007). In other cases, shortened warnings did not include all the necessary information (Baker et al., 2023), including reassurance that asserting one's rights should end the interrogation (Rogers et al. 2012). Martinez (2017) further suggested that youth may lack meta-awareness which can leave them unaware of their failure to comprehend their legal rights and thus willing to claim to understand them while being unable to explain what they understood.

Attempts to simplify warnings can improve understanding (Eastwood & Snook, 2012), for example by using a youth version that includes 5 core elements, simplified language and syntax, listing key elements to enhance recall (Eastwood et al. 2016), presenting the rights in written rather than just in oral format (Clare et al., 1998; Eastwood & Snook, 2009; Fenner et al., 2002) or using multimedia elements such as watching the rights being acted out while also reading the rights (Lively, 2023). Simplification especially improves comprehension of the right to silence and the right to legal counsel (Eastwood & Snook, 2009).

Some police officers, aware that, without a valid waiver of the suspect's rights, incriminating statements are likely inadmissible in court, are both developmentally insensitive and use manipulative and exploitative tactics that impair comprehension and appreciation, encourage children to waive their rights and/or confess (Cleary et al., 2023; Baker et al., 2023). The following tactics may decrease comprehension and encourage suspects to waive their rights:

1. Before explaining the rights, officers build rapport to decrease perceptions of confrontation (Domanico et al., 2012; Inbau et al., 2001).
2. Officers may present evidence before reading the rights so that suspects feel the need to explain the evidence and therefore waive their rights (Feld, 2013).
3. Police may minimize the significance of the rights, downplaying their delivery (Cleary & Vidal, 2016; Sim & Lamb, 2018), describing waiver procedures as a mere administrative issue (Cleary & Vidal, 2016; Feld, 2013; Inbau et al., 2013), or using neutral tones of voice when reading them (Cleary & Vidal, 2016).
4. They may suggest that waiving the rights is in the suspects' best interests because it gives them the power to tell their side of the story (Feld, 2013; Leo & White, 1999).

5. Despite often speaking fast, police officers tend to intentionally speak faster when delivering the rights than during the 30 s before and after that presentation (Domanico et al., 2012).
6. Police often imply suspects can go home if they provide the requested information (Redlich, Silverman, Chen, & Steiner, 2004), encouraging waiver of their rights.
7. Police employ many high-pressure interrogation tactics, such as accusing the suspect repeatedly, expressing certainty in the suspect's guilt, or holding suspects alone in the interrogation room (Cleary, 2014; Feld, 2013).
8. Officers also report using techniques to intentionally increase the suspect's anxiety (Meyer & Reppucci, 2007).

According to Baker et al. (2023), these tactics reflect police beliefs that the exercise of legal rights impedes effective investigations and prevents them from obtaining the confessions that are often compelling pieces of evidence (Brookman, Pike, & Maguire, 2019).

Frequent misconceptions and limited legal comprehension, in combination with police tactics, make it difficult for young people to invoke their rights proactively. A waiver can have serious consequences for the overall outcome of a case, because agreeing to talk to police significantly increases the likelihood that an individual will make self-incriminating statements and confessions, including false confessions (Baker, Haney-Caron, April, & Hellgren, 2024; Feld, 2013; Garrett, 2015). Nevertheless, over 90% of youth waive their rights and interact with the police without an attorney or parent present, making self-incriminating statements (Cleary & Vidal, 2016; Feld, 2013; Hellgren, Haney-Caron, Baker, Goldstein, & Philleo, 2024). Although many adults also waive their rights, extremely high rates of waiver by youth suspects are attributable to their developmental status.

Developmentally appropriate questioning

Many studies have shown that open-ended invitations, which activate free-recall retrieval processes, best elicit detailed and accurate accounts from both children and adults (e.g. Kelly & Valencia, 2021; Lamb et al., 2018). Wyman, Cassidy, and Talwar (2021) found that older children (10–11 years old) were more likely to disclose another's transgression in response to open-ended rather than closed questions, and Lyon and Henderson (2021) showed that recall questions (and rapport) elicited valid information without increasing the amount of false reporting. Similarly, Oxburgh, Ost, and Cherryman (2012) found that significantly more information was provided by sexual abuse suspects when they were asked appropriate open ended and probing questions rather than inappropriate closed, leading, or forced-choice questions. Almerigogna, Ost, Bull, and Akehurst (2007) added that youth with heightened anxiety more often responded incorrectly to misleading questions. Open-ended questions have repeatedly been found to elicit longer narratives than closed questions, including more accurate and detailed responses, and more elaborate explanations (Kelly & Valencia, 2020; Powell, 2013). Maintaining the use of open-ended questions during interviews leads suspects to shift from not providing to providing relevant information (Bull & Soukara, 2010). Similarly, Hershkowitz, Horowitz, Lamb, Orbach, and Sternberg (2004) showed that young suspects disclosed lots of information in response to open-ended prompts included in a developmentally adjusted interview protocol.

However, interviewers often fail to ask appropriate questions when interviewing young victims and suspects. In Hershkowitz et al.'s study (2004) of suspects, 43% of the questions asked by interviewers were option-posing and suggestive, likely compromising the accuracy of the information elicited, even though the suspects disclosed more information in response to open-ended than to focused prompts. A later study conducted in Sweden (Wienerwald, Cederborg, & Lindholm, 2019) similarly showed that police officers most frequently asked leading or suggestive questions of young suspects and put pressure on them. Almeida and Drew (2020) reported that police officers often locked suspects into their initial statements and pushed them to confirm previously mentioned information. Leahy-Harland and Bull (2017) found that open questions were mostly limited to the beginning of interviews and Launay, Py, Brunel, and Demarchi (2021) reported that more inappropriate than appropriate questions were employed overall.

The Revised Suspect Protocol: integrating best practice strategies

The RSP represents a revision of the fully structured SSP interview guide (Hershkowitz et al., 2004) that had emphasized cognitively based practices and paid less attention to socio-emotional factors which can increase stress and inhibit cooperation and performance. Interviewers were instructed to begin by explaining the purpose of the interview and reading the suspects' rights while warning them that their statements could be used against them in legal proceedings. In a subsequent rapport-building session, attempts were made to establish rapport before moving to the substantive phase and switching focus to the accusations. Open-ended prompts were encouraged throughout the interview, followed by more directive, option-posing and disparity-clarifying prompts when necessary. Whenever possible, however, interviewers were instructed to ask for open-ended elaboration of information provided in response to more focused prompts.

The RSP is characterized by an enhanced emphasis on developmentally appropriate and emotionally sensitive practices. First, legal rights are made more understandable, presented as a list of 5 short segments. Interviewers are instructed to read each segment separately, check whether or not the children understood it, and then verify comprehension by asking the child to express the content in his/her own words. If the child fails to do so accurately, interviewers are instructed to provide a simple explanation, then verify understanding again. When children waive one or more of their rights, interviewers are instructed to probe further (e.g. "You said you do not want your parents here/to talk to a lawyer. Tell me more about that.") to ensure that they were not doing so for invalid reasons (e.g. "My parents are at work/I do not know a lawyer").

Second, the RSP guided interviewers to use a variety of rapport-building practices to achieve meaningful rapport. In order to decrease children's anxiety and promote their emotional comfort, trust, and cooperation, rapport building precedes rather than follows explanation of the ground rules in the RSP. Welcoming greetings and expressions of interest in the child's well-being are offered at the beginning of the interview alongside supportive utterances reflecting personal interest in the child, empowerment, and encouragement to disclose personal and intimate information about neutral events. During rapport building, interviewers are shown how to identify expressions of reluctance and emotion by the child and how to respond in non-suggestively supportive ways (see examples below).

Third, the RSP instructs interviewers to use several types of non-suggestive but supportive comments throughout the interview to reinforce the child's efforts, convey empathy and the availability of the interviewer as a supportive figure, provide encouragement when the child expresses difficulty, offer help, or make small gestures of goodwill. In addition, interviewers are guided to acknowledge, contain, echo and explore emotions (including conflicts or reluctance) expressed by the children and to prompt for emotions if emotions were not mentioned spontaneously.

Fourth, the RSP encourages interviewers to exhaustively probe children's memory using various forms of free-recall prompts (main invitation, follow-up invitations, time-segmenting invitations and cued invitation) before asking directive questions and, finally a few option-posing questions if absolutely necessary to address crucial omissions (for a typology of questions see Hershkowitz et al, 2004). When inconsistencies make clarification necessary, interviewers are instructed to postpone such requests for clarification and to formulate them in a non-confrontational way. The RSP instructs interviewers to discuss *perceived* inconsistencies by formulating "double cued" invitations (e.g. "You told me you were wearing jeans, you also said you were only wearing a bathing suit. Please tell me more about that."), avoiding words such as *but* or *on the other hand* as well as suggestions that the two pieces of information were contradictory. Interviewers are advised that both option-posing prompts and requests for clarification should first focus on omissions or inconsistencies within the child's statement, followed by those arising from comparison with the alleged victim/s statement, and finally those arising from other external evidence. Thus, the discussion of evidence should be postponed until a later phase of questioning.

Because youth over 12 years of age are deemed criminally responsible in Israel, the Revised Suspect Protocol (RSP) had to comply with legal provisions and limitations when we tried to evaluate it in Israel. Accordingly, the new Protocol was extensively discussed with Israeli legal professionals, including prosecutors, judges, defence attorneys, and legislators, in addition to senior police and youth probation officers. At the same time, a multi-professional committee updated the precise wording of Israel's "Miranda warning" to make it easier for children to understand.

Empirical test of the Revised Suspect Protocol

Hershkowitz and Lamb (2024) predicted that, when using the RSP, rather than the SSP, interviewers would more effectively communicate the rights, establish rapport, maintain a supportive approach, and use non-suggestive questioning.

Ten interviewers and their supervisors (4) employed by the Israeli Child Investigation Service who were already trained to use the original SP (as well as the RP) with child victims and witnesses interviewed suspects between January and December 2016 using the SSP. They were then trained to use the RSP and conducted interviews using it between January 2017 and August 2018. This group training was provided in seven day-long sessions, with intervals of 1–2 months between sessions. The sessions included opportunities to practise using these specific practices as well as discussions of theory and research, coding procedures, review of recent interviews, and exercises for use inside and outside the training sessions. Interviewers also had two 2-hour long individual meetings with their supervisors after each group session, in order to evaluate interviews they had conducted following each training day. Prior to these individual sessions, the interviewer, supervisor and a research assistant coded the interviews to help interviewers develop their skills recognising different interview strategies and child responses.

A total of 198 interviews were conducted with adolescents (12–14 years old) who were suspected of having committed sexual offences against other children. Most of the young suspects (123, 62%) did not admit the accusations. Of 75 (4 females, later excluded from the analyses) young suspects who made admissions, 50 (66%) admitted all the accusations against them, while 25 (33%) admitted committing less severe sexual crimes than those suspected by the interviewer. Of the 71 boys, 28 were interviewed using the original Protocol (SSP), whereas 43 were interviewed using the RSP. The alleged offences involved vaginal, anal, or oral penetration (35.2% of the cases), fondling under the clothes (29.6%), fondling over the clothes (18.3%), and sexual offences without physical contact (such as self-exposure, or cyber sexual crimes, 16.9%). The interviews were conducted in a police station (52.1%), in a youth service or child investigation office (33.8%), or in other places (14.1%).

In the course of SSP interviews, 32 of 87 children (36.8%) confessed fully or partly, compared to 43 of 111 children (38.7%) in RSP interviews. However, in SSP interviews, 15 of 87 (17.2%) fully confessed, in comparison with 35 of 111 (31.5%) in RSP interviews. By contrast, 17 of 87 (19.5%) partially confessed in SSP interviews compared with 8 of 111 (7.2%) in RSP interviews. Protocol type thus did not have a significant effect on the overall confession rate, but children who confessed were significantly more likely to do so fully, rather than partially, when interviewed using the RSP, showing the superiority of that version (81.4% versus 46.4%).

Focusing on interviews of young suspects who admitted the alleged offences (n = 71), Hershkowitz and Lamb (2024) first examined how the interviewers communicated the suspects' rights. On average, interviewers used all recommended practices significantly more often in RSP than in SSP interviews. They read or re-read some or all 5 segments of the rights (5.17 versus 3.79 times), checked understanding (4.26 versus 2.25 times), verified comprehension (2.93 versus 0.64 times); provided explanations (1.78 versus 0.57 times); and offered support while reviewing the rights (2.57 versus 0.75 times). Overall, then, interviewers using the RSP attempted in multiple ways to ensure that the suspects were aware of and understood their rights. Indeed, the suspects interviewed using the RSP understood their rights better than those interviewed using the SSP. However, when all practices were used as predictors in the same model, verifying understanding was the strongest predictor of whether the suspects understood their rights; it was followed in order of importance by providing explanations, then checking understanding. Reading the rights and support had no significant effects on overall comprehension. In addition, the correlation between claims of understanding and actually understanding the rights was significant and positive when the RSP was used, whereas that correlation was nonsignificant and negative when the SSP was used, suggesting that youth were better able to monitor their actual comprehension when interviewed using the RSP.

In the rapport-building phase, use of the RSP was associated with higher levels of responsiveness by the children and by production of more details about a neutral event than was use of the SSP, indicating that use of the RSP facilitated a higher level of engagement, cooperation, and trust on the part of the suspects.

In the substantive phase of the interviews, there were no differences between the questioning strategies employed in SSP and SRP interviews. About 0.72 of all prompts were of a recall nature, with 0.25 free-recall open-ended invitations and 0.47 focused-recall (directive) prompts. Option-posing questions comprised 0.19 of the utterances and suggestive prompts 0.09. As expected, the average open-ended invitation elicited more forensically relevant details than the average directive, option-posing, or suggestive prompt (3.66, 1.61, 1.03, and 0.69, respectively), and this advantage was also reflected when observing the total number of details provided in the interview (127.65, 100.1, 22.54 and 8.34, respectively). These figures reflect the dominance of appropriate questioning strategies in these protocol-guided investigative interviews of young suspects. Moreover, a large proportion of the forensically relevant information was provided in response to recall prompts. Impressively, about 84% of the details were elicited using recall processes, among them about half from free-recall processes, details that are most likely to be accurate and credible.

In addition, use of the RSP was associated with more interviewer support than was the SSP; support had positive direct and indirect effects on the dynamics and outcomes of the interview. Specifically, support positively predicted the level of child responsiveness which in turn predicted lower reluctance, higher emotional expression, and more forensically relevant details provided by the children, while reluctance predicted fewer details being reported. Support also predicted emotional expression, which in turn indirectly predicted the number of details reported by enhancing the level of responsiveness. Thus, it appears that support improves cooperation and disclosures by young suspects in various ways, possibly explaining why RSP interviews yielded more complete than partial confessions from those who made any disclosure.

Directly analysing differences between interviews yielding full versus partial confessions (for which the RSP was superior relative to the SSP), full confessions were positively predicted by the number of appropriate practices employed in the rights portion of the interview, by full understanding by the children of their rights, by interviewer support, and by the proportion of open-ended invitations asked, further underscoring the value of the RSP's main components.

In all, Hershkowitz and Lamb's (2024) study showed that the Revised NICHD Suspect Protocol (RSP) represented a better way to structure and conduct interviews with young suspects, who are reluctant to describe their involvement in sexually abusive events involving other children. This protocol takes youth's vulnerabilities into account by incorporating research-based recommendations, instructing interviewers to use effective strategies to reduce young people's misconceptions, stress, reluctance and poor decision making, while promoting autonomy, trust, comprehension, cooperation and better-informed decisions. Specifically, the protocol successfully operationalized four key evidence-based practices. Firstly, it showed how suspects' rights to avoid self-incrimination could be explained in a developmentally sensitive manner by orally presenting a simplified text in small segments and at a slow pace, while also offering a readable written version and checking, verifying and correcting (mis)understanding to enhance comprehension of the rights and help the youth better monitor their own understanding. Secondly, it guided interviewers to establish meaningful rapport at the onset of the interview, fostering greater responsiveness by guiding interviewees to provide more details about a neutral event and share more information about themselves while ensuring that the children were more comfortable, trusting, and forthcoming. Thirdly, interviewers were shown how to provide non-suggestive social and emotional support throughout the interview, thereby reducing reluctance and improving responsiveness, emotional expressiveness, and forensic informativeness while, fourthly, pursuing an open-ended, non-suggestive, and non-intrusive line of questioning to ensure that most of the information elicited (more than 80% of the forensically relevant details) was derived using recall processes to maximize the likelihood that this information would be accurate and credible. Use of the RSP yielded more complete confessions, and the study suggested that those confessions were not only made in an informed and voluntary manner but were also likely to be valid.

Summary and conclusions

As detailed earlier in this chapter, young suspects face unique difficulties when questioned about their behaviour due to their youth and immaturity. As we showed, investigators often either ignore these difficulties and limitations or take advantage of them in manipulative ways in order to obtain confessions, regardless of their validity. Fortunately, it is possible to develop alternative developmentally appropriate practices that can and have been used in ways that treat young suspects in a more humane and just way, as illustrated in some of the studies reviewed above. Among these practices we have highlighted the need to present the youths' legal rights comprehensibly, establishing and maintaining meaningful rapport and support, and structuring a line of careful open-ended questioning.

Drawing upon this research, Hershkowitz and Lamb (2024) developed and field-validated an investigative interview protocol, the Revised NICHD Suspect Protocol. Following extensive training, Hershkowitz and Lamb showed that forensic interviewers were able to establish better rapport, involving increased trust and cooperation and emotional expression, ensure that the young people better understood their rights before making voluntary and informed decisions about whether to waive or take advantage of them, and if they chose to waive them, that they were able to provide rich and more complete accounts of their experiences. Because the legal system in Israel emphasizes treatment rather than punishment for younger suspects (age 12–14) the acceptance of responsibility and detailed accounts provided by young suspects makes it possible to implement effective treatment that can eliminate their harmful behaviour and protect other children from victimization by them. A substantial proportion of CSA offences are committed by youth, so appropriate practices in relation to these offenders can meaningfully address the problem as a whole.

References

Abram, K. M., Teplin, L. A., King, D. C., Longworth, S. L., Emanuel, K. M., Romero, E. G., & Olson, N. D. (2013). *PTSD, trauma, and comorbid psychiatric disorders in detained youth.* Washington, DC: US Department of Justice, Office of Justice Programs, Office of Juvenile Justice and Delinquency Prevention. Retrieved from www.ojjdp.gov/pubs/239603.pdf

Abramovitch, R., Higgins-Biss, K. L., & Biss, S. R. (1993). Young persons' comprehension of waivers in criminal proceedings. *Canadian Journal of Criminology, 35*, 309–322. https://doi.org/10.3138/cjcrim.35.3.309

Ahern, E. C., Hershkowitz, I., Lamb, M. E., Blasbalg, U., & Karni-Visel, Y. (2019). Examining reluctance and emotional support in forensic interviews with child victims of substantiated physical abuse. *Applied Developmental Science, 23*(3), 227–238. https://doi.org/10.1080/10888691.2017.1387057

Ahern, E. C., Sadler, L. A., Lamb, M. E., & Gariglietti, G. M. (2017). Practitioner perspectives on child sexual exploitation: Rapport building with young people. *Journal of Child Sexual Abuse, 26*(1), 78–91. https://doi.org/10.1080/10538712.2016.1257529

Alison, L. J., Alison, E., Noone, G., Elntib, S., & Christiansen, P. (2013). Why tough tactics fail and rapport gets results: Observing Rapport-Based Interpersonal Techniques (ORBIT) to generate useful information from terrorists. *Psychology, Public Policy, and Law, 19*(4), 411. https://doi.org/10.1037/a0034564

Allen, B. (2017). Children with sexual behavior problems: Clinical characteristics and relationship to child maltreatment. *Child Psychiatry & Human Development, 48*(2), 189–199. https://doi.org/10.1007/s10578-016-0633-8

Almeida, F. F., & Drew, P. (2020). The fabric of law-in-action: "Formulating" the suspect's account during police interviews in England. *International Journal of Speech Language and the Law, 27*(1). http://dx.doi.org/10.1558/ijsll.38527

Almerigogna, J., Ost, J., Bull, R., & Akehurst, L. (2007). A state of high anxiety: How non-supportive interviewers can increase the suggestibility of child witnesses. *Applied Cognitive Psychology, 21*(7), 963–974. https://doi.org/10.1002/acp.1311

Arndorfer, A., Malloy, L. C., & Cauffman, E. (2015). Interrogations, confessions, and adolescent offenders' perceptions of the legal system. *Law and Human Behavior, 39*(5), 503. https://doi.org/10.1037/lhb0000138

Baker, S., Haney-Caron, E., April, K., & Hellgren, J. (2024). The impact of race on predictors of parents' advice to children regarding Miranda waivers. *Psychology, Public Policy, and Law*, *30*(3), 288–302. https://doi.org/10.1037/law0000418

Baker, S., Tazi, K. Y., & Haney-Caron, E. (2023). A critical discussion of youth Miranda waivers, racial inequity, and proposed policy reforms. Psychology, *Public Policy, and Law*, *29*(3), 320–335. https://doi.org/10.1037/law0000389

Baker-Eck, B., & Bull, R. (2022). Effects of empathy and question types on suspects' provision of information in investigative interviews. *International Journal of Police Science & Management*, 24(4), 406–416. https://doi.org/10.1177/14613557221106073

Barnert, E. S., Abrams, L. S., Tesema, L., Dudovitz, R., Nelson, B. B., Coker, T., Bath. E., Biely, C., Li. N., & Chung, P. J. (2018). Child incarceration and long-term adult health outcomes: a longitudinal study. *International Journal of Prisoner Health*, *14*(1), 26–33. https://doi.org/10.1108/IJPH-09-2016-0052

Bettens, T., Cleary, H. M., & Bull, R. (2024). Humane interrogation strategies are associated with confessions, cooperation, and disclosure: Evidence from a field study of incarcerated individuals in the United States. *Criminal Justice and Behavior*, *51*(6), 949–969. https://doi.org/10.1177/00938548241232068

Blasbalg, U., Hershkowitz, I., Lamb, M. E., Karni-Visel, Y., & Ahern, E. C. (2019). Is interviewer support associated with the reduced reluctance and enhanced informativeness of alleged child abuse victims?. *Law and Human Behavior*, *43*(2), 156. https://doi.org/10.1037/lhb0000303

Blasbalg, U., Hershkowitz, I., & Karni-Visel, Y. (2018). Support, reluctance, and production in child abuse investigative interviews. *Psychology, Public Policy, and Law*, *24*(4), 518. https://doi.org/10.1037/law0000183

Braams, B. R., Van Leijenhorst, L., & Crone, E. A. (2014). Neural mechanisms underlying the peer influence on risk-taking behavior in adolescents. *Developmental Cognitive Neuroscience*, *8*, 15–23. https://doi.org/10.1016/j.neuroimage.2014.06.020

Brimbal, L., Meissner, C. A., Kleinman, S. M., Phillips, E. L., Atkinson, D. J., Dianiska, R. E., … & Jones, M. S. (2021). Evaluating the benefits of a rapport-based approach to investigative interviews: A training study with law enforcement investigators. *Law and Human Behavior*, *45*(1), 55. https://doi.org/10.1037/lhb0000437

Brimbal, L., Dianiska, R. E., Swanner, J. K., & Meissner, C. A. (2019). Enhancing cooperation and disclosure by manipulating affiliation and developing rapport in investigative interviews. *Psychology, Public Policy, and Law*, *25*(2), 107–115. https://doi.org/10.1037/law0000193

Brookman, F., Pike, S., & Maguire, E. R. (2019). Dancing around "Miranda": the effects of legal reform on homicide detectives in the USA and the UK. *Criminal Law Bulletin*, *55*(5), 725–763. https://researchspace.bathspa.ac.uk/id/eprint/12152

Brubacher, S. P., Benson, M. S., Powell, M. B., Goodman-Delahunty, J., & Westera, N. J. (2020). An overview of best practice investigative interviewing of child witnesses of sexual assault. In I. Bryce & W. Petherick (eds), *Child sexual abuse: Forensic issues in evidence, impact, and management* (pp. 445–466). Academic Press.

Bull, R., & Soukara, S. (2010). Four studies of what really happens in police interviews. In G. D. Lassiter & C. A. Meissner (eds), *Police interrogations and false confessions: Current research, practice, and policy recommendations* (pp. 81–95). American Psychological Association. https://doi.org/10.1037/12085-005

Campbell, F., Booth, A., Hackett, S., & Sutton, A. (2020). Young people who display harmful sexual behaviors and their families: A qualitative systematic review of their experiences of professional interventions. *Trauma, Violence, & Abuse, 21*(3), 456–469. https://doi.org/10.1177/1524838018770414

Carpentier, M. Y., Silovsky, J. F., & Chaffin, M. (2006). Randomized trial of treatment for children with sexual behavior problems: ten-year follow-up. *Journal of Consulting and Clinical Psychology, 74*(3), 482. https://doi.org/10.1037/0022-006X.74.3.482

Casey, B. J. (2015). Beyond simple models of self-control to circuit-based accounts of adolescent behavior. *Annual Review of Psychology, 66*(1), 295–319. https://doi.org/10.1146/annurev-psych-010814-015156

Casey, B. J., & Caudle, K. (2013). The teenage brain: Self control. *Current Directions in Psychological Science, 22*(2), 82–87. https://doi.org/10.1177/0963721413480170

Cauffman, E., Steinberg, L., & Piquero, A. R. (2005). Psychological, neuropsychological, and physiological correlates of serious antisocial behavior in adolescence: The role of self-control. *Criminology, 43*, 133–176. https://doi.org/10.1111/j.0011-1348.2005.00005.x

Chaffin, M. (2008). Our minds are made up – Don't confuse us with the facts: Commentary on policies concerning children with sexual behavior problems and juvenile sex offenders. *Child Maltreatment, 13*(2), 110–121. https://doi.org/10.1177/1077559508314510

Chaffin, M., Berliner, L., Block, R., Johnson, T. C., Friedrich, W. N., Louis, D. G., Lyon, T. D., Page, I. J., Prescott, D. S., Silovsky, J. F., & Madden, C. (2008). Report of the ATSA Task Force on Children With Sexual Behavior Problems. *Child Maltreatment, 13*(2), 199–218. https://doi.org/10.1177/1077559507306718

Chaulk, S. J., Eastwood, J., & Snook, B. (2014). Measuring and predicting police caution comprehension in adult offenders. *Canadian Journal of Criminology and Criminal Justice, 56*(3), 323–340. https://doi.org/10.3138/CJCCJ.2013.E02

Christiansen, A. K., & Vincent, J. P. (2013). Characterization and prediction of sexual and nonsexual recidivism among adjudicated juvenile sex offenders. *Behavioral Sciences & the Law, 31*(4), 506–529. https://doi.org/10.1002/bsl.2070

Clare, I. C. H., Gudjonsson, G. H., & Harari, P. M. (1998). Understanding of the current police caution (England and Wales). *Journal of Community & Applied Social Psychology, 8*, 323–329. https://doi.org/10.1002/(SICI)1099-1298(1998090)8:5%3C323::AID-CASP448%3E3.0.CO;2-2

Clarke, C., & Milne, R. (2001). *A national evaluation of the PEACE Investigative Interviewing Course* (p. 187). London: Home Office.

Cleary, H. M., & Crane, M. G. (2023). 13 police interviewing and interrogation of adolescent suspects. *The Oxford Handbook of Developmental Psychology and the Law*, 257. https://doi.org/10.1093/oxfordhb/9780197549513.013.13

Cleary, H., Guarnera, L., Aaron, J., & Crane, M. (2021). How trauma may magnify risk of involuntary and false confessions among adolescents. *The Wrongful Conviction Law Review, 2*(3), 173–204. https://doi.org/10.29173/wclawr53.

Cleary, H. M. D. (2017). Applying the lessons of developmental psychology to the study of juvenile interrogations: New directions for research, policy, and practice. *Psychology, Public Policy, and Law*, *23*(1), 118–130. https://doi.org/10.1037/law0000120

Cleary, H. M. D., & Warner, T. C. (2016). Police training in interviewing and interrogation methods: A comparison of techniques used with adult and juvenile suspects. *Law and Human Behavior*, *40*(3), 270–284. https://doi.org/10.1037/lhb0000175

Cleary, H. M. D., & Vidal, S. (2016). Miranda in actual juvenile interrogations: Delivery, waiver, and readability. *Criminal Justice Review*, *41*(1), 98–115. https://doi.org/10.1177/0734016814538650

Cleary, H. M. D. (2014). Police interviewing and interrogation of juvenile suspects: A descriptive examination of actual cases. *Law and Human Behavior*, *38*, 271–282. https://doi.org/10.1037/lhb0000070

Cohen, A. O., Breiner, K., Steinberg, L., Bonnie, R. J., Scott, E. S., Taylor-Thompson, K. A., & Casey, B. J. (2016). When is an adolescent an adult? Assessing cognitive control in emotional and nonemotional contexts. *Psychological Science*, *27*, 549–562. https://doi.org/10.1177/0956797615627625

Collins, K., & Carthy, N. (2019). No rapport, no comment: The relationship between rapport and communication during investigative interviews with suspects. *Journal of Investigative Psychology and Offender Profiling*, *16*(1), 18–31. https://doi.org/10.1002/jip.1517

Collins, K. & Carthy, N. (2018). No rapport, no comment: The relationship between rapport and communication during investigative interviews with suspects. *Journal of Investigative Psychology Offender Profiling*, *16*(3), 18–31. https://doi.org/10.1002/jip.1517

Collins, K., Doherty-Sneddon, G., & Doherty, M. J. (2014). Practitioner perspectives on rapport building during child investigative interviews. *Psychology, Crime & Law*, *20*(9), 884–901. https://doi.org/10.1080/1068316X.2014.888428

Copeland, W. E., Keeler, G., Angold, A., & Costello, E. J. (2007). Traumatic events and posttraumatic stress in childhood. *Archives of general psychiatry*, *64*(5), 577–584. https://doi.org/10.1001/archpsyc.64.5.577

Crough, Q., Dion Larivière, C., Snow, M. D., & Eastwood, J. (2022). Reflections on the nature of rapport within suspect interviews. *Current Issues in Criminal Justice*, *34*(2), 219–228. https://doi.org/10.1080/10345329.2021.2018814

Dando, C. J., & Oxburgh, G. E. (2016). Empathy in the field: Towards a taxonomy of empathic communication in information gathering interviews with suspected sex offenders. *The European Journal of Psychology Applied to Legal Context*, *8*(1), 27–33. https://doi.org/10.1016/j.ejpal.2015.10.001

Dando, C., Wilcock, R., & Milne, R. (2008). The cognitive interview: Inexperienced police officers' perceptions of their witness/victim interviewing practices. *Legal and Criminological Psychology*, *13*(1), 59–70. https://doi.org/10.1348/135532506X162498

Davis, D., & Leo, R. A. (2012). Interrogation-related regulatory decline: Ego depletion, confessions, and the interactive process of police interrogation. *Law & Human Behavior*, *36*(1), 75–88. https://doi.org/10.1037/a0027367

Deck, S. L., Quas, J. A., & Powell, M. B. (2024). Unique considerations for forensic interviews with adolescents: An exploration of expert interviewers' perspectives. *Child Maltreatment*, 10775595241270046. https://doi.org/10.1177/10775595241270046

Dianiska, R. E., Simpson, E., & Quas, J. A. (2024). Rapport building with adolescents to enhance reporting and disclosure. *Journal of Experimental Child Psychology, 238*, 105799. https://doi.org/10.1016/j.jecp.2023.105799

Dianiska, R. E., Luna, S., Winks, K. M., Quas, J. A., & Redlich, A. D. (2023). Current investigator practices and beliefs on interviewing trafficked minors. *Psychology, Public Policy, and Law, 29*(1), 32–45. https://doi.org/10.1037/law0000378

Dianiska, R. E., Swanner, J. K., Brimbal, L., & Meissner, C. A. (2021). Using disclosure, common ground, and verification to build rapport and elicit information. *Psychology, Public Policy, and Law, 27*(3), 341–353. https://doi.org/10.1037/law0000313

Dierkhising, C. B., Ko, S. J., Woods-Jaeger, B., Briggs, E. C., Lee, R., & Pynoos, R. S. (2013). Trauma histories among justice-involved youth: Findings from the National Child Traumatic Stress Network. *European Journal of Psychotraumatology, 4*(1), 20274. https://doi.org/10.3402/ejpt.v4i0.20274

Domanico, A. J., Cicchini, M. D., & White, L. T. (2012). Overcoming Miranda: A content analysis of the Miranda portion of police interrogations. *Idaho Law Review, 49*, i. https://heinonline.org/HOL/P?h=hein.journals/idlr49&i=1

Dopp, A. R., Perrine, C. M., Parisi, K. E., Hill, M. A., & Caldwell, M. F. (2020). Evidence-based assessment and treatment approaches for adolescents who have engaged in sexually abusive behavior. *The Wiley handbook of what works with sexual offenders: Contemporary perspectives in theory, assessment, treatment, and prevention*, 265–278. Chichester: John Wiley. https://doi.org/10.1002/9781119439325.ch15

Drake, K., Gudjonsson, G. H., Sigfusdottir, I. D., & Sigurdsson, J. F. (2015). An investigation into the relationship between the reported experience of negative life events, trait stress-sensitivity and false confessions among further education students in Iceland. *Personality and Individual Differences, 81*, 135–140. https://doi.org/10.1016/j.paid.2014.09.007

Drury, J. (2003). Adolescent communication with adults in authority. *Journal of Language & Social Psychology, 22*, 66–73. https://doi.org/10.1177/0261927X02250057

Eastwood, J., Snook, B., Luther, K., & Freedman, S. (2016). Engineering comprehensible youth interrogation rights. *New Criminal Law Review, 19*(1), 42–62. https://doi.org/10.1525/nclr.2016.19.1.42

Eastwood, J., & Snook, B. (2012). The effect of listenability factors on the comprehension of police cautions. *Law and Human Behavior*, 36(3), 177–183. https://psycnet.apa.org/doi/10.1037/h0093955

Eastwood, J., & Snook, B. (2010). Comprehending Canadian police cautions: Are the rights to silence and legal counsel understandable?. *Behavioral Sciences & the Law, 28*(3), 366–377. https://doi.org/10.1002/bsl.898

Evans, J. R., Meissner, C. A., Ross, A. B., Houston, K. A., Russano, M. B., & Horgan, A. J. (2013). Obtaining guilty knowledge in human intelligence interrogations: Comparing accusatorial and information-gathering approaches with a novel experimental paradigm. *Journal of Applied Research in Memory and Cognition*, *2*(2), 83–88. https://doi.org/10.1016/j.jarmac.2013.03.002

Fazel, S., Doll, H., & Långström, N. (2008). Mental disorders among adolescents in juvenile detention and correctional facilities: a systematic review and metaregression analysis of 25 surveys. *Journal of the American Academy of Child & Adolescent Psychiatry*, *47*(9), 1010–1019. https://doi.org/10.1097/CHI.ObO13e31817eecf3

Feld, B. C. (2013). Real interrogation: What actually happens when cops question kids. *Law & Society Review*, *47*(1). https://doi.org/10.1111/lasr.12000

Fenner, S., Gudjonsson, G. H., & Clare, I. C. H. (2002). Understanding of the current police caution (England and Wales) among suspects in police detention. *Journal of Community & Applied Social Psychology*, *12*, 83–93. https://doi.org/10.1002/casp.658

Finkelhor, D., Ormrod, R. K., & Turner, H. A. (2009). Lifetime assessment of poly-victimization in a national sample of children and youth. *Child Abuse & Neglect*, *33*(7), 403–411. https://doi.org/10.1016/j.chiabu.2008.09.012

Gabbert, F., Hope, L., Luther, K., Wright, G., Ng, M., & Oxburgh, G. (2021). Exploring the use of rapport in professional information-gathering contexts by systematically mapping the evidence base. *Applied Cognitive Psychology*, *35*(2), 329–341. https://doi.org/10.1002/acp.3762

Gabbert, F., Hope, L., Luther, K., Wright, G., Ng, M., & Oxburgh, G. E. (2020, November 4). Gabbert et al., Rapport Systematic Review, ACP, pre-print. https://doi.org/10.31234/osf.io/d3w28

Garrett, B. L. (2015). Contaminated confessions revisited. *Virginia Law Review.*, *101*(2), 395–454.

Gerryts, D. D., Deck, S. L., & Powell, M. B. (2024). Expert interviewers' approach to navigating forensic interviews with adolescents who are reluctant to disclose sexual abuse. *Psychiatry, Psychology and Law*, online ahead of print. https://doi.org/10.1080/13218719.2024.2362134

Gewirtz-Meydan, A., & Finkelhor, D. (2020). Sexual abuse and assault in a large national sample of children and adolescents. *Child Maltreatment*, 25(2), 203–214. https://doi.org/10.1177/1077559519873975

Goldstein, N. E., Haney-Caron, E., Levick, M., & Whiteman, D. (2018). Waving good-bye to waiver: A developmental argument against youths' waiver of Miranda rights. *New York University Journal of Legislation and Public Policy*, 21(1), 1–68.

Goldstein, N. E., Goldstein, A. M., Zelle, H., & Condie, L. O. (2012). Capacity to waive Miranda rights and the assessment of susceptibility to police coercion. *Handbook of Psychology*, *11*, 381–411.

Goldstein, N. E. S., Condie, L. O., Kalbeitzer, R., Osman, D., & Geier, C. V. (2003). Juvenile suspect's Miranda rights comprehension and self-reported likelihood of offering false confessions. *Journal of the American Academy of Psychiatry & the Law Online*, *31*(4), 534–544. https://doi.org/10.1177/1073191103259535

Goodman-Delahunty J., Martschuk N., & Dhami M. K. (2014). Interviewing high value detainees: Securing cooperation and disclosures. *Applied Cognitive Psychology*, *28*(6), 883–897. https://doi.org/10.1002/acp.3087

Grisso, T. (1981). *Juvenile's waiver of rights: Legal and psychological competence*. Plenum Press.

Gudjonsson, Gisli H., Sigurdsson, Jon F., & Sigfusdottir, Inga D. (2009). Interrogation and false confessions among adolescents in seven European countries. *Psychology, Crime & Law*, *15*(8), 711–728, online: https://doi.org/10.1080/10683160802516257

Hackett S. (2014). *Children and young people with harmful sexual behaviours*. Dartington: Research in Practice. https://tce.researchinpractice.org.uk/wp-content/uploads/2020/05/children_and_young_people_with_harmful_sexual_behaviours_research_review_2014.pdf

Haney-Caron, E., Goldstein, N. E., & Mesiarik, C. (2018). Self-perceived likelihood of false confession: A comparison of justice-involved juveniles and adults. *Criminal Justice and Behavior*, *45*(12), 1955–1976. https://doi.org/10.1177/0093854818799806

Hellgren, J., Haney-Caron, E., Baker, S., Goldstein, N. E., & Philleo, K. (2024). Parent advice to children during interrogations: Do crime severity and perceptions of consequences matter? *Psychology, Public Policy, and Law*, online ahead of print.

Hershkowitz, I., & Lamb, M. E. (2024). Interviewing young offenders about child-on-child sexual abuse. *Development and Psychopathology*, online ahead of print. https://doi.org/10.1037/law0000417

Hershkowitz, I., & Lamb, M. E. (2020). Allegation rates and credibility assessment in forensic interviews of alleged child abuse victims: Comparing the revised and standard NICHD protocols. *Psychology, Public Policy, and Law*, *26*(2), 176–184. https://doi.org/10.1037/law0000230

Hershkowitz, I., Ahern, E. C., Lamb, M. E., Blasbalg, U., Karni-Visel, Y., & Breitman, M. (2017). Changes in interviewers' use of supportive techniques during the Revised Protocol training. *Applied Cognitive Psychology*, *31*(3), 340–350. https://doi.org/10.1002/acp.3333

Hershkowitz, I., Lamb, M. E., & Katz, C. (2014). Allegation rates in forensic child abuse investigations: Comparing the revised and standard NICHD protocols. *Psychology, Public Policy, and Law*, *20*(3), 336–344. https://doi.org/10.1037/a0037391

Hershkowitz, I., Horowitz, D., Lamb, M. E., Orbach, Y., & Sternberg, K. J. (2004). Interviewing youthful suspects in alleged sex crimes: A descriptive analysis. *Child Abuse & Neglect*, *28*(4), 423–438. https://doi.org/10.1016/j.chiabu.2003.09.021

Hughes, M., Bain, S. A., Gilchrist, E., & Boyle, J. (2013). Does providing a written version of the police caution improve comprehension in the general population? *Psychology, Crime & Law*, *19*(7), 549–564. https://doi.org/10.1080/1068316X.2011.644793

Inbau, F. E., Reid, J. E., Buckley, J. P., & Jayne, B. C. (2013). *Criminal interrogation and confessions* (5th ed.). Jones & Bartlett Learning.

Inbau, F. E., Reid, J. E., Buckley, J. P., & Jayne, B. C. (2001). Criminal interrogation and confessions. Gaithersburg, MD.

Jenkins, C. S., Grimm, J. R., Shier, E. K., van Dooren, S., Ciesar, E. R., & Reid-Quiñones, K. (2020). Preliminary findings of problematic sexual behavior-cognitive-behavioral therapy for adolescents in an outpatient treatment setting. *Child Abuse & Neglect*, *105*, 104428. https://doi.org/10.1016/j.chiabu.2020.104428

Jung, H. (2015). The long-term impact of incarceration during the teens and 20s on the wages and employment of men. *Journal of Offender Rehabilitation*, *54*(5), 317–337. https://doi.org/10.1080/10509674.2015.1043480

Kahn R., Zapf P. A., Cooper V. G. (2006). Readability of Miranda warnings and waivers: Implications for evaluating Miranda comprehension. *Law and Psychology Review*, 30, 119–142.

Kaplan, J., Cutler, B. L., Leach, A.-M., & Eastwood, J. (2023). Development of the Interview and Interrogation Assessment Instrument. *Psychology, Public Policy, and Law*, *29*(1), 46–61. https://doi.org/10.1037/law0000366

Kassin, S. M., Drizin, S. A., Grisso, T., Gudjonsson, G. H., Leo, R. A., & Redlich, A. D. (2010). Police-induced confessions: Risk factors and recommendations. *Law & Human Behavior*, *34*(1), 3–38. https://doi.org/10.1007/s10979-009-9188-6

Kassin, S. M., Leo, R. A., Meissner, C. A., Richman, K. D., Colwell, L. H., Leach, A.-M., et al. (2007). Police interviewing and interrogation: A Self-report survey of police practices and beliefs. *Law and Human Behavior*, *31*, 381–400. https://doi.org/10.1007/s10979-006-9073-5

Karni-Visel, Y., Hershkowitz, I., Lamb, M. E., & Blasbalg, U. (2022). Emotional valence and the types of information provided by children in forensic interviews. *Child Abuse & Neglect*, *129*, 105639. https://doi.org/10.1016/j.chiabu.2022.105639

Karni-Visel, Y., Hershkowitz, I., Lamb, M. E., & Blasbalg, U. (2019). Facilitating the expression of emotions by alleged victims of child abuse during investigative interviews using the Revised NICHD Protocol. *Child Maltreatment*, *24*(3), 310–318. https://doi.org/10.1177/1077559519831382

Kebbell, M., Alison, L., Hurren, E., & Mazerolle, P. (2010). How do sex offenders think the police should interview to elicit confessions from sex offenders?. *Psychology, Crime & Law*, *16*(7), 567–584. https://doi.org/10.1080/10683160902971055

Kebbell, M., Alison, L., & Hurren, E. (2008). Sex offenders' perceptions of the effectiveness and fairness of humanity, dominance, and displaying an understanding of cognitive distortions in police interviews: A vignette study. *Psychology, Crime & Law*, *14*(5), 435–449. https://doi.org/10.1080/10683160801950523

Kelly, C. E., & Valencia, E. J. (2021). You ask and do not receive, because you ask wrongly. *International Journal of Police Science & Management*, *23*(1), 42–54. https://doi.org/10.1177/1461355720955077

Kelly, C. E., Miller, J. C., Redlich, A. D., & Kleinman, S. M. (2013). A taxonomy of interrogation methods. *Psychology, Public Policy, and Law*, *19*(2), 165–178. https://doi.org/10.1037/a0030310

Kettrey, H. H., & Lipsey, M. W. (2018). The effects of specialized treatment on the recidivism of juvenile sex offenders: A systematic review and meta-analysis. *Journal of Experimental Criminology*, *14*, 361–387.

Kloppen, K., Haugland, S., Svedin, C. G., Mæhle, M., & Breivik, K. (2016). Prevalence of child sexual abuse in the Nordic countries: A literature review. *Journal of Child Sexual Abuse*, *25*(1), 37–55. https://doi.org/10.1080/10538712.2015.1108944

Lamb, M. E., Brown, D. A., Hershkowitz, I., Orbach, Y., & Esplin, P. W. (2018). *Tell me what happened: Questioning children about abuse*. John Wiley & Sons.

Launay, C., Py, J., Brunel, M., & Demarchi, S. (2021). Beyond investigation-relevant information: a content analysis of police questioning. *Police Practice and Research, 22*(4), 1341–1355. https://doi.org/10.1080/15614263.2020.1869002

Leahy-Harland, S., & Bull, R. (2017). Police strategies and suspect responses in real-life serious crime interviews. *Journal of Police & Criminal Psychology, 32*(2), 138–151. https://doi.org/10.1007/s11896-016-9207-8

Leo, R. A. (2012). False confessions and the constitution: Problems, possibilities and solutions. In J. T. Parry & L. S. Richardson (eds), *The constitution and the future of criminal justice in America* (pp. 169–186). Cambridge University Press.

Leo, R. A., & White, W. S. (1999). Adapting to Miranda: Modern interrogators' strategies for dealing with the obstacles posed by Miranda. *Minnesota Law Review, 84*, 397–472.

Letourneau, E. J., Schaeffer, C. M., Bradshaw, C. P., Ruzicka, A. E., Assini-Meytin, L. C., Nair, R., & Thorne, E. (2024). Responsible behavior with younger children: results from a pilot randomized evaluation of a school-based child sexual abuse perpetration prevention program. *Child Maltreatment, 29*(1), 129–141. https://doi.org/10.1016/j.chiabu.2008.09.012

Letourneau, E. J., Schaeffer, C. M., Bradshaw, C. P., & Feder, K. A. (2017). Preventing the onset of child sexual abuse by targeting young adolescents with universal prevention programming. *Child Maltreatment, 22*(2), 100–111. https://doi.org/10.1177/1077559517692439

Letourneau E J., McCart M R., Asuzu K., Mauro P M., Sheidow A J. (2013). Caregiver involvement in sexual risk reduction with substance using juvenile delinquents: Overview and preliminary outcomes of a randomized trial. *Adolescent Psychiatry*, 3(4), 342–352.

Letourneau E. J., Henggeler S. W., Borduin C. M., Schewe P. A., McCart M. R., Chapman J. E., Saldan L. (2009). Multisystemic therapy for juvenile sexual offenders: 1-year results from a randomized effectiveness trial. *Journal of Family Psychology*, 23(1), 89–102. https://doi.org/10.1037/a0014352

Letourneau, E. J., & Miner, M. H. (2005). Juvenile sex offenders: A case against the legal and clinical status quo. *Sexual Abuse: A Journal of Research and Treatment, 17*, 293–312. https://doi.org/10.1177/107906320501700304

Lively, C. J., Snook, B., Luther, K., Mccardle, M. I., & House, J. C. (2023). A preliminary exploration of the multimedia principle's applicability for improving comprehension of youth interrogation rights. *Criminal Justice and Behavior, 50*(2), 252–271. https://doi.org/10.1177/00938548221093283

Luna, B., Padmanabhan, A., & Geier, C. (2014). The adolescent sensation seeking period: Development of reward processing and its effects on cognitive control. In V. F. Reyna & V. Zayas (eds), *The neuroscience of risky decision making* (pp. 93–121). American Psychological Association https://doi.org/10.1037/14322-005

Lyon T. D., Henderson H. (2021). Increasing true reports without increasing false reports: Best practice interviewing methods and open-ended wh- questions. *American Professional Society of the Abuse of Children Advisor*, 33(1), 29–39.

Magnusson, M., Ernberg, E., Landström, S., & Akehurst, L. (2020). Forensic interviewers' experiences of interviewing children of different ages. *Psychology, Crime & Law, 26*(10), 967–989. https://doi.org/10.1080/1068316X.2020.1742343

Malloy, L. C., Shulman, E. P., & Cauffman, E. (2014). Interrogations, confessions, and perceptions of coercion in a sample of adolescent offenders. *Law & Human Behavior*, *38*(2), 181–193. https://doi.org/10.1037/lhb0000065

Malloy, L. C., Brubacher, S. P., & Lamb, M. E. (2011). Expected consequences of disclosure revealed in investigative interviews with suspected victims of child sexual abuse. *Applied Developmental Science*, *15*(1), 8–19. https://doi.org/10.1080/10888691.2011.538616

Marcantonio, D. H., Matteson, A., Presler, M., Burke, J. M., Hagen, D. R., Hua, F., & Apgar, J. F. (2022). Early feasibility assessment: a method for accurately predicting biotherapeutic dosing to inform early drug discovery decisions. *Frontiers in Pharmacology*, *13* https://doi.org/10.3389/fphar.2022.864768

Martinez, D. C. (2017). Emerging critical meta-awareness among Black and Latina/o youth during corrective feedback practices in urban English language arts classrooms. *Urban Education*, *52*(5), 637–666. https://doi.org/10.1177/0042085915623345

McCardle, M. I., Luther, K., & Snook, B. (2021). Examining the administration of youth interrogation rights: A field study of Canadian police practices. *Youth Justice*, *21*(3), 299–320. https://doi.org/10.1177/1473225420902841

McElvaney, R., & Culhane, M. (2017). A retrospective analysis of children's assessment reports: What helps children tell?. *Child abuse review*, *26*(2), 103–115. https://doi.org/10.1002/car.2390

McLachlan, K., Roesch, R., & Douglas, K. S. (2011). Examining the role of interrogative suggestibility in Miranda rights comprehension in adolescents. *Law and Human Behavior*, *35*(3), 165–177. https://doi.org/10.1007/s10979-009-9198-4

Meissner, C. A. (2021). "What works?" Systematic reviews and meta-analyses of the investigative interviewing research literature. *Applied Cognitive Psychology*, *35*(2), 322–328. https://doi.org/10.1002/acp.3808

Meissner, C. A., Redlich, A. D., Michael, S. W., Evans, J. R., Camilletti, C. R., Bhatt, S., & Brandon, S. (2014). Accusatorial and information-gathering interrogation methods and their effects on true and false confessions: A meta-analytic review. *Journal of Experimental Criminology*, *10*, 459–486. https://doi.org/10.1007/s11292-014-9207-6

Meissner, C. A., Redlich, A. D., Bhatt, S., & Brandon, S. (2012). Interview and interrogation methods and their effects on true and false confessions. *Campbell Systematic Reviews*, *8*(1), 1–53. https://doi.org/10.4073/csr.2012.13

Meyer, J. R., & Reppucci, N. D. (2007). Police practices and perceptions regarding juvenile interrogations and interrogative suggestibility. *Behavioral Sciences and the Law*, *25*, 757–780. https://doi.org/10.1002/bsl.774

Oxburgh, G., Ost, J., & Cherryman, J. (2012). Police interviews with suspected child sex offenders: Does use of empathy and question type influence the amount of investigation relevant information obtained?. *Psychology, Crime & Law*, *18*(3), 259–273. https://doi.org/10.1080/1068316X.2010.481624

Oxburgh, G., & Ost, J. (2011). The use and efficacy of empathy in police interviews with suspects of sexual offences. *Journal of Investigative Psychology and Offender Profiling*, *8*(2), 178–188. https://doi.org/10.1002/jip.143

Palmer, L. (2013). The relationship between stress, fatigue, and cognitive functioning. *College Student Journal*, *47*(2), 312–325.

Petrosino, A., Turpin-Petrosino, C., & Guckenburg, S. (2010). PROTOCOL: The impact of juvenile system processing on delinquency. *Campbell Systematic Reviews*, *6*(1), 1–24.

Place, C. J., & Meloy, J. R. (2018). Overcoming resistance in clinical and forensic interviews. *International Journal of Forensic Mental Health*, *17*(4), 362–376. https://doi.org/10.1080/14999013.2018.1485189

Powell, K. (2022). The age-graded consequences of justice system involvement for mental health. *Journal of Research in Crime and Delinquency*, *59*(2), 167–202. https://doi.org/10.1177/00224278211023988

Powell, M. B. (2013). An overview of current initiatives to improve child witness interviews about sexual abuse. *Current Issues in Criminal Justice*, *25*(2), 711–720. https://doi.org/10.1080/10345329.2013.12035992

Puzzanchera, C., Sladky, A., & Kang, W. (2017). *Easy access to juvenile populations: 1990–2016.* Retrieved from www.ojjdp.gov/ojstatbb/ezapop

Radford, L., Corral, S., Bradley, C., & Fisher, H. L. (2013). The prevalence and impact of child maltreatment and other types of victimization in the UK: Findings from a population survey of caregivers, children and young people and young adults. *Child Abuse & Neglect*, *37*(10), 801–813. https://doi.org/10.1016/j.chiabu.2013.02.004

Redlich, A. D., Silverman, M., Chen, J., & Steiner, H. (2004). The police interrogation of children and adolescents. In G. D. Lassiter (ed.), *Interrogations, confessions, and entrapment* (pp. 107–125). New York: Kluwer Academic. https://doi.org/10.1007/978-0-387-38598-3_5

Redlich, A. D., Silverman, M., & Steiner, H. (2003). Pre-adjudicative and adjudicative competence in juveniles and young adults. *Behavioral Sciences and the Law*, *21*, 393–410. https://doi.org/10.1002/bsl.543

Redlich, A. D., & Goodman, G. S. (2003). Taking responsibility for an act not committed: The influence of age and suggestibility. *Law & Human Behavior*, *27*(2), 141–156. https://doi.org/10.1023/A:1022543012851

Rogers, R., Steadham, J. A., Carter, R. M., Henry, S. A., Drogin, E. Y., & Robinson, E. V. (2016). An examination of juveniles' Miranda abilities: Investigating differences in Miranda recall and reasoning. *Behavioral Sciences & the Law*, *34*(4), 515–538. https://doi.org/10.1002/bsl.2243

Rogers, R., Steadham, J. A., Fiduccia, C. E., Drogin, E. Y., & Robinson, E. V. (2014). Mired in Miranda misconceptions: A study of legally involved juveniles at different levels of psychosocial maturity. *Behavioral Sciences & the Law*, 32(1), 104–120. https://doi.org/10.1002/bsl.2099

Rogers, R., Blackwood, H. L., Fiduccia, C. E., Steadham, J. A., Drogin, E. Y., & Rogstad, J. E. (2012). Juvenile Miranda warnings: Perfunctory rituals or procedural safeguards? *Criminal Justice and Behavior*, *39*(3), 229–249 https://doi.org/10.1177/0093854811431934

Rogers, R., Rogstad, J. E., Steadham, J. A., & Drogin, E. Y. (2011). In plain English: Avoiding recognized problems with Miranda miscomprehension. *Psychology, Public Policy, and Law*, 17(2), 264–285. https://doi.org/10.1037/a0022508

Rogers, R., Hazelwood, L. L., Sewell, K. W., Harrison, K. S., & Shuman, D. W. (2008). The language of Miranda warnings in American jurisdictions: A replication and vocabulary analysis. *Law and Human Behavior*, *32*, 124–136. https://doi.org/10.1007/s10979-007-9091-y

Rogers, R., Harrison, K. S., Shuman, D. W., Sewell, K. W., & Hazelwood, L. L. (2007). An analysis of Miranda warnings and waivers: Comprehension and coverage. *Law and Human Behavior*, *31*, 177–192. https://doi.org/10.1007/s10979-006-9054-8

Ronis, S. T., & Borduin, C. M. (2013). Antisocial behavior trajectories of adolescents and emerging adults with histories of sexual aggression. *Psychology of Violence*, *3*(4), 367. https://doi.org/10.1037/a0033597

Saywitz, K. J., Larson, R. P., Hobbs, S. D., & Wells, C. R. (2015). Developing rapport with children in forensic interviews: Systematic review of experimental research. *Behavioral Sciences & the Law*, *33*(4), 372–389. https://doi.org/10.1002/bsl.2186

Sauerland, M., Brackmann, N., & Otgaar, H. (2018). Rapport: Little effect on children's, adolescents', and adults' statement quantity, accuracy, and suggestibility. *Journal of Child Custody*, *15*(4), 268–285. https://doi.org/10.1080/15379418.2018.1509759

Sharf, A. J., Rogers, R., & Williams, M. M. (2017). Reasoning your way out of Miranda rights: How juvenile detainees relinquish their fifth amendment protections. *Translational Issues in Psychological Science*, *3*(2), 121. https://doi.org/10.1037/tps0000118

Shulman, E. P., Harden, K. P., Chein, J. M., & Steinberg, L. (2016). Sex differences in the developmental trajectories of impulse control and sensation-seeking from early adolescence to early adulthood. *Journal of Youth & Adolescence*, *44*(1), 1–17. https://doi.org/10.1007/s10964-014-0116-9

Silovsky, J. F., Letourneau, E. J., & Bonner, B. L. (2020). Introduction to CAN special issue: Children with problem sexual behavior. *Child Abuse & Neglect*, *105*. https://doi.org/10.1016/j.chiabu.2020.104508

Silovsky, J. F., Hunter, M. D., & Taylor, E. K. (2019). Impact of early intervention for youth with problematic sexual behaviors and their caregivers. *Journal of Sexual Aggression*, *25*(1), 4–15. https://doi.org/10.1080/13552600.2018.1507487

Sim, M. P. Y., & Lamb, M. E. (2018). An analysis of how the police "caution" is presented to juvenile suspects in England. *Psychology, Crime & Law*, *24*(8), 851–872. https://doi.org/10.1080/1068316X.2018.1442449

Snook, B., Brooks, D., & Bull, R. (2015). A lesson on interrogations from detainees: Predicting self-reported confessions and cooperation. *Criminal Justice and Behavior*, *42*(12), 1243–1260. https://doi.org/10.1177/0093854815604179

Snook, B., Luther, K., Eastwood, J., Collins, R., & Evans,S. (2014). Advancing legal literacy: The effect of listenability on the comprehension of interrogation rights. *Legal and Criminological Psychology*, 21(1), 174–188. https://doi.org/10.1111/lcrp.12053

Snook, B., Eastwood, J., & MacDonald, S. (2010). A descriptive analysis of how Canadian police officers administer the right-to-silence and right-to-legal-counsel cautions. *Canadian Journal of Criminology and Criminal Justice*, *52*(5), 545–560. https://doi.org/10.3138/cjccj.52.5.545

St. Amand, A., Bard, D. E., & Silovsky, J. F. (2008). Meta-analysis of treatment for child sexual behavior problems: Practice elements and outcomes. *Child Maltreatment*, *13*(2), 145–166. https://doi.org/10.1177/1077559508315353

Steinberg, L. (2014). *Age of opportunity: Lessons from the new science of adolescence*. Houghton Mifflin Harcourt.

Steinberg, L., Cauffman, E., Woolard, J., Graham, S., & Banich, M. (2009). Are adolescents less mature than adults? Minor's access to abortion, the juvenile death penalty, and the alleged APA "flip-flop". *American Psychologist, 64*, 583–594. https://doi.org/10.1037/a0014763

Steinberg, L. (2008). A social neuroscience perspective on adolescent risk-taking. *Developmental Review, 28*(1), 78–106. https://doi.org/10.1016/j.dr.2007.08.002

Time, V. M., & Payne, B. K. (2002). Police chiefs' perceptions about Miranda: An analysis of survey data. *Journal of Criminal Justice, 30*(1), 77–86. https://doi.org/10.1016/S0047-2352(01)00124-6

Vidal, S., Cleary, H., Woolard, J., & Michel, J. (2017). Adolescents' legal socialization: Effects of interrogation and Miranda knowledge on legitimacy, cynicism, and procedural justice. *Youth Violence and Juvenile Justice, 15*(4), 419–440. https://doi.org/10.1177/1541204016651479

Viljoen, J. L., Zapf, P. A., & Roesch, R. (2007). Adjudicative competence and comprehension of Miranda rights in adolescent defendants: A comparison of legal standards. *Behavioral Sciences and the Law, 25*, 1–19. https://doi.org/10.1002/bsl.714

Walsh, D., & Bull, R. (2012). Examining rapport in investigative interviews with suspects: Does its building and maintenance work?. *Journal of Police and Criminal Psychology, 27*, 73–84. https://doi.org/10.1007/s11896-011-9087-x

Winerdal, U., Cederborg, A.-C., & Lindholm, J. (2019). The quality of question types in Swedish police interviews with young suspects of serious crimes. *The Police Journal, 92*(2), 136–149. https://doi.org/10.1177/0032258X18770915

Woolard, J. L., Cleary, H. M., Harvell, S. A., & Chen, R. (2008). Examining adolescents' and their parents' conceptual and practical knowledge of police interrogation: A family dyad approach. *Journal of Youth and Adolescence, 37*, 685–698. https://doi.org/10.1007/s10964-008-9288-5

Wyman, J., Cassidy, H., & Talwar, V. (2021). Utilizing the activation-decision-construction-action theory to predict children's hypothetical decisions to deceive. *Acta Psychologica, 218*, 103339. https://doi.org/10.1016/j.actpsy.2021.103339

Zelle, H., Romaine, C. L. R., & Goldstein, N. E. (2015). Juveniles' Miranda comprehension: Understanding, appreciation, and totality of circumstances factors. *Law and Human Behavior, 39*(3), 281. https://doi.org/10.1037/lhb0000116

Appendix

Revised Suspect Protocol

Adapted from Hershkowitz and Lamb (2024).

A. Introduction

A.1. My name is [name]. Today's date is [date], and it is now [time]. I'm interviewing [child's name] at [location].

Verify that the recorder is on.

A.2. Hello, [child's name], I am glad to meet you today. How are you? My name is [name] and my job is to talk to children about things that have happened. As you can see, we have a video-camera here. It will record us talking so I can remember everything you tell me. Sometimes I forget things and the recorder allows me to listen to you without having to write everything down.

In the introduction, gestures of goodwill are appropriate, e.g.

> Are you comfortable?/Can I do anything to make you more comfortable?
>
> The police have received a complaint that you [concrete brief accusation that might mention: the act, the allegation, and the alleged frequency. e.g. "you touched a girl's/several girls' breasts/private parts several times"] and I was asked to talk to you about that. We will talk about that later on.

It is important that the child not give any information before the interviewer has read aloud the section "Informing juvenile suspects of their rights before the interview" fully. If the child interrupts, say:

> We will talk about that in a little while. Now please listen carefully to what I have to tell you:

B. *Informing juvenile suspects of their rights before the interview*

Each segment of the rights below (B.1.a to B.3) should be read loudly, slowly, and clearly. A written version of each segment can be offered. After reading each segment, the comprehension check, verification and correction, if necessary, should follow:

> [Child's name], I want to know if you understood what I just told you/ you read.

Wait for the child to respond. If the child says s/he didn't understand, slowly repeat the wording above and check the child's comprehension at the end of every sentence. If the child says s/he understands, say:

> Please tell me what you understood.

Wait for the child's response, reinforce the child for any correct report and correct anything that was misunderstood.

Please make sure the child doesn't fail to exercise a right for reasons that could be overcome; suggest possible solutions.

B.1. [Child's name], you should know that:

B.1.a. You have the right to remain silent in this interview and you don't have to tell me anything. According to the law, everyone who is suspected of doing something that's wrong or forbidden can refuse to speak about it.

Please check, verify, and correct comprehension.

B.1.b. If you decide to remain silent, and a trial is held later, the court may consider the fact that you remained silent.

Please check, verify, and correct comprehension.

B.1.c. [Child's name], I will tell the police everything you tell me so that they can investigate further. Everything you say during this interview will be recorded and videotaped. If a trial takes place, what you tell me now may be brought up in court.

Please check, verify, and correct comprehension.

> Before we continue, I would like to let you know that you have additional rights:

If the right to consult an attorney hasn't been revoked, say:

B.2.a. You have the right to talk to a lawyer in private before we begin the interview. Would you like to talk to a lawyer?

Wait for the child to respond. If the child wants to consult an attorney, allow him/her to do so. If the child says no, ask:

Tell me about your refusal to talk to a lawyer.

And/or, if necessary:

What's the reason you don't want to talk to a lawyer?

Please make sure the child doesn't fail to exercise a right for reasons that could be overcome; suggest possible solutions. For example, if the child says "because I don't know any lawyer" you can suggest your help and guidance in contacting one.

If you know the child consulted an attorney prior to the interview, you can ask:

I understand you spoke to a lawyer before the interview. Is that true? What's the lawyer's name?

If the right to consult an attorney has been revoked, say:

Children being questioned can usually talk to a lawyer before the interview begins, but in your case, it has been decided, according to the law, that you're not allowed to talk to a lawyer now.

Please check, verify, and correct comprehension.

If the minor is under arrest or the police intend to arrest him/her, say:

B.2.b. If you don't have a lawyer, a public attorney can be appointed for you and you can consult with him or her for free. If you would like that, I can arrange it for you.

Please check, verify, and correct comprehension.

To a minor who is not under arrest and is entitled to have the parents notified about the interview, say:

B.3. Before we begin the interview, you have the right to talk to one of your parents or to a relative or friend who is over 18. In addition, you have the right to have one of them with you during the interview. You can also decide that you don't want them here during the interview.

Please check, verify, and correct comprehension.

> Would you like to consult one of these people before we start the interview?

Wait for the child to respond. If the child says no, say:

> Tell me about your refusal to talk to them. [And/or, if necessary] What's the reason you don't want to consult any of these people?

Please make sure the child doesn't fail to exercise a right for reasons that could be overcome; suggest possible solutions.

If the child says yes, allow the child to consult an appropriate adult before the interview.

> Would you like one of those people to be with you in the interview?

Wait for the child to respond, if the child says no, ask:

> Tell me about your refusal to have one of them with you in the interview. [And/or, if necessary] What's the reason you don't want any of them here with you in the interview?

Please make sure the child doesn't fail to exercise a right for reasons that could be overcome; suggest possible solutions.

If the child says yes, let the person that the child named be present for the interview.

Say to that person:

> Hello, [name of the person]. [Child's name] asked you to be present for this interview. I have to tell you that you cannot intervene during the interview, under any circumstances. Also, you can't leave the room unless I allow you to do so, and under the conditions I set for you. Is that clear?

If it was decided that a parent/another adult should not be permitted to be present, say:

> Children under investigation usually have the right to have a parent or other relative/adult present during the interview, but in your case, it has been decided, according to the law, that they are not allowed to be present for the interview.

Please check, verify, and correct comprehension.

B.4. [Child's name], do you have questions about what I have said so far?

Please answer the child's question/s and provide explanations.

C. Rapport building and narrative training

C.1. Now, [child's name], before we talk about the complaint, I want to get to know you better. Tell me about things you like to do.

If the child responds, express appreciation and reinforce the cooperation:

> Thank you for sharing that with me, it helps me get to know you/I am starting to get to know more about you.

If the child does not answer, gives a short answer, or gets stuck, you can say:

> We haven't met before, and I really want to get to know you.

If the child displays nonverbal cues of avoidance or resistance (e.g. gaze aversion), address them right away:

> [Child's name], let me see your eyes.
> [Child's name], come and sit closer to me.
> [Child's name], I can see you're [crying, quiet], tell me what is happening, so I can help.

C.2. I really want to know you better, [child's name]. I would like you to tell me about things you like to do.

Wait for an answer.

If the child continues showing avoidance or resistance, invite him/her to talk about a neutral topic you learned about before the interview.

> I heard you like [activity, hobby e.g. animals/sports]. Tell me about [activity, hobby].

Ask about distinctive items (e.g. of clothing):

> I can see you are wearing [a unique item, e.g. soccer team T-shirt]. Tell me about [item].

C.3. Now, [child's name], tell me more about [an activity the child already mentioned].

C.4. [Child's name], tell me about something fun that has happened to you [at school].

C.5. Tell me about [something the child mentioned].

Use various cued invitations to ask about different topics; one of those cued invitations should focus on internal contents: thoughts, feelings, sensations, or emotions.

C.6. You told me about something [happy, pleasant, fun] that has happened to you at school. Now, tell me about something unpleasant that has happened to you at school.

Important! Do not mention the location in which the alleged abuse may have taken place.

C.7. Please tell me about [something the child has mentioned].

Ask various cued invitations to elicit richer information about a variety of topics; one cued invitation should focus on internal contents: thoughts, feelings, sensations, or emotions.

If the child reveals distressing information, please explore that briefly while making supportive statements (see Addendum). You may want to check whether the child has previously reported it:

> You told me about [the distressing incident]. Have you told an adult about that?

If the child says no, say:

> Would you like me to help you tell someone?

C.8. [child's name], you told me about [pleasant event already described] and about [unpleasant event already described], and shared your [emotions, thoughts] with me (if s/he did). Thank you for letting me know. It's important that you know you can talk to me about anything, both good things and bad things.

D. *Further rapport building and episodic memory training*

Prior to the interview, please identify a recent, short, positive, and meaningful event in which the child actively participated, such as a Bar Mitzvah ceremony, or a sports competition. If possible, choose an event that took place at about the same time as the alleged/suspected abuse. If the alleged abuse took place during a specific day or event, ask about a different event. Alternatively, it is possible to select a hobby or activity the child mentioned earlier and focus on the last time the child engaged in it.

> [Child's name], before we talk about the complaint that brought you here, I would like to get to know you even better.

D.1. Main invitation

If an event was reported previously:

> You told me earlier about [the event previously mentioned]. Tell me, [child's name], everything that happened [during the event], from the beginning to the end, as best as you can.

In case an event wasn't identified previously, ask:

> Did you do something special [Bar-Mitzvah party school activity/youth movement activity] recently? Tell me, [child's name], everything that happened [during the event], from the beginning to the end, as best as you can.

If the child doesn't mention an event, say:

> [Child's name], you told me earlier about something pleasant and unpleasant that has happened to you. Thank you for sharing that with me, it helps me get to know you. I would like to get to know you even better. Please tell me about a pleasant experience you've had recently.

If the child doesn't answer, say:

> [Child's name] if there is anything that's bothering you, you can tell me/share with me.

If the child asks to discuss the complaint, move to the substantive phase, part F.

D.2. Follow-up invitations

Please repeat the first action that started the event. Then ask:

> And then what happened, [child's name]?

Use this question as often as needed throughout this section until you have been given a full account of the event.

> Thank you, [child's name], you have told me many things (if s/he did). I want to ask you some more questions about what you just told me.

D.3. Time segmenting invitations

Try to use three time-segmenting invitations, although you may adjust the quantity and type of invitations to the child's capabilities and reactions.

> [Child's name], I would like you to tell me everything about [the event].
>
> Please tell me everything that happened from the moment [an activity the child mentioned] to the moment [a subsequent activity].

If the child has difficulty understanding delineated segments, say:

> Please tell me everything that happened from the moment [an activity the child mentioned] began.
>
> Thank you, [child's name], for telling me that. You speak/express yourself very clearly, and that helps me understand what you are saying.

D.4. Cued invitations

Try to use three cued invitations, but you may adjust the number depending on the child's capabilities and reactions. Please focus on thoughts and feelings as well.

Cued invitations can be used in one of two formats:

> Tell me more about [activity, object, thought, feeling].
>
> Earlier you spoke about [activity, object, thought, feeling]. Tell me more about that.

D.5. [Child's name], thank you for telling me about [title of the event]. When we talk today, it is very important that you tell me everything about things that have really happened to you.

D.6. [Child's name], how are you feeling so far in our conversation?

E. Explaining and practising ground rules

Adjust the questions according to the child's developmental level.

E.1. In our conversation today, I'll be asking you questions. If I ask a question that you don't understand, please tell me so that I can explain it to you. Okay, [child's name]?

If I ask a question, and you don't know the answer, just tell me, "I don't know".

Pause

In our conversation, please tell me only the things that you know or remember.

E.2. And if I say things that are wrong, you should correct me/tell me what is right. Okay, [child's name]?

If I said that you were born in [a wrong detail about the child's country of birth], what would you say?

Reinforce the child if s/he gives the right answer:

That's right, [child's name], you were not born in [wrong detail].

Ask for the correction if needed:

What is correct?

Correct a wrong answer:

No, [child's name], you are not [wrong detail], you are [correct detail].

[Child's name], now you understand that if I say something incorrect/wrong, you need to correct me and tell me what is right.

E.3. It is very important [child's name] that your answers be accurate today.

F. *Substantive phase*

Transition to substantive issues.

Important! If the child expresses explicit verbal resistance without denying the allegations at any point, employ support to deal with the resistance (Addendum) without using additional transitional prompts.

F.1. Now that I know you better, [child's name], I want us to talk about the complaint that brought [me/you] here today.

I told you earlier that I am interviewing you about the complaint made about you, and I read you your rights. As I said then, you are accused of [briefly repeat the accusations]. I also said that, by law, you have several rights. First, you don't have to tell me anything, although the court may take into account that you didn't say anything. You also have the right to consult with a lawyer and with your parents or other adults. Finally, you have the right to have a parent or adult present when you're being interviewed. Do you want me to explain some rights again? Accommodate the child's request.

F.2. Are you willing to talk about the accusations?
Wait for the child's response. If the child says yes, whether or not s/he associates him/herself to the abuse, go to F3. If the child asks to remain silent, go to F4.

F.3. [Child's name], tell me everything that happened from the beginning to the end.

If the child mentions one or more events, go to part G. If the child denies involvement in the alleged events: go to question F.5.

F.4. If the child asks to remain silent, say:

[Child's name], things have been said about you/accusations have been made against you, and this is your opportunity to tell me what had happened. Wait for the child to respond.

If the child remains silent, inform him/her that he can provide an alternative version and that therapy is an available option:

F.4.1. [Child's name], even if you think the accusations are false/not true, it is important for me to hear your side/story [alternative account].

F.4.2. [Child's name], children who perform sexual acts on other children need therapy in order to stop doing that, and there are people whose job is to help them.
(If the child continues to remain silent/states his right to remain silent, consider ending the interview.)

F.4.3. [Child's name], if so, we will end this conversation now.

If the child denies involvement in the alleged events and seems avoidant or resistant, provide support to deal with the resistance before and while progressing through the following transitional prompts.

F.5. [Child's name], even if you think the accusations are false/not true, it is important for me to hear your side [alternative account].

F.6. [Child's name], I want you to take a few minutes to think about that, because it is very important. If you feel more comfortable writing, here's a pen and paper.

Wait for the child to respond, if s/he is writing wait until s/he stops writing, then ask:

> Will you share with me what you just wrote? Wait for the child to respond, if the child says s/he is willing to share, add: Will you show me what you wrote? You don't have to. If you do, you should know that it can be used as evidence.

If there was an earlier investigation, say:

F.7. [Child's name], I've heard that you talked to [school manager, social worker, other professional] at [time, location]. Please tell me what you talked about.

F.8. [Child's name], do you know about [material or circumstantial evidence connected to the events: e.g. injury from a bottle of alcohol] that happened to someone?

F.9. Did something happen at [time/place/context of the incident such as a party/camping]?

F.10. Did something happen with [a child/name of the victim]?

F.11. [Child's name], did [present gradually more specific details of the complaint] happen?

Repeat this question as needed.

F.12. [Child's name], I understood that [you told someone/someone said] that you were involved in [a short summary of the allegations]. I want to check if something like that happened.
If the child keeps denying involvement in the suspected/alleged event/s, go to G.3.b.

G. Exploring the incidents

Throughout the substantive part it is important to preserve and enhance the rapport established with the child and to continue offering support (Addendum) to address expressed inhibitions, distress, and conflicts. If the child mentions a specific incident:

G.1.a. [Child's name], you told me that [briefly summarize the child's version]. Tell me everything from the beginning to the end as best you can.

If the child mentions a specific incident or s/he gives a generic description and you cannot determine the number of incidents:

[Child's name], you told me that [briefly summarize the child's version]. Did that happen one time or more than one time?

If the child mentions a number of incidents:

Child's name], tell me everything about [the last/first time/incident at place/at time/specific incident] from the beginning to the end.

G.1.b. Follow-up invitations

Please repeat the child's description of the action/occurrence that started the event. Then ask:

And then what happened?

Use this question as often as needed until you have a complete description of the incident.

G.1.c. Time segmenting invitations

You have told me many things and helped me understand what happened. Now, [child's name], I want to ask you more questions about [incident title].

[Child's name], think back to that time [day, night] and please tell me everything that happened from the moment [an activity the child mentioned] to the moment [a subsequent activity the child mentioned].

You may use this question as often as needed to ensure that all parts of the incident are described.

G.1.d. Cued invitations

Cued invitations can have two formats:

[Child's name], tell me more about [activity, object, feeling, thought].

[Child's name], you mentioned [activity, object, feeling, thought]. Tell me more about that.

Use this question as often as needed throughout this section.

Important! Free-recall invitations should be exhausted before proceeding to directive questions.

G.2. Directive questions

If some central details of the accusation are still missing or unclear after the exhaustive use of open-ended questions, use directive questions.

[Child's name], you said that/mentioned [activity, object, feeling, thought]. [How, when, where, who, what, which, how many, what did you mean]?

It is important to pair open-ended invitations with directive questions whenever possible:

Tell me more about that.

Important! If the child mentioned more than one incident, repeat questions G.1–G.2 for each incident before moving to option-posing questions, G.3.

G.3. Option-posing questions

Review the information you have received, see if there is any missing information, and plan the rest of the interview. Be sure to formulate option-posing questions in writing and consider replacing them with open-ended (or directive) prompts. Option-posing questions should be followed by invitations. First ask about information missing from the suspect's statement, then information missing based on the alleged victim's statements, and finally about information missing based on external evidence.

G.3.a. Option-posing questions – eliciting information based on the child's version.

[Child's name], when you told me about [specific incident embedded in time and place] you mentioned [activity, object, feeling, thought]. [Did, have, has, is, are] [present a detail for child to confirm or deny]?

Follow with an invitation:

Tell me everything about that.

G.3.b. Option-posing questions – eliciting information based on the alleged victim's version.

If the child denied the allegations or only partially associated him/herself with the incidents, ask a general option-posing question:

[Child's name], did other things happen with [a child/alleged victim]?
[Child's name], did more things happen with [a child/alleged victim]?

If the child denies, ask specific option-posing questions.

[Child's name], did you go to your house with [a child/alleged victim]?

G.3.c. Option-posing questions – eliciting information based on evidence

[Child's name], did you [send WhatsApp message]/did something happen to [the child/alleged victim's clothes]?

G.4. Clarifying contradictions

If substantial disparities remain between the suspect's version and that of the alleged victim/suggested by case evidence, a general clarifying question might be required:

G.4.a. [Child's name], thank you for everything you've told me. In a conversation with [the alleged victim], different/additional things were said. It is important that you help me understand everything that has happened. I would like you to think back, try to elaborate and be as accurate as you can.

If the child still denies the allegations or seem reluctant, say:

G.4.b. Take a few minutes and think whether there is anything else you would like to tell me.
(Break)

Is there anything else you would like to tell me?

If the child provides some information, listen and elaborate accordingly. If substantial disparities remain between the suspect's version and that of the alleged victim/suggested by case evidence, you may formulate double-cued invitations, which include the two differing items, without suggesting that they are contradictory. Avoid identifying contradictions using terms such as "but", "yet" or "on the other hand". First address contradictions within the suspect's statement, then those between the child's and alleged victim's statements, and finally those between the suspect's statement and external evidence.

G.4.c.1. Clarifying contradictions within the suspect's statement

[Child's name], you said you met her once. You also mentioned a second time. Please tell me about that.

G.4.c.2. Clarifying discrepancies between the suspect's and the victim's statement

[Child's name], you said you touched her over her clothes. She said you touched her under her clothes. Please help me understand.

G.4.c.3. Clarifying contradictions between the statement and external evidence

[Child's name], you said you do not know her. On your phone, there is a message sent to her. Please tell me about that.

If the child keeps denying/sticks to his/her version, you can say the following:

That is your choice and I'll respect it.

G.5. Did anything like that happen with other kids? On other occasions?

Please follow any disclosure by the child and investigate accordingly.

H. *Disclosure information*

[Child's name], you've given me [lots of] information and that really helps me to understand what happened, and now I would like to know if other people knew about what happened.

Explore the disclosure process, addressing the disclosure time, circumstances, recipients, potential discussions of the event, and reactions to disclosure by both the child and recipients. Use open ended questions whenever possible. If the child did not disclose the incident previously, ask why not.

I. *Exposure to inappropriate sexual content*

If, during the interview, the child mentions exposure to inappropriate sexual content such as watching online pornography, sexual behaviour that isn't age appropriate, or poor sexual hygiene in the child's environment, explore that using cued invitations.

Example:

Earlier you mentioned (watching pornography, playing sexual games, watching your sister and her boyfriend), tell me everything about that.

If the child didn't mention inappropriate sexual content during the interview but there is a concern that s/he may have been exposed to such content, ask:

I.1. Have you watched sexual activity before?
I.2. Have you seen sexual acts in a photo/movie/the internet/live?

J. Exploring the possibility the child has been victimized:

J.1. Did someone hurt you?
J.2. Did someone (do something sexual with you/undress you/touch you)?

If the child discloses that he has been victimized, consider a victim protocol interview.

K. Ending the interview

[Child's name], you've talked to me today and I want to thank you.

K.1. Is there anything else you think I should know?
K.2. Is there anything else you would like to tell me?
K.3. Are there any questions that you would like to ask me?
K.4. Before we finish, it is important for me that you tell me how you felt before you came to talk to me?
K.5. How did you feel during our conversation?
K.6. How do you feel now that we have finished?

If the child confessed but expressed ambivalence while confessing, ask:

[Child's name], at the beginning of our conversation you had a hard time telling me/you didn't want to tell me [use the child's words] about [the event/s], but then you did tell me. What helped you talk?

Thank you for talking to me today, [child's name], and for helping me get to know you. We will end this conversation now and if you would like to talk with me again you can tell [the school's principal/counsellor/teacher]. You can add if necessary: I may want to talk to you again.

L. Neutral topic

[Child's name], what are you going to do after we finish talking?

Talk to the child for a couple of minutes about a neutral topic.

Say to the recorder:

Interview ended at [time]

Addendum: Supportive non-suggestive techniques for the Revised NICHD Suspect Protocol

Adapted for the RSP from table 9.1 in Lamb et al. (2018).

A. *Addressing the child in a personal way*

Address the child in a personal way using the name s/he prefers. Avoid using terms of endearment (e.g. "sweety").

B. *Establishing rapport*

- Welcoming the child

I am glad to meet you today/to get to know you/to get to talk. It's nice to meet you, my name is _________.

- Expressing personal interest in the child

I really want to get to know you/about things that happened to you.

Today is the first time we've met and it is important for me to know you better.

- Making small gestures of goodwill

Are you warm enough?
Let me show you the toilets.
Here is a glass of water for you.
Do you want to look at the video camera? Do you need a short break?

C. *Reinforcement*

- Reinforcement during the interview

You are telling me clearly/in detail and that's important.
You're really helping me understand/know you.
You corrected me and that's really important.
I understand what you're saying.

Avoid "grading" ("very good") or associating reinforcement with specific content ("You told me that you ran away, which was good").

- Expressing thanks and appreciation

I want to thank you for your help.
I really appreciate that you are talking to me.
I appreciate that you are trying to remember and tell me. Thank you for sharing with me.

- Emphasizing the child's agency

It's up to you whether you talk to me or not. I will respect your choice/decision.

D. *Using rapport*

- Mentioning and building on trust

  You told me a lot about yourself and I feel I know you better.

  Now that we know each other better, you can share with me what happened.

- Expression of care or worry

  I'm here for you.

  I care about you.

  You are important to me.

  People are/I am worried that something may have happened to you. [You can specify the cause for concern (e.g. "The teacher said you were crying this morning").]

- Presenting the interviewer as someone to disclose to

  If something happened, I'm here to listen to you.

  You can trust me and tell me if something happened.

  It's okay to share secrets/problems with me.

  I talk to many kids who tell me about things that have happened to them.

  It's my job to listen to the children if they have problems.

  If there is something that should stop/not happen again, you can tell me.

  It is important for me to hear your side.

E. *Emotional support*

- Generalized comments about the child's perceived difficulties

  Many children find it difficult to talk/feel ashamed at the beginning but then it becomes easier.

  Many children have secrets.

- Empathy

  I understand it is difficult for you to tell me (when the child said that).

  I know it's been a long interview.

- Checking for the child's feeling

  How are you feeling so far/now that we are done?

How did you feel before we began/during our conversation?

- Exploring emotions
  Tell me more about your fears.
  Tell me what you're afraid of.
  I can see you're crying. Tell me what is happening.
  You said you don't want to/cannot tell me. Tell me more about that.

- Open questioning about expressing feelings or thoughts
  You said you were sad/disgusted/wanted to run away. Tell me more about that.

- Echoing emotions
  You said you were sad/you were crying.

- Acknowledging/accepting/recognizing emotions
  You say that it was very painful, I understand what you you're saying.
  I see what you are saying.

- Reassurance
  Don't worry, I won't tell other children.
  You won't be late for the bus.
  Nobody is going to arrest you.
  Sometimes it helps children when they speak and don't have to keep a secret.
  Sometimes it's possible to help children who have done such things.
  Therapy can help children who do sexual things to other children.

- Exploring unexpressed emotions and conflicts
  If there is something you are worried about, please tell me.

F. *Encouragement*

- Emphasizing the child is the source of knowledge
  I'm asking you these questions because I was not there.

- Legitimating expression
  You can talk about bad things and good things.
  In this office you can say everything.
  It is okay to tell me about this kind of things/to say these words/bad words.
  Many children tell me what happened to them.

- Expression of confidence/optimism
  I think you can explain it well.

- Offering help
  I want to make it easier for you. What would help you tell me?
  Would it make it easier if you wrote it down?
  You can start talking and I'll help you by asking questions.
  I am here to help.
  There are people whose job is to help in these cases.

- Encouraging non-verbal communication
  Could you please turn toward me?
  Come on, look at me.
  I'd like to see your eyes!

- Encouraging disclosure
  It is really important that you tell me if something has happened.

G. *Counter-supportive*

1. Suggestive support – presuming content, selective reinforcement.
2. Confrontation – interviewer challenges the information given by the child by suggesting it's implausible, mentioning competing external information or pointing to inconsistencies in the child's statements.
3. Causing discomfort – interrupting or criticizing the child's statements or behaviour, being coercive, using the wrong name for the child.
4. Ignoring or not recognizing. A. Clarification requests or inquiries by the child. B. Resistance, omissions, denials. C. References to internal content (including conflict, emotions (positive or negative), or physiological responses associated with emotions or pain).
5. Unfounded support – unrealistic promises or reassurance.

Strategies to overcome the reluctance to disclose abuse

The Revised NICHD Investigative Interview Protocol

Irit Hershkowitz, Michael E. Lamb, Yael Karni-Visel, and Uri Blasbalg

Most child abuse, especially child sexual abuse, occurs in private, without witnesses other than the perpetrator and the victim. Some instances of abuse result in visible recognizable injuries revealing what has happened, but in many cases, there are no such physical signs of abuse. Further, as contributors to this book have repeatedly pointed out, children tend to delay reporting their abuse experiences for a variety of reasons, both cognitive (e.g. their memories are hazy or they can't express themselves clearly) and motivational (e.g. they are too embarrassed or ashamed to report). These interrelated factors that keep many instances of abuse wholly or partially unrecognized underscore the importance of questioning possible victims to find out about their experiences. Sadly, notorious examples like the McMartin and Kelly Michaels cases in the 1980s made clear that this questioning had to be accomplished with care by trained and unbiased interviewers (Ceci & Bruck, 1995), a realization that fuelled both research and the development of evidence-based interview guidelines designed to facilitate the elicitation of detailed and accurate accounts of abuse from young victims.

Initial efforts to improve investigative interviewing were informed by years of careful research designed to understand the emotional, cognitive, linguistic, and social characteristics that impeded children's abilities to provide detailed and accurate accounts. Evidence-based guidance for forensic interviewers thus sought to help them recognize and work around those limitations and build on relevant strengths (e.g. Lamb et al., 1994, 1995; Poole & Lamb 1998; Saywitz et al., 1992). Lecture-style training regarding desirable and undesirable practices proved to have little effect on practice in the field (Lamb, 2016; Lamb et al., 2002a, 2002b), however, so researchers developed increasingly structured interview guides or protocols, including the NICHD Investigative Interview Protocol (here called the Standard Protocol or SP; Lamb et al., 2002a, 2002b; Orbach et al., 2000; Sternberg et al., 1997). The SP was a structured interview protocol designed to translate research-based professional recommendations into operational guidelines

DOI: 10.4324/9781003427155-9

(Lamb et al., 2008) covering all phases of the interview. The initial protocol (SP) (Lamb et al., 2003; Orbach et al., 2000) included six phases: Introduction, clarification of the ground rules, rapport building, narrative training, episodic-memory training, transitional phase, and substantive questioning. The guide encouraged interviewers to exhaust the child's memory using free-recall prompts before asking any directive questions, followed (only if necessary) by option-posing questions.

In part because coercive and suggestive questioning had proved so problematic in the egregious miscarriages of justice mentioned earlier, questioning style was originally the focus of the new interview guidance. Practitioners were not only taught how to avoid suggestive questions but also how to maximize the elicitation of high-quality information by asking broad open-ended requests for recall, also known as invitations (see Lamb et al., 2018, for a review). Later studies also showed that children produced more detailed reports when rapport was built using invitations rather than other types of questions (e.g. Anderson et al., 2014; Sternberg et al., 1997). Indeed, questions that relied on recognition rather than recall memory processes tended not only to elicit less information but also to elicit less accurate information, especially when the questions involved were leading or suggestive (e.g. Brown et al., 2013).

Although initial guidelines like the SP paid some attention to socio-emotional factors, those were not the major focus; little attention was paid to addressing children's reticence and the protocols were thus especially effective only with cooperative children. However, the increasing acknowledgement that many reluctant children offered few if any details, often denying any abuse when interviewed (e.g. Hershkowitz et al., 2006), led researchers to focus attention on the socio-emotional dynamics of forensic interviews and their associations with the informativeness of investigative interviews. Early studies by Hershkowitz et al. (2006, 2007) were particularly influential. They showed that children's initial uncooperativeness was often followed by interviewers' counter-productive interventions such as intrusive questioning, unsupportiveness, and premature reference to sensitive topics which seemed to reinforce rather than moderate the children's reluctance, creating a dynamic that often resulted in non-disclosure, even if abuse was known to have taken place. This led to an increased focus on the part of researchers, experts, and professionals on the socioemotional factors that influence the effectiveness of forensic interviews with alleged victims of child abuse. This focus in turn led to the development of a revised interview protocol taking account of these factors, the Revised Protocol (RP). The RP guides interviewers to establish meaningful rapport with children and to enhance the expression of emotions, including negative emotions and conflicted feelings about disclosure, responding to them supportively.

Rapport, support, and emotional expression

Both laboratory-analogue and field studies of forensic interviews contributed to the development of the socio-emotional practices emphasized in the RP. Supportive interviewer behaviour was first shown to be positively associated with the production of abuse-related information in studies suggesting that the correlations were stronger when disclosing children seemed less cooperative (e.g. Hershkowitz, 2009; Teoh & Lamb, 2013). A pilot study with reluctant children showed that supportive interviewing was associated with reduced reluctance in both the pre-substantive and substantive interview phases (Hershkowitz et al., 2014, 2015). Additional research showed that support offered immediately in response to expressions of reluctance was positively associated with reduced reluctance (Ahern et al., 2014). Overall, good child-interviewer rapport (friendly, harmonious interaction) is associated with children's informativeness about the alleged abuse (Sternberg et al., 1997) whereas poor rapport is associated with reticence and uncooperativeness (e.g. Hamilton et al., 2016; Katz et al., 2012).

Attention by interviewers to emotional factors was also motivated by basic research on the complex and multifaceted associations between memory and emotional processes. For example, researchers investigating various mnemonics had shown the advantage of emotional cues in the retrieval process (e.g. Mather & Sutherland, 2011) while other researchers had observed that both adults (see Dolcos et al., 2020; Holland & Kensinger, 2010 for reviews; Kensinger, 2009; Mickley Steinmetz et al., 2016) and children (Hamann & Stevens, 2013; see Massol et al., 2020; but cf. Van Bergen et al., 2015) remember emotional experiences in richer detail than non-emotional events. Differences in the extent and quality of children's reports are evident when children recall positive rather than neutral events (Jones & Pipe, 2002), but the effect is especially strong when children recall negative personal experiences (Fivush & Baker-Ward, 2005) such as painful medical treatments (Peterson, 2012), violent and abusive events (Fivush et al., 2003; Lamb et al., 2000; Quas et al., 1999), or natural disasters (Cordón et al., 2004).

Analogue studies have also shown that children's emotional expressiveness is associated with enhanced responsiveness and informativeness during an interview (Ahern & Lyon, 2013; Klemfuss et al., 2013) while participating in a dialogue that encourages emotional expression promotes children's memory retrieval (Ahern & Lyon, 2013; Klemfuss et al., 2013). Similar results were obtained in studies conducted in forensic contexts. Lyon et al. (2012) found that "how did you feel?" questions often elicited reports of abuse-related evaluative content (descriptions of emotional, cognitive, and physical reactions). However, when speaking with adults and describing past events, including incidents of abuse, children typically minimize their spontaneous emotional expression, and their expressions tend to be brief and sporadic (e.g. Pasupathi & Wainryb, 2010), especially in forensic contexts (Katz et al., 2016). As explained below, supportive forensic interviewing is aimed at helping children, reassuring them, and facilitating emotional expression to assist them in overcoming emotional barriers that may have made the interview taxing (e.g. Karni-Visel et al., 2019; Klemfuss & Musser, 2020). In turn, facilitating emotional expression during the interview is intended to help children elaborate on and regulate their emotions, thereby reducing the intensity of inhibiting emotions and enabling the disclosure of sensitive information.

Emotional cueing can also enhance the recollection of events. Liwag and Stein (1995) tested the role of emotional cues including labels, faces and the reinstatement of emotions previously described by their parents, on preschool-aged children's recall of emotional events. They found that all types of emotional cues increased information retrieval, but that reinstatement of the original emotion experienced during the event was most effective. In another laboratory study, O'Carroll and colleagues (2006) observed a similar effect with 10- to 11-year-olds reporting more specific details than younger children (7 to 8 years old) when emotional cues (consisting of negatively and positively valanced words) were provided. Neurophysiological (Bowen et al., 2018) as well as imaging research (Fenker et al., 2005; Ford & Kensinger, 2016) has also suggested neural pathways by which emotional cues in the form of words, pictures, or faces affect memory for episodic contents in adults (see Murty et al., 2010 for review) and children (see Dolcos et al., 2020; Hamann & Stevens, 2013 for reviews).

Not only does emotional cueing enhance the retrieval of information about events, but emotional valence is associated with the type of information reported as well. Whereas negative emotions seem to be associated with enhanced memory for central details (Buchanan & Lovallo, 2001; Christianson, 1992), positive emotions tend to be linked with enhanced memory for peripheral details (Talarico et al., 2009). Thus, children have more accurate and lasting memories of central features than peripheral or background features of traumatic experiences such as natural disasters (e.g. Bahrick et al., 1998), child sexual abuse (e.g. Alexander et al., 2005), and physical injuries (Peterson & Bell, 1996). However, negative stimuli can enhance memory for peripheral details as well when the events are especially meaningful and salient (Kensinger et al., 2007; Knight & Mather, 2009; Mickley Steinmetz et al., 2016; Wessel et al., 2000).

Emotions also affect the retrieval of information about discrete instances when repeated events have occurred although few studies to date have explored this effect (Brubacher & Earhart, 2019). When children (and adults) experience many similar events, they tend to form over-generalized representations of typical events rather than specific representations of particular incidents (see Bouyeure & Noulhiane, 2020 for review; Canada et al., 2019; Hudson & Mayhew, 2008). As a result, they may be able to recall the general gist of recurring events but poorly recall details specific to single occurrences (Brubacher et al., 2013; Odegard et al., 2009). In forensic contexts, generic statements are usually not sufficient and the likelihood that a case will proceed to prosecution frequently depends on the specificity with which a child reports discrete instances of the alleged abuse (Guadagno et al., 2006).

In a laboratory study, O'Carroll et al. (2006) sought to show the effects of emotional cueing on the amount of specific information (representing event-specific memory) as opposed to generic information reported. They showed that emotional cueing elicited event-specific information, and that the valence of emotions also mattered: Negative emotional cueing was especially effective as children grew older. Complementary imaging studies suggested that emotional arousal triggers stronger activity in the brain region that is critical for pattern separation and thus enables better retrieval of information about separate events (Leal, 2016).

Whereas laboratory-analogue studies have used external information as emotion-related retrieval cues (Liwag & Stein, 1995; O'Carroll et al., 2006), only self-references to emotions can be used in actual forensic interviews to avoid risky suggestions. However, because children often do not mention emotions when recalling their abuse (Lamb et al., 1997; Lyon et al., 2012; Westcott & Kynan, 2004), researchers have introduced strategies designed to elicit emotional expressions and references to them (Karni-Visel et al., 2019; Lyon et al., 2012). As explained below, attention to emotional contents may help to explain the effectiveness of the RP.

Forensic interviews with reluctant children

As Hershkowitz et al. (2006) initially observed, interviewers who fail to engage reluctant children sensitively often react to demonstrations of reluctance counter-productively (e.g. Teoh & Lamb, 2013). By contrast, supportive engagement (interviewer demeanour showing that they want to help and encourage the child) is associated with better interview outcomes (Hershkowitz et al., 2017). The improved outcomes include moderation of reluctance (e.g. Ahern et al., 2014; Blasbalg, Hershkowitz, Lamb, Karni-Visel, & Ahern, 2019), increases in the rates of initial disclosures (Hershkowitz & Lamb, 2020), the production of more forensically relevant information (e.g. Blasbalg, Hershkowitz, Lamb, Karni-Visel, & Ahern, 2019; Karni-Visel et al., 2019) and statement coherence (Blasbalg, Hershkowitz, Karni-Visel, & Lamb, 2019).

Reluctance to disclose abuse is associated with factors such as child age, type and severity of the offence, as well as relationship to the suspect:

younger children abused by parent figures, especially those abused sexually or more severely, are less likely to disclose abuse than are older children and those abused by adults to whom they are less closely related (e.g. Hershkowitz & Lamb, 2020; Wallis & Woodworth, 2020). Children who are more reluctant are typically prompted using more and more direct/specific questions (Hershkowitz et al., 2006) and provide less information about the abuse (e.g. Lewy et al., 2015).

Establishing rapport at the beginning of forensic interviews helps facilitate communication with children and encourages them to affirm and describe traumatic experiences (e.g. Brown et al., 2013; Lavoie et al., 2021). Research focused on rapport building has shown that better rapport is achieved when forensic interviewers invite interviewees to share personal information in detail using invitations (e.g. Roberts et al., 2004; Sternberg et al., 1997). Rapport is often built within a narrative practice session and/or when practicing episodic memory retrieval about neutral events (e.g. Saywitz et al., 2011; Snider & Everson, 2011). Hershkowitz et al. (2006) reported that, during the pre-substantive rapport-building phase, children who later failed to disclose abuse were less responsive to interviewers' questions than their disclosing peers. Later studies showed that enhanced support during the rapport-building phase was associated with reduced reluctance (e.g. Hershkowitz et al., 2015) and these findings all informed development of the Revised NICHD Investigative interview Protocol (RP) which grew out of efforts to address both the cognitive and emotional/motivational factors that should be addressed together so as to maximize the likelihood that children will both report abuse they have experienced and describe it in sufficient detail to allow effective interventions in both the child protection and criminal justice domains.

The Revised NICHD Protocol

The Revised NICHD Protocol (RP), like the SP, was designed to enhance the amount of event-specific (rather than generic) information retrieved by instructing interviewers to seek accounts of specific events and directing children to recount discreet events that are most accessible to memory (for more details see Lamb et al., 2018; a complete version of the RP appears in the Appendix and translations are available at https://nichdprotocol.com/). In addition to these principles, the RP encourages the interviewer to address discomfort and emotions expressed by children with supportive yet non-suggestive techniques. The guide shows how to engage in more supportive pre-substantive and transitional phases, as well as an inventory of non-suggestive supportive statements that can be used as needed by interviewers. In order to encourage emotional discourse, the RP also instructs interviewers to echo and explore all emotions reported (e.g. "[Child's name], you say you were [the emotion expressed]/I hear/see what you are saying/. Tell me more about being [the emotion expressed]"), in the pre-substantive part of the interview, and to prompt for emotions if children do not mention them spontaneously (e.g. "How did you feel about [an episode reported], [child's name]?"). Interviewers are then guided to use these supportive techniques during the substantive part of the interviews. Interviewers are also encouraged to reply in other supportive ways to emotions by showing appreciation (e.g. "Thank you [child's name] for sharing your emotions/experiences/with me, I appreciate that"), showing overt interest in what children say ("I really want to know about your emotions/experiences better, [child's name]"), emphasizing the child-interviewer rapport ("You've already told me a lot about your emotions/experiences, [child's name]"), and noting the availability of the interviewer as a supportive figure ("[Child's name], I am here to understand your emotions/experiences"). Interviewers are also encouraged to be supportive by providing direct encouragement ("Please tell me more about your emotions/experiences, [child's name]"/"Sometimes children find it difficult to talk at the beginning, but then they succeed"), offering help ("What would help you tell, [child's name]? Would you like to write/draw?") or making small gestures of good will ("Are you comfortable, [child's name]? Would you like a break/A glass of water?").

Effectiveness and use

Although each element of the RP was informed by empirical research, some of which has been reviewed (briefly) in this chapter, other research has made clear how difficult it would be to bring about meaningful and persistent changes in the ways interviewers interacted with children in the course of forensic interviews. Specifically, changes in interviewing practice tend to be achieved only in the context of well-structured and extended training which includes efforts to ensure maintenance of any gains achieved (Cederborg et al., 2013; Lamb, 2016; Lamb et al., 2002). These studies suggest that the training needs to move beyond the classroom, to be spaced over time, and to involve extensive opportunities to consolidate learning and practice skills in contexts that ensure prompt feedback and guidance.

Hershkowitz et al. (2017) thus examined the impact of an extended training program on interviewers' responses when using the RP. They implemented and assessed a training program that addressed the documented needs and difficulties experienced by child investigators in Israel who had been using the RP. The instructors encouraged interviewers to provide appropriate support and to avoid missing opportunities to demonstrate support during the pre-substantive and substantive phases of the interview. This training program described a broad range of supportive techniques for interviewers to draw upon and included detailed guidance about how support should be employed in each phase of the interview.

The training followed a *train the trainer* approach, with interviewers trained to evaluate their own interviews. This self-review involved identifying instances of support offered, missed opportunities to provide support in response to reluctance or emotions, as well as instances of inappropriate (or unsupportive) interviewer behaviour, such as suggestive support, unfounded reassurance, or causing discomfort. Supervisors were trained for 5 days; the sessions included instructions on how to identify various types of supportive and unsupportive behaviour in their own previous interviews, as well as a 1-day workshop on how to deliver training to their teams. Supervisors then trained the interviewers that they typically supervised in eight 1-day workshops. The workshops included a review of theory and research, practice with the various supportive interventions, learning how to code, reviewing recent interviews, and exercises for use throughout the training period. Interviewers also had 2-hour long individual meetings with their supervisor following each workshop.

Hershkowitz et al.'s analyses examined the presence or absence of support and inadequate interviewer responses, as well as the absence of supportive responses when they would have been appropriate, throughout each interview. In all, 321 interviews with 3- to 14-year-old alleged victims were examined; they took place at varying stages of the training program and were spread across nearly a year (8 training sessions).

Results showed that insensitivity (failing to provide support when it was needed) decreased relative to baseline after the second and third training sessions, while support was higher at each time point relative to baseline and also increased between the second and third training sessions. Inadequate support decreased relative to baseline following each subsequent training session. More support was also given to younger children while insensitivity was higher for older children (9 years or older). More inadequate responses were made to younger children during the baseline and following the first training session, but age differences were no longer apparent thereafter. The researchers speculated that the interviewers' differential sensitivity to signs of reluctance may have reflected differences in the ways in which younger and older children verbalized their reluctance. This would imply that the passive resistance exhibited by older children (pausing; "I don't know") may be more difficult for interviewers to detect and address supportively than active resistance ("I want to go") by younger children. It is also possible that interviewers were more empathic toward younger children because they appeared more immature and vulnerable.

Clearly, over the course of the training program, interviewers became better able to recognize the need for support and to respond appropriately. Interviewers' increasing insight into their own practice and children's responding may have been helped, at least in part, by a focus in the self-review and supervision sessions on the use of desired behaviours but also by the identification of missed opportunities. Some skills were more easily acquired in the course of training, whereas others took longer to mature. For example, trainees quickly increased the rates at which they provided support and decreased the rates at which they responded inadequately, whereas sensitivity to signs of reluctance only increased after further training sessions. Similarly, improvements in responding to young children took place later than improvements in patterns of responding to older children.

The evaluation of interviews conducted by those who completed this training showed that use of the RP was associated with enhanced verbal (Karni-Visel et al., 2019) and nonverbal emotional expressiveness (Karni-Visel et al., 2023). Importantly, in Karni-Visel et al.'s (2019) study, more frequent verbal expressions of emotion by children were not only positively associated with the enhanced production of abuse-related information, but also mediated the positive association between support and informativeness. These findings suggested that, by supportively encouraging the expression of emotions, interviewers may promote children's cooperativeness and their production of abuse-related information. Similarly, interviewer support was associated with children's expressiveness, and when children expressed more nonverbal emotions, they were more responsive during the pre-substantive phases and more informative about the abuse. Overall, increased informativeness in RP interviews was associated with the extent to which the interviewers offered supportive comments throughout the interview, reduced the use of intrusive questions during the transitional phase when exploring the possibility that abuse had occurred, and relied more on invitations when exploring the abusive event in the substantive phase (Blasbalg et al., in preparation). This study also showed that children who were interviewed supportively and were more informative when narrating their memories were more talkative and emotionally expressive in the pre-substantive rapport-building phase, were less reluctant to disclose abuse during the transitional phase, and showed greater willingness to express their emotions in the substantive phase.

Karni-Visel et al. (2022) showed that it was especially important to address negative rather than positive emotions, consistent with other evidence that emotional valence can influence the degree of detail with which events are remembered (for review see Kensinger, 2009). Because the events remembered by the children studied by Karni-Visel et al. (2022) involved physical violence toward the children, it is possible that even peripheral details (such as the colour of the suspect's clothing or descriptions of non-abusive aspects of the incidents) were meaningful or threatening, so retrieval of those details was also triggered by references to negative emotions. However, while negative emotions had stronger associations with informativeness, references to positive emotions were also useful, although negative emotional language was associated with the production of less generic information than was positive emotional language (Karni-Visel et al., 2022).

Repeated experiences of stressful experiences may create an emotional barrier that prevents children from freely exploring their memories (Conway & Pleydell-Pearce, 2000). This mechanism known as functional avoidance (see review by Sumner, 2012) perhaps led children to over-generalized memory of repeated experiences (Valentino et al., 2009). Exploring negative emotions during retrieval may have helped the children studied by Karni-Visel et al. (2022) to overcome their tendency to retrieve generic details. This in turn may have improved the quality of their episodic memory retrieval (Yassa & Stark, 2011) such that exploring emotions allowed them to focus their attention (Bowen et al., 2018). Thus, they may have engaged in the efficient top-down scanning process required to move from generalized to specific information (Liu et al., 2008), and to extract episodic details about particular events, which may be especially important in forensic contexts.

Overall, by emphasizing the creation and maintenance of rapport, attention and prompt responding to emotional expressions, and careful reliance on recall memory processes through the use of open-ended questions, researchers showed that use of the RP rather than the original (or Standard) Protocol (SP) was associated with declines in reluctance, and increases in both the amount of forensically relevant information provided (e.g. Blasbalg et al., 2018; Karni-Visel et al., 2022) and the coherence of children's accounts (Blasbalg et al., 2018). These correlates were obviously apparent to those making decisions on the basis of the information provided by the alleged victims being interviewed: Analysing administrative data regarding all interviews conducted in Israel over a 3-year period, Hershkowitz and Lamb (2020) reported that significantly more children made allegations when interviewed using the RP rather than the SP and that their allegations were rated as more credible. This was consistent with earlier research involving children whose abuse had been documented by evidence independent of the children's allegations. Specifically, Hershkowitz, Lamb, and Katz (2014) showed that significantly more of these known victims of abuse made allegations when interviewed using the RP rather than the SP. However, in that study as well as in Hershkowitz and Lamb's (2020) more comprehensive analysis, many suspected victims failed to make allegations even when there was substantial reason to believe that they had in fact been abused.

In the view of many professionals, some actual victims may so mistrust interviewers that additional efforts need to be invested in rapport building before the children may be willing to engage (e.g. Carnes et al., 1999). In such cases, a second interview may be needed to allow continued rapport building before the possibility of abuse is explored. An extended interview in which the focus is on rapport building rather than forensic investigation may allow trust to develop gradually as interviewer support and reassurance help dissipate negative emotions such as fear, embarrassment, or general distress associated with disclosure and/or the abuse itself (Karni-Visel et al., 2019). Leander (2010) and Azad and Leander (2015) reported that children were less avoidant and made fewer denials in a second or third interview than in the first, while Faller and Nelson-Gardell (2010) suggested that even more interviews may sometimes be necessary.

Accordingly, Hershkowitz et al. (2021) and Blasbalg et al. (2021) undertook studies involving 204 children for whom there were good reasons to believe that abuse had taken place and who were later reinterviewed using the RP. Over half (104 out of 204) of the children who denied abuse in the initial interview disclosed in the second, an interview characterized by more positive dynamics than in the first. Interviewer support during the first interview was associated with improved rapport in the second, which, in turn, predicted more spontaneous and detailed allegations. This highlighted the importance of establishing and maintaining rapport with reluctant children, confirming that some children may need more time to build rapport even with supportive interviewers.

Although the initial development and field assessment of the RP took place in Israel in collaboration with the government agency responsible for investigating all alleged crimes involving children, the RP has since been translated into dozens of languages and embraced, in whole or in part, by investigative agencies around the world, although it is unclear what efforts have been made to provide the necessary intensive training or to evaluate the protocol's effectiveness when utilized by skilled and trained interviewers. Prior research makes us doubt whether success can be obtained without intensive training and investment in maintenance of effective practices (Lamb, 2016).

Conclusion

As all contributors to this volume have acknowledged, many child abuse victims do not disclose maltreatment when interviewed, even when there is evidence that they were actually abused. Such failures to disclose frequently appear related to mistrust of professionals and fears about the consequences for themselves and others involved. Researchers have shown that interviewers can reinforce children's reluctance by failing to address it sensitively, whereas skilful management of their reluctance by enhancing rapport and providing social support may help reduce these barriers. The RP provides interviewers with detailed guidance about how to effectively develop and maintain rapport while supporting interviewees emotionally. Using these socio-emotionally sensitive practices during forensic interviews may not only promote children's sense of well-being and improve their experience during interviews, but also, importantly, enhance the quality of their testimony, motivating victims to provide accurate information about their experiences of abuse while avoiding suggestive techniques that might foster false allegations.

References

Ahern, E. C., Hershkowitz, I., Lamb, M. E., Blasbalg, U., & Winstanley, A. (2014). Support and reluctance in the pre-substantive phase of alleged child abuse victim investigative interviews: Revised versus standard NICHD protocols. *Behavioral Sciences & the Law*, *32*, 762–774. https://doi.org/10.1002/bsl.2149

Ahern, E.C, & Lyon, T.D. (2013). Facilitating maltreatment children's use of emotional language. *Journal of Forensic Social Work*, *3*, 176–203. https://doi.org/10.1080/1936928X.2013.854124

Alexander, K. W., Quas, J. A., Goodman, G. S., Ghetti, S., Edelstein, R. S., Redlich, A. D., et al. (2005). Traumatic impact predicts long-term memory for documented child sexual abuse. *Psychological Science*, *16*, 33–40.

Anderson, G. D., Anderson, J. N., & Gilgun, J. F. (2014). The influence of narrative practice techniques on child behaviors in forensic interviews. *Journal of Child Sexual Abuse*, *23*(6), 615–34. https://doi.org/10.1080/10538712.2014.932878

Azad, A., & Leander, L. (2015). Children's reporting about sexual versus physical abuse: Patterns of reporting, avoidance and denial. *Psychiatry, Psychology and Law*, *22*(6), 890–902. https://doi.org/10.1080/13218719.2015.1016392

Bahrick, L. E., Parker, J. F., Fivush, R., & Levitt, M. (1998). The effects of stress on young children's memory for a natural disaster. *Journal of Experimental Psychology: Applied*, *4*(4), 308.

Blasbalg, U., Hershkowitz, I., Karni-Visel, Y. (2018). Support, reluctance and production in child abuse investigative interviews. *Psychology, Public Policy, and Law*, *24*, 518–527. https://doi.org/10.1037/law0000183

Blasbalg, U., Hershkowitz, I., Karni-Visel, Y., & Lamb, M. E. (2019, June). The effects of interviewer's support on the coherence of child abuse forensic statements: Comparing the Revised and Standard NICHD Protocols. Paper presented at the International Investigative Interviewing Research Group Annual Conference, Stavern, Norway.

Blasbalg, U., Hershkowitz, I., Lamb, M. E., Karni-Visel, Y. (In preparation). Does supportive behavior throughout forensic interviews have a cumulative effect on children's cooperativeness?

Blasbalg, U., Hershkowitz, I., Lamb, M. E., Karni-Visel, Y., & Ahern, E. C. (2019). Is interviewer support associated with the reduced reluctance and enhanced informativeness of alleged child abuse victims? *Law and Human Behavior*, *43*, 156–165. https://doi.org/10.1037/lhb0000303

Blasbalg, U., Hershkowitz, I., Lamb, M. E., & Karni-Visel, Y. (2021). Adherence to the Revised NICHD Protocol recommendations for conducting repeated supportive interviews is associated with the likelihood that children will allege abuse. *Psychology, Public Policy, and Law*, *27*(2), 209.

Bouyeure, A., & Noulhiane, M. (2020). Memory: Normative development of memory systems. In A. Gallagher, C. Bulteau, D. Cohen, & J. L. Michaud (eds), *Handbook of clinical neurology* (pp. 201–213). Elsevier B.V. https://doi.org/10.1016/B978-0-444-64150-2.00018-6

Bowen, H. J., Kark, S. M., & Kensinger, E. A. (2018). NEVER forget: Negative emotional valence enhances recapitulation. *Psychonomic Bulletin and Review*, *25*(3), 870–891. https://doi.org/10.3758/s13423-017-1313-9

Brown, D. A., Lamb, M. E., Lewis, C., Pipe, M. E., Orbach, Y., & Wolfman, M. (2013). The NICHD investigative interview protocol: An analogue study. *Journal of Experimental Psychology: Applied*, *19*, 367–382. https://doi.org/10.1037/a0035143

Brubacher, S. P., & Earhart, B. (2019). Investigative interviewing about repeated experiences. In J. J. Dickinson, N. Schreiber Compo, R. Carol, B. L. Schwartz, & M. McCauley (eds), *Evidence-based investigative interviewing: Applying cognitive principles* (1st ed., pp. 216–233). Routledge. https://doi.org/10.4324/9781315160276

Brubacher, S. P., Malloy, L. C., Lamb, M. E., & Roberts, K. P. (2013). How do interviewers and children discuss individual occurrences of alleged repeated abuse in forensic interviews? *Applied Cognitive Psychology*, *27*(4), 443–450. https://doi.org/10.1002/acp.2920

Buchanan, T. W., & Lovallo, W. R. (2001). Enhanced memory for emotional material following stress-level cortisol treatment in humans. *Psychoneuroendocrinology*, *26*(3), 307–317. https://doi.org/10.1016/S0306-4530(00)00058-5

Canada, K. L., Ngo, C. T., Newcombe, N. S., Geng, F., & Riggins, T. (2019). It's All in the Details: Relations between Young Children's Developing Pattern Separation Abilities and Hippocampal Subfield Volumes. *Cerebral Cortex*, *29*(8), 3427–3433. https://doi.org/10.1093/cercor/bhy211

Carnes, C. N., Wilson, C., & Nelson-Gardell, D. (1999). Extended forensic evaluation when sexual abuse is suspected: A model and preliminary data. *Child Maltreatment*, *4*(3), 242–254.

Ceci, S. J., & Bruck, M. (1995). *Jeopardy in the courtroom: A scientific analysis of children's testimony*. American Psychological Association.

Cederborg, A. C., Alm, C., Lima da Silva Nises, D., & Lamb, M. E. (2013). Investigative interviewing of alleged child abuse victims: An evaluation of a new training programme for investigative interviewers. *Police Practice and Research*, *14*(3), 242–254.

Christianson, S. A. (1992). Emotional stress and eyewitness memory: A critical review. *Psychological Bulletin*, *112*(2), 284–309. https://doi.org/10.1037/0033-2909.112.2.284

Conway, M. A., & Pleydell-Pearce, C. W. (2000). The construction of autobiographical memories in the self-memory system. *Psychological Review*, *107*(2), 261.

Cordón, I. M., Pipe, M. E., Sayfan, L., Melinder, A., & Goodman, G. S. (2004). Memory for traumatic experiences in early childhood. *Developmental Review*, *24*(1), 101–132. https://doi.org/10.1016/j.dr.2003.09.003

Dolcos, F., Katsumi, Y., Moore, M., Berggren, N., de Gelder, B., Derakshan, N., Hamm, A. O., Koster, E. H. W., Ladouceur, C. D., Okon-Singer, H., Pegna, A. J., Richter, T., Schweizer, S., Van den Stock, J., Ventura-Bort, C., Weymar, M.,

& Dolcos, S. (2020). Neural correlates of emotion-attention interactions: From perception, learning, and memory to social cognition, individual differences, and training interventions. *Neuroscience and Biobehavioral Reviews*, *108*, 559–601. https://doi.org/10.1016/j.neubiorev.2019.08.017

Faller, K. C., & Nelson-Gardell, D. (2010). Extended evaluations in cases of child sexual abuse: How many sessions are sufficient?. *Journal of Child Sexual Abuse*, *19*(6), 648–668.

Fenker, D. B., Schott, B. H., Richardson-Klavehn, A., Heinze, H. J., & Düzel, E. (2005). Recapitulating emotional context: Activity of amygdala, hippocampus and fusiform cortex during recollection and familiarity. *European Journal of Neuroscience*, *21*(7), 1993–1999. https://doi.org/10.1111/j.1460-9568.2005.04033.x

Fivush, R., & Baker-Ward, L. (2005). The search for meaning: Developmental perspectives on internal state language in autobiographical memory. *Journal of Cognition and Development*, *6*(4), 455–462. https://psycnet.apa.org/doi/10.1207/s15327647jcd0604_1

Fivush, R., Hazzard, A., McDermott Sales, J., Sarfati, D., & Brown, T. (2003). Creating coherence out of Chaos? Children's narratives of emotionally positive and negative events. *Applied Cognitive Psychology*, *17*(1), 1–19. https://doi.org/10.1002/acp.854

Ford, J. H., & Kensinger, E. A. (2016). Effects of internal and external vividness on hippocampal connectivity during memory retrieval. *Neurobiology of Learning and Memory*, *134*(Part A), 78–90. https://doi.org/10.1016/j.nlm.2015.12.007

Guadagno, B. L., Powell, M. B., & Wright, R. (2006). Police officers' and legal professionals' perceptions regarding how children are, and should be, questioned about repeated abuse. *Psychiatry, Psychology and Law*, *13*(2), 251–260. https://doi.org/10.1375/pplt.13.2.251

Hamann, S., & Stevens, J. S. (2013). Memory for emotional stimuli in development. In P. J. Bauer & R. Fivush (eds), *The Wiley handbook on the development of children's memory* (pp. 724–742). Wiley Blackwell. https://doi.org/10.1002/9781118597705.ch32

Hamilton, G., Brubacher, S. P., & Powell, M. B. (2016). Expressions of shame in investigative interviews with Australian Aboriginal children. *Child Abuse and Neglect*, *51*, 64–71. https://doi.org/10.1016/j.chiabu.2015.11.004

Hershkowitz, I. (2009). Socioemotional factors in child abuse investigations. *Child Maltreatment*, *14*, 172–181. https://doi.org/10.1177/1077559508326224

Hershkowitz, I., Ahern, E. C., Lamb, M. E., Blasbalg, U., Karni-Visel, Y., & Breitman, M. (2017). Changes in interviewers' use of supportive techniques during the Revised Protocol Training. *Applied Cognitive Psychology*, *31*(3), 340–350. https://doi.org/10.1002/acp.3333

Hershkowitz, I., Lamb, M. E., Katz, C., & Malloy, L. C. (2015). Does enhanced rapport-building alter the dynamics of investigative interviews with suspected victims of intra-familial abuse? *Journal of Police and Criminal Psychology*, *30*, 6–14. https://doi.org/10.1007/s11896-013-9136-8

Hershkowitz, I., & Lamb, M. E. (2020). The effects of the NICHD Revised Protocol on allegation rates and credibility assessment in child abuse cases. *Psychology, Public Policy, and Law*, *26*, 176–184. https://doi.org/10.1037/law0000230

Hershkowitz, I., Lamb, M. E., Blasbalg, U., & Karni-Visel, Y. (2021). The dynamics of two-session interviews with suspected victims of abuse who are reluctant to make allegations. *Development and Psychopathology*, *33*, 739–747. https://doi.org/10.1017/S0954579420001820

Hershkowitz, I., Lamb, M. E., & Katz, C. (2014). Allegation rates in forensic child abuse investigations: Comparing the revised and standard NICHD protocols. *Psychology, Public Policy, and Law*, *20*, 336. https://doi.org/10.1037/a0037391

Hershkowitz, I., Lanes, O., & Lamb, M. E. (2007). Exploring the disclosure of child sexual abuse with alleged victims and their parents. *Child Abuse & Neglect*, *31*, 111–123. https://doi.org/10.1016/j. chiabu.2006.09.004

Hershkowitz, I., Orbach, Y., Lamb, M. E., Sternberg, K. J., & Horowitz, D. (2006). Dynamics of forensic interviews with suspected abuse victims who do not disclose abuse. *Child Abuse & Neglect*, *30*, 753–769. https://doi.org/10.1016/j.chiabu.2005.10.016

Hershkowitz, I., & Terner, A. (2007). The effects of repeated interviewing on children's forensic statements of sexual abuse. *Applied Cognitive Psychology: The Official Journal of the Society for Applied Research in Memory and Cognition*, *21*(9), 1131–1143.

Holland, A. C., & Kensinger, E. A. (2010). Emotion and autobiographical memory. *Physics of Life Reviews*, *7*(1), 88–131. https://doi.org/10.1016/j.plrev.2010.01.006

Hudson, J. A., & Mayhew, E. M. Y. (2008). The development of memory for recurring events. In M. L. Courage & N. Cowan (eds), *Studies in developmental psychology. The development of memory in infancy and childhood* (2nd ed., pp. 69–91). Psychology Press. https://doi.org/10.4324/9780203934654

Jones, C. H., & Pipe, M. E. (2002). How quickly do children forget events? A systematic study of children's event reports as a function of delay. *Applied Cognitive Psychology*, *16*(7), 755–768. https://doi.org/10.1002/acp.826

Karni-Visel, Y., Hershkowitz, I., Lamb, M. E., & Blasbalg, U. (2022). Emotional valence and the types of information provided by children in forensic interviews. *Child Abuse and Neglect*, 129. https://doi.org/10.1016/j.chiabu.2022.105639

Karni-Visel, Y., Hershkowitz, I., Lamb, M. E., & Blasbalg, U. (2019). Facilitating the expression of emotions by alleged victims of child abuseduring investigative interviews using the Revised NICHD Protocol. *Child Maltreatment*, *24*, 310–318. https://doi.org/10.1177/1077559519831382

Karni-Visel, Y., Hershkowitz, I., Lamb, M. E., & Blasbalg, U. (2023). Nonverbal emotions while disclosing child abuse: the role of interviewer support. *Child Maltreatment*, *28*, 66–75. doi:10.1177/10775595211063497

Katz, C., Paddon, M. J., & Barnetz, Z. (2016). Emotional language used by victims of alleged sexual abuse during forensic investigation. *Journal of Child Sexual Abuse*, *25*, 243–261. https://doi.org/10.1080/10538712.2016.1137666

Katz, C., Hershkowitz, I., Malloy, L. C., Lamb, M. E., Atabaki, A., & Spindler, S. (2012). Non-verbal behavior of children who disclose or do not disclose child abuse in investigative interviews. *Child Abuse & Neglect*, *36*, 12–20. https://doi.org/10.1016/j.chiabu.2011.08.006

Kensinger, E. A., Garoff-eaton, R. J., & Schacter, D. L. (2007). Effects of emotion on memory specificity: Memory trade-offs elicited by negative visually arousing stimuli. *Journal of Memory and Language, 56*(4), 575–591. https://doi.org/10.1016/j.jml.2006.05.004

Kensinger, E. A., & Schacter, D. L. (2007). Remembering the specific visual details of presented objects: Neuroimaging evidence for effects of emotion. *Neuropsychologia*, *45*(13), 2951–2962. https://doi.org/10.1016/j.neuropsychologia.2007.05.024

Kensinger, E. A. (2009). Remembering the details: Effects of emotion. *Emotion Review*, *1*(2), 99–113. https://doi.org/10.1177/1754073908100432

Klemfuss, J. Z., Milojevich, H. M., Yim, I. S., Rush, E. B., & Quas, J. A. (2013). Stress at encoding, context at retrieval, and children's narrative content. *Journal of Experimental Child Psychology*, *116*, 693–706. https://doi.org/10.1016/j.jecp.2013.07.009

Klemfuss, J. Z., & Musser, E. D. (2020). Talking about emotions: Effects of emotion-focused interviewing on children's physiological regulation of stress and discussion of the subjective elements of a stressful experience. *Journal of Experimental Child Psychology*, *198*, 104920. https://doi.org/10.1016/j.jecp.2020.104920

Knight, M., & Mather, M. (2009). Reconciling findings of emotion-induced memory Enhancement and impairment of preceding items. *Emotion*, *9*(6), 763–781. https://doi.org/10.1037/a0017281

Lamb, M. E. (2016). Difficulties translating research on forensic interview practices to practitioners: Finding water, leading horses, but can we get them to drink? *American Psychologist, 71*, 710–718. https://doi.org/10.1037/amp0000039

Lamb, M. E., Brown, D. A., Hershkowitz, I., Orbach, Y., & Esplin, P. W. (2018). *Tell me what happened: Questioning children about abuse*. John Wiley & Sons.

Lamb, M. E., Hershkowitz, I., Orbach, Y., & Esplin, P. W. (2008). What has been achieved: What else needs to be done? In G. Davies & R. Bull (Series Eds.), *Tell me what happened: Structured investigative interviews of child victims and witnesses* (pp. 267–282). John Wiley & Sons. https://doi.org/10.1002/9780470773291

Lamb, M. E., Sternberg, K. J., & Esplin, P. W. (1994). Factors influencing the reliability and validity of statements made by young victims of sexual maltreatment. *Journal of Applied Developmental Psychology*, *15*, 255–280. https://doi.org/10.1016/0193-3973(94)90016-7

Lamb, M. E., Sternberg, K. J., & Esplin, P. W. (1995). Making children into competent witnesses: Reactions to the amicus brief *in re Michaels*. *Psychology, Public Policy, and the Law*, *1*, 438–449. https://doi.org/10.1037/1076-8971.1.2.438

Lamb, M. E., Sternberg, K. J., Orbach, Y., Esplin, P. W., & Mitchell, S. (2002a). Is ongoing feedback necessary to maintain the quality of investigative interviews with allegedly abused children? *Applied Developmental Science*, *6*, 35–41. https://doi.org/10.1207/S1532480XADS0601_04

Lamb, M. E., Sternberg, K. J., Orbach, Y., Hershkowitz, I., Horowitz, D., & Esplin, P. W. (2002b). The effects of intensive training and ongoing supervision on the quality of investigative interviews with alleged sex abuse victims. *Applied Developmental Science*, *6*, 114–125. https://doi.org/10.1207/S1532480XADS0603_2

Lamb, M. E., Sternberg, K. J., & Esplin, P. W. (2000). Effects of age and delay on the amount of information provided by alleged sex abuse victims in investigative interviews. *Child Development*, *71*(6), 1586–1596. https://doi.org/10.1111/1467-8624.00250

Lamb, M. E., Sternberg, K. J., Esplin, P. W., Hershkowitz, I., Orbach, Y., & Hovav, M. (1997). Criterion-based content analysis: A field validation study. *Child Abuse & Neglect*, *21*(3), 255–264. https://doi.org/10.1016/S0145-2134(96)00170-6

Lamb, M. E., Sternberg, K. J., Orbach, Y., Esplin, P. W., Stewart, H., & Mitchell, S. (2003). Age differences in young children's responses to open-ended invitations in the course of forensic interviews. *Journal of Consulting and Clinical Psychology*, *71*(5), 926–934. https ://doi.org/10.1037/0022–006X.71.5.926.

Lavoie, J., Wyman, J., Crossman, A. M., & Talwar, V. (2021). Meta-analysis of the effects of two interviewing practices on children's disclosures of sensitive information: Rapport practices and question type. *Child Abuse & Neglect*, *113*, 104930. https://doi.org/10.1016/j.chiabu.2021.104930.

Leal, S. L. (2016). Emotional modulation of episodic memory and translational applications to aging and depression-related cognitive impairment [Doctoral dissertation, John Hopkins University]. http://jhir.library.jhu.edu/handle/1774.2/40274

Leander, L. (2010). Police interviews with child sexual abuse victims: Patterns of reporting, avoidance and denial. *Child Abuse & Neglect*, *34*(3), 192–205.

Lewy, J., Cyr, M., & Dion, J. (2015). Impact of interviewers' supportive comments and children's reluctance to cooperate during sexual abuse disclosure. *Child Abuse & Neglect*, *43*, 112–122. https://doi.org/10.1016/j.chiabu.2015.03.002

Liu, D. L. J., Graham, S., & Zorawski, M. (2008). Enhanced selective memory consolidation following post-learning pleasant and aversive arousal. *Neurobiology of Learning and Memory*, *89*(1), 36–46. https://psycnet.apa.org/doi/10.1016/j.nlm.2007.09.001

Liwag, M. D., & Stein, N. L. (1995). Children's memory for emotional events: The importance of emotion-related retrieval cues. *Journal of Experimental Child Psychology*, *60*(1), 2–31.

Lyon, T.D., Scurich, N., Choi, K., Handmaker, S., & Blank, K. (2012). "How did you feel?" Increasing child sexual abuse witnesses' production of evaluative information. *Law & Human Behavior*, *36*, 448–457. https://doi.org/10.1037/h0093986

Massol, S., Vantaggio, S., & Chainay, H. (2020). Emotional modulation of episodic memory in school-age children and adults: Emotional items and their associated contextual details. *Journal of Experimental Psychology: General*, *149*(9), 1684–1703. https://doi.org/10.1037/xge0000744

Mather, M., & Sutherland, M. R. (2011). Arousal-biased competition in perception and memory. *Perspectives on Psychological Science*, *6*(2), 114–133.

Mickley Steinmetz, K. R., Knight, A. G., & Kensinger, E. A. (2016). Neutral details associated with emotional events are encoded: Evidence from a cued recall paradigm. *Cognition and Emotion*, *30*(7), 1352–1360. https://doi.org/10.1080/02699931.2015.1059317

Murty, V. P., Ritchey, M., Adcock, R. A., & LaBar, K. S. (2010). FMRI studies of successful emotional memory encoding: A quantitative meta-analysis. *Neuropsychologia*, *48*(12), 3459–3469. https://doi.org/10.1016/j.neuropsychologia.2010.07.030

O'Carroll, R., Dalgleish, T., Drummond, L. E., Dritschel, B., & Astell, A. (2006). Effects of age, dysphoria, and emotion-focusing on autobiographical memory specificity in children. *Cognition and Emotion*, *20*(3–4), 488–505. https://doi.org/10.1080/02699930500341342

Odegard, T. N., Cooper, C. M., Lampinen, J. M., Reyna, V. F., & Brainerd, C. J. (2009). Children's eyewitness memory for multiple real-life events. *Child Development*, *80*(6), 1877–1890. https://doi.org/10.1111/j.1467-8624.2009.01373.x

Orbach, Y., Hershkowitz, I., Lamb, M. E., Sternberg, K. J., Esplin, P.W., & Horowitz, D. (2000). Assessing the value of structured protocols for forensic interviews of alleged child abuse victims. *Child Abuse & Neglect*, *24*, 733–752. https://doi.org/10.1016/S0145-2134(00)00137-X

Pasupathi, M., & Wainryb, C. (2010). On telling the whole story: Facts and interpretations in autobiographical memory narratives from childhood through mid-adolescence. *Developmental Psychology*, *46*, 735–746.

Peterson, C. (2012). Children's autobiographical memories across the years: Forensic implications of childhood amnesia and eyewitness memory for stressful events. *Developmental Review*, *32*(3), 287–306.

Peterson, C., & Bell, M. (1996). Children's memory for traumatic injury. *Child Development*, *67*, 3045–3070. https://doi.org/10.1111/j.1467-8624.1996.tb01902.x

Poole, D. A., & Lindsay, D. S. (1998). Assessing the accuracy of young children's reports: Lessons from the investigation of child sexual abuse. *Applied and Preventive Psychology*, *7*(1), 1–26.

Quas, J. A., Goodman, G. S., Bidrose, S., Pipe, M.-E., Craw, S., & Ablin, D. S. (1999). Emotion and memory: Children's long-term remembering, forgetting, and suggestibility. *Journal of Experimental Child Psychology*, *72*(4), 235–270. https://doi.org/10.1006/jecp.1999.2491

Roberts, K. P., Lamb, M. E., & Sternberg, K. J. (2004). The effects of rapport-building style on children's reports of a staged event. *Applied Cognitive Psychology*, *18*, 189–202. https://doi.org/10.1002/acp.957

Saywitz, K. J., Lyon, T. D., & Goodman, G. S. (2011). Interviewing children. In J. Myers (ed.), *The APSAC handbook on child maltreatment*, 3rd edition (pp. 337–360). Thousand Oaks CA: Sage.

Saywitz, K.J., Geiselman, R.E., & Bornstein, G.K. (1992). Effects of cognitive interviewing and practice on children's recall performance. *Journal of Applied Psychology*, *77*, 744–756.

Snider, S. M. & Everson, M. D. (2011). What is my next question? Using question frameworks to improve children's narrative accounts of abuse. *APSAC Advisor*, *4*(2), 11.

Sternberg, K. J., Lamb, M. E., Hershkowitz, I., Yudilevitch, L., Orbach, Y., Esplin, P. W., & Hovav, M. (1997). Effects of introductory style on children's abilities to describe experiences of sexual abuse. *Child Abuse & Neglect*, *21*(11), 1133–1146.

Sumner, J. A. (2012). The mechanisms underlying overgeneral autobiographical memory: An evaluative review of evidence for the CaR-FA-X model. *Clinical Psychology Review*, *32*(1), 34–48. https://doi.org/10.1016/j.cpr.2011.10.003

Talarico, J. M., Berntsen, D., & Rubin, D. C. (2009). Positive emotions enhance recall of peripheral details. *Cognition and Emotion*, *23*(2), 380–398.

Teoh, Y. S., & Lamb, M. (2013). Interviewer demeanor in forensic interviews of children. *Psychology, Crime & Law*, *19*, 145–159. https://doi.org/10.1080/1068316X.2011.614610

Valentino, K., Toth, S. L., & Cicchetti, D. (2009). Autobiographical memory functioning among abused, neglected, and nonmaltreated children: The overgeneral memory effect. *Journal of Child Psychology and Psychiatry, and Allied Disciplines, 50*)8(, 1029–1038. https://doi.org/10.1111/j.1469-7610.2009.02072.x

Van Bergen, R. S., Ma, W. J., Pratte, M. S., & Jehee, J. F. M. (2015). Sensory uncertainty decoded from visual cortex predicts behavior. *Nature Neuroscience, 18*(12), 1728–1730. https://doi.org/10.1038/nn.4150

Wallis, C. R. D., & Woodworth, M. D. (2020). Child sexual abuse: An examination of individual and abuse characteristics that may impact delays of disclosure. *Child Abuse & Neglect, 107*, 104604. https://doi.org/10.1016/j.chiabu.2020.104604.

Wessel, I., De Kooy, P. V., & Merckelbach, H. (2000). Differential recall of central and peripheral details of emotional slides is not a stable phenomenon. *Memory, 8*(2), 95–109. https://doi.org/10.1080/096582100387641

Westcott, H. L., & Kynan, S. (2004). The application of a "story-telling" framework to investigative interviews for suspected child sexual abuse. *Legal and Criminological Psychology, 9*(1), 37–56. https://psycnet.apa.org/doi/10.1348/135532504322776843

Yassa, M. A., & Stark, C. E. L. (2011). Pattern separation in the hippocampus. *Trends in Neurosciences, 34*(10), 515–525. https://doi.org/10.1016/j.tins.2011.06.006

Appendix

Revised Investigative Interview Protocol

A. *Introduction*

My name is [name]. Today's date is [date], and it is now [time]. I'm interviewing [child's name] at [location].

Verify that the recorder is on.

Hello, [child's name], I am glad to meet you today, How are you?

My name is ________ and my job is to talk to children about things that have happened to them. As you can see, we have a video-camera here. It will record us talking so I can remember everything you tell me. Sometimes I forget things and the recorder allows me to listen to you without having to write everything down.

In the introduction, gestures of goodwill are appropriate:

Are you comfortable?

Can I do anything to make you more comfortable?

B. *Rapport Building and Narrative Training*

B.1 Now, [child's name], I want to get to know you better. Tell me about things you like to do.

Wait for child to respond
If the child responds, express appreciation and reinforcement:

Thank you for sharing that with me, it helps me get to know you.

I am glad I am starting to get to know more about you.

Then skip to B.3, if you think the child should go directly into narrative training from here.

If the child does not answer, gives a short answer, or gets stuck, you can say:

I know this is the first time we have met and I really want to know about you.

I am glad I can talk to you today [Child's name].

Skip to B.2, if you think more rapport building is necessary.

If the child displays nonverbal cues of avoidance or resistance (e.g. gaze aversion), address it right away:

[Child's name], let me see your eyes.
[Child's name], go ahead and sit closer to me.
[Child's name], I can see you're [crying, quiet], tell me what is happening so I can help.
[Child's name], thanks for letting me listen to you today. Please tell me about what you're going through.

B.2 I really want to know you better [child's name]. I would like you to tell me about things you like to do at school, during recess, after school].

Wait for an answer

If the child continues showing avoidance or resistance, invite him/her to talk about a neutral topic chosen before the interview began (e.g. child's caregiver may have been asked to report about activities the child enjoys):

I heard you like [activity, hobby]. Tell me about [activity, hobby].

Ask about distinctive items (e.g. of clothing):

I can see you are wearing [a unique item, e.g. soccer team T-shirt]. Tell me about [that item].

Offer the child the opportunity to draw:

[Child's name] would you like to draw a picture of something [you like to do, something fun that happened]? Here are some crayons and paper for you.

B.3 Now, [child's name], Tell me more about [activity the child already mentioned].

Avoid TV shows, videos or fantasy.
Wait for an answer.

B.4 [Child's name], Tell me about something fun that has happened to you [at school, kindergarten]?

B.5 Tell me about [something the child mentioned]. Use various invitations to ask about different topics; one of those invitations should focus on internal contents: thoughts, feelings, sensations, or emotions.

B.6 You told me about something [happy, pleasant, fun] that has happened to you. Now, tell me about something unpleasant that has happened to you [at school, kindergarten].

Important! Do not mention the location in which the alleged abuse may have taken place.

B.7 Please tell me about [Something the child has mentioned]. Ask various invitations to elicit richer information about a variety of topics; one invitation should focus on internal contents: thoughts, feelings, sensations, or emotions, too.

If the child reveals distressing information, please explore that briefly while making supportive statements. You may want to check whether the child has previously reported it:

You told me about [the distressing incident]. Have you told an adult about that?

If the child says no, say:

Would you like me to help you tell someone?

B.8 [Child's name], you told me about [pleasant event already described] and about [unpleasant event already described], and shared your [emotions, thoughts] with me (if s/he did). Thank you for letting me know. It's important that you know you can talk to me about anything, both good things and bad things.

C. *Explaining and Practicing Ground Rules*

Adjust the questions according to the child's developmental level.

C.1 [Child's name], I'm interested in you and I'll be asking you all kinds of questions today.

If I ask a question that you don't understand, just say, "[interviewer's name], I don't understand". Okay, [child's name]?

Pause

If I don't understand what you say, I'll ask you to explain.

Pause

If I ask a question, and you don't know the answer, just tell me, "I don't know". So, [child's name], if I ask you, [e.g. what did I have for breakfast today], what would you say?

Wait for an answer.
If the child says "I don't know", say:

Right. You don't know, [child's name], do you?

If the child offers a guess, say:

No, [child's name], you don't know me and [e.g. you weren't with me when I had my breakfast this morning], so you don't know. When you don't know the answer, please don't guess, just say that you don't know.

Pause

But if you do know or do remember, it is very important that you tell me, okay, [child's name]?

C.2 And if I say things that are wrong, you should tell me. Okay, [child's name]?

Wait for an answer

So if I said that you are a 2-year-old girl [when interviewing a 5-year-old boy, etc.], what would you say?

If the child only denies and does not correct you, say:

What would you say if I made a mistake and called you a 2-year-old girl [when interviewing a 5-year-old boy, etc.]?

Wait for an answer.

Reinforce the child if s/he gives the right answer:

That's right, [child's name]. Now you know you should tell me if I make a mistake or say something that is not right.

Pause

Correct a wrong answer:

No, [child's name], you are not [wrong age], you are [real age]. So if I say you are [wrong gender], what would you say?

Reinforce the child if s/he gives the right answer, correct a wrong answer and practice again:

So if I said you were standing up, what would you say?

Wait for an answer

Okay. [Child's name], now you understand that if I say something incorrect, you need to correct me and tell me what is right.

C.3 Part of my job is to talk to [children, teenagers] about things that have happened to them. I meet with lots of [children, teenagers] so that they can tell me the truth about things that have happened to them. [Child's name], it is very important that you tell me the truth today about things that have happened to you.

D. *Further Rapport Building and Episodic Memory Training*

Prior to the interview, please identify a recent, short, positive and meaningful event in which the child actively participated. If possible, choose an event that took place at about the same time as the alleged or suspected abuse. If the alleged abuse took place during a specific day or event, ask about a different event.

I am glad to meet with you today, [child's name], and I would like to get to know you even better.

D.1 *Main invitation*

A few [days, weeks] ago was [a holiday, birthday party, other event]. Tell me everything that happened [during the event], from the beginning to the end, as best as you can.

In case an event wasn't identified previously, ask:

Did you do something special recently, like did you get to go somewhere or go to a birthday party?

If the child doesn't identify a suitable event, say:

So, I want you to tell me everything that happened [today, yesterday], from the time you woke up.

D.2 *Follow-up invitations*

Please repeat the first action that started the event. Then ask:

And then what happened, [child's name]?

Use this question as often as needed throughout this section until you have been given a full account of the event.

Thank you, [child's name], you have told me many things (if s/he did). I want to ask you some more questions about what just you told me.

D.3 *Time segmentation invitations*

Try to use three time segmentation invitations, although you may adjust the quantity and type of invitations to the child's capabilities and reactions.

[Child's name], I would like you to tell me everything about [the event].

Please tell me everything that happened from the moment [an activity the child mentioned] to the moment [a subsequent activity].

If the child has difficulty understanding delineated segments, say:

Please tell me everything that happened from the moment [an activity the child mentioned] began.

Thank you, [child's name], for telling me that. You speak/express yourself very clearly, and that helps me understand what you are saying.

D.4 *Cued invitations*

Try to use three cued invitations, but you may adjust the number depending on the child's capabilities and reactions. Please focus on thoughts and feelings as well.

Cued invitations can be used in one of two formats:

Tell me more about [activity, object, thought, feeling].

Earlier you spoke about [activity, object, thought, feeling]. Tell me more about that.

D.5 [Child's name], thank you for telling me about [title of the event]. When we talk today, it is very important that you tell me everything about things that have really happened to you.

D.6 [Child's name], how are you feeling so far in our conversation?

If during the pre-substantive phase, the child is not cooperative and remains reluctant, end the interview now. Skip to section G in order to end the interview, and schedule an additional interview for continued rapport building.

E. *Substantive Phase*

E.1 *Transition to Substantive Issues*

Important!, If the child expresses explicit verbal resistance without denying the abuse at any point, skip to section E.1.a, "support for managing overt refusals", and deal with the resistance without using additional transitional prompts.

Now that we know each other a little better, I want to talk about why [you are, I am] here today.

At any stage, if the child makes an allegation, skip to section E.2.

If the child reports an irrelevant event, say:

I hear what you are saying to me, [child's name]. If you want, we can talk about that later. Right now though, I want to know about something else that may have happened to you.

1. I understand that something may have happened to you. Tell me everything that happened from the beginning to the end.
2. As I told you, my job is to talk to children about things that might have happened to them. It is very important that you tell me why you think [your mum, dad, grandmother] [brought you here today, I came to talk to you today].
   If the child doesn't make an allegation and looks avoidant or resistant, you may address him/her with general supportive statements which do not refer specifically to him/her, and do not mention abuse:

a. [Child's name], my job is to listen to children about things that happened to them.
b. [Child's name], I really want to know when something happens to children. That's what I am here for.
c. [Child's name], here kids can talk about good things and bad things that have happened to them.
d. My job is to try to help kids.

3. I've heard that you talked to [a doctor, teacher, social worker, other professional] at [time, location]. Please tell me what you talked about.
4. I [saw, heard] that you have/had [documented injuries, bruises] on your [body part]. Tell me everything about [those, that].
5. [Child's name], has anything happened to you at [location, time of alleged incident]?
If the child doesn't make an allegation and looks avoidant or resistant, you may use some of the supportive statements above (a–c) or one of the following statements, which refer specifically to the child, but still do not mention abuse:

d. You told me a lot about yourself. I feel I know you better and you can tell me more [about things, about both good things and bad things] that have happened to you.
e. You told me a lot about yourself, thank you for letting me know. When you talk to me today please go on and tell me about other things that have happened to you.
f. [Child's name], if there is anything you want to tell me, [I want to know/listen, It's important for me to know/listen].

If there is no allegation or a denial: Evaluate and plan your next steps.

You may use the child's verbal and nonverbal indications of reluctance to evaluate the situation and decide whether or not to proceed. Consider ending the interview (skip to E.1.b) and planning an additional interview if you believe that the child is resisting or avoiding cooperation and that an additional session of rapport building might be beneficial.

Proceed through the transitional prompts gradually when you suspect that:

- *Abuse may not have occurred. [Because it may be important to understand why suspicions arose.]*
- *The child doesn't recognize the aim of the interview.*
- *The child is resisting your efforts or avoiding cooperation but there is serious concern about his/her welfare or the investigation.*

1. [Child's name], has anybody been bothering you?
2. [Child's name], did someone do something to you that you don't think was right?

3. [Child's name], did someone [briefly summarize allegations or suspicions without specifying names of alleged perpetrator or providing too many details]?

If the child doesn't make an allegation but looks avoidant or resistant and there is independent evidence arousing suspicion, you may use the above supportive statements (a–f) or one of the following:

- g. [Child's name], [I am, people] are worried about you and I want to know if something may have happened to you.
- h. [Child's name], if something has happened to you and you want it to stop, you can tell me about it.
- i-1. [Child's name], if it is hard for you to tell, what makes it so hard?
- i-2. [Child's name] is there anything you are concerned about?
- i-3. [Child's name] what would happen if you told me?
- i-4. [Child's name] has someone told you not to tell?
- j. Sometimes children think that if something happened to them, it's their fault, but children are not responsible if things happen to them.
- k. It's your choice if you want to tell me and it is my job to let you choose.

9. [Child's name], I understand [you, someone] [reported, saw] [briefly summarize allegations or suspicions without specifying names of alleged perpetrator or providing too many details]. I want to find out if something may have happened to you.

E.1.a Supportive statements to help manage overt refusals.

If the child has explicitly expressed difficulty or reluctance to disclose but hasn't denied the abuse, you may use the supportive statements above (a–k) and the following statements dealing with overt refusals to engage:

- l. [Child's name], I understand you are [difficulty the child mentioned, e.g. embarrassed]. Let's start talking and I'll try to help you with it.
- m. Many children are [difficulty the child mentioned] and I try to help them.
- n. I understand you are [difficulty the child mentioned], tell me more about that.
- o. If the child expressed lack of confidence: I'm sure you can talk about it well.
- p. If the child said s/he was worried about something specific and the reassurance you can give is true: Do not worry, I will [not tell the other children/make sure you are not late for the bus].
- q. It's your choice whether to tell and I will go with your choice.

E.1.b *Ending the interview without an allegation*

If at any point while exploring whether abuse might have occurred you believe that the child is resistant or uncooperative and that rapport building will benefit from additional meeting, end the interview and plan an additional one. Skip to section G if you want to end the interview.

E.2 *Exploring the incidents*

Throughout the entire substantive part it is important to preserve and enhance the rapport established with the child, continue providing supportive statements, and address expressed inhibitions, distress and conflicts.

E.2.a *Free recall invitations*
10.a. Invitation for a first narrative about the incidents.

If the child mentions a specific incident:

> [Child's name], you told me that [briefly summarize the allegation the child has made]. Tell me everything from the beginning to the end.

If the child mentions a number of incidents:

> [Child's name], you told me that [a brief summary of the allegation the child has made]. Tell me everything about [the last/first time/at place/at time/specific incident] from the beginning to the end.

If the child gives a generic description and you cannot determine the number of incidents:

> [Child's name], you told me that [briefly summarize the allegation the child has made]. Did that happen one time or more than one time? *Depending on the answer please invite a first narrative (10.a).*

If the description is still generic, please say:

> [Child's name], you told me that [briefly summarize the generic description]. Tell me everything from the beginning to the end.

10.b. *Follow-up invitations*

Please repeat the child's description of the action/occurrence that started the event. Then ask

And then what happened?

Use this question as often as needed until you have a complete description of the alleged incident.

10.c. *Time segmenting invitations*

You have told me many things and helped me understand what happened. Now, [child's name], I want to ask you more questions about [incident title].

[Child's name], Think back to that time [day, night] and please tell me everything that happened from the moment [an activity the child mentioned] to the moment [a subsequent activity the child mentioned].

You may use this question as often as needed to ensure that all parts of the incident are elaborated.

10.d. *Cued invitations*

Cued invitations can have two formats:

- Tell me more about [activity, object, feeling, thought].
- Child's name], you mentioned [activity, object, feeling, thought]. Tell me more about that.

Use this question as often as needed throughout this section.

Important! Free-recall invitations should be exhausted before proceeding to directive questions.

E.2.b *Directive questions*

If some central details of the allegation are still missing or unclear after the exhaustive use of open-ended questions, use directive questions.

11. [Child's name], you said that/mentioned [activity, object, feeling, thought]. [How, when, where, who, what, which, how many, what did you mean]?

It is important to pair open-ended invitations with directive questions whenever possible:

Tell me more about that.

E.2.c *Exploring multiple incidents*

If in reply to question 10a–11 the child mentions a single incident:

12. [Child's name], what you just told me, did that happen one time or more than one time?

If the child has said that such incidents happened more than one time, go back to question 10.a and explore additional incidents. It is often best to explore the last, first, or best remembered incident.

E.2.d *Break*

[Child's name], now I want to make sure I have understood everything you said and see if there's anything else I need to ask. I will take a couple of minutes to think about what you told me/go over my notes.

During the break time, review the information you have received, see if there is any missing information, and plan the rest of the interview. Be sure to formulate option-posing questions in writing and consider replacing them with open-ended or directive prompts.

E.2.e *Option-posing questions – eliciting information that has not been mentioned by the child.*

You should ask these focused questions only if you have already tried other approaches and you realize that some forensically important information is still missing. It is very important to pair option-posing questions with open invitations ("Tell me all about that") whenever possible.

In case of multiple incidents, you should direct the child to the relevant incidents in his own words.

13. [Child's name], when you told me about [specific incident embedded in time and place] you mentioned [activity, object, feeling, thought]. [Did, have, has, is, are] [a detail for child to confirm or deny]?

Example: Sarah, when you told me about being in the kitchen with Lewis, were there other people with you?

Whenever appropriate, follow with an invitation:

Tell me everything about that [activity, object, feeling, thought].

Before you move to the next incident, make sure you have obtained all the missing details about each specific incident.

F. *Disclosure Information*

You've told me why you came to talk to me today. You've given me [lots of] information and that really helps me to understand what happened.

If the child has mentioned telling someone about the incident(s), you may say:

Now I want to understand how other people found out about [last incident].

If he has not mentioned telling anyone, probe about possible disclosure by saying:

Does anybody else know what happened?

Then explore the disclosure process, addressing the disclosure time, circumstances, recipients, potential discussions of the event, and reactions to disclosure by both the child and recipients. Use open-ended questions whenever possible.

G. *Ending the Interview*

[Child's name], what are you going to do after we finish talking?

Talk to the child for a couple minutes about a neutral topic.

Risks and benefits of therapeutic interventions for non-disclosing suspected victims of sexual abuse

Rosaleen McElvaney

Introduction

This chapter discusses the context of working therapeutically with children and adolescents where there are concerns that the child has been sexually abused but no verbal disclosure has been shared. We know from research with both children and adults that children are reluctant to disclose experiences of sexual abuse and many do not do so until adulthood (Alaggia et al., 2019; Central Statistics Office, 2022; Lemaigre et al., 2017; McElvaney, 2015; Morrison et al., 2018). Allard-Gaudreau et al. (2024) found that children are more likely to delay their disclosure if they have been abused by a family member, have been abused over a period of time, or have been made to perform sexual acts on the abuser. Even when there is corroborative evidence that children have been sexually abused and children are interviewed about these concerns, many children deny that they have been abused (Lyon et al., 2020). It is now well established that disclosure is a process, not a discrete event (Alaggia et al., 2019). Many disclose in an incremental fashion, following several opportunities for conversations (Lyon et al., 2020), and may need multiple opportunities before they are able to disclose in a formal interview (Carnes et al., 2001; Coulborn Faller & Nelson-Gardell, 2010; Hershkowitz et al., 2021).

Where a concern has emerged as a result of physical evidence, witnessing abuse, or partial/ambiguous disclosures from the child, a referral may be made for therapy in the hope that this safe environment will facilitate disclosure. Children may have difficulty recalling their experiences, providing a coherent narrative, or fear the consequences of disclosure. Children who have experienced trauma typically avoid focusing on their memories due to the distress triggered by these memories, feelings of self-blame and shame, or consequences of disclosing the experience (Deblinger et al., 2015). Their memories may be of poor quality due to the manner in which information was encoded and processed at the time, particularly if the child was in a heightened state of distress (van der Kolk, 2015). Complex trauma has been

DOI: 10.4324/9781003427155-10

associated with difficulties in assimilating and retrieving memories with clarity (Cook et al., 2005). This can result in incoherent or disorganized narratives about their experiences. Finally, children may be actively withholding information about their experiences as a way of containing their fears about the consequences of disclosure (McElvaney et al., 2012).

Therapy can provide a safe containing environment and trusting relationships with individuals outside their familial and social networks. Talking about events can strengthen certain aspects of recall or prompt the introduction of new information as individuals reflect on the meaning of their experiences (CPS, 2022a). In therapy, children can explore their worries either through creative or talking therapies, learn to manage distress, make sense of their experiences (Carpenter et al., 2016; Vliegen et al., 2023) and be able to communicate this in ways that are understood by others.

Where there are concerns about sexual abuse in the absence of a clear disclosure, therapists have to balance the tensions between therapeutic and forensic considerations in fulfilling their ethical and legal responsibilities. In particular, given the potential for criminal investigation if a child does make an allegation of abuse, the therapist must manage the tension between providing an opportunity for the child to narrate their experience while not influencing the child's memory and narrative about that experience. Little has been written about working therapeutically with children who have not yet made a disclosure, or whose disclosure is ambiguous; however, the British Psychological Society's guidance on working with adult clients who disclose non-recent experiences of abuse in mental health contexts (Rouf & Waites, 2023) acknowledges the complexity of balancing duty of care and safeguarding with clients' therapeutic needs.

This chapter explores the areas where these tensions arise and how therapists can navigate this work, holding in mind the best interests of the child and family along with the therapist's own ethical and legal obligations. A trauma-informed approach that is based on a good understanding of children's memory and language development, the barriers and facilitators to disclosure, and the impact of sexual abuse on children, will help a therapist make sense of a child's presentation and keep in mind various hypotheses in their formulation of the child's and family's needs. Therapists need to keep an open mind in relation to whether abuse has occurred or not and be attuned to the importance of not influencing the child's narrative about their experiences. They must balance the need to promote the child's autonomy and respect their rights with managing the limits of confidentiality and working collaboratively with other professionals tasked with protecting the child and enforcing the law. Good record keeping is essential to ensure accuracy, transparency and facilitate the sharing of information that may be relied on for evidential purposes. Collaboration with the multidisciplinary interagency network, supervision and personal therapy are important sources of support as therapists navigate this work. The chapter provides a framework for therapeutic work where there are concerns about sexual abuse in the absence of a clear disclosure by the child.

The integrity of the child's narrative

Following some highly publicized cases of false allegations of sexual abuse in day care centres in California and New Jersey in the 1980s, fuelled by persistent and suggestive questioning of children by parents and professionals (Wood et al., 2009) and claims of therapists "implanting false memories" of childhood sexual abuse in adult clients (Bass & Davis, 2008), attention focused on how victims' narratives about their experiences are influenced by conversations with professionals. Structured interview protocols for investigative interviewing of children where there were concerns about sexual abuse were developed, typically involving a single interview with a child. These protocols took account of research on children's developmental capacities, particularly with respect to language and memory, and emphasized the use of open questioning styles to address concerns about suggestibility, memory distortion, and interviewer bias. Subsequent research found that the use of these protocols resulted in more accurate and more detailed accounts from children (Lamb et al., 2018). Because prosecution of sexual abuse offences is so heavily reliant on the child's narrative of their experience, it was considered essential to find ways of helping children articulate their experiences that would preserve the integrity of their narrative.

However, even when given the opportunity to disclose experiences of abuse, a sizeable minority of children are reluctant to disclose, despite concerning evidence that they have been abused (Lyon et al., 2020). An extended forensic evaluation model was developed by Carnes and colleagues (1999) involving several sessions with the child and a more comprehensive assessment. In this less pressurized environment, providing more opportunity to build safety and trust than in a one-off interview, children were able to disclose previously undisclosed experiences of abuse in response to nonleading questions (Coulborn Faller & Nelson-Gardell, 2010). More recently, studies of the Revised National Institute of Child and Health Development (NICHD) Protocol (RP), using two or more interviews with the child, focusing on relationship building prior to the substantive phase of exploring possible experiences of abuse, while directly addressing reluctance in the first interview through emotional support, have demonstrated an increase in children's credible allegations (Hershkowitz & Lamb, 2020). Use of the revised protocol has also led to more spontaneous allegations in subsequent interviews and a higher use of open-ended questions by interviewers, which allowed them to obtain more free recall information from children (Hershkowitz et al., 2021).

Lamb and colleagues (2018) have summarized the research on how children develop memories and how children's memories are affected by interaction with their environment. Memories from early childhood are encoded perceptually, not verbally. Children form long-term memories as they begin to talk about their experiences with others. They remember more details of an event if their parents have spoken to them during or after the event, thus rehearsing their memories, obtaining labels for experiences, and focusing on the specific details of the experience, all of which enhance their memory for the event. Both the passage of time and experience of repeated incidents of abuse affect their ability to remember specific details of specific events. Younger children, in particular, may struggle to separate out different experiences, and struggle to know the source of their memory (i.e. whether this is based on actual experience or on conversations about their experiences). Finally, children are often vulnerable to social expectations when communicating their experiences. They are more accustomed to being asked about events that adults already know have happened to them. This can influence how they communicate (i.e. by not providing rich detail), and how this communication is received (i.e. by misunderstanding). Children may want to appear co-operative and tell adults what they think those adults want to hear.

Addressing concerns that repeated opportunities to talk about allegations of abuse may contaminate children's memories or accounts of their experiences, resulting in false allegations (Ceci & Bruck, 1995; Bruck & Ceci, 1999), researchers have concluded that while leading and suggestive questioning can contaminate some children's allegations of abuse, multiple non-suggestive questioning usually does not (La Rooy et al., 2009; Malloy & Quas, 2009). When repeated interviews are conducted with appropriate methods, they do not compromise the accuracy, consistency or coherence of statements obtained (La Rooy et al., 2009; Szojka et al., 2022). Indeed, multiple interviews have been found to increase the completeness of children's testimony (Blasbalg et al., 2021; Waterhouse et al., 2023).

These concerns about suggestibility have raised questions about how therapy is conducted with children when there are concerns about sexual abuse, in particular, how therapists ensure that they do not influence children's narratives about their experiences. Experiential narratives change with the retelling of stories; many children provide more details pertaining to their experiences of abuse when given more opportunities to talk about it (Carnes et al., 2001; Goodman et al., 2017). Therapists are not trained forensic interviewers; however, open questioning is a micro-skill that is part of a therapist's skills repertoire (Smyth, 2013) and therapists working with children are well attuned to children's language development and the dangers of misinterpreting children's utterances and behaviours during the therapy session. While this attunement serves to privilege the child's voice over adult interpretations of children's experiences and needs (Capella & Boddy, 2021), it can also serve the therapist well in helping preserve the integrity of the child's narrative about their experience, which may be needed for evidential purposes.

Open questioning styles that have been found in research on interviewing children to increase accuracy and reliability and decrease suggestibility can be used by the therapist to help the child explore their experience more fully (Lamb et al., 2018). Examples include the classic invitations, "tell me what happened" and "tell me more about that". The therapist must always hold in mind both the possibility that the child has been abused and equally that they have not. Younger children due to a limited vocabulary repertoire, or older children due to emotional presentation, often need scaffolding in verbally expressing their thoughts and emotions. Therapists typically offer words to help put names on their thoughts and feelings, holding in mind the need to avoid imposing their own interpretation of the child's experience.

Where there are concerns about sexual abuse, therapists need to be extra cautious about language used and the dangers of misinterpreting children's presentations. The details that children share in these conversations may be needed for court proceedings; accuracy and reliability are therefore more important when discussing sexual abuse than when discussing other experiences in therapy.

Creative techniques are often used as a non-directive method of facilitating emotional expression (Wymer et al., 2020). Therapists must be extra mindful of the dangers of interpreting children's play or artwork as illustrating lived experiences and offering suggestions to children to this effect, thus influencing children's own narratives and beliefs about their experiences. Where there is doubt or lack of clarity as to the child's experience, the therapist must remain open to different possibilities and not "put words into the child's mouth". Where a therapist misinterprets a child's behaviour or narrative as indicative of sexual abuse, this can influence their interactions with the child, leading to suggestive questioning or interpretations, unduly influencing the child's account of their experience. Research on interviews with children in forensic contexts shows that the more impoverished a child's language, the more likely they are to be misinterpreted and the child is more likely to repeat that incorrect information later in an interview (Lamb et al., 2018).

There is disagreement about how easy it is to implant false information, the prevalence of how this is misconstrued as an autobiographical memory, and how experimental research findings generalize to real life sexual abuse experiences (Brewin et al., 2020). In their longitudinal study, Goodwin et al. (2017) found that participants who had engaged in therapy as children before or during the prosecution period showed significant consistency in the details of their allegations when interviewed as adults. According to the

CPS (2022a) in the UK, "there is no substantive evidence that therapy will generate false memories". Nevertheless, given the power imbalance inherent in therapeutic relationships and particularly younger children's susceptibility to saying what they believe adults want them to hear (Bruck & Ceci, 1999), caution is warranted when undertaking such therapeutic work.

When children have experienced sexual abuse, they are often confused and struggle to make sense of their experiences (Capella et al., 2016), which in turn affects their ability to articulate their experiences. Therapy can, where appropriate, provide an opportunity to help children understand and make sense of their difficulties. Through a non-directive approach to therapy, using active listening skills and open questions (Smyth, 2013), the therapist can help the child find words to capture their experiences (van der Kolk, 2015), while preserving the integrity of their narratives.

Understanding barriers to disclosure and helping children tell

We now have an extensive literature on the barriers to disclosure (see chapters in this book by London, Lyon, Quas, Herskowitz and Korkman) and to a lesser extent, what helps children tell when they have experienced sexual abuse. Awareness of these potential barriers and facilitators of disclosure will help therapists attune to recognizing and identifying children who have been sexually abused but are unable or reluctant to share these experiences. Factors that influence disclosure operate on an intrapersonal (e.g. self-blame), interpersonal (e.g. fear of losing an important relationship or concern about the impact on others, particularly parents), societal (e.g. disbelief that something like this could happen in this community) and cultural (e.g. fear that disclosure will bring additional discrimination to an already marginalized group in society) level. Alaggia et al. (2019) conceptualized this as a socio-ecological framework. Each individual child may be reluctant to disclose for different reasons. In addition, these factors affect each family in a different way. Children are acutely sensitive to family culture; prohibitions on communication within a family affect the child's implicit understanding of what they are permitted to talk about outside the family (Sheinberg & Fraenkel, 2001).

Research on what helps children tell highlights the importance of creating opportunities for children to share experiences of abuse (McElvaney, 2015; Brennan & McElvaney, 2020; Morrison et al., 2018). The implications of this research for professionals working with children include the importance of noticing changes in their behaviour and mood and communicating these observations, both to children themselves and to their carers; sharing concerns about individual children with other professionals; responding to children's attempts to tell, using open questioning and good listening skills;

and promoting children's resilience and sense of agency following disclosure through involving them as much as possible in decision-making processes (McElvaney, 2019).

The therapist can help build a picture of why this child, in this family, in these circumstances, may be reluctant to disclose. Therapy can provide an opportunity for the child to explore the benefits and risks of disclosing. Psychoeducation can help to raise awareness of why children feel and think the way they do. We know from research on disclosure that an invitation to talk about sexual abuse or their wellbeing in general has been identified by young people as contributing to the "pressure cooker effect" (McElvaney et al., 2012) that helped them eventually tell someone. Pressure from within may be experienced as psychological distress or not being able to keep the secret in any longer, pressure from without may refer to concern for other children or caring adults asking about their distress or behaviour. Balancing readiness to tell with needing support to tell suggests that some pressure seems to help. However, children who are actively withholding information about abuse are not passive victims; an analysis of the literature shows that choosing not to disclose may be a way of protecting the self from further harm (Kukura, 2023).

Understanding the impact of sexual abuse

A good knowledge of the impact of sexual abuse is important for therapists, bearing in mind that children who have experienced sexual abuse may present in a very similar manner to those that have experienced a range of adverse experiences, such as emotional abuse (Dye, 2020) or experiences unrelated to abuse. The therapist must not assume a causal link between sexual abuse and children's presentations, but rather keep an open mind as to the origins of these difficulties. Therapy may help with identifying the underlying reasons for the child's presentation or it may be necessary to help the child develop ways of coping in the absence of a formulation that includes an understanding of why the child is presenting in this way.

There are various frameworks for helping us understand the impact of sexual abuse. The four traumagenic dynamics devised by Finkelhor and Browne (1985) – traumatic sexualization (becoming sexualized prematurely), betrayal (being harmed by a trusted other), stigmatization (related to shame, guilt and self-blame), and powerlessness (being unable to stop the abuse or disclose it) – provide a useful classification of how a child may be affected. Narang et al. (2019) identified seven domains of functioning affected by sexual abuse, including physical (e.g. sexually transmitted infections); behavioural (e.g. aggression); psychological (e.g. altered sense of self); cognitive distortions (e.g. beliefs such as self-blame); interpersonal and social difficulties (e.g. lack of trust; peer relationship difficulties); body and sexuality (e.g. "damaged goods syndrome") and mental health concerns (e.g. PTSD).

The impact of sexual abuse can serve as an inhibitor to disclosure, in particular where avoidance is employed as a coping strategy to manage the distress elicited when children are reminded of their experiences (Deblinger et al., 2015; van der Kolk, 2015). Helping children address the impact of their experiences in the absence of a clear narrative about those experiences can provide them with the opportunity they need to disclose.

Keeping an open mind

A good knowledge of child development, including understanding of children's language and memory capacities will help the therapist engaged in this work keep an open mind as to the nature of the child's experience. While younger children have more limited and less descriptive vocabularies than older children and adults, their rapid vocabulary growth often leads adults to believe their capacity to understand is better than it is. Young children frequently use words that they themselves do not understand (Walker, 1994), which can therefore be misconstrued by therapists and other professionals. A common technique in person-centred therapeutic work is that of paraphrasing, i.e. repeating back to the client the essence of what they have communicated, but often with modifications added by the therapist (Smyth, 2013). Therapists need to be careful to stay as closely as possible to what the child has actually said, as paraphrasing may unwittingly include additional information that the child has not stated but the therapist has interpreted from the child's communication.

Research in the field of investigative interviewing highlights the impact that interview bias has on children's accounts of child sexual abuse. Lacey and Nunkoosing (2022) note that such bias not only refers to a priori beliefs and attitudes about whether sexual abuse has occurred but is a dynamic process that may affect the child's account through interactions with the child. Measures to minimize bias, according to the authors, include adhering to established interview protocols, drawing on multidisciplinary teamwork and co-working, reflecting explicitly on potential biases, maintaining a neutral stance, questioning and testing information, and seeking alternative explanations. Holding competing hypotheses in mind is part of ongoing therapeutic formulation (Vliegen et al., 2023) and is an important part of the therapist's skills repertoire. The focus of therapeutic work should not be on helping the child disclose when it is not known whether the child has been sexually abused. It is not the responsibility of the therapist to elicit details of the sexual abuse experience; that task is best left to those with expertise in questioning children. However, it is important not to ignore the child's attempts to disclose; this may be the first time they have considered sharing this information and research with young people about what helped them tell reveals that "being asked" often helps children to disclose when they are reluctant to share this information (Brennan & McElvaney, 2020; Morrison et al., 2018).

The therapeutic relationship is a powerful relationship in the child's life. A therapist who "believes" that a child has been abused, in the absence of clear evidence to support this, will be doing a child and family a disservice. Self awareness and monitoring of one's own feelings about sexual abuse can help the therapist remain open to receiving a disclosure in the therapeutic session, not only because of the risk of contaminating the child's account for evidentiary purposes but also to preserve the integrity of the child's account and understanding of themselves and their ability to make sense of their experience. This reflective capacity will help the therapist keep an open mind and not unduly influence the child's narrative about their experience.

Respecting children's rights

The United Nations Convention on the Rights of the Child (UNICEF, 1989), the Gillick principle (based on a 1986 UK court judgement; see Jenkins, 1997) and EU regulations such as General Data Protection Regulations 2016, respect the autonomy of the child and their right to privacy. When children have experienced sexual abuse, their autonomy has been undermined, power has been misused and the child has likely experienced helplessness and disempowerment (Finkelhor & Browne, 1985). For some children, there are negative consequences to disclosing experiences of abuse. Kakuru (2023) cautioned against pathologizing non-disclosure, as choosing not to disclose can be seen as a form of agency, a strategy to protect oneself from further abuse and harm. Safety planning is often necessary to support the therapeutic work. This may involve ensuring that the young person has access to trusted adults and contact with unsupportive peers or adults is minimized. In criminal investigations, children's mobile devices may be taken from them for evidential purposes. This can cause considerable distress for young people, isolating them from their peers, contributing to feelings of helplessness, and loss of faith in the effectiveness of law enforcement processes.

To counteract the power dynamics inherent in the therapeutic relationship and support the young person's autonomy, it is recommended that therapists engage in shared decision-making with the child and family (McElvaney & Moorhouse, 2022). Children need to be offered as much choice as is reasonable about attending, whom they attend, and assenting to therapy (Fonagy et al., 2017). Where decisions need to be made that override children's wishes, they should be informed of these in advance, where possible, and a rationale offered for those decisions (Bond & Mitchels, 2014).

Children and young people may present for therapy due to their own distress or due to concerns of others. In the latter case, the therapist and other adults in the child's life need to be transparent with the young person about why they are attending therapy and acknowledge their concerns. Coercion or pressure placed on a child who has experienced trauma can unfortunately and unintentionally mirror the abuse dynamic where a child has been coerced into doing something they didn't want to do (Harper & Steadman, 2003). While many young people are reluctant to attend therapy and need encouragement, they often reflect back and appreciate this encouragement when they experience the benefits of therapy (McElvaney et al., 2023). A clear understanding of the purpose of therapy along with giving them a choice fosters collaboration and trust. It increases the likelihood that the child will actively engage in the process, will be motivated to attend, and will have more successful outcomes (Midgley et al., 2017; O'Keeffe et al., 2019). Particularly for older children and adolescents, it is important to respect their growing autonomy, consult with them where possible and mediate the impact that many young people feel in relation to loss of control following disclosure, a fear identified by young people as inhibiting them from confiding about their experiences of abuse (Ungar et al., 2009).

Limits to confidentiality

An important ethical and legal consideration when working with children where there may be concerns about sexual abuse is that of the limits of confidentiality. Confidentiality is a cornerstone of psychotherapy. However, limits to this confidentiality apply to the therapeutic space, particularly where there are concerns that a child or others are at risk of or have experienced harm, and where this harm constitutes a criminal offence (Jenkins, 1997; see Bond & Mitchels, 2014 for discussion of US case law, including the 1976 Tarasoff judgement that has changed psychotherapy practice in this regard). In many countries, therapists are "mandated reporters" and are required to share information with appropriate authorities where they have a concern that a child has been or is being sexually abused. Children may disclose abuse for the first time to a therapist, or they may share information that was previously unknown to investigating law enforcement personnel, which is a valuable piece of evidence for the prosecution case and needs to be shared with investigating officers (CPS, 2022a).

Establishing the therapeutic contract at the outset of the work together involves clearly outlining these limits and explaining to the child in developmentally appropriate language, as well as to the parents or carers, what obligations the therapist has with respect to sharing confidential information and the circumstances where information may be released (e.g. response to court orders) (Magee, 2021; Theimer et al., 2020). Rouf and Waites (2023) recommend that these should ideally be provided in writing, e.g. in the form of a leaflet. Therapists may be concerned that this could deter children and families from engaging or could represent a further barrier to disclosing. It may be necessary for the therapist to explain the rationale for reporting as part of an overall strategy for protecting children in general. The task of the therapist is to attend to both the therapeutic relationship with the young person and the working collaboration with parents, while adhering to their ethical and legal obligations. Clear communication to clients regarding the limits of confidentiality, it has been suggested, helps create a strong therapeutic relationship (Henderson, 2013; Steinberg et al., 1997). Studies have found that clients who trusted their therapist were less likely to drop out of therapy following a report (Levine et al., 1995; Steinberg et al., 1997).

Inviting children to talk about their experiences and using open questions where further information is needed will help the therapist determine if the information constitutes a grounded concern of abuse that should be reported to authorities. Therapists must balance the need to elicit sufficient information to meet the threshold of a mandated report with the need to avoid asking too many specific questions, which may in themselves contaminate children's recollections of their experiences (Ceci & Bruck, 1995). Given the process nature of disclosure, it is likely that once a child has begun disclosing, they will provide more and more detail over time, within the therapy sessions. Where there are criminal investigations, information may need to be shared with law enforcement as new details are shared. As noted above, good record keeping is essential in this regard.

Various authors have outlined decision-making models when considering sharing sensitive information outside of the therapeutic boundary. Wheeler and Bertram (2014) provide guidance for therapists that includes: communicating clearly to clients the limits of confidentiality and the steps that may need to be taken if information is shared; reflection on the issue and of all courses of action and their consequences; consulting with expert external sources (e.g. professional codes of ethics; legal obligations) and perspectives (e.g. colleague or supervisor; child protection professional; legal advisor); taking account of personal influences; seeking additional information from the client if needed; weighing up options and consequences; considering institutional policy; making a decision and documenting this decision and the rationale for rejecting other courses of action; and making referrals where appropriate. Clinical notes may contain information that, if disclosed, could be psychologically harmful to the child or family, or might adversely affect the therapeutic relationship. However, consideration needs to be given to the risks involved in withholding such information as it could be more harmful if disclosed at a later stage in the criminal process (CPS, 2022a).

Conscious and unconscious dynamics may influence the therapist's decision-making processes in managing the interface between therapeutic work and the criminal justice system. The dynamics of abuse can be re-enacted or mirrored in the therapeutic relationship (Harper & Steadman, 2003). Such dynamics include the secrecy surrounding abuse (Furniss, 1991), the betrayal of trust, powerlessness, and stigma (Finkelhor & Browne, 1985). Therapists may get drawn into maintaining secrecy in the guise of confidentiality. Families may view reporting as a betrayal of trust and confidentiality (Collin-Vezina et al., 2015; McTavish et al., 2019). Therapists may view reporting as disempowering the child. Transference issues, whereby parents or young people may experience the therapist as "abusive" in adhering to mandatory reporting obligations, may need to be addressed. Countertransference or co-transference issues (Harper & Steadman, 2003) may need to be identified and discussed in supervision or personal therapy, whereby therapists' own unresolved conflicts or wounds are triggered by the reporting process.

Understanding the idiosyncratic reasons why children do not disclose abuse may help the therapist anticipate a young person's concerns about reporting, as may an appreciation of the role of reporting in breaking the cycle of abuse and empowering the client to find their voice and take action. Creating opportunities to explore the child's and family's anxieties about reporting and the implications for them and others may help foster an understanding of why the report needs to be made. Research has found that families avoided engaging in therapy because they felt intimidated by authorities, felt excluded from the investigative process, powerless and unheard, or were anxious about what might happen next (McTavish et al., 2019). Wheeler and Bertram (2014) advise that, if clinically appropriate, it is best to involve the client in the decision-making process. According to Rouf and Waites (2023), care should be taken with the timing of decisions to make a report, as haste can result in disengagement from therapy, increased risk of harm, loss of trust in services, and lost opportunity to access important safeguarding information that could potentially protect others. The therapist can collaborate with the client in making the report e.g. making a phone call with the child in the office; going through the details that will be reported and offering the child some choice in the wording of the report.

Cultural sensitivity is also important; therapists need to inform themselves about their client's cultural context and expectations in relation to engagement with authorities, particularly when clients are distrustful of governmental institutions. Being open to hearing about families' frustrations about the system's response is important, particularly for therapists employed in state agencies and who may be experienced as being part of that same system. Parents may have heard stories of unsuccessful investigation or prosecutions and may be reluctant to co-operate with criminal justice systems and lack hope that the wider system will keep their child safe (Theimer et al., 2020).

While the therapist is obliged to assist with investigations, their primary concern needs to focus on the therapeutic work, while supporting the young person and their parents on this journey. Responsibility (and expertise) for investigating child protection/abuse concerns rests with child protection and criminal justice professionals. The therapist must balance the tensions arising from the child's right to privacy and need for increasing autonomy, their psychological wellbeing, and other professionals' need for information to pursue a prosecution of sexual abuse offences.

Record keeping

Keeping frequent and clear records of concerns about children is particularly important where children have not disclosed sexual abuse, yet concerns remain that they have experienced abuse. As noted above, it is common for children to disclose incrementally, drip-feeding information about experiences that they are reluctant to share (Lyon et al., 2020). It is often the task of professionals working with children over time to collate information in order to understand what the child is communicating. Younger children may depict their experiences through play or artwork rather than verbal media (Deblinger et al., 2015). Photographs of artwork or sand play constitute an important therapy record that, on discussion with professional colleagues, can help the therapist explore possible interpretations and how to proceed therapeutically with the child in a way that is non-leading.

Practice and policy on record keeping in psychotherapy varies across jurisdictions. For example, in the US, the Health Insurance Portability and Accountability Act of 1996 (HIPPA) is federal legislation designed to create national standards for protecting patient health information. The implementation of this legislation is operationalized through the Standards for Privacy of Individually Identifiable Health Information (the "Privacy Rule"). In the US, a distinction is made between mental health records and progress notes or psychotherapy notes, the latter being described as the private notes that therapists keep of their clinical impressions, hypotheses and analysis of the content of psychotherapy. According to the Health Insurance Portability and Accountability Act of 1996 (HIPAA) Privacy Rule (US Department of Health and Human Services, 1996), these are separate from the client's record and the American Psychological Association (APA; 2007) recommends that these be kept separate from the rest of the medical record. In European Union and UK legislation, under the General Data Protection Regulations (European Union, 2022) and the Data Protection Act of 2018 (National Archives, 2025), no distinction is made between healthcare records and psychotherapy notes.

If the child discloses abuse for the first time to the therapist, it is essential that the therapist maintains clear records of these disclosures as they may be asked to make a witness statement to the police and give evidence in court if there is a criminal prosecution. Therapists' notes may also be requested to provide corroborative evidence to support the child's allegations. The Crown Prosecution Service (CPS) in the UK provides guidance for therapists on their obligations in relation to sharing notes for pre-trial therapy (CPS, 2022a, 2022b). In preparation for the trial, the CPS may request therapy notes even when a child has given a full statement to the police prior to engaging in therapy. This is an area of contention, given the sensitivity of material discussed in therapy and the likelihood that this information could be made available to the defence and therefore indirectly to the person who has been accused of abusing the child. Therapist concerns in this regard may impede the content and quality of record keeping when disclosures contain details of alleged offences, through recording minimal information about the content of therapeutic sessions in an effort to protect the child and family from further distress if those notes were to be released. Therapists may be concerned that minor discrepancies between the child's account in therapy and the original police statement will result in undue questioning of the child's credibility. Despite clear guidance from state prosecution agencies that discovery of therapy notes should not be used by defence as a "trawling exercise", entire files may be sought from therapists in the process.

Good practice dictates that an opportunity to review the notes with the child and discuss the implications of sharing the notes should be offered by the therapist (CPS, 2022a). The therapist must balance the needs of the child, the parents and the potential for harm to the child through sharing the notes. Children and families often do not understand the implications of providing consent without a detailed conversation or understanding of the sensitivity of these records and information therein that may have no relevance to the trial proceedings. Although families do have a right to a disclosure hearing in many countries, where the judge makes the decision as to whether the notes are disclosed, this is often framed as potentially delaying the criminal process and many parents who have waited years for a trial date consent to the release of notes to avoid delays, mindful of the impact of such delays on their child's wellbeing (McElvaney, undated).

Therapist capacities

Participants in a recent study funded by the NSPCC in the UK (Baker et al., 2019) spoke of their uncertainty about how to speak with children about sexual abuse, how to open, continue, and close the conversation, what questions to ask, how to explain confidentiality in a sensitive way, and anxiety about saying the "right" or "wrong" thing. Some of this anxiety stems from a fear of retraumatizing the child but much of it is related to the criminal nature of sexual abuse and the possibility that the professional will get drawn into legal proceedings, an unfamiliar territory for many professionals, including therapists. Added to this are anxieties fuelled by historical accounts of zealous therapists being accused, in some cases rightly so, of misinterpreting children's presentations and contributing to miscarriages of justice (Ceci & Bruck, 1995) and lack of confidence in addressing trauma in therapeutic work.

Most psychotherapists do not receive input during their professional training on dealing with family law or criminal justice systems; they have limited experience in giving testimony, either as a corroboration witness or expert witness, and view this as a frightening prospect for which they are ill prepared. They typically do not work in contexts where there is a regular interface with the criminal justice system and may be unfamiliar with police procedures and forensic interviewing, research on suggestibility, and confirmation bias. No research is available, to the author's knowledge, on therapists' use of non-leading or suggestive questions to children during therapy sessions. Research with professionals has found that despite training, professionals were not able to avoid directive, leading and suggestive prompts in interviews with children and were unaware of this failure (Lamb, 2016). Lamb suggests that extensive training over time with repeated opportunities to consolidate learning and receive feedback are needed to improve the quality of investigative interviews with children where there are concerns about sexual abuse. Such training would be helpful for therapists engaged in working with children where there are concerns about sexual abuse.

We know from research with children and young people that they make agentic decisions about who they can confide in and how others respond to them influences their decisions about further disclosures (Staller & Nelson-Gardell, 2005). A therapist who is uncomfortable with talking about sexual abuse or witnessing intense emotions may deter the child from confiding such difficult experiences or expressing strong feelings in the therapeutic work. A therapist with their own history of childhood abuse may feel triggered by a child's story or a parent's response, and through their own instinct to avoid, collude with helping the child and family avoid confiding about abuse experiences and addressing them in the therapeutic work. Having a clear protocol about who to contact and what procedures to follow if a child does confide an experience of sexual abuse helps the therapist prepare themselves for such a situation arising in their practice (Wheeler & Bertram, 2014).

It is challenging to work with the uncertainty of whether a child has experienced sexual abuse when there are very real concerns about a child's safety and wellbeing. Therapists can come under pressure from other professionals who are tasked with protecting children and professional systems can mirror the abuse dynamics resulting in conflict and over-alignment with various actors in the system (Furniss, 1991). Tolerating frustration, anger, and the desire to fix everything in the child's world, as well as the need to prevent vicarious trauma and secondary traumatization (Pearlman & Saakvitne, 1995) are all predictable challenges in this work and require appropriate support to ensure that children and families receive the service they need and deserve.

The focus of therapy

The first stage of any therapeutic encounter is an assessment of therapeutic need. This involves developing a therapeutic formulation, a guiding framework for the work of therapy, consisting of a range of hypotheses as to the root of the concern, what needs to change to support the child or young person and their family, and how the therapist can facilitate such change (McElvaney & Moorhouse, 2022). The goal of therapy will be to strengthen the child's sense of self and connection to others through supporting relationships and communication between the child and their family/community and providing a safe, nurturing and protective environment for the child (Sheinberg & Fraenkel, 2001).

The therapeutic relationship itself may trigger feelings of shame. Children often blame themselves for the experience of sexual abuse, which may be experienced as shame (McElvaney et al., 2022); parents may feel ashamed of their feelings of inadequacy and helplessness, all of which may serve to inhibit the child's disclosure (McElvaney & Nixon, 2020). The sharing of sexually explicit images or recruitment of peers in technology assisted sexual abuse, may also be shaming. Young people who have experienced being trafficked may feel shame at being duped into co-operating with traffickers and engaging in criminal activity (see Quas' chapter in this book for an overview of the distinctive challenges experienced by young people in disclosing their trafficked experiences). The therapist may unwittingly enact shame-inducing experiences in the young person and their parents through their use of language (e.g. problem-based language), eye contact (persisting in seeking eye contact with a young person who consistently avoids eye contact), and how much space they take up in the interactions (e.g. by talking too much). Dearing and Tangney (2011) note that if counsellors are not attuned to cues of shame, they may overlook or avoid addressing shame, which is an uncomfortable topic for both the therapist and client. Naming how difficult it might be to share personal information with a stranger, staying attuned to non-verbal cues and reactions to what is being said in the room and intervening with supportive empathic reflections (Smyth, 2013), when appropriate, may help to minimize shame-inducing experiences.

Where there is uncertainty about whether the child has been sexually abused, person-centred non-directive approaches with an emphasis on providing a facilitating environment for the child, offering empathy, congruence and unconditional positive regard (Rogers, 1951; Smyth, 2013) are appropriate. Where children present with posttraumatic symptoms, techniques drawn from trauma-focused approaches are effective (Lawson & Quinn, 2013). Trauma-focused approaches draw heavily on humanistic psychotherapy, systemic therapy, attachment theory and empowerment models (Deblinger et al., 2015), all of which can inform the therapeutic work with children who have not yet disclosed sexual abuse. It is not necessary for the therapist to elicit details of the child's experience of abuse. Even where a disclosure is forthcoming, some authors advocate not focusing on the details of the allegation so as not to prejudice legal proceedings; the therapist can instead focus on emotional stabilization and making sense of experiences without discussing abuse details (Rouf & Waites, 2023). However, this is not always possible as children may feel pressurized to talk about the abuse (McElvaney et al., 2012), may be exhibiting symptoms such as intrusive thoughts or flashbacks that require directly talking about their experiences (Deblinger et al., 2015) and may be particularly sensitive to cues from the therapist of a prohibition to speak, which may in turn discourage them from disclosing. When responding to children's need to discuss the details of the abuse, non-directive open questioning is advisable to ensure that, as noted above, the therapist does not unduly influence the child's narrative. Also, as noted above, attention to good record keeping can support the integrity of the child's narrative.

Some forms of therapy, such as group therapy may present difficulties as children's accounts may be unduly influenced by being exposed to other children's accounts of abuse. The CPS (2022a) notes that while the defence may seek to undermine children's credibility when memories are recalled or shared during therapy, the paramount concern must be the health and wellbeing of the victim and this must take precedence over ongoing police investigation or prosecution. Group therapy has been described as particularly effective in reassuring children that they are not alone in their experiences (Brown et al., 2022). According to the CPS guidance, group therapy that focuses on psychoeducation, support and developing coping strategies should not be considered as undermining the child's credibility (CPS, 2022a). The CPS also cautions against relying on allegations of abuse that have been shared as a result of hypnotherapy or hypnotic age regression, where an individual has been invited to "relive" events from the past as these "memories" should be treated with caution.

Three general areas of functioning are useful to focus on when working therapeutically with children who have experienced sexual abuse (McElvaney, 2023): relational capacity (ability to trust and form relationships, capacity to avail of support), emotion regulation (ability to manage distress and range of symptoms), and sense of self (self-esteem and identity). Focusing on supporting the child's wellbeing rather than on the sexual abuse concerns will assist the therapist in maintaining a non-directive approach in their work and provide the child with a non-pressurized environment which can facilitate disclosure, if appropriate. Through the therapeutic relationship, the largest contributor to effective outcomes in psychotherapy (Midgley et al., 2017), children can learn to trust, depend on others, and confide in a therapist about difficult experiences or worries they have.

The therapeutic relationship can also provide an opportunity for a corrective emotional experience where a child has been hurt by someone they trusted; the child may learn about how boundaries are breached when adults hurt children. As most children are abused by someone they know and often someone they trust, this corrective emotional experience can be particularly central to healing issues of trust, self-blame, boundary violation, and their sense of self in relation to self and others (Harper & Steadman, 2003). Part of the work on relational capacity is supporting the child's relational network, particularly parents or carers, building the foundation to support the young person in confiding in those close to them if they need to. As adolescents tend to confide more in their peers in the first instance (McElvaney, 2015), the focus of therapy may need to be on supporting peer relationships.

Emotion regulation involves early attunement and co-regulation of the care-giver with the child who learns to internalize this experience and regulate their own body and emotions. Trauma, by definition, overwhelms the individual and impedes their ability to regulate (van der Kolk, 2015). Children's coping strategies for managing distress, either through withdrawal or acting out to relieve tensions may enable them to contain the secret of the abuse (McElvaney et al., 2012). It can be helpful to use psychoeducation with older children and adolescents about how the body and brain works when we experience emotions, how, when in a heightened state of emotion, brain functioning is affected, which can explain impulsive behaviours and the inability to think clearly or solve problems. Assistance with emotion regulation can help children and young people tolerate their emotional distress and be prepared to experience this rather than avoid it, thus expanding their window of tolerance (Siegel, 2020). Children can gain confidence and learn to take control of their emotions so that they do not feel overwhelmed (Foroughe, 2023). Therapy can equip them to coherently communicate their distress in ways that are better understood by those close to them. Creative techniques, commonly used in trauma-focused approaches (Carpenter et al., 2016), represent an unintrusive non-directive way of working with children that facilitates emotional expression yet minimizes the risk of therapists influencing children's narratives about their experiences. Educating parents about techniques and skills to regulate emotion will support the child's learning (Deblinger et al., 2015).

When it is unknown whether children have been abused, exploring their self-esteem and sense of self with non-suggestive support may go some way to addressing the impact of experiences that have not been verbalized. There may be significant feelings of self-blame, shame, powerlessness (Finkelhor & Browne, 1995) and challenges to the child's sense of identity (Capella et al., 2016). Particularly when abused by an attachment figure, children may internalize the bad experiences, resulting in feelings of worthlessness, conceptualized by Suzanne Sgroi (1982) as the "damaged goods syndrome". Part of the work on sense of self involves helping the child feel curious about themselves, identifying their strengths and competencies, and supporting parents, teachers, and other important people in their lives to nurture the child in developing their potential (Capella et al., 2016). Through the therapeutic relationship based on empathy, congruence and unconditional positive regard (Rogers, 1951), and parent–child conjoint therapeutic work, children can internalize a positive sense of themselves, which may counteract the impact of sexual abuse that may be inhibiting the child from disclosing.

Supporting parents and carers

Parents exert a strong influence on children's ability to disclose sexual abuse. Children may be reluctant to disclose due to a concern about the distress this may cause to their parents (McElvaney et al., 2014) or a conviction that their parents will not believe them (Hershkowitz et al., 2007). In the forensic interviewing context, children who have good caregiver support are more likely to disclose than those without (Carnes et al., 2001). Parents or carers may experience anxiety and uncertainty when having conversations about sexual abuse that affects their responsiveness to their child and the child's willingness or ability to confide further in them. Therapy can help support parents in their role as parents, helping to build their confidence, facilitating conversations between parents and children, and teaching both the child's and parents coping skills so that parents can support the child between sessions in building competence and understanding their child (McElvaney, 2016). Trauma-focused approaches emphasize the need for parental involvement if children are to benefit from therapy (Deblinger et al., 2015; Carpenter et al., 2016).

Parents sometimes hold beliefs that their child has been sexually abused in the absence of concrete evidence to support this. This may result from a sensitized awareness of the prevalence of sexual abuse, their own childhood history of sexual abuse, or concern about how their child is presenting. It is not difficult to misinterpret children's behaviours as indicative of sexual abuse, given the considerable overlap in children's presentations following a distressing experience. Parents who either believe that their child has not been abused, despite concerns on the part of others, or parents who believe that their child has been abused, despite a lack of disclosure, will need support in maintaining an open stance in relation to this. This uncertainty can be difficult for parents to tolerate; the belief that their child has been abused has a considerable impact not only on parents' mental health but also on their confidence in themselves and identity as protective parents (McElvaney & Nixon, 2020).

Supporting the therapeutic work

The importance of multidisciplinary and interagency collaboration is essential when working in the field of sexual abuse (ICMEC, 2023). Building collaborative relationships with other professionals engaged with the child and family will ensure that therapeutic needs, child protection needs and legal obligations are met when information needs to be shared. The Barnahus model in Europe (www.barnahus.eu) and the Children's Advocacy Center model in the US and Canada (www.nationalcac.org) have at their centre the multidisciplinary interagency collaboration ethos. The models aim to minimize any secondary victimization that may be experienced by families navigating the various professional systems through co-ordinating child protection, forensic medical, therapeutic and, in some jurisdictions, law enforcement and prosecution services.

Clarification of roles in the professional network is conducive to effective multidisciplinary interagency working (ICMEC, 2023). Where there are high levels of concern, the therapist may come under pressure from the professional network to elicit a disclosure from the child. Social workers and police may be dependent on the therapist to share information necessary to inform child protection and prosecution decisions. The perspectives that different professionals bring to discussions regarding the child's best interests enrich the service the therapist can provide (Furniss, 1991) and provides the necessary challenging of attitudes and beliefs that can pervade the field.

Clinical supervision, a cornerstone of psychotherapy practice, is essential for supporting good quality work (Hawkins & McMahon, 2022), providing a learning environment to support therapists in responding to the ever-changing needs of children and families, and protecting clients from harmful practice. While little has been written specifically about supervision of psychotherapy in the field of sexual abuse, supervision itself is referenced in various contexts such as managing bias in interviewing children (Lacey & Nunkoosing, 2022) and as a prevention strategy in managing the impact of the work and prevention of secondary traumatization (Miller, 2021; Pearlman & Saakvitne, 1995). In working with children where there is uncertainty about their experiences, supervision can provide a place to explore alternative explanations for the child's presentation, reflecting on how the therapist can preserve the integrity of the child's narrative, and identifying and addressing possible explicit and implicit bias. Personal therapy is also an important support mechanism for therapists working in the field of sexual abuse. Strong emotions may be evoked in the work, which can interfere with the neutral stance that is needed to support children and families where there is uncertainty about sexual abuse experiences. The therapist who is a parent may experience over identification or frustration with parents whom they perceive as acting protectively or neglectfully. Awareness of one's own vulnerabilities helps the therapist identify when they need to seek support, either through clinical supervision, personal therapy or peer support.

Conclusion

This chapter explores the context of working therapeutically with children where there are concerns about sexual abuse in the absence of a clear disclosure. This can be a complex area of work for therapists who are unfamiliar with interfacing with the criminal justice system. Balancing the therapeutic needs of the child and family, respecting children's rights, while attending to their ethical and legal obligations to maintain a neutral stance where there is uncertainty in relation to details of abuse, can be challenging. Providing a safe and trusting opportunity for the child to disclose sexual abuse experiences while preserving the integrity of the child's narrative requires the therapist keep an open mind as to the origins of children's difficulties and rely on open questioning when children do disclose. Research on why children delay disclosing and what helps children tell, the impact of sexual abuse on children, as well as findings from research on investigative interviewing can assist therapists in approaching this work with a trauma-informed and developmentally sensitive lens, and help them make sense of children's presentations when there are concerns about sexual abuse. Keeping an open mind as to the source of these concerns is essential.

Research has shown that where limits of confidentiality and potential consequences of sharing information are clearly articulated at the outset of therapy and where there is trust in the therapeutic relationship, these issues can be managed in a respectful and transparent manner, minimizing potential negative impacts from the wider system and supporting the young person's autonomy. Therapists need to attend to their legal obligations to share information with law enforcement personnel if disclosures of abuse are forthcoming. Given the prevalence of sexual abuse in our society, and the evidence that many individuals do not disclose childhood abuse until adulthood, it is important for all therapists to ensure they have the necessary skills and support to provide trauma informed non-directive therapy when working with children, regardless of whether there is a current concern about sexual abuse.

References

Alaggia, R., Collin-Vezina, D., & Lateef, R. (2019). Facilitators and barriers to child sexual abuse (CSA) disclosures: A research update (2000–2016). *Trauma, Violence, & Abuse*, *20*(2), 260–283. https://doi.org/10.1177/1524838017697312

Allard-Gaudreau, N., Poirier, S., & Cyr, M. (2024). Factors associated with delayed disclosure of child sexual abuse: A focus on the victims having been led to perform sexual acts on the perpetrator, *Child Abuse & Neglect*, *147*, 106537. https://doi.org/10.1016/j.chiabu.2023.106537.

APA. (2007). Record keeping guidelines. *American Psychologist*, 993–1004.

Baker, H., Miller, P., Starr, E., Witcombe-Hayes, S. & Gwilym, C. (2019). Let children know you're listening: The importance of an adult's interpersonal skills in helping to improve a child's experience of disclosure. Retrieved from https://learning.nspcc.org.uk/research-resources/2019/let-children-know-you-re-listening

Bass, E. & Davis, L. (2008). *The courage to heal: A guide for women survivors of child sexual abuse*. HarperCollins.

Blasbalg, U., Hershkowitz, I., Lamb, M. E., & Karni-Visel, Y. (2021). Adherence to the Revised NICHD Protocol recommendations for conducting repeated supportive interviews is associated with the likelihood that children will allege abuse. *Psychology, Public Policy, and Law*, *27*(2), 209–220. https://doi-org/10.1037/law0000295

Bond, T. & Mitchels, B. (2014). *Confidentiality and record keeping in counselling and psychotherapy*. Sage Publications.

Brennan, E., & McElvaney, R. (2020). What helps children tell? A qualitative meta-analysis of child sexual abuse disclosure. *Child Abuse Review*, *29*(2), 97–113. https://doi.org/10.1002/car.2617

Brewin, C. R., Andrews, B., & Mickes, L. (2020). Regaining consensus on the reliability of memory. *Current Directions in Psychological Science*, *29*(2), 121–125. https://doi.org/10.1177/0963721419898122

Brown, S. J., Carter, G. J., Halliwell, G., Brown, K., Caswell, R., Howarth, E., Feder, G., O'Doherty, L. (2022). Survivor, family and professional experiences of psychosocial interventions for sexual abuse and violence: A qualitative evidence synthesis. *Cochrane Database of Systematic Reviews, 10*. https://doi.org/10.1002/14651858.CD013648.pub2.

Bruck, M., & Ceci, S. J. (1999). The suggestibility of children's memory. *Annu. Rev. Psychol.*, *50*, 419–439. https://doi.org/10.1146/annurev.psych.50.1.419

Capella C., & Boddy J. (2021). Listening to the opinista? Relational understandings of voice and silence in a multiperspective narrative study of child psychotherapy. *Children & Society*, 35, 835–849. https://doi.org/10.1111/chso.12458

Capella, C., Lama, X., Rodríguez, L., Águila, D., Beiza, G., Dussert, D., & Gutierrez, C. (2016). Winning a race: Narratives of healing and psychotherapy in children and adolescents who have been sexually abused. *Journal of Child Sexual Abuse*, *25*(1), 73–92. https://doi.org/10.1080/10538712.2015.1088915

Carnes, C. N., Wilson, C., & Nelson-Gardell, D. (1999). Extended forensic evaluation when sexual abuse is suspected: A model and preliminary data. *Child Maltreatment*, *4*(3), 242–254. https://doi.org/10.1177/1077559599004003005

Carnes, C. N., Nelson-Gardell, D., Wilson, C. & Orgassa, U. C. (2001). Extended forensic evaluation when sexual abuse is suspected: A multisite field study. *Child Maltreatment*, *6*(3), 230–242. https://doi.org/10.1177/1077559501006003004

Carpenter, J., Hackett, S., Jessiman, T., Patsios, D. & Phillips, J. (2016) Letting the future in: A therapeutic intervention for children affected by sexual abuse and their carers. An evaluation of impact and implementation. Retrieved from https://learning.nspcc.org.uk/research-resources/2016/evaluation-of-the-letting-the-future-in-service

Ceci, S. J., & Bruck, M. (1995). *Jeopardy in the courtroom: A scientific analysis of children's testimony*. American Psychological Association.

Central Statistics Office (2022). Sexual violence survey 2022. Retrieved from www.cso.ie/en/statistics/crimeandjustice/sexualviolencesurvey/

Collin-Vezina, D., de la Sablonnière, M., Palmer, A., & Milne, L. (2015). A preliminary mapping of individual, relational, and social factors that impede disclosure of childhood sexual abuse. *Child Abuse & Neglect*, *43*, 123–134. https://doi.org/10.1016/j.chiabu.2015.03.010

Cook, A., Spinazzola, J., Ford, J. D., Lanktree, C., Blaustein, M., Cloitre, M., & van der Kolk, B. (2005). Complex trauma in children and adolescents. *Psychiatric Annals*, *35*(5), 390–398. https://doi.org/10.3928/00485713-20050501-05

Coulborn Faller, K., & Nelson-Gardell, D. (2010). Extended evaluations in cases of child sexual abuse: How many sessions are sufficient? *Journal of Child Sexual Abuse*, 19, 648–668. https://doi.org/10.1080/10538712.2010.522494

CPS. (2022a). Pre-trial therapy: Legal guidance. Retrieved from www.cps.gov.uk/legal-guidance/pre-trial-therapy (accessed 13 February 2025).

CPS. (2022b). Pre-trial therapy: Accompanying note for therapists. Retrieved from www.cps.gov.uk/legal-guidance/pre-trial-therapy-accompanying-note-therapists (accessed 13 February 2025).

Dearing, R. L., & Tangney, J. P. (Eds.). (2011). *Shame in the therapy hour.* American Psychological Association. https://doi.org/10.1037/12326-000

Deblinger, E., Mannarino, A. P., Cohen, J.A., Runyon, M. K., & Heflin, A. H. (2015). *Child sexual abuse: A primer for treating children, adolescents, and their non-offending parents* (2nd ed.). Oxford University Press.

Dye, H. L. (2020). Is emotional abuse as harmful as physical and/or sexual abuse? *Journal of Child and Adolescent Trauma*, *13*(4), 399–407. https://doi.org/10.1007/s40653-019-00292-y

European Union. (2022). General data protection regulation (GDPR). Retrieved from https://eur-lex.europa.eu/EN/legal-content/summary/general-data-protection-regulation-gdpr.html (accessed 13 February 2025).

Finkelhor, D., & Browne, A. (1985). The traumatic impact of child sexual abuse: A conceptualization. *American Journal of Orthopsychiatry*, *55*(4), 530–541. https://doi.org/10.1111/j.1939-0025.1985.tb02703.x

Fonagy, P., Pugh, K., & O'Herlihy, A. (2017). *The Children and Young People's Improving Access to Psychological Therapies (CYPIAPT) programme in England.* In D. Skuse, H. Bruce, & L. Dowdney (eds), *Child psychology and psychiatry: Frameworks for clinical training and practice* (pp. 429–435). Wiley Blackwell.

Foroughe, M. (2023). *Emotion focused therapy for youth: The clinical manual* (1st ed.). Routledge.

Furniss, T. (1991). *The multiprofessional handbook of child sexual abuse.* Routledge.

Goodman, G. S., Goldfarb, D., Quas, J. A., & Lyon, A. (2017). Psychological counseling and accuracy of memory for child sexual abuse. *American Psychologist*, *72*(9), 920–931. https://doi.org/10.1037/amp0000282

Harper, K., & Steadman, J. (2003). Therapeutic boundary issues in working with childhood sexual-abuse survivors. *American Journal of Psychotherapy*, *57*(1), 64–79. https://doi.org/10.1176/appi.psychotherapy.2003.57.1.64

Hawkins, P. & McMahon, A. (2020). *Supervision in the helping professions.* McGraw-Hill Education.

Henderson, K. L. (2013). Mandated reporting of child abuse: Considerations and guidelines for mental health counselors. *Journal of Mental Health Counseling*, *35*(4), 296–309. https://doi.org/10.17744/mehc.35.4.x356102458 63n034

Hershkowitz, I., Horowitz, D., & Lamb, M. E. (2007). Individual and family variables associated with disclosure and nondisclosure of child abuse in Israel. In M. E. Pipe, M. E. Lamb, Y. Orbach, & A. C. Cederborg (Eds.), *Child sexual abuse: Disclosure, delay, and denial* (pp. 65–75). Erlbaum.

Hershkowitz, I., & Lamb, M. E. (2020). Allegation rates and credibility assessment in forensic interviews of alleged child abuse victims: Comparing the Revised and Standard NICHD protocols. *Psychology, Public Policy, and Law*, *26*(2), 176–184. https://doi.org/10.1037/law0000230

Hershkowitz, I., Lamb M. E., Blasbalg, U., & Karni-Visel, Y. (2021). The dynamics of two-session interviews with suspected victims of abuse who are reluctant to make allegations. *Development and Psychopathology*, *33*, 739–747. https://doi.org/10.1017/S0954579420001820

ICMEC. (2023). The multidisciplinary team framework for addressing child sexual abuse, exploitation and trafficking. Retrieved from https://www.icmec.org/heroes/multidisciplinary-team-framework.

Jenkins, P. (1997). *Counselling, psychotherapy and the law.* Sage Publications.

Kakuru, D. M. (2023). Choice of non-disclosure as agency: A systematic review of non-disclosure of sexual violence in girlhood in Africa, *Women*, *3*, 322–334. https://doi.org/10.3390/women3020024

Lacey, E., & Nunkoosing, K. (2022). "What am I bringing into the room?" perception and management of interviewer bias in child sexual abuse interviews: An interpretative phenomenological analysis. *Child Abuse Review*, *31*(2), 1–14. https://doi.org/10.1002/car.2725

Lamb, M. E. (2016). Difficulties translating research on forensic interview practices to practitioners: Finding water, leading horses, but can we get them to drink? *American Psychologist, 71*(8), 710–718. https://doi.org/10/1037/amp0000039

Lamb, M. E., Hershkowitz, I., Orbach, Y. & Esplin, P. W. (2018). *Tell me what happened.* Wiley.

La Rooy, D., Lamb, M. E., & Pipe, M. E. (2009). Repeated interviewing: A critical evaluation of the risks and potential benefits. In K. Kuehnle, & M. Connell (Eds.), *The evaluation of child sexual abuse allegations: A comprehensive guide to assessment and testimony* (pp. 327–361). Wiley.

Lawson, D. M., & Quinn, J. (2013). Complex trauma in children and adolescents: Evidence-based practice in clinical settings. *Journal of Clinical Psychology, 69*(5), 497–509. https://doi.org/10.1002/jclp.21990

Lemaigre, C., Taylor, E. P., & Gittoes, C. (2017). Barriers and facilitators to disclosing sexual abuse in childhood and adolescence: A systematic review. *Child Abuse & Neglect, 70*, 39–52. https://doi.org/10.1016/j.chiabu.2017.05.009

Levine, M., Doueck, H. J., Anderson, E. M., Chavez, F. T., Deisz, R. L., George, N. A., Sharma, A., Steinberg, K. L., & Wallach, L. (1995). *The impact of mandated reporting on the therapeutic process: Picking up the pieces.* Sage Publications.

Lyon, T. D., Williams, S., & Stolzenberg, S. N. (2020). Understanding expert testimony on child sexual abuse denial after New Jersey v. J.L.G.: Ground truth, disclosure suspicion bias, and disclosure substantiation bias. *Behavior Science & Law, 38*(6), 630–647. https://doi.org/10.1002/bsl.2490.

Magee, K. (2021). Maintaining the therapeutic alliance when reporting child maltreatment: Recommendations for mental health clinicians. *Journal of Contemporary Psychotherapy, 51*(1), 1–5. https://doi.org/10.1007/s10879-020-09476-2

Malloy, L. C., & Quas, J. A. (2009). Children's suggestibility: Areas of consensus and controversy. In K. Kuehnle & M. Connell (eds), *The evaluation of child sexual abuse allegations: A comprehensive guide to assessment and testimony* (pp. 267–297). Wiley.

McElvaney, R. (2015). Disclosure of child sexual abuse: Delays, non-disclosure and partial disclosure. What the research tells us and implications for practice. *Child Abuse Review, 24*(3), 159–169. https://doi.org/10.1002/car.2280

McElvaney, R. (2016). *Helping children tell about child sexual abuse: Guidance for helpers.* Jessica Kingsley.

McElvaney, R. (2019). Helping children tell about their experiences of sexual abuse. *Child Abuse Review, 28*, 166–172. https://doi.org/10.1002/car.2559

McElvaney, R. (2023). Childhood sexual abuse. In T. Hanley, & L.S. Winter (Eds.), *SAGE handbook of counselling and psychotherapy*(pp.313–318). Sage Publications.

McElvaney, R. (undated). Guest blog: Rosaleen McElvaney. Retrieved from www.oneinfour.ie/blog/guest-blog-rosaleen-mcelvaney (accessed 13 February 2025).

McElvaney, R., Greene, S., & Hogan, D. (2012). Containing the secret of child sexual abuse. *Journal of Interpersonal Violence, 27*(6), 1155–1175. https://doi.org/10.1177/0886260511424503

McElvaney, R., Greene, S., & Hogan, D. (2014). To tell or not to tell? Factors influencing young people's informal disclosures of child sexual abuse. *Journal of Interpersonal Violence*, *29*(5), 928–947. https://doi.org/10.1177/0886260513506281

McElvaney, R., Lateef, R., Collin-Vézina, S., Alaggia, R., & Simpson, M. (2022). Bringing shame out of the shadows: Identifying shame in child sexual abuse disclosure processes and implications for psychotherapy, *Journal of Interpersonal Violence*, *37*(19–20), NP18738–NP18760, https://doi.org/10.1177/08862605211037435

McElvaney, R., Monaghan, A., Treacy, C., & Delaney N. (2023). Adolescents' experiences of psychotherapy following child sexual abuse. *Research in Psychotherapy: Psychopathology, Process and Outcome*, *26*(2). https://doi.org/10.4081/ripppo.2023.630.

McElvaney, R., & Moorhouse, A. (2022). The multidimensional process of assessing therapeutic need following child sexual abuse. *Irish Psychologist*, *48*(5), 119–123.

McElvaney, R., & Nixon, E. (2020). Parents' experiences of their child's disclosure of child sexual abuse. *Family Process*, *59*(4), 1773–1788. https://doi.org/10.1111/famp.12507

McTavish, J. R., Kimber, M., Devries, K., Colombini, M., MacGregor, J. C. D., Wathen, N. & MacMillan, H. L. (2019). Children's and caregivers' perspectives about mandatory reporting of child maltreatment: A meta-synthesis of qualitative studies. *BMJ Open*, 1–13. https://doi.org/10.1136/bmjopen-2018-025741.

Midgley, N., Hayes, J. & Cooper, M. (2017). *Essential research findings in child and adolescent counselling and psychotherapy.* Sage Publications.

Miller, B. (2021). *Reducing secondary traumatic stress: Skills for sustaining a career in the helping professions.* Taylor & Francis.

Morrison, S.E., Bruce, C. & Wilson, S. (2018). Children's disclosure of sexual abuse: A systematic review of qualitative research exploring barriers and facilitators. *Journal of Child Sexual Abuse*, *27*(2), 176–194. https://doi.org/10.1080/10538712.2018.1425943

Narang, J., Schwannauer, M., Quayle, E., & Chouliara, Z. (2019). Therapeutic interventions with child and adolescent survivors of sexual abuse: A critical narrative review, *Children and Youth Services Review*, *107*, 104559. https://doi.org/10.1016/j.childyouth.2019.104559

National Archives. (2025). Data Protection Act 2018. Retrieved from www.legislation.gov.uk/ukpga/2018/12/contents (accessed 13 February 2025).

O'Keeffe, S., Martin, P., Target, M., & Midgley, N. (2019). "I just stopped going": A mixed methods investigation into types of therapy dropout in adolescents with depression. *Frontiers in Psychology*, *10*, 75. https://doi.org/10.3389/fpsyg.2019.00075

Pearlman, L., & Saakvitne, K. (1995). *Trauma and the therapist: Countertransference and vicarious traumatization in psychotherapy with incest survivors.* W. W. Norton & Company.

Rogers, C. (1951). *Client-centered therapy: Its current practice, implications and theory.* Constable.

Rouf, K., & Waites, B. (2023). *Guidance on responding to disclosures of non-recent (historic) child sexual abuse: Safeguarding and support implications.* British Psychological Society.

Sgroi, S. M. (1982). *Handbook of clinical intervention in child sexual abuse.* Simon and Schuster.

Sheinberg, M., & Fraenkel, P. (2001). *The relational trauma of incest: A family-based approach to treatment.* The Guilford Press.

Siegel, D. J. (2020). *The developing mind: How relationships and the brain interact to shape who we are* (3rd ed.). The Guilford Press.

Szojka, Z. A., Nicol, A., & La Rooy, D. (2020). Narrative coherence in multiple forensic interviews with child witnesses alleging physical and sexual abuse. *Applied Cognitive Psychology, 34*(5), 943–960. https://doi: 10.1002/acp.3673

Smyth, D. (2013). *Person-centred therapy with children and young people.* Sage Publications.

Staller, K. M., & Nelson-Gardell, D. (2005). "A burden in your heart": Lessons of disclosure from female preadolescent and adolescent survivors of sexual abuse. *Child Abuse & Neglect, 29*(12), 1415–1432. https://doi.org/10.1016/j.chiabu.2005.06.007

Steinberg, K. L., Levine, M., & Doueck, H. J. (1997). Effects of legally mandated child-abuse reports on the therapeutic relationship: A survey of psychotherapists. *American Journal of Orthopsychiatry, 67*, 112–122. http://doi.org/10.1080/1068316X.2021.1984479

Theimer, K., Akemi, E.M., Sonnen, E., McCoy, K., Meidlinger, K., Biles, B., Zachary Huit, T., Flood, M. F., & Hansen, D. J. (2020). Identifying and addressing barriers to treatment for child sexual abuse survivors and their non-offending caregivers. *Aggression and Violent Behavior, 52*, 101418. https://doi.org/10.1016/j.avb.2020.101418

Ungar M., Tutty, L. M., Mc Connell, S., et al. (2009). What Canadian youth tell us about disclosing abuse, *Child Abuse and Neglect, 33*, 699–708. https://doi.org/10.1016/j.chiabu.2009.05.002

UNICEF (1989). The United National Convention on the Rights of the Child (UNCRC). Retrieved from www.unicef.org/child-rights-convention

US Department of Health and Human Services (1996). The standards for privacy of individually identifiable health information. Retrieved from www.hhs.gov/ocr/hipaa (accessed 17 February 2025).

Van der Kolk, B. (2015). *The body keeps the score: Brain, mind, and body in the healing of trauma.* Penguin.

Vliegen, N., Tang, E., Midgley, N., Luyten, P. & Fonagy, P. (2023). *Therapeutic work for children with complex trauma: A three-track psychodynamic approach.* Routledge.

Walker, A. G. (1994). *Handbook on questioning children: A linguistic perspective.* American Bar Association Center on Children and the Law.

Waterhouse, G. F., Ridley, A. M., Bull, R., Satchell, L., & Wilcock, R. (2023). Rapport-building in multiple interviews of children. *Applied Cognitive Psychology,* 37(6), 1210–1222. https://doi-org/10.1002/acp.4116

Wheeler, A. M. N., & Bertram. B. (2014). *The counselor and the law: A guide to legal and ethical practice* (7th ed.). American Counseling Association.

Wood, J. M., Nathan, D., Nezworksi, M. T., & Uhl, E. (2009). Child sexual abuse investigations: Lessons learned from the McMartin and other daycare cases. In B. L. Bottoms, C. J. Najdowski & G. G. Goodman (eds), *Children as victims, witnesses, and offenders: Psychological science and the law* (pp. 81–101). Guilford Publications.

Wymer, B., Ohrt, J. H., Morey, D. & Swisher, S. (2020). Integrating expressive arts techniques into trauma-focused treatment with children *Journal of Mental Health Counseling*, *42*(2), 124–139. https://doi.org/10.17744/mehc.42.2.03

Name Index

Note: Page numbers followed by "n" denote endnotes.

Subject Index

Note: Page numbers followed by "n" denote endnotes.

Made in United States
Cleveland, OH
31 March 2026

35150086R00195